SMP interact

Higher

2

for **AQA, Edexcel** and **OCR two-tier GCSE mathematics**

CAMBRIDGE
UNIVERSITY PRESS

D1413046

...ool Mathematics Project

Writing and editing for this edition   John Ling, Paul Scruton, Susan Shilton, Heather West
SMP design and administration   Melanie Bull, Pam Keetch, Nicky Lake, Cathy Syred, Ann White

The following people contributed to the original edition of SMP Interact for GCSE.

Benjamin Alldred	David Cassell	Spencer Instone	Susan Shilton
Juliette Baldwin	Ian Edney	Pamela Leon	Caroline Starkey
Simon Baxter	Stephen Feller	John Ling	Liz Stewart
Gill Beeney	Rosemary Flower	Carole Martin	Biff Vernon
Roger Beeney	John Gardiner	Lorna Mulhern	Jo Waddingham
Roger Bentote	Colin Goldsmith	Mary Pardoe	Nigel Webb
Sue Briggs	Bob Hartman	Paul Scruton	Heather West

CAMBRIDGE UNIVERSITY PRESS
Cambridge, New York, Melbourne, Madrid, Cape Town, Singapore, São Paulo, Delhi

Cambridge University Press
The Edinburgh Building, Cambridge CB2 8RU, UK

www.cambridge.org
Information on this title: www.cambridge.org/9780521689922

© The School Mathematics Project 2007

First published 2007
Reprinted 2008

Printed in Dubai by Oriental Press

A catalogue record for this publication is available from the British Library

ISBN 978-0-521-68992-2 paperback

ACC. NO. 925811 OX   FUND SECS
LOC. ET   CATEGORY CC   PRICE £13.50
10 AUG 2011
CLASS No. 510 SMP
OXFORD BROOKES UNIVERSITY LIBRARY

Typesetting by The School Mathematics Project
Technical illustrations by The School Mathematics Project and Jeff Edwards
Other illustrations by Robert Calow and Steve Lach at Eikon Illustration
Cover design by Angela Ashton
Cover image by Jim Wehtje/Photodisc Green/Getty Images

The authors and publisher thank the following for supplying photographs: pages 31, 90 and 127 Paul Scruton; page 128 Graham Portlock; page 139 Royalty-free/CORBIS; page 140 Tiffany Passmore

The authors and publisher are grateful to the following examination boards for permission to reproduce questions from past examination papers, identified in the text as follows.
AQA   Assessment and Qualifications Alliance
Edexcel Edexcel Limited
OCR   Oxford, Cambridge and RSA Examinations
WJEC   Welsh Joint Education Committee
The authors, and not the examination boards, are responsible for the method and accuracy of the answers to examination questions given; these may not necessarily constitute the only possible solutions.

Thames barrier data on page 33 courtesy of the consulting engineers High-Point Rendel and the Environment Agency; illustration on page 92, which originally appeared in *Time*, 9 April 1979, redrawn from *The Visual Display of Quantitative Information*, Edward R. Tufte (Graphics Press 1983), p. 62; extracts on page 92 from *On Being the Right Size and Other Essays*, J. B. S. Haldane (Oxford University Press, 1985), pp. 1–2

NOTICE TO TEACHERS
It is illegal to reproduce any part of this work in material form (including photocopying and electronic storage) except under the following circumstances:
(i)   where you are abiding by a licence granted to your school or institution by the Copyright Licensing Agency;
(ii) where no such licence exists, or where you wish to exceed the terms of a licence, and you have gained the written permission of Cambridge University Press;
(iii) where you are allowed to reproduce without permission under the provisions of Chapter 3 of the Copyright, Designs and Patents Act 1988, which covers, for example, the reproduction of short passages within certain types of educational anthology and reproduction for the purposes of setting examination questions.

Using this book

This book, *Higher 2*, is the second of two main books for Higher tier GCSE. It completes the course up to the level of A and A*, and includes revision of topics from earlier in the course.

The contents list on the next few pages gives full details of the topics covered; at the end of the contents list is a precedence diagram to help those who want to use chapters selectively or in a different order from that of the book.

Each chapter begins with a summary of what it covers and ends with a self-assessment section ('Test yourself').

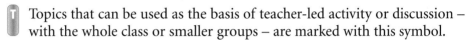 Topics that can be used as the basis of teacher-led activity or discussion – with the whole class or smaller groups – are marked with this symbol.

There are clear worked examples – and past exam questions, labelled by board, to give the student an idea of the style and standard that may be expected, and to build confidence.

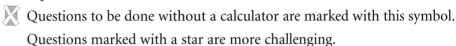 Questions to be done without a calculator are marked with this symbol.

Questions marked with a star are more challenging.

   Suggestions for work with a geometry program, web searches and use of a graph plotter are marked like this.

After every few chapters there is a review section, containing questions on work in that group of chapters; a special feature of the reviews in this book is that they also contain questions on work from *Higher 1*, so that important skills and concepts can be 'kept alive' in the run up to the GCSE examination.

The small number of resource sheets linked to this book can be downloaded in PDF format from www.smpmaths.org.uk and may be printed out for use within the institution purchasing this book.

Practice booklets

There is a practice booklet for each students' book. The practice booklet follows the structure of the students' book, making it easy to organise extra practice, homework and revision. The practice booklets do not contain answers; the answers can be downloaded in PDF format from www.smpmaths.org.uk

Contents

continues >

The precedence diagram below is designed to help with planning, especially where the teacher wishes to select from the material to meet the needs of particular students or to use chapters in a different order from that of the book.
A blue line connecting two chapters indicates that, to a significant extent, working on the later chapter requires competence with topics dealt with in the earlier one.

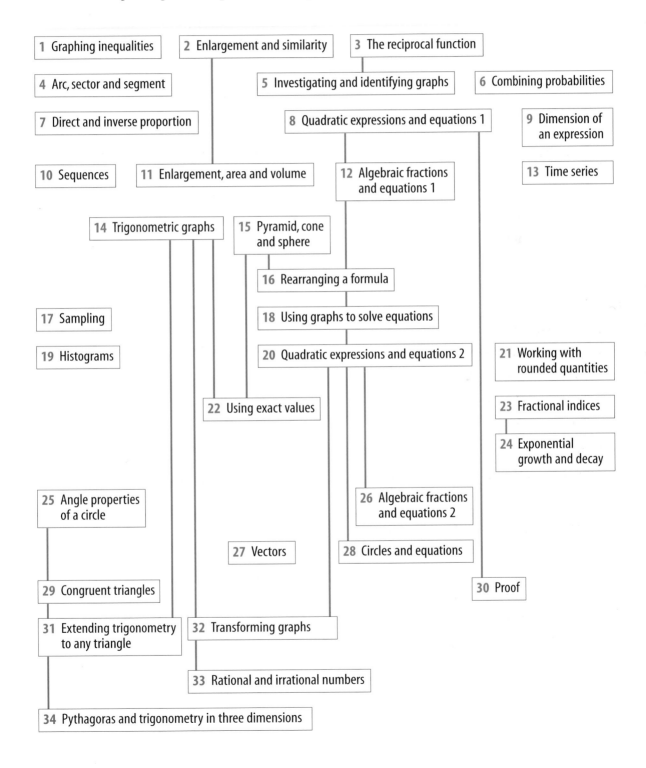

1 Graphing inequalities

You should know

- how to draw the graph of a straight line given its equation
- that < stands for 'is less than' and ≤ stands for 'is less than or equal to'
- that > stands for 'is greater than' and ≥ stands for 'is greater than or equal to'

This work will help you interpret inequalities as regions on a grid.

A Inequalities on a grid

Some ducks and swans share a pond in a park.
There are never more than five of each.

All possible combinations of ducks and
swans are shown by the points on the grid.

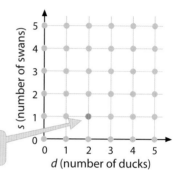

This point represents
2 ducks and 1 swan.

- Match up each set of orange points with two statements.

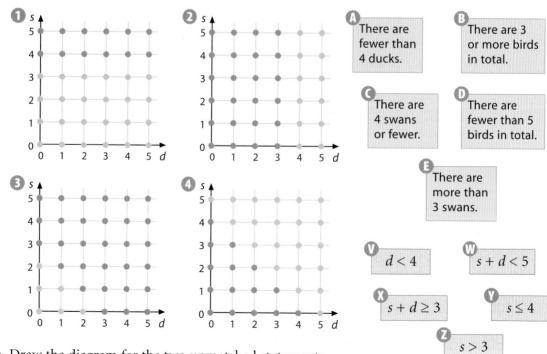

A There are fewer than 4 ducks.

B There are 3 or more birds in total.

C There are 4 swans or fewer.

D There are fewer than 5 birds in total.

E There are more than 3 swans.

V $d < 4$

W $s + d < 5$

X $s + d \geq 3$

Y $s \leq 4$

Z $s > 3$

- Draw the diagram for the two unmatched statements.

In a wildlife park, hippos and rhinos share the same enclosure.
There are never more than six of each kind of animal.

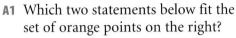

A1 Which two statements below fit the
set of orange points on the right?

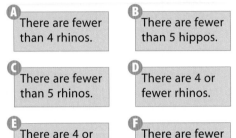

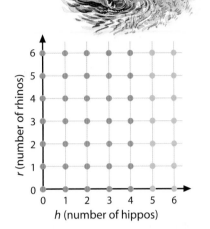

A2 Match each set of orange points below to one of the inequalities.

(a)

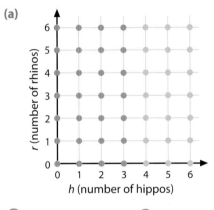

(b)

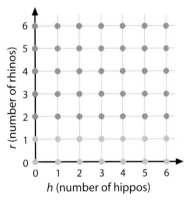

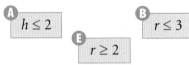 $h \leq 2$
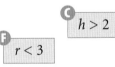 $r \leq 3$
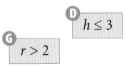 $h > 2$
 $h \leq 3$

E $r \geq 2$
F $r < 3$
G $r > 2$
H $h < 3$

A3 Hippos and rhinos live quite happily in a new enclosure as long as
the total number of animals is 6 or less.

(a) Which of these inequalities fits this statement?

 $h + r \geq 6$
 $h + r < 6$
 $r \leq 6$
 $h + r \leq 6$
E $h < 6$

(b) Draw a diagram for the hippos and the rhinos and colour
the points that fit this statement.

A4 Draw diagrams for these inequalities in the wildlife park.

(a) $r \leq 3$ **(b)** $h \geq 2$ **(c)** $r \geq 1$ **(d)** $h \leq 5$ **(e)** $h + r \geq 4$

B Regions with vertical and horizontal boundaries

T The shaded region consists of all the points on the line $x = 3$ and all the points to the left of it.

• Which of the points below are in this region?

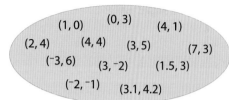

(1, 0) (0, 3) (4, 1)
(2, 4) (4, 4) (3, 5) (7, 3)
($^-$3, 6) (3, $^-$2) (1.5, 3)
($^-$2, $^-$1) (3.1, 4.2)

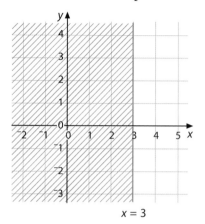

$x = 3$

• Which one of these inequalities is true for all the points in the region?

A $x \geq 3$ B $y < 3$ C $x < 3$ D $y \geq 3$ E $x \leq 3$ F $y \leq 3$ G $x > 3$ H $y > 3$

• Draw a diagram showing the region that consists of all the points where $y \geq 4$.

B1 Match each shaded region with one of the inequalities below.

(a)
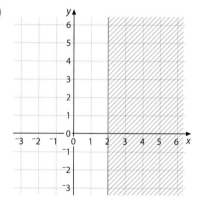

(b)
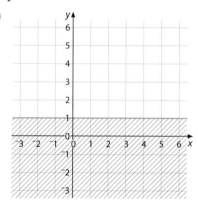

(c)
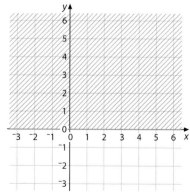

A $y \geq 1$ B $x \geq 3$ C $x \leq 2$

D $x \leq 1$ E $y \geq 2$ F $x \leq 0$

G $y \leq 2$ H $y \leq 1$ I $x \geq 0$

J $y \geq 0$ K $x \geq 2$

B2 Write an inequality for each shaded region.

(a)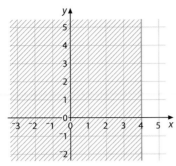

(b)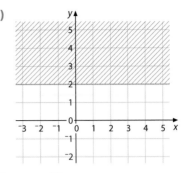

(c)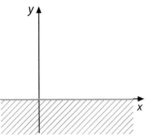

(d)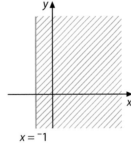

$x = {}^-1$

B3 Draw a diagram for the region given by each inequality.

(a) $x \geq 4$ (b) $y \leq 2$ (c) $x \geq 0$ (d) $y \geq {}^-1$

B4 (a) Draw a pair of axes, each numbered from 0 to 8.

(b) Draw the line with equation $x = 3$.

(c) Shade the region described by $x \geq 3$.

(d) On the same set of axes, draw the line with equation $y = 5$.

(e) Shade the region described by $y \leq 5$.

(f) (i) Show clearly the region described by both $x \geq 3$ **and** $y \leq 5$.

(ii) Give the coordinates of three points in this region.

B5 (a) Which of the four regions A, B, C or D satisfies both these inequalities?

$x \leq 2$ $y \geq 1$

(b) Write down the coordinates of two points that satisfy both the inequalities.

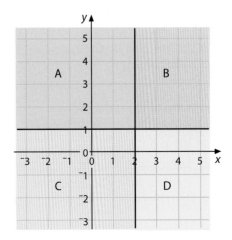

B6 The shaded region can be defined by four inequalities. One of these is $x \geq 1$.

Write down the other three inequalities.

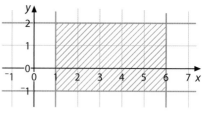

B7 (a) Which of the inequalities below describes the shaded region?

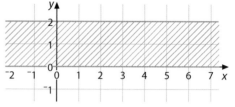

U $0 \leq x \leq 2$

V $0 \leq y \leq 2$

W $^-1 \leq x \leq 7$

X $^-1 \leq y \leq 7$

(b) Sketch diagrams for the regions given by each of the other inequalities.

C Sloping boundary lines

This is how to draw the region satisfied by the inequality $y \leq 2x + 1$.

*   First draw the boundary line $y = 2x + 1$.
*   Choose a point on one side of the line.

    Choose $(3, 2)$, for example.
*   Check the inequality for your point.

    $y = 2$ and
    $2x + 1 = 2 \times 3 + 1 = 7$

    $2 \leq 7$, so $y \leq 2x + 1$ is true for this point.
*   Shade the correct region.

    The inequality is true for $(3, 2)$ so shade the region that includes this point.

You can use this method to draw the region satisfied by any inequality.

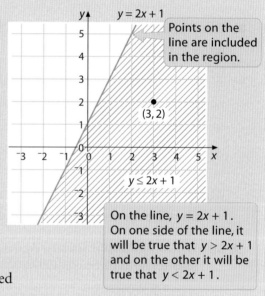

Points on the line are included in the region.

On the line, $y = 2x + 1$. On one side of the line, it will be true that $y > 2x + 1$ and on the other it will be true that $y < 2x + 1$.

C1 One of these diagrams shows the region defined by $y \geq x + 2$.

Which is it, A or B? Explain how you decided.

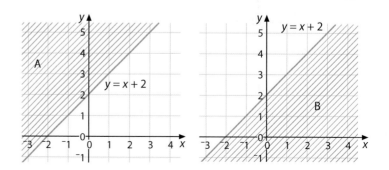

C2 Write an inequality for each shaded region.

(a)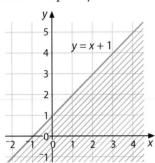

(b)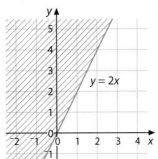

(c)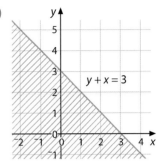

C3 Draw a pair of axes and number each axis from ⁻2 to 7.

(a) Draw the line with equation $y = x + 3$.

(b) Shade the region described by $y \geq x + 3$.

(c) Write down the coordinates of two points that satisfy the inequality $y \geq x + 3$.

C4 Draw a diagram for the region given by each inequality.
Number each axis from ⁻2 to 7.

(a) $y \leq 3x + 1$ (b) $y \leq x$ (c) $x + y \geq 3$ (d) $y \leq 6 - x$ (e) $3x + 4y \leq 12$

C5 For each diagram, find the equation of the line and write the inequality for the shaded region.

(a)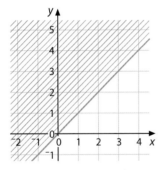

(b)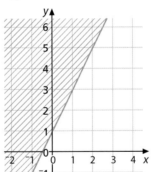

(c)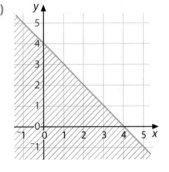

C6 A lorry carries a tonnes of sand together with b tonnes of gravel.
The total weight carried must not be greater than 30 tonnes.

(a) Write down an inequality in a and b that represents this.

(b) On graph paper draw suitable axes and show the region that represents your inequality.

C7 A teacher is buying some prizes for a maths competition.
Calculators cost £3 each and geometry sets £5 each.

(a) Write down an expression for the total cost of n calculators and m geometry sets.

(b) The teacher cannot spend more than £60.
Use this fact to write down an inequality in n and m.

(c) On graph paper show the region that represents this inequality.

D Overlapping regions

Shade the region satisfied by all the inequalities $x \geq 1$ $y \geq 0$ $x + y \leq 4$

- Shade the three different regions on the same set of axes.
- Where the shading overlaps defines the region where **all** the inequalities are satisfied.

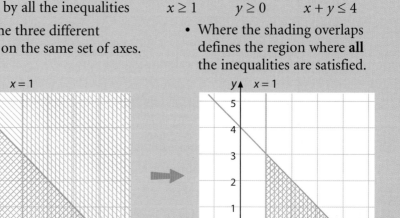

$x \geq 1$

$y \geq 0$

$x + y \leq 4$

D1

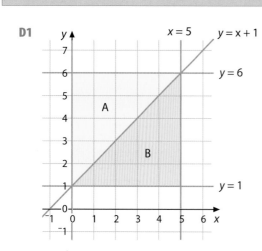

(a) Which region, A or B, is satisfied by these three inequalities?

$$y \leq 6 \qquad x \geq 0 \qquad y \geq x + 1$$

Write down the coordinates of three points that satisfy all these inequalities.

(b) Write down the three inequalities that fully describe the other lettered region.

D2 Write down the three inequalities that define each shaded region.

(a)

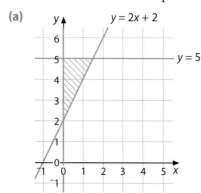

(b)

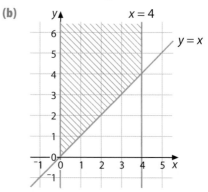

D3 Draw a pair of axes, each numbered from 0 to 8.

(a) Show clearly the single region that is satisfied by all these inequalities.

$x \geq 3$ $y \leq 6$ $y \leq x$

(b) Write down the coordinates of two points that satisfy all these inequalities.

D4 Draw a pair of axes, each numbered from ⁻3 to 6.

(a) Show clearly the single region that is satisfied by all these inequalities.

$x \leq 0$ $y \geq 0$ $y \leq x + 3$

Label this region Q.

(b) Write down the coordinates of all the points inside Q whose coordinates are both integers.

D5 Draw a pair of axes, each numbered from ⁻2 to 6.

The region R is defined by these inequalities.

$y \geq x + 1$ $x + y \leq 5$ $x \geq 1$

Show the region R on the grid.

OCR

D6 The shaded region can be defined by four inequalities. One of these is $y \geq 2$.

Write down the other three inequalities.

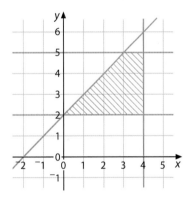

D7 Write down the three inequalities that define each region.

(a)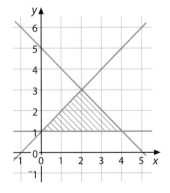

(b)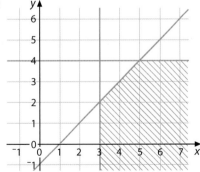

D8 Draw a pair of axes, each numbered from ⁻1 to 6.

Show clearly the single region that is satisfied by all these inequalities.

$x \leq 4$ $y \geq ⁻1$ $3x + 2y \leq 12$ $y \leq 2x$

E Boundaries: included or not included

An inequality such as $y < 2x + 1$ does not include values for which $y = 2x + 1$.

So points on the boundary line are **not** included in the region defined by $y < 2x + 1$.

One way to show this is to draw a dotted boundary line, as in the diagram.

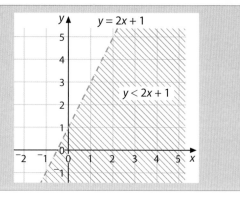

E1 Write an inequality for each region.

(a)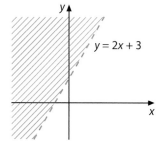

(b)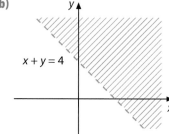

E2 Draw a pair of axes, each numbered from ⁻2 to 3.

   (a) On the grid, shade the region R that satisfies the inequalities

       $x < 1$, $y > 0$ and $y < x + 2$

   (b) The point X with coordinates (p, q) lies inside the region R where p and q are integers. Find the values of p and q.

E3 Draw a pair of axes, each numbered from ⁻3 to 4.

   (a) On the grid, shade the region Q that satisfies the inequalities

       $^-1 < x \leq 3$, $3y + x \leq 3$ and $x - 2y < 4$

   (b) Which of the points below are part of region Q?

       $(2, 0)$ $(^-1, 0)$ $(3, 0)$ $\left(1, \frac{-1}{2}\right)$ $\left(3, \frac{-3}{4}\right)$ $\left(2, \frac{1}{3}\right)$

   (c) Name the shape defined by region Q.

E4 Draw a pair of axes, each numbered from ⁻3 to 6.

   (a) Shade the part of your diagram that is the region defined by $4x + 3y > 12$.

   (b) Similarly, shade the areas defined by

       (i) $y - x > 2$ (ii) $y < \frac{1}{2}x + 1$.

   (c) What inequalities are true for the region that is left **unshaded** in your diagram?

Test yourself

T1 (a) Draw a pair of axes, numbered from 0 to 8 on each.

On the grid, draw straight lines and use shading to show the region R that satisfies the inequalities

$$x \geq 2 \qquad y \geq x \qquad x + y \leq 6$$

(b) The point P with coordinates (x, y) lies inside the region R. x and y are **integers**.

Write down the coordinates of **all** the points of R whose coordinates are both integers.

Edexcel

T2 On graph paper, draw a pair of axes, numbered from ⁻6 to 6 on each.

On the grid, indicate clearly the region defined by the three inequalities

$$y \leq 4 \qquad x \geq ^-3 \qquad y \geq x + 2$$

Mark the region with an R.

AQA

T3 On graph paper, draw a pair of axes, numbered from ⁻4 to 8 on each.

On the grid indicate clearly the single region which satisfies all these three inequalities.

$$y \geq \tfrac{1}{2}x \qquad y \leq 2x + 4 \qquad 5x + 2y \geq 10$$

OCR

T4 Draw a pair of axes, each numbered from ⁻6 to 6.

Indicate, by shading, the region R defined by these inequalities.

$$y \leq x + 4 \qquad y \geq ^-1 \qquad x \leq 3 \qquad x + y \leq 5$$

T5 The region R is shown shaded below.

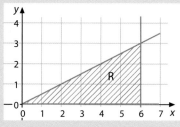

Write down three inequalities which together describe the shaded region.

AQA

T6 (a) $^-2 < x \leq 1$

x is an integer.

Write down all the possible values of x.

(b) $^-2 < x \leq 1 \qquad y > ^-2 \qquad y < x + 1$

x and y are integers.

Draw a pair of axes, numbered from ⁻5 to 5 on the x-axis and ⁻4 to 4 on the y-axis.

On the grid, mark with a cross (×) each of the six points which satisfies **all** these 3 inequalities.

Edexcel

2 Enlargement and similarity

You will revise finding and using the scale factor of an enlargement.

This work will help you

- solve problems involving similar triangles
- understand enlargement by a negative scale factor

A Enlargement and scale factor

When a shape is enlarged, the result is said to be **similar** to the original shape.
All lengths in the shape are multiplied by the same number, called the **scale factor**.
If the scale factor is less than 1, the result is smaller than the original,
but we often still use the word 'enlargement'.

A1 Shape Q is similar to shape P.
(They are not drawn accurately.)
The scale factor of the
enlargement is 2.5.
Find a, b, c and d.

A2 A shop offers to enlarge photos 10 cm by 15 cm into posters 50 cm by 75 cm.
What is the scale factor of the enlargement?

A3 Shape B is similar to shape A.

   (a) What is the scale factor
      of the enlargement?

   (b) Find a and b.

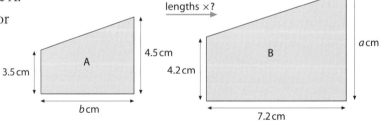

A4 Shape D is similar to shape C.

   (a) What is the scale factor?

   (b) Find a and b.

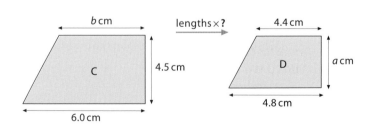

Scale factor as a fraction

In questions A2 to A4 the calculation $\frac{\text{enlarged length}}{\text{original length}}$ gave you the scale factor.

So the scale factor for the 'enlargement' shown here

is given by $\frac{\text{enlarged length}}{\text{original length}} = \frac{20}{35}$.

It sometimes helps to leave the scale factor as
a simplified fraction, in this case $\frac{4}{7}$.

- Using this scale factor, find w.
- Find x.

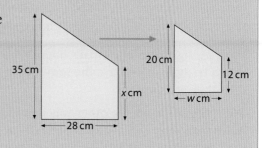

A5 Shape F is similar to shape E.
(They are not drawn accurately.)

   (a) Give the scale factor
that 'enlarges' E to F
as a fraction.

   (b) Find a, b and c.

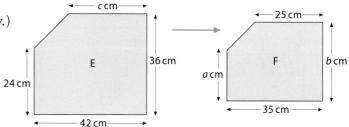

When a fractional scale factor is greater than 1 you can give it as an
improper fraction (like $\frac{7}{6}$).

A6 Shape H is similar to shape G.

   (a) Give the scale factor
that enlarges G to H
as an improper fraction.

   (b) Find a, b and c.

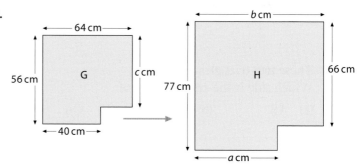

A7 Are these two shapes similar?
If not, why not?

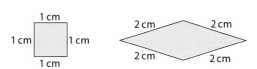

B Similar triangles

Two shapes are still similar if you **reflect** or **rotate** (as well as enlarge) one shape to transform it to the other.

If two shapes are similar then each has the same set of angles.

With triangles this also works the other way round: if two triangles each have the same set of three angles then they are similar.

But it doesn't work the other way round for shapes with more than three sides: for example, these quadrilaterals each have the same set of four angles but they are not similar.

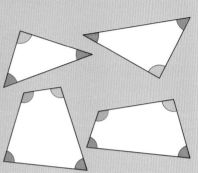

B1 Are any of these triangles similar to one another? If so, which?

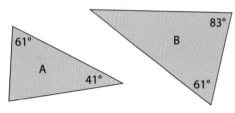

B2 These two triangles are similar.
Equal angles are marked the same way.
Which side is the enlargement of

   (a) PQ   **(b)** QR   **(c)** RP

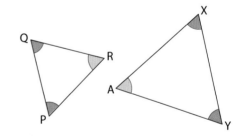

B3 These two triangles are similar.
Which side is the enlargement of

   (a) AB   **(b)** BC   **(c)** CA

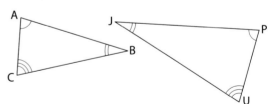

B4 (a) Explain why the two unmarked angles in these triangles must be equal.

   (b) Find the scale factor that enlarges the smaller triangle to the larger one.

   (c) Find the values of a and b.

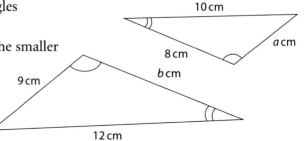

B5 Find the values of a and b here.

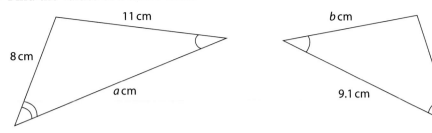

An **internal ratio** can be used to find missing sides in similar triangles.
These three triangles are similar.

The internal ratio $\dfrac{x}{y} = 3 \div 8 = 0.375$.

So $a = 14 \times 0.375 = 5.25$ cm
and $b = 1.8 \div 0.375 = 4.8$ cm

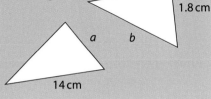

B6 By measuring x and y and calculating $\dfrac{x}{y}$
in each of these right-angled triangles, decide
which triangles are similar to the blue one.

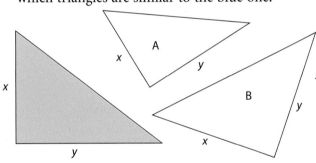
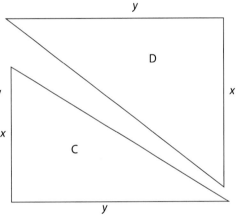

B7 These triangles (not drawn accurately) are all similar to
the pink triangle.

   (a) What is the ratio $\dfrac{XY}{YZ}$ in the pink triangle?

   (b) Use this ratio to find the values shown by letters.

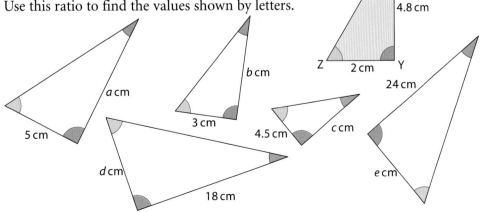

B8 At a certain time in the afternoon a flagpole 10 m high casts a shadow 8 m long.

At the same time of day another flagpole casts a shadow 13 m long.

How high is this flagpole?

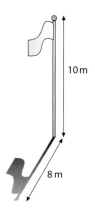

Equal angles occur when a line crosses a set of parallel lines.

Equal angles like these are called **corresponding angles**.

Equal angles like these are called **alternate angles**.

Example

(a) Explain why triangles PQR and PST must be similar.

(b) Calculate the length RT.

(c) Calculate the length PQ.

(a) ∠RQP = ∠TSP (corresponding angles with parallel lines)
∠QRP = ∠STP (corresponding angles with parallel lines)
∠QPR = ∠SPT (common)

So triangles PQR and PST are similar (same set of three angles).

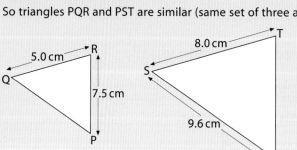

> It can help to draw and label the two triangles separately.

(b) Scale factor that enlarges triangle PQR to triangle PST = $\frac{ST}{QR}$ = 1.6
PT = 7.5 × 1.6 = 12.0 cm
so RT = 12.0 − 7.5 = 4.5 cm

(c) PQ = 9.6 ÷ 1.6 = 6.0 cm

> You could answer these questions using internal ratios.
>
> For example, $\frac{PR}{QR}$ = 1.5
>
> so PT = ST × 1.5 = 8.0 × 1.5 = 12.0 cm

B9 In this diagram BC is parallel to DE.

(a) Explain why triangles ABC and ADE must be similar.

(b) What is the scale factor of the enlargement from triangle ABC to ADE?

(c) Find the length BC.

(d) If CE = 6 cm, how long is AE?

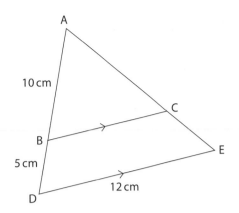

B10 In this diagram lines PQ and ST are parallel.

(a) Explain why triangles PQR and STR are similar.

(b) Calculate length PQ.

(c) PT = 12.5 cm. How long is PR?

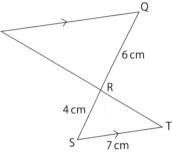

B11 BC is parallel to DE.
AB is twice as long as BD.
AD = 36 cm and AC = 27 cm

(a) Work out the length of AB.

(b) Work out the length of AE.

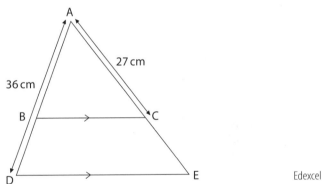

Edexcel

B12 JKLM is a trapezium with JK parallel to ML.

(a) Explain why triangles JKM and KLM are similar.

(b) Find the length of JK.

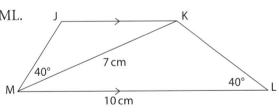

*B13 Find the length AC.

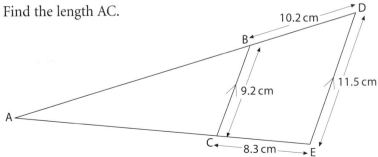

C Map scale

Example

On an architect's scale drawing a table 1.6 m long is drawn 8 mm long.

(a) What is the drawing's scale, in the form $1:n$?

(b) How long would a sofa 2.4 m long be drawn?

(a) Length of table = 1.6 m = 1600 mm
Scale factor from plan to reality
= 1600 ÷ 8 = 200
So scale is 1:200.

(b) Length of sofa = 2.4 m = 2400 mm
Length on plan = 2400 ÷ 200 = 12 mm

C1 An architecture student draws a building to a scale of $1:50$.
How big **in millimetres** would she draw a door that is 1 m by 2.2 m in real life?

C2 On a scale drawing a window 1.6 m tall is drawn 64 mm tall.

(a) What is the scale of the drawing?

(b) The window is drawn 42 mm wide. How wide is that, in metres, in real life?

C3 A map uses a scale of $1:25\,000$.

(a) The distance between two farmhouses on the map is 5 cm.
How far apart are the actual farmhouses, in km?

(b) How long, in cm, will the route of a 15 km walk be on the map?

D Repeated enlargement

D1 (a) A line 10 cm long is enlarged by a scale factor of 1.5. The resulting line is then enlarged by a scale factor of 2. What is the length of the final line?

(b) What scale factor would take you in a single enlargement from the original line to the final line?

(c) How is this value related to the scale factors of the separate enlargements?

D2 A shape is enlarged with scale factor 3.5. Its image is then enlarged with scale factor 1.2. What scale factor would achieve the same effect in a single enlargement?

D3 Shape X is enlarged with scale factor 3 to produce shape Y.
Y is then reduced by scale factor 0.8 to produce shape Z.
With what single scale factor could shape Z be produced directly from shape X?

*D4 To set the scaling on a photocopier you use a percentage.
For example, 125% means a scale factor of 1.25.

(a) What percentage setting should you use if you want to increase the width of a drawing from 15.4 cm to 20.0 cm? Give your answer to the nearest 1%.

(b) Paul wants to reduce a picture on a photocopier so that all the lengths are 36% of the original. The smallest the photocopier will do is 50%.
What should he do?

E Enlargement with a negative scale factor

You saw in the previous book how a shape can be enlarged using a centre of enlargement.

Here point C has been used as the centre to enlarge the shaded triangle by a scale factor of 2.

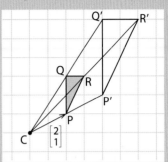

The vector from C to P is $\begin{bmatrix} 2 \\ 1 \end{bmatrix}$.

For an enlargement with scale factor 2 we multiply each vector by 2.

So the vector from C to P′ is $2 \times \begin{bmatrix} 2 \\ 1 \end{bmatrix} = \begin{bmatrix} 4 \\ 2 \end{bmatrix}$.

The vectors from C to Q and from C to R are multiplied by 2 in the same way.

For an enlargement with scale factor 3 each vector from C would be multiplied by 3, and so on.

The same process applies to a negative scale factor: for an enlargement with scale factor ⁻2 we multiply each vector by ⁻2.

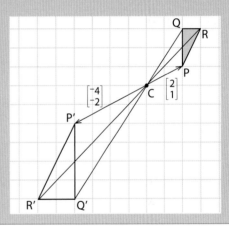

The vector from C to P is again $\begin{bmatrix} 2 \\ 1 \end{bmatrix}$.

So the vector from C to P′ is $^-2 \times \begin{bmatrix} 2 \\ 1 \end{bmatrix} = \begin{bmatrix} ^-4 \\ ^-2 \end{bmatrix}$.

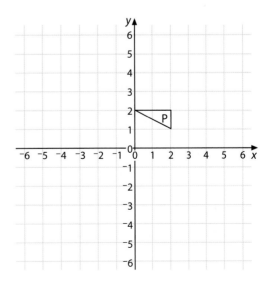

The positions of Q′ and R′ are obtained the same way.

E1 Copy this diagram.

(a) Draw an enlargement of triangle P using a scale factor of ⁻3 and (0, 0) as the centre of enlargement. Label this image Q.

(b) Draw an enlargement of P with centre (1, 0) and scale factor ⁻1. Label the image R.

(c) What transformation maps R directly on to Q? Describe it fully.

Test yourself

T1 Triangle Q is similar to triangle P.

  (a) What is the scale factor that enlarges P to Q?

  (b) Find a and b.

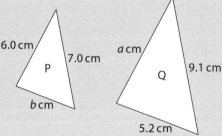
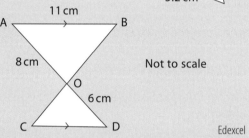

T2 AB is parallel to CD.
The lines AD and BC intersect at point O.
AB = 11 cm, AO = 8 cm, OD = 6 cm.

Calculate the length of CD.

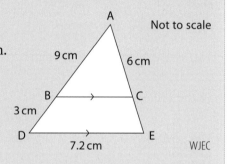

Not to scale

Edexcel

T3 In the diagram, BC is parallel to DE, and the
triangles ABC and ADE are similar.
AB = 9 cm, AC = 6 cm, BD = 3 cm and DE = 7.2 cm.

Showing all your working, find the length of

  (a) BC   **(b)** AE

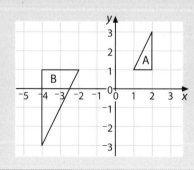

Not to scale

WJEC

T4 On a kitchen designer's scale drawing a tumble dryer 60 cm wide is drawn 30 mm wide.

  (a) Give the scale of the drawing in the form $1:n$.

  (b) The real tumble dryer is 84 cm high.
  How high is it in millimetres on the drawing?

T5 Shape P is enlarged using scale factor 3.5 to produce shape Q.
Q is then enlarged with scale factor 2.4 to give shape R.
What scale factor would be needed to produce R directly from P by a single enlargement?

T6 Describe fully the **single** transformation
that maps triangle A on to triangle B.

OCR

3 The reciprocal function

You will revise how to find the reciprocal of a number.

This work will help you use the reciprocal key on a calculator and work with graphs involving $\frac{1}{x}$.

In section B you may need a graphic calculator or a graph plotting facility on a computer.

A Review: reciprocals

If two numbers multiply together to give 1, each is called the **reciprocal** of the other.

$$n \times \frac{1}{n} = 1$$

$\frac{1}{n}$ is the reciprocal of n.

n is the reciprocal of $\frac{1}{n}$.

$$\frac{a}{b} \times \frac{b}{a} = 1$$

$\frac{b}{a}$ is the reciprocal of $\frac{a}{b}$.

$\frac{a}{b}$ is the reciprocal of $\frac{b}{a}$.

A1 Write down the reciprocal of 3.

A2 What is the reciprocal of each of these?

(a) $\frac{1}{4}$　　(b) $\frac{1}{6}$　　(c) $\frac{2}{3}$　　(d) $\frac{3}{4}$　　(e) $\frac{9}{5}$

A3 (a) Write $2\frac{1}{4}$ in the form $\frac{a}{b}$.

(b) Hence write down the reciprocal of $2\frac{1}{4}$.

A4 (a) Write 0.3 as a fraction.

(b) Hence write down the reciprocal of 0.3.

A5 Find the reciprocal of each of these.

(a) 0.25　　(b) 0.1　　(c) 0.01　　(d) 0.6　　(e) 1.7

A6 $\frac{1}{32} = 0.031\,25$. Hence write down the value of $\frac{1}{0.031\,25}$.

A7 Which is bigger, the reciprocal of 7 or the reciprocal of 70?

A8 Which is bigger, the reciprocal of 0.001 or the reciprocal of 0.0001?

A9 Solve these equations.

(a) $\frac{1}{x} = 5$　　(b) $\frac{1}{x} = \frac{2}{9}$　　(c) $\frac{1}{x} = 0.9$

Most calculators have a reciprocal key.

A10 Find the reciprocal key on your calculator and use it to find the reciprocal of 2.

A11 Use a calculator to find the reciprocal of each of these as a decimal.

(a) 8   (b) 16   (c) 0.8   (d) 0.08   (e) 6.4   (f) ⁻25

A12 (a) What is the value of $x^2 - \dfrac{1}{x}$ when $x = 5$?

(b) Use trial and improvement to find the positive solution to
the equation $x^2 - \dfrac{1}{x} = 20$.

Give your answer correct to two decimal places.

B Graphs of reciprocal functions

B1 (a) Copy and complete this table for $y = \dfrac{1}{x}$.

Give values correct to two decimal places where appropriate.

x	⁻4	⁻3	⁻2	⁻1	⁻0.5	⁻0.25	0.25	0.5	1	2	3	4
$y = \frac{1}{x}$	⁻0.25	⁻0.33				⁻4	4					

(b) On graph paper, draw the graph of $y = \dfrac{1}{x}$ for values of x from ⁻4 to 4.

(c) What is the decimal value of y when

(i) $x = 10$ (ii) $x = 1000$ (iii) $x = 100\,000$ (iv) $x = 10\,000\,000$

(d) What happens to the value of y as positive values of x get bigger and bigger?

(e) What is the value of y when

(i) $x = 0.1$ (ii) $x = 0.0001$ (iii) $x = 0.000\,001$ (iv) $x = 0.000\,000\,01$

(f) What happens to the value of y as positive values of x get closer and closer to 0?

(g) What happens to the value of y as negative values of x get bigger and bigger?

(h) What happens to the value of y as negative values of x get closer and closer to 0?

(i) What happens if you use your calculator to try to find the value of y when $x = 0$?
Can you explain this?

(j) Sketch the graph of $y = \dfrac{1}{x}$ showing what happens for large positive and
negative values of x.

(k) Does the graph have any reflection symmetry?
If so what are the equations of the mirror lines?

(l) Does the graph have any rotation symmetry?
If so what is the centre and order of rotation symmetry?

B2 (a) Work out the value of each expression when $x = 0$.

(i) $\dfrac{1}{x+1}$

(ii) $\dfrac{1}{x-1}$

(b) Sort the equations and sketch graphs into four matching pairs.

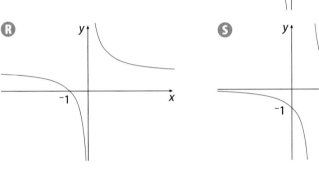

A $y = \dfrac{1}{x} + 1$

B $y = \dfrac{1}{x+1}$

C $y = \dfrac{1}{x-1}$

D $y = \dfrac{1}{x} - 1$

***B3 (a)** Use a graph plotter to draw the graphs of $y = x^2$ and $y = \dfrac{1}{x^2}$.
What do you notice about the two graphs?

(b) Use a graph plotter to draw the graphs of $y = x^3 - x$ and $y = \dfrac{1}{x^3 - x}$.
What do you notice about the two graphs?

(c) Investigate the relationship between the graph of any function and its reciprocal.

Test yourself

T1 Find the reciprocal of

(a) 4   (b) 0.1   (c) $\frac{1}{2}$ (d) $\frac{3}{7}$ (e) $\frac{4}{3}$

T2 Dario is using trial and improvement to find a solution to the equation

$$x + \frac{1}{x} = 5$$

The table shows his first trial.

x	$x + \frac{1}{x}$	Comment
4	4.25	Too low

Copy and continue the table to find a solution to the equation.
Give your answer to one decimal place.

AQA

4 Arc, sector and segment

You need to be able to use Pythagoras and trigonometry.

This work will help you

• calculate the length of an arc

• calculate the area of a sector and segment of a circle

• solve problems involving the surface area and volume of part of a cylinder

A Arc and sector of a circle

When r is the radius of a circle,

circumference $C = 2\pi r$ area $A = \pi r^2$

Part of a circle is called an **arc**.
The length of the arc is a fraction of the circumference of the circle.

A shape cut like this from a circle is called a **sector**.
The area of the sector is a fraction of the area of the circle.

arc

sector

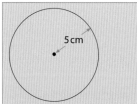
5 cm

Circumference = $2 \times \pi \times 5 = 31.4$ cm to 1 d.p.
Area = $\pi \times 5^2 = 78.5$ cm^2 to 1 d.p.

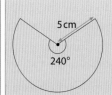
5 cm

240°

The sector is $\frac{240}{360}$ or $\frac{2}{3}$ of the complete circle.

Length of arc = $\frac{2}{3} \times 2 \times \pi \times 5 = 20.9$ cm to 1 d.p.
Area of sector = $\frac{2}{3} \times \pi \times 5^2 = 52.4$ cm^2 to 1 d.p.

A1 For each of these, calculate

    (i) the length of the arc to the nearest 0.1 cm

    (ii) the area of the sector to the nearest 0.1 cm^2

(a)
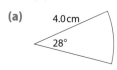
4.0 cm
28°

(b)

115° 6.0 cm

(c)
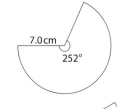
7.0 cm
252°

(d)
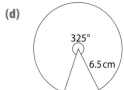
325°
6.5 cm

(e)
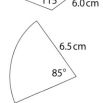
6.5 cm
85°

(f)
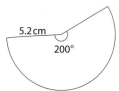
5.2 cm
200°

A2 Calculate

    (a) the area of a sector with radius 4.1 m and angle 48° (to the nearest 0.1 m²)

    (b) the length of its arc (to the nearest 0.1 m)

A3 Calculate

    (a) the area of a sector with radius 2.5 m and angle 220°

    (b) the length of its arc

A4 Calculate

    (a) the area of this sector

    (b) its total perimeter

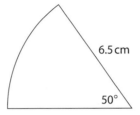

A5 These are the dimensions of the fabric part of this fan.

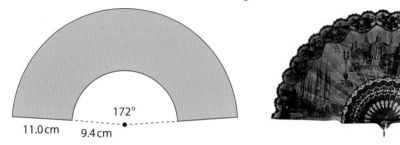

What is the area of the fabric part to the nearest cm²?

A6 Give each of these as an exact value, leaving π in your answer.

    (a) The length of the arc of a circle with radius 5 cm and angle 144°

    (b) The area of a sector with radius 3 cm and angle 120°

A7 The sector of a circle with radius 6 cm and angle 150°
is folded to form a cone.

    (a) Find, in terms of π, an exact value for
the length of the arc PQ.

    (b) Calculate the base radius, r, of the cone.

A8 Find the radius of a circle that has area 100 cm².

*A9 Find the radius of a sector that has area 50 cm² and angle 125°.

*A10 Find, to the nearest degree, the angle of a sector that has area 35 cm² and radius 5 cm.

*A11 A fitter bends a 50 cm length of curtain track into an arc of a circle.
The track has turned through 48°.
What is the radius of the arc to the nearest cm?

B Segment of a circle

A **segment** of a circle is part of the circle cut off by one straight line.

Example

Find the area of the segment shown.

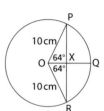

Area of segment = area of sector OAB – area of triangle OAB

Area of triangle = $\frac{1}{2} \times 8 \times 3 = 12\,cm^2$

$\tan x = \frac{4}{3}$

$x = 53.1...°$ Use trigonometry to find the angle in the sector.

So angle AOB = $2 \times 53.1...° = 106.2...°$

Area of minor sector AOB = $\frac{106.2...}{360} \times \pi \times 5^2 = 23.18...\,cm^2$

Area of segment = $23.18... - 12 = 11.2\,cm^2$ to 1 d.p.   'Minor sector' means the one with an angle less than 180°.

B1 (a) Calculate the area of sector OPQR.

(b) Use trigonometry to calculate lengths PX, XR and OX.

(c) Calculate the area of triangle OPR.

(d) Calculate the area of segment PQR.

B2 Calculate the area of the shaded segment.
You will first need to use trigonometry and
Pythagoras to find some extra measurements.
Mark them on a copy of the diagram and
show all your working.

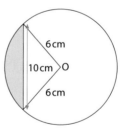

B3 A segment can be more than half of a circle, like these.
Devise methods to find their areas.

(a)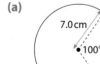

(b)

(c)

*B4 (a) This doorway has an arc of a circle at the top.
O is the centre of the circle.

What is the total area of the doorway,
to the nearest 0.1 m²?

(b) What is the height of the middle of the doorway?

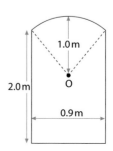

C Part of a cylinder

For any cylinder with radius r and height h,

$$\text{volume} = \pi r^2 h \qquad \text{area of curved surface} = 2\pi rh \qquad \text{total surface area} = 2\pi r(h + r)$$

C1 Assuming that this slice of cake is a sector of a cylinder (like a sector of a circle), find its volume.

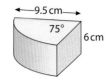

C2 The cross-section of a solid is the sector of a circle with radius 7 cm and angle 120°.
The height of the solid is 4 cm.

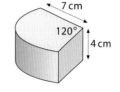

   (a) What is the area of the sector of the circle?

   (b) What is the area of the curved surface of the solid?

   (c) What is the total surface area of the solid?

*C3 The largest gates on the Thames barrier have these dimensions.
Each gate is a segment of a cylinder.
(It is rotated into this position to keep back a flood tide.
Normally it is under the water with its curved surface downwards.)

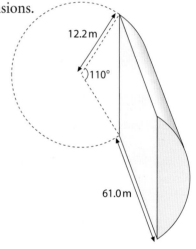

   (a) Work out the area of the curved surface.

   (b) Work out the areas of the three flat faces.

   (c) The curved surface is made from sheet steel weighing 314 kg per m². The flat faces are made from thinner sheet steel weighing 275 kg per m².

   Find the total mass of the surface steel in tonnes.

Test yourself

T1 AOB is a sector of a circle of radius 12 cm.
The area of the minor sector AOB is 98 cm².

Calculate the size of angle AOB.

Not drawn accurately

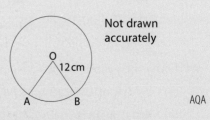

AQA

T2 The diagram shows a circle with centre O and radius 6 cm.

Find the area of the shaded segment.
Give the units of your answer.

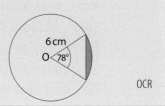

OCR

5 Investigating and identifying graphs

You will learn how to recognise the general shape of a quadratic, cubic or reciprocal graph.

You need a graphic calculator or a graph plotting facility on a computer.

A Investigating graphs

A1 Use a graph plotter to investigate graphs that have equations of the form $y = ax^2$.
Use positive and negative values for a.
Include fractional values such as $\frac{1}{2}$ and $\frac{-1}{4}$.
What does the value of a tell you about the graph?

A2 Use a graph plotter to investigate graphs that have equations of the
form $y = ax^2 + c$ for values of a and c both positive and negative.
What do the values of a and c tell you about the graph?

A3 Without using a graph plotter, match each equation to a sketch graph.

$y = x^2 + 1$

$y = x^2 - 1$

$y = 1 - x^2$

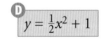
$y = \frac{1}{2}x^2 + 1$

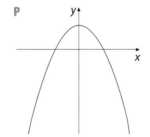

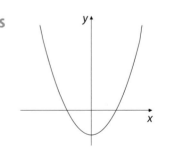

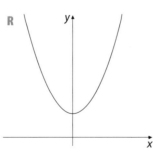

A4 Draw the graphs of $y = x^2 - 3$ and $y = x^2 - 2x - 3$ using a graph plotter.

(a) Which of these graphs has the y-axis as its line of symmetry?

(b) What is the equation of the line of symmetry of the other graph?

(c) How can you tell from the equations that both graphs will have the same y-intercept?

(d) **(i)** Sketch the graph of $y = x^2 - 2x - 3$.
On the same set of axes draw this graph after a reflection in the x-axis.

(ii) Show that the equation of the reflected graph is $y = {}^-x^2 + 2x + 3$.

A5 Without using a graph plotter, decide which of these is a sketch of $y = x^2 - x$.

A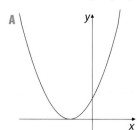

B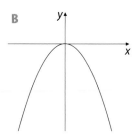

C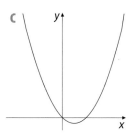

A6 Use a graph plotter to investigate graphs that have equations of the form $y = px^3 + q$ for values of p and q both positive and negative. What do the values of p and q tell you about the graph?

A7 (a) Without using a graph plotter, match each equation to a sketch graph.

A $y = x^3$

B $y = {}^-x^3$

C $y = x^3 + 1$

D $y = 1 - x^3$

W

X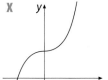

Y

Z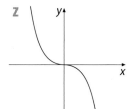

(b) Write down the centre of rotation symmetry of each graph.

A8 Use a graph plotter to investigate graphs that have equations of the form $y = x^3 + bx$ for values of b both positive and negative. What does the value of b tell you about the graph?

A9 Without using a graph plotter, match each equation to a sketch graph.

A $y = x^3 + x$

B $y = x^3 - x$

C $y = 2x - x^3$

P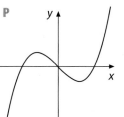

Q

R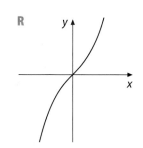

A10 The diagram shows a sketch of the graph of $y = \frac{1}{2}x^3 + 4$.
Without using a graph plotter, find the values of p, q and r.

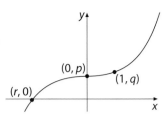

A11 Use a graph plotter to investigate graphs that have equations of the
form $y = \dfrac{k}{x} + c$ for values of k and c both positive and negative.
What do the values of k and c tell you about the graph?

A12 Without using a graph plotter, match each equation to a sketch graph.

A

$$y = \frac{1}{x} - 1$$

B

$$y = 1 - \frac{1}{x}$$

C
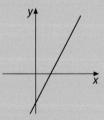
$$y = 1 + \frac{1}{x}$$

L
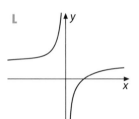

M
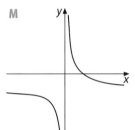

N
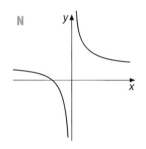

B Identifying graphs

When identifying a graph, think about the following.

• Is the graph one of these?

Linear	Quadratic	Cubic	Reciprocal

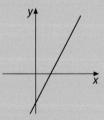

This involves x.
Examples are:
$y = 2x$
$y = 8 - x$

This involves x^2.
Examples are:
$y = x^2 + 5$
$y = x - x^2$

This involves x^3.
Examples are:
$y = x^3 - 1$
$y = x^3 + 5x + 1$

This involves $\dfrac{1}{x}$.
Examples are:
$y = \dfrac{1}{x} + 5$

$y = \dfrac{-3}{x}$

• Does the graph go through $(0, 0)$?

• Is the number in front of x, x^2, x^3 or $\dfrac{1}{x}$ positive or negative?

• For a graph involving a reciprocal, what happens to y when x is
very large and positive; very large and negative?

B1 Here are six equations and six sketch graphs. Match them up.

A $y = 2x^2$

B $y + x = 2$

C $y = x^2 + 2$

D $y = x^3 + 2$

E $y = 2x^3 + 1$

F $y = \dfrac{3}{x}$

P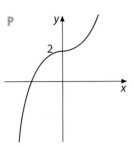

Q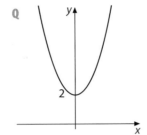

R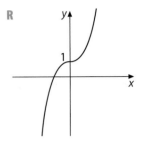

S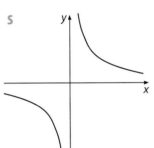

T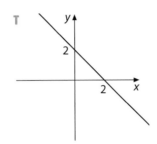

U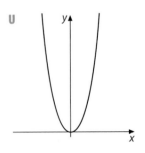

B2 A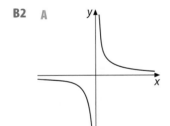

B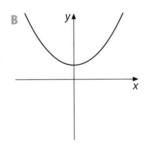

C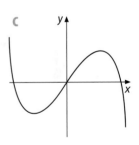

D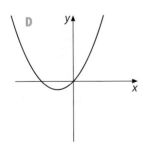

E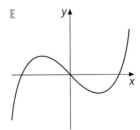

F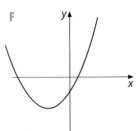

Each of the equations below represents one of the graphs A to F.
For each equation, write down the letter of the correct graph.

$y = x^2 + 3x$ $y = x - x^3$ $y = x^3 - 2x$

$y = x^2 + 2x - 4$ $y = \dfrac{4}{x}$ $y = x^2 + 3$ Edexcel

Test yourself

T1 For each of the sketch graphs below, choose the correct equation from this list.

$$y = 2 + x^3 \qquad y = \frac{-2}{x} \qquad y = 2 - x^3 \qquad y = \frac{2}{x}$$

(a)
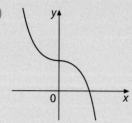

(b)
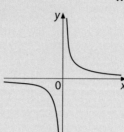

OCR

T2 Each of the graphs represents one of the following equations.

A $y = 3x + 4$ **B** $2x + 3y = 12$ **C** $y = x^2 - 2$ **D** $y = x^3$

Write down the letter of the equation represented by each graph.

(a)
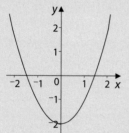

(b)
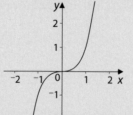

(c)
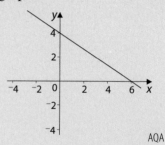

AQA

T3 Match the sketch graph to its equation.

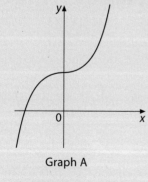

Graph A

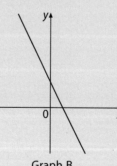

Graph B

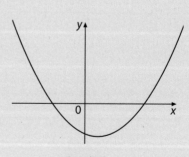

Graph C

Equation 1 $y = 4x + 7$
Equation 3 $y = x^2 - x - 6$
Equation 5 $y = x^3 + 4$

Equation 2 $y = 4 - 3x$
Equation 4 $y = x^2 - 5$
Equation 6 $y = {}^-x^3 + 4$

OCR

6 Combining probabilities

This work will help you calculate probabilities in the case of

- mutually exclusive events

- independent events

- dependent events

A Review: finding probabilities

A1 A pack contains 40 cards, numbered from 1 to 40.
A card is picked at random from the pack.
What is the probability that the number on the card is

(a) even   (b) 10 or less   (c) a multiple of 5   (d) a multiple of 7

A2 The fish in a pond are classified as red or silver
and as male or female.
The number of fish of each type is shown here.

	Red	Silver
Male	20	55
Female	40	25

A fish in the pond is caught at random.
What is the probability that the fish is

(a) male   (b) silver   (c) a red female   (d) a silver male

A3 (a) Sharmila takes a cube and writes these numbers on its six faces: 1, 1, 2, 2, 2, 3.
Sharmila rolls the cube.
What is the probability that the number 1 is uppermost?

(b) David writes numbers on the faces of a cube.
He rolls the cube many times and makes this record of how it lands.

Number uppermost	1	2	3	4
Frequency	42	79	85	34

What numbers do you think he wrote on the six faces of the cube?

A4 Britalite tested 250 of their 100 watt bulbs, to see how long they lasted.
The results of the test are shown in this table.

Lifetime, L, of bulb (hours)	$0 \leq L < 1000$	$1000 \leq L < 2000$	$2000 \leq L < 3000$	$3000 \leq L$
Frequency	24	62	145	19

Estimate the probability that a Britalite 100 watt bulb will last

(a) less than 1000 hours   (b) less than 3000 hours   (c) 2000 hours or more

B Mutually exclusive events

Imagine that these cards are turned over and shuffled.
One card is picked at random.

| 2 | 3 | 4 | 5 | 6 | 7 | 8 | 9 | 10 | 11 |

An **event** is something that may or may not be true about the outcome.
Here are some examples of events, their **favourable outcomes** and probabilities.

Event	Favourable outcomes			Probability
A: The number picked is a multiple of 3.	3	6	9	$\frac{3}{10}$
B: The number picked is a factor of 20.	2	4 5	10	$\frac{4}{10}$

The lists of favourable outcomes for A and B are completely different.
There is no number common to both lists.
We say the events A and B are **mutually exclusive**.
In other words A and B can't both happen.

Suppose you win a prize if the number picked is **either** a multiple of 3 **or** a factor of 20.
The probability of winning is $\frac{3}{10} + \frac{4}{10} = \frac{7}{10}$.
You can add the probabilities because the two events are mutually exclusive.

Now look at these two events.

Event	Favourable outcomes					Probability
C: The number picked is even.	2	4	6	8	10	$\frac{5}{10}$
D: The number picked is a factor of 60.	2 3	4 5	6		10	$\frac{6}{10}$

Events C and D are not mutually exclusive.
They can both happen (if the outcome is 2, 4, 6 or 10).

Suppose you win a prize if the number picked is **either** even **or** a factor of 60.
You can't find the probability of winning by adding the probabilities of C and D, because the events are not mutually exclusive.

The favourable outcomes for winning the prize are 2, 3, 4, 5, 6, 8, 10. So the probability is $\frac{7}{10}$.

B1 (a) Are the events A and C mutually exclusive?

(b) Are the events A and D mutually exclusive?

(c) E is the event 'The number picked is a factor of 21'.
Are the following events mutually exclusive?

(i) A and E   (ii) B and E   (iii) C and E   (iv) D and E

B2 In a fairground game, players each choose a number on this board. An electronic device lights up and turns off the numbers in a random way. When it stops, one number is lit up.

1	2	3	4
5	6	7	8
9	10	11	12
13	14	15	16

What is the probability that the lit-up number is

(a) in the first row
(b) in the first column
(c) either in the first row or the first column

B3 These cards are turned over and shuffled. A card is picked at random.

| 20 | 21 | 22 | 23 | 24 | 25 | 26 | 27 | 28 | 29 |

Event A is 'The number picked is less than 24'.

Event B is 'The number picked is a multiple of 5'.

Event C is 'The number picked is prime'.

Event D is 'The number picked is a multiple of 3'.

(a) Are these pairs of events mutually exclusive?

   (i) A, B   (ii) A, C   (iii) A, D   (iv) B, C   (v) B, D

(b) What is the probability that the number picked is either prime or a multiple of 3?

(c) Jake said:

'The probability of picking a number less than 24 is $\frac{4}{10}$.

The probability of picking an even number is $\frac{5}{10}$.

So the probability of picking either a number less than 24 or an even number is $\frac{9}{10}$.'

Is he right? If not, why not?

B4 A bag contains sweets that are red, yellow, green or orange.
A sweet is picked at random from the bag.
The probability that the sweet is red is 0.28, yellow 0.26 and green 0.4 .

Colour	Red	Yellow	Green	Orange
Probability	0.28	0.26	0.4	

What is the probability that the sweet is

(a) orange   (b) red or yellow   (c) not green   (d) neither red nor green

B5 The students in a college are on degree courses that lead to either a BA or a BSc degree.
The table gives a breakdown of the students by course and by sex.

	BA	BSc
Male	150	120
Female	190	140

(a) A student is picked at random to represent the college at a conference. Find the probability that the student is

   (i) a male student on a BSc course   (ii) a student on a BA course

   (iii) a female student   (iv) either a male student or a student on a BSc course

(b) (i) How many male students are there in the college?

   (ii) If one of the male students is picked at random, what is the probability that he is on a BSc course?

C Independent events

For the rest of this chapter, assume that coins, dice and spinners are fair, unless told otherwise.

Paul flips a coin and rolls a dice.

The coin and the dice do not affect each other. Their outcomes are **independent**.

There are 12 equally likely outcomes of the coin and dice. They are shown in this diagram.

The probability of each outcome (for example H, 5) can be found by **multiplying** the separate probabilities:

$$\frac{1}{2} \quad \times \quad \frac{1}{6} \quad = \quad \frac{1}{12}$$

| probability of head | probability of 5 | probability of head and 5 |

Dice		
6	H, 6	T, 6
5	H, 5	T, 5
4	H, 4	T, 4
3	H, 3	T, 3
2	H, 2	T, 2
1	H, 1	T, 1
	H(ead)	T(ail)
	Coin	

The **multiplication rule for independent events** says

If two events are independent, the probability that they **both** happen is found by multiplying their probabilities.

C1 (a) What is the probability of getting an even number on the dice?

(b) What is the probability of getting a head on the coin?

(c) Use the multiplication rule to find the probability of getting an even number on the dice and head on the coin.

Check from the diagram of outcomes that your result is correct.

C2 (a) What is the probability that spinner A shows blue?

(b) What is the probability that spinner B shows blue?

(c) Find the probability that both spinners show blue.

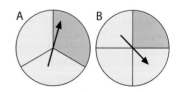

C3 (a) What is the probability that spinner P shows blue?

(b) What is the probability that spinner Q shows blue?

(c) Find the probability that both spinners show blue.

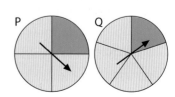

Example

These two spinners are spun.
What is the probability that spinner A shows blue and spinner B shows white?

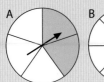

Probability that A shows blue = $\frac{2}{5}$

Probability that B shows white = $\frac{5}{8}$

Probability of (A blue, B white) = $\frac{2}{5} \times \frac{5}{8} = \frac{10}{40} = \frac{1}{4}$

C4 These spinners are both spun.
Find the probability that

 (a) P shows blue and Q shows white

 (b) P shows white and Q shows blue

 (c) both spinners show blue

 (d) both spinners show white

C5 Sharmila takes a card at random from each
of these packs.
Find the probability that

Pack A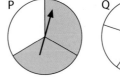

Pack B

 (a) she takes a 1 from pack A and a 2 from pack B

 (b) she takes a 2 from pack A and a 3 from pack B

 (c) she takes a 3 from both packs

C6 Susie has 2 blue skirts and 3 pink skirts in a drawer.
In another drawer she has 3 blue tops and 4 pink tops.
She takes a skirt at random and a top at random.
Find the probability that the skirt and the top are (a) both blue (b) both pink

C7 Class 1A consists of 10 boys and 15 girls.
Class 1B consists of 18 boys and 12 girls.

One child is picked at random from each class.
What is the probability that the children picked are (a) both boys (b) both girls

C8 A train and a coach go from London to Brighton.
The probability that the train is late is 0.3.
The probability that the coach is late is 0.2.
These two events are independent.

 (a) What is the probability that the train is not late?

 (b) Find the probability that the coach is late but the train is not late.

 (c) Find the probability that both the train and the coach are late.

 (d) Find the probability that neither the train nor the coach is late.

D Tree diagrams

The possible outcomes when these two spinners are spun can be shown in a **tree diagram**.

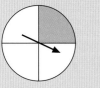

Spinner A

Spinner B

Probabilities along the branches are found by multiplying.

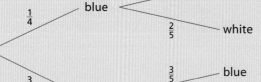

$\frac{3}{5}$ — blue   probability of (A blue, B blue) $= \frac{1}{4} \times \frac{3}{5} = \frac{3}{20}$

$\frac{1}{4}$ — blue

$\frac{2}{5}$ — white   probability of (A blue, B white) $= \frac{1}{4} \times \frac{2}{5} = \frac{2}{20}$

$\frac{3}{5}$ — blue   probability of (A white, B blue) $= \frac{3}{4} \times \frac{3}{5} = \frac{9}{20}$

$\frac{3}{4}$ — white

$\frac{2}{5}$ — white   probability of (A white, B white) $= \frac{3}{4} \times \frac{2}{5} = \frac{6}{20}$

The four routes through the tree diagram represent mutually exclusive events.

Their probabilities $\frac{3}{20}$, $\frac{2}{20}$, $\frac{9}{20}$ and $\frac{6}{20}$ add up to 1.

The probability that both spinners give the same colour is found by adding:

probability of same colour = probability of (A blue, B blue) + probability of (A white, B white)

$$= \frac{3}{20} + \frac{6}{20} = \frac{9}{20}$$

It is better **not** to simplify the fractions: it makes them easier to compare and add.

D1 (a) Copy and complete the tree diagram for these two spinners.

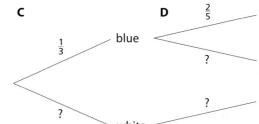

C $\frac{1}{3}$ — blue   **D** $\frac{2}{5}$ — blue

? — white

? — blue

? — white

? — white

(b) What is the probability that C and D show

(i) the same colour   **(ii)** different colours

D2 (a) Draw a tree diagram for these two spinners.

(b) Find the probability that the two spinners show the same colour.

E 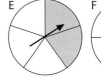 F

D3 Gill has a coin which is weighted so that the probability that it lands head is $\frac{3}{5}$ and tail $\frac{2}{5}$.

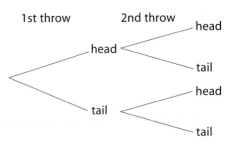

(a) Copy and complete the tree diagram for two throws of the coin, writing the probabilities on the branches.

(b) Find the probability of getting one head and one tail.

D4 Two trains, A and B, go from London to Reading by different routes.

The probability that train A is late is $\frac{3}{10}$.

The probability that train B is late is $\frac{1}{5}$.

These two events are independent.

(a) What is the probability that train A is not late?

(b) Find the probability that both trains are late.

(c) Find the probability that only one of the two trains is late.

D5 Patrick has two cubes, A and B.

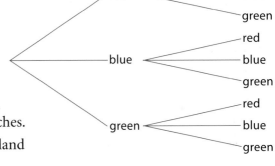

The faces of cube A are coloured red, red, blue, blue, green, green.

The faces of cube B are coloured red, blue, blue, blue, green, green.

Patrick rolls the two cubes to see which colours come on top.

(a) Copy and complete the tree diagram, writing the probabilities on the branches.

(b) Find the probability that both cubes land with the same colour on top.

(c) Find the probability that one of the cubes lands blue and the other green.

D6 A chicken coop is protected by two alarms A and B.
The alarms are intended to sound when a fox approaches the coop.

The probability of alarm A sounding is 0.9.
The probability of alarm B sounding is 0.8.
These two events are independent.

(a) What is the probability that both alarms fail to sound?

(b) What is the probability that at least one of the alarms sounds when a fox approaches?

(c) A third alarm is installed.
The probability that this new alarm sounds when a fox approaches is 0.7.
It is now more likely or less likely that at least one alarm sounds when a fox approaches?

E Dependent events

A box contains 2 black counters and 4 white counters.

One counter is picked at random.
This tree diagram shows the probabilities.

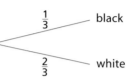

Suppose the counter is **not** put back in the box.
The contents of the box will be different, depending on whether
the counter taken out was black or white.

If it was black, the box would now contain 1 black and 4 white counters.

If it was white, it would contain 2 black and 3 white counters.

If another counter is now taken out at random, the probability that it is black is
dependent on the colour of the first counter.

The complete tree diagram looks like this.

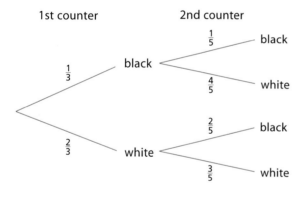

probability of (black, black) $= \frac{1}{3} \times \frac{1}{5} = \frac{1}{15}$

probability of (black, white) $= \frac{1}{3} \times \frac{4}{5} = \frac{4}{15}$

probability of (white, black) $= \frac{2}{3} \times \frac{2}{5} = \frac{4}{15}$

probability of (white, white) $= \frac{2}{3} \times \frac{3}{5} = \frac{6}{15}$

$\left(\text{Check: total} = \frac{15}{15}\right)$

E1 From the tree diagram above, find the probability that the two counters are

(a) the same colour

(b) different colours

E2 A bag contains 3 red cubes and 2 blue cubes.
A cube is taken at random from the bag and not replaced.
Then a second cube is taken at random.

(a) Draw a tree diagram for this situation.

(b) Find the probability that both of the cubes taken out are the same colour.

(c) Find the probability that the two cubes are of different colours.

E3 Two counters are taken at random from a box containing 4 red and 6 blue counters.
Use a tree diagram to find the probability that the two counters are the same colour.

E4 The probability that it will be raining tomorrow morning is $\frac{1}{3}$.
If it is raining, the probability that Simon will be late for school is $\frac{1}{4}$.
If it is not raining, the probability that he will be late is $\frac{1}{5}$.

(a) Copy and complete this tree diagram.

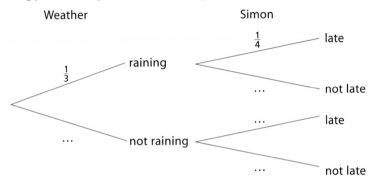

(b) Find the probability that Simon will be late for school tomorrow.

E5 In a TV game show, contestants are given two tasks.
In each task they either succeed or fail.

The probability of succeeding in the first task is 0.8.

If a contestant succeeds in the first task, the probability of succeeding in the second is 0.6.
If a contestant fails in the first task, the probability of succeeding in the second is 0.3.

What is the probability that a contestant

(a) succeeds in both tasks   (b) fails in at least one task

E6 A pack of cards consists of 3 'wolf' cards and 2 'goat' cards.
Here are the rules for a game.

> A player takes a card at random from the pack.
> If it is a wolf, the player keeps it. If it is a goat, it goes back in the pack.
> The player then takes a card at random again.
>
> If the player took a wolf both times, they win 5 points.
> If they took a wolf once (either first or second time), they win 2 points.
> If they took a goat both times, they do not win any points.

Find the probability that a player wins

(a) 5 points   (b) 2 points

E7 Jack takes a card at random from this pack. ☐1 ☐2 ☐3 ☐4

He keeps the card and then takes a second card at random.

What is the probability that the second number he takes is higher than the first?

F Mixed questions

F1 These nine cards are placed face down and shuffled.

`1` `2` `3` `4` `5` `6` `7` `8` `9`

One card is picked at random.

Pat says:

'The probability that the number on the card is even is $\frac{4}{9}$.
The probability that the number is less than 6 is $\frac{5}{9}$.
So the probability that the number is either even or less than 6 is $\frac{4}{9} + \frac{5}{9} = 1$.'

What is wrong with Pat's reasoning?

F2 What's wrong here?

The probability that a person stopped at random is male is about 0.5.
The probability that a person stopped at random is wearing a skirt is about 0.25.
Therefore the probability that a person stopped at random is male and wearing
a skirt is 0.5×0.25 which is 0.125 or 12.5%.

F3 This table gives information about the
children in a primary school class.

	Left-handed	Right-handed
Girls	5	15
Boys	4	9

(a) One of the children is picked at random from the class.
What is the probability that the child is a girl?

(b) One of the boys in the class is picked at random.
What is the probability that he is left-handed?

(c) A boy in the class is picked at random, and a girl is picked at random.
What is the probability that they are both left-handed?

(d) One of the right-handed children is picked at random.
What is the probability that the child is a boy?

F4 Josh assembles alarms which consist of a lamp, a buzzer and a battery.
He takes each component from a separate bin and puts them together.
The probability that the lamp he takes is faulty is 0.4.
The probability that the buzzer is faulty is 0.5, and the battery 0.3.

An alarm fails to work if any of the components is faulty.
What is the probability that the next alarm Josh makes is faulty?

F5 Josie takes a card at random from this pack and keeps it.
Then she takes a second card at random.
Find the probability that she takes one odd number and
one even number (in either order).

Test yourself

T1 A spinner has three colours: red, green and blue. When it is spun, the probability it lands on red is 0.3 and the probability it lands on green is 0.15.

(a) Find the probability that the spinner lands on either red or blue.

(b) If the spinner is spun 200 times, how many times would you expect it to land on blue?

(c) The spinner is spun twice. Find the probability that

(i) both spins result in red

(ii) one spin results in blue and one in red, in either order

T2 One domino is to be chosen at random from this collection.

Three events are defined as

    Event S   The total number of spots on the chosen domino is 6.
    Event D   The chosen domino is a double.
    Event T   The total number of spots on the chosen domino is 10.

What is the probability that

(a) S is true   (b) D is true   (c) both S and D are true   (d) either S or T is true

T3 On his way to work, Nick goes through a set of traffic lights and then passes over a level crossing. Over a period of time, Nick has estimated the probability of stopping at each of these.

The probability that he has to stop at the traffic lights is $\frac{2}{3}$.
The probability that he has to stop at the level crossing is $\frac{1}{5}$.

These probabilities are independent.

(a) Construct a tree diagram to show this information.

(b) Calculate the probability that Nick will not have to stop at either the lights or the level crossing on his way to work.   OCR

T4 A packet contains stamps from three different countries. The packet contains 4 Spanish stamps, 10 French stamps and 6 German stamps.

Two stamps are to be removed at random, without replacement.
Calculate the probability that both stamps will be from the same country.   Edexcel

T5 In Britain the probability of a 17-year-old passing the driving test at the first attempt is 0.6.

Three people are chosen at random from the population of 17-year-olds in Britain who are about to take their driving test. What is the probability that exactly two of them pass the driving test at the first attempt?   AQA

Review 1

1 This diagram shows a pair of similar triangles.
Calculate the lengths marked a and b.

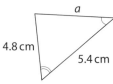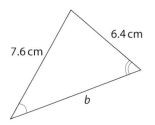

2 (a) Calculate the cost of 16 calculators at £5.89 each.

(b) How many 34p stamps can be bought with a £5 note?

3 x and y are integers.

(a) List all the values of x such that $^-3 \leq x < 5$.

(b) List all the values of y such that $^-2 < 2y \leq 4$.

4 Here are sketches of the front elevation and side elevation of a prism.

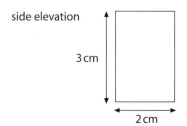

front elevation   3 cm   4 cm   side elevation   3 cm   2 cm

(a) Sketch the prism and find its volume.

(b) Draw a full-size plan view of the prism.

5 Jodi thinks of a number.
She multiplies it by 5 and adds 21.
The answer is double the number she first thought of.
Find the number she was thinking of.

6 As a fraction, write down the reciprocal of

(a) 5   (b) 0.4   (c) 100   (d) 1.2

7 Find the equation of the straight line that goes through points $(^-2, 5)$ and $(6, 1)$.

8 Points A $(^-1, 5)$, B $(1, 1)$ and C $(5, 3)$ are three vertices of the square ABCD.

(a) What are the coordinates of D, the fourth vertex?

(b) Find the coordinates of the mid-point of AD.

(c) Calculate the length of each side of the square, to two decimal places.

(d) Find the coordinates of the centre of the square.

9 Sunil passes two sets of traffic lights on his route into town.
The probability that the first set of lights is green is 0.7.
The probability that the second set of lights is green is 0.4.
These two events are independent.

(a) Copy and complete the tree diagram.

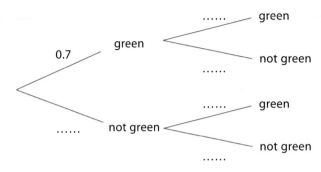

(b) Work out the probability that

(i) neither set of lights is green

(ii) only one of the sets of lights is green

10 This cumulative frequency graph shows the distribution of marks (out of 100) scored by 200 students in a test.

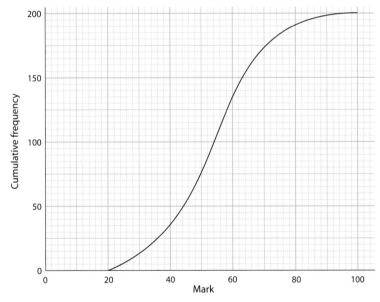

(a) Estimate the median mark.

(b) Estimate the lower and upper quartiles.

(c) Estimate the percentage of students who will pass the test if the pass mark is 35.

11 Solve the inequality $3x - 1 \leq 20$.

12 Increase £6.50 by 24%.

13 Multiply out and simplify the expression $x(x - 3) + 9x$.

14 (a) Explain why triangle PTS and triangle PRQ are similar triangles.

(b) Calculate the length of QR.

(c) Given that the length of QP is 28 cm, work out the length of SP.

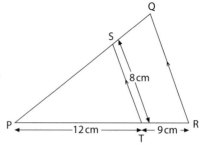

15 Work these out, giving each answer in its simplest form.

(a) $\frac{5}{6} \times \frac{3}{4}$ **(b)** $1\frac{2}{3} \times 1\frac{4}{5}$ **(c)** $\frac{9}{10} \div \frac{3}{4}$ **(d)** $\frac{3}{5} \div \frac{2}{3}$

16 The diagram shows a quadrilateral.
The length of each side is marked on the diagram.

(a) Find an expression, in its simplest form, for the perimeter of the quadrilateral.

(b) The perimeter of the quadrilateral is 32 cm.
Form an equation and solve it to find the value of x.

(c) What is the length of the longest side of the shape?

2x + 6 cm

x cm

3x – 1 cm

3x cm

17 A company is doing badly.
In March, the employees agree to a 7% reduction in their wages.
In September, business picks up and they are given an 11.5% rise.

Find the overall percentage change between March and September, to the nearest 0.1%.

18 A group of three adults and one child pay £12 altogether for concert tickets.
Another group of two adults and four children pay £13 altogether.

Form a pair of simultaneous equations.
Solve them to find the cost of an adult ticket and the cost of a child ticket.

19 A fish farmer collected this information about salmon.

Weight (kg)	5.0	3.3	4.3	5.1	3.4	5.1	4.7	4.2	3.1	2.9	4.5	4.9	3.4	5.0	5.0
Length (cm)	74	49	62	67	54	74	71	57	54	48	69	69	58	79	71

(a) Show this information on a scatter diagram.

(b) Describe the correlation.

(c) Draw a line of best fit.

(d) Estimate the weight of a salmon of length 75 cm.

20 (a) Write, as an improper fraction, the reciprocal of $\frac{3}{8}$.

(b) As an exact decimal, $\frac{3}{8} = 0.375$.
Work out the reciprocal of 0.375, correct to three decimal places.

21 Find the size of each exterior angle in a regular nine-sided polygon.

22 Lee has a biased dice.
The table shows probabilities
for scores on his dice.

Score	1	2	3	4	5	6
Probability	0.11	0.12	0.17	x	0.14	0.27

(a) Work out the value of x.

(b) Lee is going to roll the dice 500 times.
Work out an estimate for the number of times he will roll a 6.

23 Solve these simultaneous equations. $\quad 6x + y = 28$
$$x - 3y = 11$$

24 Gold has a density of 19.3 g/cm³.
Calculate the mass of a gold disc that has a radius of 5 cm and a thickness of 4 mm.

25 Rianna has £x.
Jerome has £10 more than Rianna.
Kelly has three times as much money as Rianna.

(a) Write down, in terms of x, how much money Jerome has.

(b) Show that the total amount of money Rianna, Jerome and Kelly have is £$5(x + 2)$.

26 Two bags contain coloured marbles.
Bag A contains 3 red marbles and 2 blue marbles.
Bag B contains 2 red marbles, 3 blue marbles and 1 green marble.

Ken picks a marble at random from each bag.
Calculate the probability that both marbles will be the same colour.

27 (a) Write down the equation of the line L.

(b) Write down three inequalities that describe
the pink region.

(c) On a similar diagram, show clearly the region
that is satisfied by these three inequalities.
$$x + y \geq 2, \quad y \leq 2x - 1 \quad \text{and} \quad x \leq 2$$

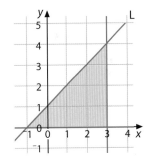

28 Shape ABCD is a piece of sheet metal.
OAB and OCD are each sectors of a circle.

(a) Calculate the length of the arc AB.

(b) Calculate the total area of sheet metal.

(c) The metal weighs 6.2 kilograms per **square metre**.
Calculate the weight of the metal, in kilograms.

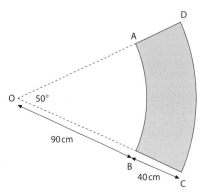

29 Factorise fully the expression $6x^2y + 15xy^2$.

30 A bag contains two Russian coins and three Mexican coins.
Josie takes two coins at random from the bag.
Find the probability that both coins are Mexican.

31 Simplify each of these.

(a) $\dfrac{4x}{2}$
   (b) $\dfrac{x^3}{x}$
   (c) $\dfrac{10x}{5x}$
   (d) $\dfrac{8x+4}{2}$
   (e) $\dfrac{x^2-7x}{x}$

32 This stem-and-leaf table shows the weights
of the members of a football team.

6	4 9
7	1 4 5 6 8
8	3 4 4 6

Stem: 10 kg

(a) Find the median weight.

(b) Find the mean weight.

33 Points (2, 1) and (4, 1) are opposite vertices of a rhombus.
The area of the rhombus is 4 square units.

(a) Draw the rhombus on axes, each numbered from ⁻6 to 6.

(b) (i) Draw an enlargement of the rhombus using a scale factor of ⁻2 and
(1, 1) as the centre of enlargement.

(ii) What is the image of point (3, ⁻1)?

(iii) What is the area of the enlarged rhombus?

34 Multiply out the brackets and simplify each of these expressions.

(a) $3(x-5) + x(x+2)$
   (b) $n(5-n) - 2(n+3)$
   (c) $p(p+5) - p(p-4)$

35 Express the area 2.5 m² in cm².

36 Match each equation with its sketch graph.

 A $y = \dfrac{3}{x}$ **B** $y = 3 - x^2$ **C** $y = x^3 + 3$ **D** $y = 3x + 1$ **E** $y = x^2 + 3$

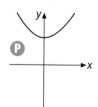 **P**   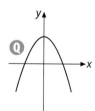 **Q**   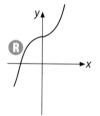 **R**   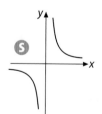 **S**   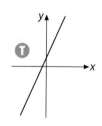 **T**

37 $\frac{2}{3}$ of the children in a primary class are boys and $\frac{1}{3}$ are girls.
$\frac{1}{4}$ of the boys are left-handed and $\frac{1}{6}$ of the girls are left-handed.

(a) What fraction of all the children are left-handed?

(b) What is the smallest possible value for the number of children in the class?

7 Direct and inverse proportion

You will revise ratio.

This work will help you

- recognise direct and inverse proportion
- do calculations involving direct and inverse proportion
- solve problems involving other types of proportionality

A Review: ratio

Adult lizard

Young lizard

15 cm

6 cm

The ratio of the adult's length to the young lizard's length can be written in different ways.

length of adult : length of young = 15 : 6
$$= 5 : 2$$

$$\frac{\text{length of adult}}{\text{length of young}} = \frac{15}{6} = 2.5$$

A1 Write each of these ratios in its simplest form.

(a) $10:5$ (b) $12:20$ (c) $9:15$ (d) $200:25$ (e) $144:360$

A2 The 'aspect ratio' of a rectangular picture is the ratio $\frac{\text{height}}{\text{width}}$.

Find the aspect ratio of each of these pictures.

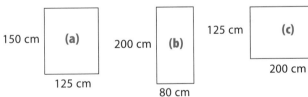

150 cm (a) 125 cm

200 cm (b) 80 cm

125 cm (c) 200 cm

A3 The ratio of the number of rainy days to the number of dry days over a period of time is $2:5$.
If there were 16 rainy days, how many dry days were there?

A4 Split £60 in the following ratios. (a) $2:3$ (b) $4:1$ (c) $2:3:7$

A5 Write each of these ratios in the form $k:1$. (a) $12:3$ (b) $7:2$ (c) $4:5$

*A6 The ratio of sheep to goats on a farm is $5:4$. The ratio of goats to pigs is $3:2$.
What is the ratio of sheep to pigs?

B Quantities related by a rate

T Ribbon can be bought by length from a roll.
50 cm of ribbon costs 20p.

- How much ribbon can you buy for 1p?
- How much can you buy for 12p?
- How much does 1 cm of ribbon cost?
- What numbers are missing from this table?

Length (L cm)	0	1			20		50	80
Cost (C pence)	0		1	6		12	20	

The graph of C against L is a straight line that
goes through the origin $(0, 0)$.

- What is the gradient of the graph?
- What is the equation connecting C and L?
- Use the equation to find C when $L = 130$.

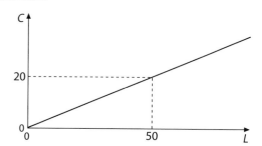

B1 Stephanie works in a factory and is paid by the hour.
She works for 6 hours and is paid £45.

(a) How much does she earn in 1 hour?

(b) How much will she earn in a 40-hour week?

(c) How long does it take her to earn £1? (Give your answer as a fraction of an hour.)

(d) Copy and complete this table of values.
T is the time in hours, W the wages in £.

T	6	1	40			30
W	45			1	90	

(e) Draw a graph of W against T.

(f) What is the equation connecting W and T?

(g) Use the equation to find

  (i) Stephanie's wages when she works 15 hours

  (ii) the time Stephanie has to work to earn £60

B2 (a) Using suitable axes, plot values of
S and T as given in this table.
Draw the graph of T against S.

S	0	2	4	5	7	10
T	0	9	18	22.5	31.5	45

(b) Write down the equation of the graph.

(c) Use the equation to find

  (i) T when $S = 30$

  (ii) S when $T = 54$

C Direct proportion

The cost of ribbon, C pence, is **directly proportional** to the length, L cm.
This means

- If L is multiplied by a number, then C is multiplied by the same number.
  (For example, if you buy 3 times as much, you pay 3 times as much.)

- The ratio $\dfrac{C}{L}$ is the same for every pair of values of L and C.

- The graph of C against L is **a straight line going through (0, 0)**.

- C is connected to L by a formula of the type $C = kL$.
  k is called the **constant of proportionality**.
  (In the ribbon example, $k = 0.4$.)

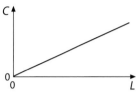

The symbol $\propto$ is used to mean 'is directly proportional to'. So we write $C \propto L$.

You can think of $C \propto L$ as another way of writing $C = kL$.

C1 In which of these graphs is Q directly proportional to P? Give reasons.

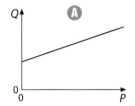 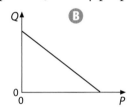 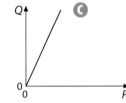 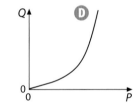

C2 Are these statements true or false?

(a) The cost of petrol is directly proportional to the quantity purchased.

(b) The height of a person is directly proportional to their age.

(c) The area of a square is directly proportional to the length of the side.

(d) The distance travelled in a certain time by a car travelling at constant speed is directly proportional to the speed of the car.

(e) The time taken for a journey is directly proportional to the speed of travel.

C3 In each of these tables, is Q directly proportional to P?
If so, give the equation connecting Q and P.

(a)

P	0	3	4	10
Q	0	12	16	40

(b)

P	0	2	4	6
Q	4	10	16	22

(c)

P	0	3	4	6
Q	0	18	32	72

(d)

P	4	6	7	10
Q	8	12	14	20

(e)

P	1	2	3	4
Q	3	7	11	15

(f)

P	2	10	12	20
Q	7	35	42	70

D Calculating with direct proportion

Example

When a spring is stretched, the extension, E cm, of the spring is directly proportional to the stretching force, F newtons.

Given that $E = 12$ when $F = 5$, find   **(a)** E when $F = 8$ **(b)** F when $E = 15$

The information and the unknowns can be shown in a table.

F	5	8	?
E	12	?	15

E and F are connected by an equation of the form $E = kF$.
Use the known pair of values to find k:

$$12 = k \times 5, \text{ so } k = \tfrac{12}{5} = 2.4$$

Now use the equation $E = 2.4F$ to find the unknowns.

(a) When $F = 8$, $E = 2.4 \times 8 = \mathbf{19.2}$ (b) When $E = 15$, $15 = 2.4F$

So $F = \tfrac{15}{2.4} = \mathbf{6.25}$

D1 The volume, V litres, of water that comes out of a tap is directly proportional to the time, T minutes, for which the tap is turned on.

Given that $V = 125$ when $T = 2.5$, find

(a) the equation connecting V and T **(b)** the value of V when $T = 4.5$

(c) the value of V when $T = 10.5$ **(d)** the value of T when $V = 475$

D2 The quantity, P litres, of paint needed to paint a floor is directly proportional to the area, A m², of the floor.

Given that $P = 3.0$ when $A = 40$, find

(a) the equation connecting P and A **(b)** the value of P when $A = 140$

D3 The length, L m, of a shadow is directly proportional to the height, H m, of the object (at a given time of day).

Find

(a) the equation connecting L and H

(b) the length of the shadow of flagpole B

(c) the height of flagpole C

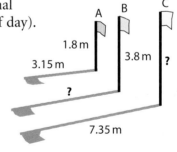

D4 The electric current I (measured in amps) in a lamp is directly proportional to the voltage V (measured in volts).

When $V = 2.5$, $I = 1.5$. Find

(a) the equation for I in terms of V **(b)** the value of I when $V = 4.5$

(c) the value of V when $I = 6.9$

D5 The quantity Q is directly proportional to P.
When $P = 2.5$, $Q = 20$.

(a) If $Q = kP$, find the value of k.　　(b) What is Q when $P = 28$?

(c) What is P when $Q = 4.5$?

D6 In this table, $Y \propto X$.

(a) If $Y = kX$, find the value of k.

(b) Copy and complete the table.

X	5	1		11
Y	18		12	

D7 On Mid Western Trains, the fare for a journey of 40 km is £7.20.
Fares are directly proportional to the distance travelled.

(a) What is the fare for a journey of 70 km?　　(b) How far could you travel for £18?

E $Q \propto P^2$, $Q \propto P^3$, ...

This table shows the mass, m grams, of a disc of diameter d cm cut from a sheet of plastic.

d (diameter in cm)	0	5	10	15	20
m (mass in grams)	0	50	200	450	800

- Draw the graph of m against d.
  Explain why m is not directly proportional to d.

- If d is doubled, how does m change?

The mass is directly proportional to the square of the diameter: $m \propto d^2$.

We can see this if we put an extra row in the table showing d^2.

d	0	5	10	15	20
d²	0	25	100	225	400
m	0	50	200	450	800

× 2

The equation connecting m and d is of the form $m = kd^2$.

The constant of proportionality is 2, so $m = 2d^2$.

E1 The length of the skid mark made by a car after braking hard on a particular type of road surface is proportional to the square of the speed.

This table shows some values of the speed, S km/h, and the skid length L cm.

S	0	20	40	60	80
S²					
L	0		800		

(a) Copy the table and complete the values of S^2.

(b) Find the value of k in the equation $L = kS^2$.

(c) Use the equation to fill in the missing values of L.

(d) Find the speed of a car whose skid mark is 450 cm long.

E2 The distance, s m, fallen by a stone dropped from a high point is proportional to the square of the time, t seconds, since it was dropped.

This table shows some values of t, t^2 and s.

t	0	4	7	
t^2	0			
s	0	80		980

(a) Use the known values to find the equation connecting s and t.

(b) Copy the table and use the equation to fill in the missing values of s and t.

E3 The force of air resistance, R newtons, on a car is directly proportional to the square of the speed, S km/h.

When the speed is 30 km/h, the air resistance is 1350 N.

(a) Find the equation connecting R and S in the form $R = kS^2$.

S	10	30	40	
S^2				
R		1350		2904

(b) Copy the table and fill in the missing values.

E4 A quantity Q is proportional to the square of quantity P. When $P = 14$, $Q = 1078$.

(a) Sketch the graph of Q against P.

(b) Find the equation connecting Q and P.

(c) Use the equation to find

    (i) the value of Q when $P = 8$ (ii) the value of P when $Q = 1782$

E5 Given that $Y \propto X^2$ and that $Y = 38.4$ when $X = 8$, find

(a) the equation connecting Y and X (b) the value of Y when $X = 13$

(c) the value of Y when $X = 22$ (d) the value of X when $Y = 173.4$

E6 The time taken for one complete swing (to and fro) of a simple pendulum is proportional to the **square root** of its length.

$T \propto \sqrt{L}$, where T is the time in seconds and L is the length in metres.

This table shows some values of L, $\sqrt{L}$ and T.

L	4	6.25	9	
$\sqrt{L}$	2			
T			6	50

(a) Use the known values to find the equation connecting T and L.

(b) Copy the table and use the equation to fill in the missing values of T and L.

E7 A weight is hung at the end of a beam of length L. This causes the end of the beam to drop a distance d. d is directly proportional to the cube of L. $d = 20$ when $L = 150$.

(a) Find a formula for d in terms of L.

(b) Calculate the value of L when $d = 15$.

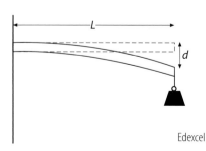

Edexcel

F Inverse proportion

A club is arranging a coach trip. The coach costs £200 to hire.
The cost will be shared equally among the people who go on the trip.

If n people go, the amount A (in £) that each person will have to pay
is given by the formula

$$A = \frac{200}{n}$$

This table shows some pairs of values of n and A.

n	8	10	20	25	40	50
A	25	20	10	8	5	4

Notice that

- If n is multiplied by a number, then
  A is **divided** by the same number.
  (For example, if twice as many people go,
  the amount per person is divided by 2.)

- The product nA is constant.
  (In this example it is always 200.)

- The graph of A against n is a curve
  (called a 'rectangular hyperbola').

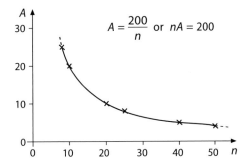

$A = \dfrac{200}{n}$ or $nA = 200$

A is **inversely proportional** to n. This can be written $A \propto \dfrac{1}{n}$.

When you see $A \propto \dfrac{1}{n}$ you can replace it by $A = \dfrac{k}{n}$ or $\boldsymbol{nA = k}$.

F1 This table shows some pairs of values of
two quantities P and Q.

P	4	5	6	8	20	30
Q	15	12	10	7.5	3	2

(a) By working out PQ for each pair, check that Q is inversely proportional to P.

(b) Check that when P is multiplied by a number, then Q is divided by the
same number.

(c) What is the value of Q when P is   **(i)** 2   **(ii)** 3   **(iii)** 1   **(iv)** 0.5

F2 The time taken, T hours, for a journey is inversely proportional to
the speed of travel, S km/h.

The table shows some values of S and T.

(a) Find the value of k in the equation $ST = k$.

S	4	5	8	20	40
T	10	8			

(b) Use the equation to find the three missing
values in the table.

(c) Find

   (i) the value of T when $S = 25$ **(ii)** the value of S when $T = 1.25$

Direct and inverse proportion compared

If Q is directly proportional to P, the **ratio** $\dfrac{Q}{P}$ is constant.

P	2	4	10
Q	5	10	25

$\dfrac{Q}{P} = 2.5$

or $Q = 2.5P$

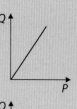

If Q is inversely proportional to P, the **product** PQ is constant.

P	2	3	20
Q	15	10	1.5

$PQ = 30$

or $Q = \dfrac{30}{P}$

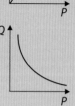

F3 For each table below, say whether it shows direct proportion, inverse proportion or neither. If it shows direct or inverse proportion, write down the equation connecting Q and P.

(a)

P	4	5	8	20	40
Q	6	7.5	12	30	60

(b)

P	1	5	7	10	20
Q	20	5	4	3	1

(c)

P	2	4	8	10	40
Q	50	25	12.5	10	2.5

(d)

P	0.1	0.4	0.6	1.2	1.8
Q	3.6	0.9	0.6	0.3	0.2

F4 The frequency of a musical note is measured in hertz (vibrations per second). The frequency, F hertz, of the note produced by a guitar string is inversely proportional to the vibrating length, L cm, of the string.

Given that $F = 200$ when $L = 40$, find

(a) the equation connecting F and L

(b) the value of F when $L = 16$

(c) the value of L when $F = 125$

(d) the value of L when $F = 1000$

F5 If $Y \propto \dfrac{1}{X}$ and $Y = 30$ when $X = 2$, find

(a) the value of Y when $X = 8$

(b) the value of X when $Y = 0.5$

F6 If $Q \propto \dfrac{1}{P}$ and $Q = 0.75$ when $P = 1.6$, find

(a) the value of Q when $P = 0.3$

(b) the value of P when $Q = 0.25$

F7 The quantity B is inversely proportional to the **square** of another quantity A.

$\left(\text{This is written } B \propto \dfrac{1}{A^2}. \right)$

This table shows some values of A, A^2 and B.

A	2	3	4	5	
A²	4	9	16		
B	90	40	22.5		10

(a) Check that A^2B is constant for the first three sets of values in the table.

(b) Write the equation in the form $A^2B = k$.

(c) Find the missing values in the table.

Example

$Q \propto \dfrac{1}{\sqrt{P}}$, and $Q = 15$ when $P = 16$.

(a) Find the equation connecting Q and P.

(b) Find Q when $P = 25$.

(c) Find P when $Q = 20$.

> Make a table showing P, $\sqrt{P}$ and Q. Fill in the known values.

P	16	25	
$\sqrt{P}$	4	5	
Q	15		20

> P and Q are connected by an equation of the form $Q\sqrt{P} = k$. Use the known pair of values of $\sqrt{P}$ and Q to find k.

> (a) $15 \times \sqrt{16} = 15 \times 4 = k$ So $k = 60$

> Now use the equation $Q\sqrt{P} = 60$ to find the unknowns.

> (b) When $P = 25$, $Q \times 5 = 60$.   So $Q = \frac{60}{5} = \mathbf{12}$

> (c) When $Q = 20$, $20 \times \sqrt{P} = 60$.   So $\sqrt{P} = \frac{60}{20} = 3$ So $P = \mathbf{9}$

F8 D is inversely proportional to the square root of M.

    (a) Given that $D = 10$ when $M = 4$, find the equation connecting D and M.

    (b) Copy this table and complete it using your equation.

M	4		16	
$\sqrt{M}$				
D	10	4		40

F9 y is inversely proportional to the square of x.
When $y = 3$, $x = 2$.
Find the value of y when $x = 4$.

AQA

F10 $V \propto \dfrac{1}{\sqrt{U}}$, and $V = 8$ when $U = 100$.

    (a) Find the equation connecting V and U.

    (b) Find   (i) the value of V when $U = 16$ (ii) the value of U when $V = 5$

F11 $V \propto \dfrac{1}{U^2}$, and $V = 8$ when $U = 3$.

    (a) Find the equation connecting V and U.

    (b) Find   (i) the value of V when $U = 20$ (ii) the value of U when $V = 2$

F12 The force, F newtons, between two magnets is inversely proportional to the square of the distance, d metres, between them.
When the magnets are 2 metres apart, the force between them is 36 newtons.

    Find   (a) F when $d = 5$ (b) d when $F = 49$ OCR

*F13 Q is inversely proportional to P.
If P is increased by 50%, what is the percentage change in Q?

G Identifying a proportional relationship

This table gives values of two quantities P and Q.
P and Q are related by the equation $Q = 3P^2$.

P	1	2	3	4	6
Q	3	12	27	48	108

- When P is multiplied by 2, what is Q multiplied by?
- When P is multiplied by 3, what is Q multiplied by?
- What is the value of Q when $P = k$?
- What is the value of Q when $P = nk$?
- When P is multiplied by n, what is Q multiplied by?

This table gives values of two quantities, L and M.
L and M are related by the equation $M = \dfrac{72}{L}$.

L	1	2	3	6	8
M	72	36	24	12	9

- When L is multiplied by 2, what is M divided by?
- When L is multiplied by 3, what is M divided by?
- What is the value of M when $L = k$?
- What is the value of M when $L = nk$?
- When L is multiplied by n, what is M divided by?

G1 This table gives values of two quantities, U and V.

U	2	4	6	8	10
V	4	32	108	256	500

   (a) What is V multiplied by when U is multiplied by 2?

   (b) What is V multiplied by when U is multiplied by 3?

   (c) What is V proportional to?

   (d) Find the equation connecting V and U.

G2 This table gives values of two quantities, S and T.

S	2	4	6	10	20
T	180	45	20	7.2	1.8

   (a) Check that when S is multiplied by 2,
T is **divided** by 4, or 2^2.

   (b) Check that when S is multiplied by 3, T is divided by 9, or 3^2.

   (c) From (a) and (b) it follows that $T \propto \dfrac{1}{S^2}$.
Find the equation connecting T and S.

G3 In each of the tables below, Q is either proportional to P, P^2 or P^3, or
inversely proportional to P, P^2 or P^3.

Find the type of proportionality for each table and the equation connecting Q and P.

(a)

P	1	2	3	6
Q	5	20	45	180

(b)

P	1	2	3	6
Q	36	18	12	6

(c)

P	2	3	4	6
Q	18	8	4.5	2

(d)

P	1	2	3	4
Q	5	40	135	320

(e)

P	2	4	10	12
Q	7	14	35	42

(f)

P	3	5	6	15
Q	54	150	216	1350

Test yourself

T1 The cost of a circular pizza is directly proportional to the square of its diameter. A pizza with diameter 9 inches costs £2.16.

(a) How much does a pizza with diameter 12 inches cost?

(b) Which of the graphs below represents the relationship between the diameter and the cost of a pizza?

A 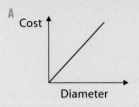   B 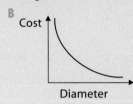   C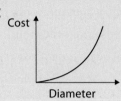

OCR

T2 The time, t seconds, that a ball takes to roll from rest down a slope is proportional to the square root of the distance, d metres, that it rolls.

It takes 4 seconds for the ball to roll 25 metres down the slope.

(a) Find an expression for t in terms of d.

(b) Find the time it takes for the ball to roll 64 metres down the slope.

(c) Find how far down the slope the ball will roll in 8 seconds.

OCR

T3 In an experiment measurements of t and h were taken.

These are the results.

Which of these rules fits the results?

t	2	5	6
h	10	62.5	90

A $h \propto t$ B $h \propto t^2$ C $h \propto t^3$

You must show all your working.

AQA

T4 The number of days, D, to complete a project is inversely proportional to the number of people, P, who work on the project.

(a) The project takes 18 days to complete if 150 people work on it.

(i) Find an equation connecting D and P.

(ii) How many people are needed to complete the project in 10 days?

(b) Sketch a graph which shows that D is inversely proportional to P. Put P on the horizontal axis and D on the vertical axis.

AQA

T5 y is inversely proportional to x^2. $y = 3$ when $x = 4$.

(a) Write y in terms of x.   (b) Calculate the value of y when $x = 5$.   Edexcel

T6 Given that y is inversely proportional to x^3, and that $y = 5$ when $x = 4$,

(a) find an expression for y in terms of x

(b) calculate   (i) the value of y when $x = 2$ (ii) the value of x when $y = 0.32$ WJEC

8 Quadratic expressions and equations 1

You should know how to

- multiply out expressions such as $(x + 1)(x - 3)$ and factorise simple quadratic expressions
- solve quadratic equations such as $x^2 + 4x + 3 = 0$

This work will help you

- multiply out expressions such as $(4x + 1)(2x - 3)$
- factorise expressions such as $5x^2 - 9x - 2$
- solve quadratic equations such as $5x^2 - 9x - 2 = 0$ by factorising
- solve problems by forming and solving a quadratic equation

A Review: simple quadratic expressions and equations

Example

Solve the equation $(x + 2)(x - 3) = 84$.

	$(x + 2)(x - 3) = 84$
Multiply out the brackets.	$x^2 - 3x + 2x - 6 = 84$
Simplify.	$x^2 - x - 6 = 84$
Rearrange to get 0 on one side.	$x^2 - x - 90 = 0$
Factorise.	$(x - 10)(x + 9) = 0$
	So $x = 10$ or $x = {}^-9$

A1 Multiply out and simplify each of these.

(a) $(x + 3)(x + 4)$ (b) $(x + 5)(x - 5)$ (c) $(x - 1)(x - 7)$

A2 Factorise each of these.

(a) $x^2 + 5x + 6$ (b) $x^2 - x - 30$ (c) $x^2 - 16$

A3 Solve these equations by factorising.

(a) $x^2 + 3x - 18 = 0$ (b) $x^2 + 7x + 12 = 0$ (c) $x^2 + 11x = 0$

(d) $x^2 - 9x - 10 = 0$ (e) $x^2 + 6x + 9 = 0$ (f) $x^2 - 13x + 40 = 0$

A4 Solve these equations by rearranging and factorising.

(a) $x^2 + 3x = 4$ (b) $x^2 + 16 = 8x$ (c) $x^2 = x$

(d) $x^2 = 5x - 6$ (e) $x^2 = 11 + 10x$ (f) $x^2 - x = 2x$

A5 The area of this rectangle is $42\,\text{cm}^2$.

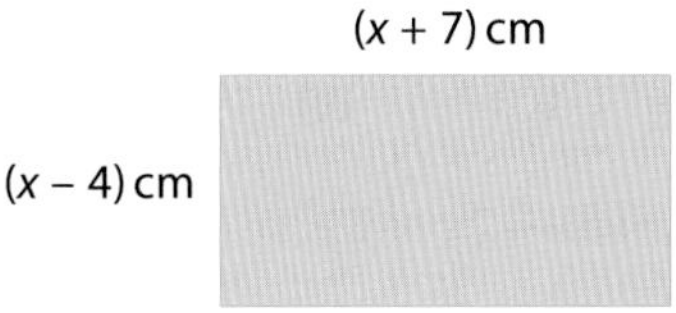

$(x + 7)\,\text{cm}$

(a) Show that $x^2 + 3x - 70 = 0$.

(b) Solve the equation to find the dimensions of the rectangle.

$(x - 4)\,\text{cm}$

A6 The length of this rectangle is 7 cm longer than the width.

(a) Write an expression for the length of the rectangle.

$x\,\text{cm}$

(b) The area of the rectangle is $44\,\text{cm}^2$.

    (i) Form an equation in x and solve it.

    (ii) What is the perimeter of this rectangle?

A7 The equation of a graph is of the form $y = x^2 + bx + c$.
The graph crosses the x-axis at $^-4$ and 5.
Sketch the graph and find the values of b and c.

B Multiplying out expressions such as $(2n - 3)(4n + 5)$

A table can be used when multiplying algebraic expressions.

$\times$	$4n$	5
$2n$	$8n^2$	$10n$
$^-3$	^-12n	$^-15$

$(2n - 3)(4n + 5)$ ➡

➡ $(2n - 3)(4n + 5)$
$= 8n^2 + 10n - 12n - 15$
$= 8n^2 - 2n - 15$

Here is another way to approach $(2n - 3)(4n + 5)$.

$(2n - 3)(4n + 5) = 2n(4n + 5) - 3(4n + 5)$
$= 8n^2 + 10n - (12n + 15)$
$= 8n^2 + 10n - 12n - 15$
$= 8n^2 - 2n - 15$

B1 Multiply out and simplify these.

(a) $(2x + 1)(x + 3)$ (b) $(x + 2)(4x + 3)$ (c) $(x + 5)(3x - 2)$

(d) $(2x - 3)(x + 1)$ (e) $(2x - 5)(x - 4)$ (f) $(x - 2)(5x - 2)$

B2 Expand and simplify these.

(a) $(2n + 1)(3n + 4)$ (b) $(5n + 3)(5n + 2)$ (c) $(4n + 5)(2n - 1)$

(d) $(3n - 4)(2n + 1)$ (e) $(2n - 3)(3n - 5)$ (f) $(5n - 1)(2n - 3)$

B3 Multiply out and simplify these.

    (a) $(1 + 5m)(m - 10)$ **(b)** $(5 - 2c)(3c + 4)$ **(c)** $(1 - 3a)(1 - 2a)$

B4 Copy and complete $(2x + 3)^2 = (2x + 3)(2x + 3)$

$$= \ldots\ldots\ldots\ldots\ldots\ldots$$

    Simplify your result.

B5 Multiply out each expression and write the result in its simplest form.

    (a) $(2x + 5)^2$ **(b)** $(3x - 1)^2$ **(c)** $(1 - 4x)^2$

B6 The diagram shows a rectangular garden.
The area of the rectangular pond is $21\,\text{m}^2$.

Show that the area of the lawn in m^2 is $5x^2 + 38x$.

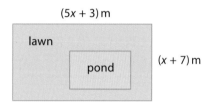

B7 The diagram shows a rectangular
paved patio and a square pond.
Lengths are in metres.

Show that the expression for the
paved area is $2x^2 + 8x + 4$.

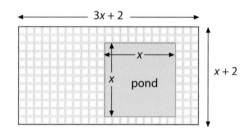

B8 Copy and complete each identity.

    (a) $(2x + 1)(\quad\quad) = 2x^2 + 7x + 3$ **(b)** $(\quad\quad)(2x + 5) = 6x^2 + 19x + 10$

    (c) $(\quad\quad)(3x - 1) = 6x^2 + x - 1$ **(d)** $(3x - 2)(\quad\quad) = 15x^2 - 22x + 8$

B9 Find pairs of expressions from the bubble that multiply to give

    (a) $3x^2 + 16x + 5$ **(b)** $3x^2 + 8x + 5$

    (c) $2x^2 + 15x + 25$ **(d)** $6x^2 + 5x + 1$

    $x + 1$ $x + 5$ $3x + 5$ $2x + 1$

    $2x + 5$ $3x + 1$

B10 Find pairs of expressions from the bubble that multiply to give

    (a) $2x^2 + x - 3$ **(b)** $2x^2 - x - 1$

    (c) $2x^2 - 3x + 1$ **(d)** $4x^2 - 8x + 3$

    $x + 1$ $x - 1$ $2x - 3$ $2x - 1$

    $2x + 3$ $2x + 1$

C Factorising quadratic expressions

Some quadratic expressions can be factorised into the product of two linear expressions.

For example, the expression $10n^2 + 17n + 3$ can be factorised to give $(2n + 3)(5n + 1)$. However, the expression $10n^2 + 16n + 3$ **cannot** be factorised like this.

• Can you factorise these quadratic expressions?

A $\quad 3x^2 + 7x + 2$ **B** $\quad 3x^2 + 5x + 2$ **C** $\quad 3x^2 + 6x + 2$

D $\quad 2x^2 + 7x + 6$ **E** $\quad 6x^2 + 11x + 5$ **F** $\quad 6x^2 + 21x + 9$ **G** $\quad 4x^2 + 4x + 1$

C1 Factorise these.

(a) $\quad 2x^2 + 15x + 7$ (b) $\quad 3x^2 + 10x + 3$ (c) $\quad 2x^2 + 9x + 4$

(d) $\quad 3x^2 + 8x + 4$ (e) $\quad 3x^2 + 7x + 4$ (f) $\quad 5x^2 + 17x + 6$

C2 Factorise these.

(a) $\quad 4k^2 + 8k + 3$ (b) $\quad 4m^2 + 13m + 3$ (c) $\quad 10n^2 + 17n + 7$

(d) $\quad 16p^2 + 8p + 1$ (e) $\quad 4x^2 + 12x + 9$ (f) $\quad 6y^2 + 23y + 10$

• Can you factorise these quadratic expressions?

P $\quad 2x^2 + 9x - 5$ **Q** $\quad 2x^2 + 6x - 5$ **R** $\quad 2x^2 - 3x - 5$

S $\quad 3x^2 - 10x + 7$ **T** $\quad 4x^2 - 21x + 5$ **U** $\quad 4x^2 + 2x - 12$ **V** $\quad 9x^2 - 6x + 1$

C3 Factorise these.

(a) $\quad 2x^2 + 3x - 5$ (b) $\quad 3x^2 + 8x - 3$ (c) $\quad 3x^2 - 2x - 5$

(d) $\quad 5x^2 - 9x - 2$ (e) $\quad 2x^2 - 7x + 3$ (f) $\quad 3x^2 - 22x + 7$

C4 Factorise these.

(a) $\quad 6k^2 + 7k - 5$ (b) $\quad 4m^2 - 4m + 1$ (c) $\quad 3n^2 - 5n - 8$

(d) $\quad 2p^2 - 13p + 6$ (e) $\quad 4x^2 - 16x + 15$ (f) $\quad 6y^2 - 5y - 6$

If every term in a quadratic expression has a common factor, deal with that first.

For example: $3x^2 + 12x + 9 = 3(x^2 + 4x + 3)$
$$= 3(x + 1)(x + 3)$$

C5 Factorise these.

(a) $\quad 4x^2 + 14x + 6$ (b) $\quad 5x^2 + 10x + 5$ (c) $\quad 9x^2 - 39x + 12$

The expressions below are examples of the **difference of two squares**:

$$4x^2 - 25 \qquad 9n^2 - 1 \qquad 16 - 25a^2$$

Both terms in the expression are squares and one is subtracted from the other.

C6 (a) Expand and simplify the following.

      (i) $(2x + 1)(2x - 1)$ (ii) $(3x + 2)(3x - 2)$ (iii) $(3 + 4x)(3 - 4x)$

  (b) What do you notice about your results?

  (c) Factorise   (i) $4x^2 - 9$ (ii) $9x^2 - 1$ (iii) $16 - 25x^2$

C7 The nth term of a sequence is $9n^2 + 6n + 1$.

  (a) Work out the first three terms of this sequence.

  (b) Show that **every** term in the sequence must be a square number.

C8 (a) (i) Find the value of $9n^2 + 9n + 2$ when $n = 5$.

      (ii) Write this value as the product of two consecutive numbers.

  (b) (i) Factorise $9n^2 + 9n + 2$.

      (ii) Hence show that, when n is an integer, the value of $9n^2 + 9n + 2$ can always be written as the product of two consecutive numbers.

Factorising a quadratic expression

- Look for common factors first.

$$2x^2 + 8x = 2x(x + 4)$$
$$2x^2 + 4x - 6 = 2(x^2 + 2x - 3)$$
$$= 2(x + 3)(x - 1)$$

- $ax^2 + bx + c = (?x + ?)(?x + ?)$

$$2x^2 + 7x + 3 = (2x + 1)(x + 3)$$

+ and + means **both** brackets have +

- $ax^2 - bx + c = (?x - ?)(?x - ?)$

$$2x^2 - 7x + 3 = (2x - 1)(x - 3)$$

− and + means **both** brackets have −

- $ax^2 \pm bx - c = (?x + ?)(?x - ?)$

$$2x^2 + 3x - 5 = (2x + 5)(x - 1)$$
$$2x^2 - 3x - 5 = (2x - 5)(x + 1)$$

− means brackets have + and −

- For expressions of the form $ax^2 - c$ look for the 'difference of two squares'.

$$x^2 - 49 = (x + 7)(x - 7)$$
$$25x^2 - 36 = (5x + 6)(5x - 6)$$

D Solving equations by factorising

Examples

Solve $2x^2 + 7x - 4 = 0$.

$2x^2 + 7x - 4 = 0$

$(2x - 1)(x + 4) = 0$

Either $(2x - 1) = 0$ or $(x + 4) = 0$

So $x = \frac{1}{2}$ or $x = {}^-4$

Solve $3k^2 + 6 = 16k + 1$.

$3k^2 + 6 = 16k + 1$

$3k^2 - 16k + 5 = 0$

$(3k - 1)(k - 5) = 0$

Either $(3k - 1) = 0$ or $(k - 5) = 0$

So $k = \frac{1}{3}$ or $k = 5$

Give the answer as an exact fraction where appropriate.

D1 Solve these equations by factorising.

(a) $2x^2 + 9x - 5 = 0$ (b) $2x^2 + 11x + 5 = 0$ (c) $3x^2 + 20x - 7 = 0$

(d) $2x^2 - 6x = 0$ (e) $2x^2 - 23x + 11 = 0$ (f) $5x^2 - 2x - 7 = 0$

D2 Solve these equations by factorising.

(a) $4x^2 + 5x + 1 = 0$ (b) $4x^2 - 8x + 3 = 0$ (c) $2x^2 - 13x + 15 = 0$

(d) $3x^2 - x - 2 = 0$ (e) $16x^2 - 8x + 1 = 0$ (f) $4x^2 + 14x = 0$

(g) $4x^2 + 16x - 9 = 0$ (h) $4x^2 - 16x + 15 = 0$ (i) $3x^2 - 19x + 20 = 0$

D3 Solve these equations by factorising.

(a) $2x^2 + 18x + 40 = 0$ (b) $4x^2 - 14x + 6 = 0$ (c) $9x^2 - 42x - 15 = 0$

D4 Solve these equations by rearranging and factorising.

(a) $2x^2 + 11x = 6$ (b) $3y^2 + 13y + 10 = 6$ (c) $5m^2 + 30m = 21 - 2m$

(d) $30k + 1 = 1 - 5k^2$ (e) $10p^2 = 28p + 6$ (f) $35 + 8a - 9a^2 = 2a$

D5 The diagram shows a sketch of the graph of $y = 3x^2 + 11x - 4$.
What are the coordinates of A and B?

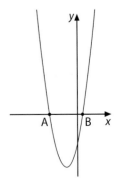

D6 Where does the graph of $y = 6x^2 - 15x + 9$ cross the x-axis?

D7 (a) Show that the area of this rectangle in cm² is equivalent to $2x^2 + 5x + 2$.

(b) The area of the rectangle is $14\,\text{cm}^2$.

$(x+2)\,\text{cm}$ $(2x+1)\,\text{cm}$

    (i) Form an equation in x and solve it.

    (ii) Write down the length and width of the rectangle.

D8 The diagram shows a cuboid.
The dimensions of the cuboid are x, $x+3$ and $x-1$.
All measurements are given in centimetres.

(a) Show that the surface area of the cuboid is $6x^2 + 8x - 6$.

(b) The surface area of the cuboid is $184\,\text{cm}^2$.

    (i) Show that x satisfies the equation $3x^2 + 4x - 95 = 0$.

    (ii) Find the volume of the cuboid.

D9 (a) (i) Factorise $4x^2 - 37x + 9$.

    (ii) Hence, or otherwise, solve the equation $4x^2 - 37x + 9 = 0$.

(b) By considering your answers to part (a), find all the solutions to the equation
$$4y^4 - 37y^2 + 9 = 0$$

AQA

E Quadratic expressions that use two letters

$(2x + y)(3x - 2y)$ $\Rightarrow$

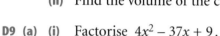

$\times$	$3x$	^-2y
$2x$	$6x^2$	^-4xy
y	$3xy$	$^-2y^2$

$\Rightarrow$

$(2x + y)(3x - 2y)$
$= 6x^2 - 4xy + 3xy - 2y^2$
$= 6x^2 - xy - 2y^2$

E1 Expand and simplify.

(a) $(x + y)(2x + 3y)$ **(b)** $(x + 2y)(2x + y)$ **(c)** $(3x + y)(x - 2y)$

(d) $(2p - q)(p + q)$ **(e)** $(2p - 3q)(p + 5q)$ **(f)** $(p - q)(5p - q)$

(g) $(2a - b)(2a - 3b)$ **(h)** $(a + b)^2$ **(i)** $(2a - b)^2$

(j) $(2y - 3x)^2$ **(k)** $(2x - y)(2x + y)$ **(l)** $(5x + 2y)(5x - 2y)$

E2 (a) Expand and simplify $(a + b)(a - b)$.

(b) (i) Use your result from (a) to calculate $99^2 - 1^2$ without a calculator.

    (ii) Hence calculate 99^2.

E3 Without using a calculator, evaluate

(a) $999^2 - 1^2$ **(b)** 999^2 **(c)** $98^2 - 2^2$ **(d)** 98^2 **(e)** 998^2

E4 Factorise these completely.

(a) $a^2 - b^2$ (b) $4x^2 - y^2$ (c) $9p^2 - 16q^2$ (d) $h^2 - 25k^2$

(e) $5g^2 - 5h^2$ (f) $18a^2 - 2b^2$ (g) $3x^2 - 12y^2$ (h) $2p^2 - 200q^2$

E5 Factorise these.

(a) $3x^2 + 7xy + 2y^2$ (b) $2a^2 - ab - b^2$ (c) $6p^2 + pq - 2q^2$

E6 Expand these.

(a) $(x + 3)(y + 2)$ (b) $(a + b)(5 + b)$ (c) $(p + 6)(p - q)$

(d) $(2h - 1)(h + k)$ (e) $(4g + 5)(4 - h)$ (f) $(2x + 1)(x - 5y)$

E7 Factorise these.

(a) $p^2 + pq + 3p + 3q$ (b) $p^2 + p + pq + q$ (c) $2p^2 - 2pq - 3p + 3q$

Test yourself

T1 Expand and simplify $(2p + 5)(p - 2)$.   OCR

T2 Expand and simplify these.

(a) $(2x - 5)(3x + 4)$ (b) $(3n - 5)^2$ (c) $(3x + 5y)(x - 6y)$

T3 Factorise these.

(a) $2n^2 - 11n + 12$ (b) $5x^2 + 17x - 12$ (c) $9x^2 - 6x + 1$

T4 Solve these equations.

(a) $3y^2 + 5y - 2 = 0$ (b) $2x^2 - 5x = 0$ (c) $2k^2 - 35k + 98 = 0$

T5 Factorise   (a) $x^2 - 9y^2$ (b) $1 - 25a^2$

T6 The diagram shows a six-sided shape.
All the corners are right angles.
All measurements are given in centimetres.
The area of the shape is $25\,\text{cm}^2$.

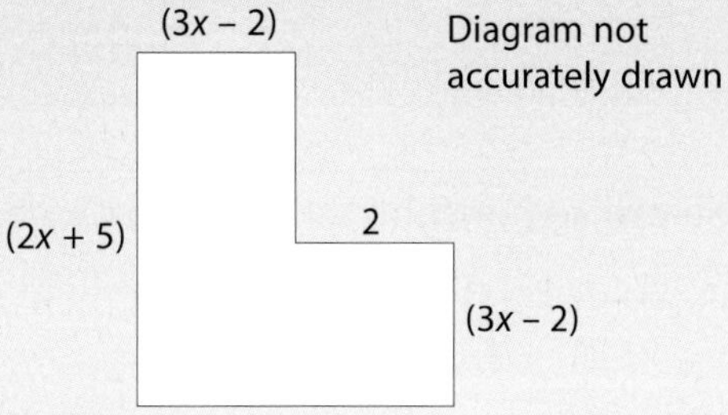

(a) Show that $6x^2 + 17x - 39 = 0$.

(b) (i) Solve the equation
$$6x^2 + 17x - 39 = 0$$

(ii) Hence work out the length of the longest side of the shape.   Edexcel

(3x – 2)   Diagram not accurately drawn

(2x + 5)   2

(3x – 2)

T7 Factorise completely $75p^2 - 3q^2$.

T8 (a) Expand and simplify $(x + y)(x - y)$.

(b) Using your answer to part (a), or otherwise, find the exact value of $780^2 - 220^2$.   AQA

9 Dimension of an expression

This work will help you

- work out the dimension of an expression representing length, area or volume
- use dimensions to check that an expression is sensible

A Length, area and volume

The area of a triangle is given by $\frac{1}{2} \times$ **base** $\times$ **height**.

In this expression,

the base is a ***length***,
the height is a ***length***,
the $\frac{1}{2}$ is a ***pure number***.

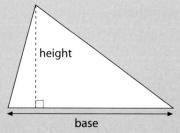

We say the **dimension** of the area is $[length]^2$ because it is found by multiplying $length \times length \times a\ number$.

(This is also shown by the units, for example cm for length and cm² for area.)

A length has dimension $[length]^1$.

A pure number (including, for example, π) has no dimension.

The volume of a cylinder of radius r and height h is $\pi r^2 h$.

The dimension of the expression $\pi r^2 h$ is $[length]^3$ because it is found by multiplying $number \times [length]^2 \times length$.

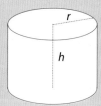

You can add or subtract quantities with the same dimension.

$$4\,\text{cm} + 2\,\text{cm} = 6\,\text{cm}$$
$$6\,\text{cm}^2 + 3\,\text{cm}^2 = 9\,\text{cm}^2$$

But it does not make sense to add or subtract quantities with different dimensions. For example, you can't add an area of 6 cm² to a length of 4 cm.

$$6\,\text{cm}^2 + 4\,\text{cm} = \text{nonsense!}$$

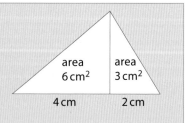

By checking dimensions you can see whether an expression could represent a length, an area or a volume (or none of these).

Examples

Suppose a, b, c represent lengths. What, if anything, could these expressions represent?

(a) $(a + b)^2$
> The dimension of $(a + b)$ is [*length*],
> so the dimension of $(a + b)^2$ is [*length*]^2.
> So the expression could represent an **area**.

(b) $a(b - 2c)$
> The dimension of $2c$ is [*length*],
> so the dimension of $(b - 2c)$ is also [*length*].
> The dimension of $a(b - 2c)$ is [*length*] $\times$ [*length*] = [*length*]^2.
> So the expression could represent an **area**.

(c) $\dfrac{a^3b}{c}$
> The dimension of a^3b is [*length*]^3 $\times$ [*length*] = [*length*]^4.
> The dimension of $\dfrac{a^3b}{c}$ is $\dfrac{[\textit{length}]^4}{[\textit{length}]} = [\textit{length}]^3$.
> So the expression could represent a **volume**.

(d) $b^2 + c$
> The dimension of b^2 is [*length*]^2. The dimension of c is [*length*].
> It is impossible to add a length to an area.
> So the expression is **dimensionally inconsistent**.
> It does not represent anything.

In these questions, the letters a, b, c, d, h, r, ... represent lengths.

A1 Write an expression for each of the following.
Check that your expression is dimensionally correct.

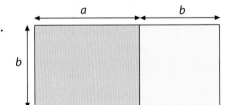

   (a) The area of the blue rectangle
   (b) The perimeter of the blue rectangle
   (c) The perimeter of the whole coloured rectangle
   (d) The total area of the coloured rectangle
   (e) The difference between the blue and yellow areas

A2 What is the dimension of each of these expressions?

   (a) abc **(b)** $a + b$ **(c)** ab^2 **(d)** $\dfrac{ab}{c}$ **(e)** $2a - b$

A3 One of the expressions below could represent a length, one an area, one a volume and one a pure number. Which is which?

   a^2b $\dfrac{ab}{c^2}$ $2ab$ $a + 3b$

A4 What is the dimension of each of these expressions?

(a) $a(b + c)$　　(b) $\dfrac{a - b}{2}$　　(c) $\dfrac{a^2 - b^2}{4}$　　(d) $(2a - b)^3$

A5 Say whether each of these expressions could represent a length, an area, a volume or a pure number, or is dimensionally inconsistent.

(a) $ab + cd$　(b) $\dfrac{a^2 + b^2}{c}$　(c) $\dfrac{abc}{d^3}$　(d) $ab^2 - 4c^3$　(e) $a^2 + 3b$

A6 A book on engineering includes the formulas below, which relate to cylinders, cones and spheres.

For each formula, say whether it could represent a length, an area, a volume, or a pure number.

(a) $4\pi r^2$　　(b) $\dfrac{\pi(b^2 - a^2)}{4}$　　(c) $2\pi r(r + h)$　　(d) $\dfrac{4\pi r^3}{3}$

(e) $\pi h(a + b)$　　(f) $\dfrac{ah}{b - a}$　　(g) $\tfrac{1}{3}\pi h(a^2 + ab + b^2)$

The length of the hypotenuse of this right-angled triangle is

$\sqrt{a^2 + b^2}$

You can check that this expression has the correct dimension:

a^2 and b^2 are both $[length]^2$.

So $a^2 + b^2$ is also $[length]^2$.

So $\sqrt{a^2 + b^2}$ is $[length]$.

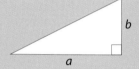

A7 What is the dimension of each of these expressions?

(a) $\sqrt{ab}$　(b) $a\sqrt{bc}$　(c) $\sqrt{b^2 - 2c^2}$　(d) $\dfrac{a^3}{\sqrt{bc}}$　(e) $\dfrac{2\sqrt{ab}}{c}$

*A8 If A represents an area and b and c represent lengths, what could each of these expressions represent?

(a) Ab　(b) $\dfrac{A}{b}$　(c) $\dfrac{Ab}{c}$　(d) $\sqrt{\dfrac{A}{\pi}}$　(e) $\dfrac{\sqrt{2A + b^2}}{c}$

You saw earlier that it makes no sense to add an area to a length.
In the same way, it makes no sense to add a distance to a time.
But you can do distance ÷ time to get speed.

In science, if you know the dimension of a measure like speed or kinetic energy
(how each is built up from fundamental quantities like length, time and mass)
you can check that a formula or equation makes sense.

Test yourself

T1 In the following expressions r, a and b represent lengths.
For each expression state whether it represents

> a **length**   an **area**   a **volume**   or **none** of these

(a) πab (b) $\pi r^2 a + 2\pi r$ (c) $\dfrac{\pi r a^3}{b}$ AQA

T2 Here are some expressions.

$$\frac{ab}{h} \qquad 2\pi b^2 \qquad (a+b)ch \qquad 2\pi a^3 \qquad \pi ab \qquad 2(a^2+b^2) \qquad \pi a^2 b$$

The letters a, b, c and h represent lengths.
π and 2 are numbers that have no dimensions.

Three of the expressions could represent areas. Which are they?   Edexcel

T3 One of these formulae gives the volume of this solid.

$$\frac{\pi(a+b)}{6} \qquad \frac{\pi ab}{6} \qquad \frac{\pi(ab)^2}{6} \qquad \frac{\pi ab^2}{6} \qquad \frac{\pi(a^2+b)}{6}$$

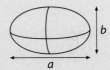

Which is the correct formula?
Give a reason for your answer.   OCR

T4 The letters f, g and h all represent lengths.
For each of the following expressions, state whether it could represent
a length, an area, a volume or none of these.

(a) $f^2(h+g)$ (b) $\sqrt{h^2 g f}$ (c) $\pi(3f+2g)$ OCR

T5

A	B	C	D
$p^3 + 3q^3$	$p^2 + 2q$	$2p + 3q$	$3p^2 + 2pq$

The boxes A, B, C and D show four expressions.
The letters p and q represent lengths.
2 and 3 are numbers which have no dimension.

(a) Write one of the letters A, B C or D for the expression which represents

     (i) an area   (ii) a length

The box X shows an expression.
The letters p and q represent lengths.
n is a number.
The expression represents a volume.

(b) Find the value of n.   Edexcel

10 Sequences

This work will help you

- find and use a rule for the *n*th term of a linear or a quadratic sequence
- find an expression for the *n*th term of a sequence generated from a context and prove it

A Linear sequences

A **linear** (or **arithmetic**) **sequence** is one where the terms increase or decrease by the same amount each time.

To find an expression for the *n*th term of the linear sequence 7, 11, 15, 19, 23, ...

... first look at the differences.

The differences are all 4 so the rule begins 4*n*.

A table can help to find the rule.

Term numbers (*n*)	1	2	3	4	5	...
Terms of the sequence	7	11	15	19	23	...
4*n*	4	8	12	16	20	...
Terms – 4*n*	3	3	3	3	3	...

Subtracting 4*n* from each term shows that each term is 3 more than 4*n*.

So the *n*th term of the sequence is 4*n* + 3.

A1 Copy and complete each linear sequence below, to show the first five terms.

(a) 2, 9, __, 23, __, ...

(b) 20, 18, __, __, 12, ...

(c) 1, __, __, 19, __, ...

(d) 30, __, __, __, 18, ...

A2 (a) Find an expression for the *n*th term of each of these arithmetic sequences.

(i) 5, 7, 9, 11, 13, ...

(ii) 1, 4, 7, 10, 13, ...

(iii) ⁻3, ⁻2, ⁻1, 0, 1, ...

(iv) 8, 15, 22, 29, 36, ...

(v) 19, 18, 17, 16, 15, ...

(vi) 23, 21, 19, 17, 15, ...

(b) Find the 10th term of each sequence in part (a).

A3 A linear sequence begins 4, 9, 14, 19, ...

(a) Find an expression, in terms of *n*, for the *n*th term of this sequence.

(b) What is the 20th term of this sequence?

(c) Show that 1000 cannot be a term in this sequence.

(d) Calculate the number of terms in the linear sequence 4, 9, 14, 19, ..., 499 .

B Quadratic sequences

For the sequence 8, 15, 26, 41, 60, ...

... the **first differences** are 7, 11, 15, 19, ...

... and the **second differences** are 4, 4, 4, ...

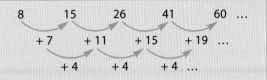

Sequences with constant second differences are **quadratic sequences**.

B1 Which of these sequences are quadratic?

A   6, 8, 12, 18, 26, 36   B   6, 8, 12, 20, 36, 68

C   6, 8, 10, 12, 14, 16   D   3, 4, 7, 12, 19, 28

B2 Find the next two terms for each of these quadratic sequences.

(a) 3, 4, 6, 9, 13, ...   (b) 3, 6, 11, 18, 27, ...

The nth term of a quadratic sequence can be written in the form $an^2 + bn + c$.
It can be proved that **the value of a is half the value of the second differences.**

To find an expression for the nth term of the quadratic sequence 8, 15, 26, 41, 60, ...

| | | 8 | 15 | 26 | 41 | 60 ... |

... first look at the differences. $+7 \quad +11 \quad +15 \quad +19$ ...

The second differences are all 4. $+4 \quad +4 \quad +4$ ...

Half of 4 is 2 so the rule begins $2n^2$.

A table can help to find the rule.

Term numbers (n)	1	2	3	4	5	...
Terms of the sequence	8	15	26	41	60	...
$2n^2$	2	8	18	32	50	...
Terms $- 2n^2$	6	7	8	9	10	...

Subtracting $2n^2$ from each term gives
the linear sequence 6, 7, 8, 9, 10, ...
This sequence has the nth term $n + 5$.

So the nth term of the quadratic sequence is $2n^2 + n + 5$.

B3 (a) Find an expression for the nth term of each of these quadratic sequences.

(i)   5, 8, 13, 20, 29, ...   (ii) 0, 3, 8, 15, 24, ...

(iii) 2, 8, 18, 32, 50, ...   (iv) 1, 10, 25, 46, 73, ...

(v)   4, 10, 18, 28, 40, ...   (vi) 2, 9, 20, 35, 54, ...

(b) Find the 10th term of each sequence in part (a).

C Mixed sequences

C1 Write down the first five terms of the sequences that have these nth terms.

    (a) $3n - 7$ (b) $n^3 + 1$ (c) $2n^2 - 5n$ (d) $n^3 + n - 2$

    (e) $n^4 - n^2$ (f) $\dfrac{12}{n}$ (g) $\dfrac{n}{n+1}$ (h) $3^n + 1$

C2 (a) Find the first three terms of the sequence whose nth term is $2n - 1$.

    (b) Find the first three terms of the sequence whose nth term is $n^3 - 6n^2 + 13n - 7$.

    (c) What do you notice?

    (d) Work out the 4th term of each sequence in parts (a) and (b).

C3 (a) Find the first three terms of the sequence whose nth term is n^3.

    (b) A **quadratic** sequence begins $1,\ 8,\ 27,\ \ldots$
       Find an expression for the nth term of this sequence.

When dots are used to show that a sequence continues it usually means the sequence continues in the simplest way possible.

For example, the sequence $2,\ 4,\ 6,\ 8,\ \ldots$

is taken to be the linear sequence that continues $10,\ 12,\ \ldots$ with nth term $2n$,

not the sequence that continues $34,\ 132,\ \ldots$ with nth term $n^4 - 10n^3 + 35n^2 - 48n + 24$.

C4 Find an expression for the nth term of the sequence $5,\ 9,\ 13,\ 17,\ \ldots$

C5 Give the nth term of each of these sequences.

    (a) $1,\ 4,\ 9,\ 16,\ 25,\ 36,\ \ldots$

    (b) $2,\ 5,\ 10,\ 17,\ 26,\ 37,\ \ldots$

    (c) $3,\ 7,\ 13,\ 21,\ 31,\ 43,\ \ldots$ AQA

C6 The first five terms of a sequence are

        $^{-}2,\ 1,\ 6,\ 13,\ 22$

Find the nth term of this sequence.

C7 The nth term of a sequence is $\dfrac{3n}{2(n+3)}$.

    (a) Write down the first two terms of this sequence.

    (b) Which term of the sequence has value 1?

C8 Write down the nth term of each of these sequences.

    (a) $\dfrac{1}{3},\ \dfrac{2}{4},\ \dfrac{3}{5},\ \dfrac{4}{6},\ \dfrac{5}{7},\ \ldots$

    (b) $\dfrac{1}{3},\ \dfrac{1}{12},\ \dfrac{1}{27},\ \dfrac{1}{48},\ \dfrac{1}{75},\ \ldots$

D Analysing spatial patterns

D1 A sequence of matchstick patterns begins:

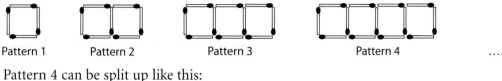

Pattern 1   Pattern 2   Pattern 3   Pattern 4   ......

Pattern 4 can be split up like this:

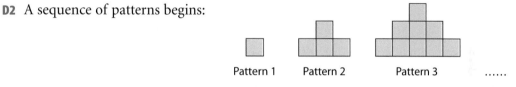

Use this to help you show that the number of matches in pattern n is $3n + 1$.

D2 A sequence of patterns begins:

Pattern 1   Pattern 2   Pattern 3   ......

Pattern 3 can be split up like this:

Use this to help you show that the number of squares in pattern n is n^2.

If you cannot show why a sequence goes on in a certain way, you cannot be sure that it does.
It may not be following the pattern that you think it is.

If you cannot show why a rule is correct, you cannot be sure that it is.
It may only fit the examples that you have tried.

D3 Each 'hollow square' model is made with cubes.

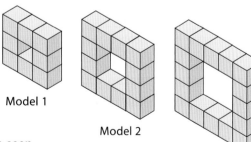

Model 1

Model 2

Model 3

    ......

(a) Find an expression for the number of cubes in model n. Explain how you found this expression and how you know it is correct.

(b) Some of the cube faces cannot be seen, even if you look all round each model. (For example, there are 16 hidden faces in model 1.)

Find an expression for the number of hidden cube faces in model n.

(c) Can you make a hollow square with 150 cubes? Explain your answer.

D4 **(a)** Find an expression for the number of cubes in the *n*th model.

Explain how you found this expression and how you know it is correct.

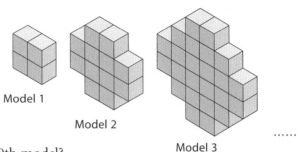

Model 1

Model 2

Model 3

......

(b) How many cubes are in the 10th model?

D5 The numbers of cubes in these designs are called 'triangle numbers'.

(a) Work out the first six triangle numbers.

(b) Find an expression for the *n*th triangle number and show it is correct

......

(c) What is the 100th triangle number?

(d) 820 is a triangle number.
How many triangle numbers are less than this?

D6 For each sequence, find an expression for the number of matches in the *n*th pattern.
Show that each expression is correct.

(a)

......

(b)

......

D7 Four points are marked on the circumference of a circle.
Each point is joined to each other with straight lines.
This divides the circle up into eight regions as shown.

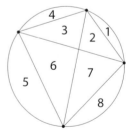

4 points
8 regions

(a) Is this the **maximum** number of regions you can make with 4 points in this way?

(b) How many regions can you make in this way with 1, 2 and 3 points?

(c) What is the maximum number of regions you can make with 5 points?

(d) Draw a diagram to show the maximum number of regions with 6 points.
Lee thinks that with 6 points the maximum number of regions will be 32.
Why does he think this? Do you agree with him?

(e) The expression $\frac{1}{24}(n^4 - 6n^3 + 23n^2 - 18n + 24)$ gives the maximum number of regions with *n* points on the circumference of a circle.
Find the maximum number of regions you can make with 7 points.

Test yourself

T1 Here are the first five terms of an arithmetic sequence

     6, 11, 16, 21, 26

Find an expression, in terms of n, for the nth term of the sequence.   Edexcel

T2 (a) Write down the next two terms of this sequence.

     18   17   15   12   8   ...   ...

(b) The nth term of another sequence is $15 - 3n$.
Find the 5th term of this sequence.

(c) These are the first five terms of another sequence.

     5   9   13   17   21

Find the nth term of this sequence.   OCR

T3 (a) Here are the first four patterns
in a dot sequence.

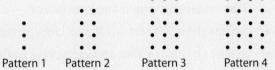

     Pattern 1   Pattern 2   Pattern 3   Pattern 4

Explain why an expression for the number of dots in the nth pattern is $n(n + 2)$.

(b) Here are the first four terms of another sequence.

     4   10   18   28

They may be written in the following way.

     1×4 2×5 3×6 4×7

Find an expression for the nth term of this sequence.   OCR

T4 Write down the nth term of each of these sequences.

(a) 2, 5, 10, 17, 26, 37, ...

(b) 4, 16, 36, 64, 100, 144, ...

T5 Find the nth term of this sequence.

     2, 7, 14, 23, 34, 47, ...

T6 Find an expression for the number
of matches in the nth diagram.

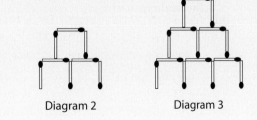

     Diagram 1   Diagram 2   Diagram 3

11 Enlargement, area and volume

This work will help you see how the scale factor, area factor and volume factor of an enlargement are related.

A Enlargement and area

A1 (a) Calculate the area of the shape sketched here.

(b) The shape is to be enlarged with scale factor 2. Sketch the enlarged shape and mark the new dimensions on it.

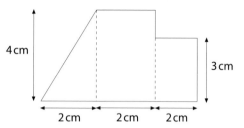

(c) Calculate the area of the enlarged shape. By what number has the area been multiplied as a result of the enlargement? This number is called the **area factor**.

(d) Repeat steps (b) and (c) for an enlargement of the original shape with scale factor 3.

(e) Repeat (b) and (c) for an enlargement of the original with scale factor 1.5.

(f) What do you notice about the area factors?

When rectangle P is scaled down (reduced) with scale factor $\frac{2}{3}$, you get rectangle Q.

The area of P is $18\,cm^2$ and the area of Q is $8\,cm^2$.

So the area factor is $\frac{4}{9}$ (because 8 is $\frac{4}{9}$ of 18).

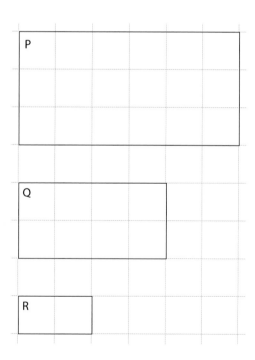

A2 (a) Copy and complete this table.

Original shape	Scaled shape	Scale factor	Original area	Scaled area	Area factor
P	Q	$\frac{2}{3}$	$18\,cm^2$	$8\,cm^2$	$\frac{4}{9}$
P	R				
Q	R				

(b) How is each area factor related to the scale factor?

A3 This sketch shows a rectangle being enlarged with scale factor k.

   (a) What is the area (in square units) of the original rectangle?

   (b) Copy the lower rectangle.
       Label its width with an expression that has k in it.
       Label its height with an expression that has k in it.

   (c) Multiply these expressions together to get an
       expression for the area of the enlarged rectangle.

   (d) By what area factor has the area been multiplied as
       a result of the enlargement?

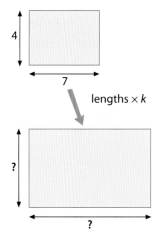

lengths $\times$ k

A4 This sketch shows a circle being enlarged with scale factor k.

   The area of the original circle can be written $\pi \times 3^2 = 9\pi$.

   (a) Write down the radius of the enlarged circle
       as an expression with k in it.

   (b) Write an expression for the area of the enlarged circle.
       (Keep the symbol π in the expression: do not replace it
       by an approximate value of π.)

   (c) By what area factor has the area been multiplied as
       a result of the enlargement?

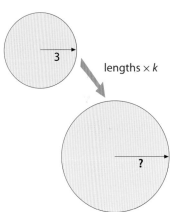

lengths $\times$ k

A5 Here a shape is being enlarged with scale factor k.

   (a) What is the area in square units of the original shape?

   (b) Copy the lower shape. Label the missing dimensions
       with expressions that have k in them.

   (c) Carefully work out expressions involving k for
       the areas of the rectangles and triangle in
       the lower shape. Add them together to get an
       expression for the total area.

   (d) By what area factor has the area been multiplied as
       a result of the enlargement?

   (e) Does it matter whether k is greater than or less than 1?

lengths $\times$ k

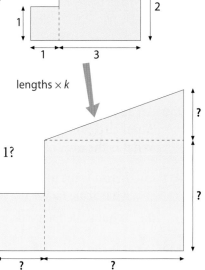

What you have seen for some shapes is true for any shape.

If a shape is enlarged by scale factor k, its area is multiplied by k^2.

We say: k^2 is the **area factor** of the enlargement.

This happens because every unit length becomes k units long,

and every square unit becomes k^2 square units in area.

A6 On squared paper, draw a pair of axes labelled from 0 to 10.

(a) Draw the pentagon with vertices at $(5, 1)$, $(4, 2)$, $(5, 3)$, $(7, 3)$, $(7, 2)$.
Draw an enlargement of the pentagon, scale factor 3, centre $(6, 0)$.

(b) What is the area in square units of the original pentagon?

(c) What is the area of the enlargement?

(d) From your answers to (b) and (c), calculate the area factor and explain whether this is the expected result.

A7 Kate has a favourite postage stamp that is a rectangle 36 mm by 24 mm.
She scans it and prints out an enlargement that is 150 mm by 100 mm.

(a) What is the scale factor for the enlargement?

(b) What is the area factor?

A8 What is the area factor of an enlargement whose scale factor is

(a) 5   (b) 9   (c) 100   (d) 4.5   (e) $\sqrt{3}$

A9 A design for a mosaic has an area of 176 cm^2.
The actual mosaic is an enlargement of the design with scale factor 2.5.
What is the area of the completed mosaic?

A10 An artist does a preparatory drawing for a mural to a scale of 1:10.
A red circle on the drawing has an area of 35 cm^2.
What is the area of that circle on the full-size mural?

A11 (a) If you want to enlarge a photo so its area is multiplied by 4, what scale factor do you use for the enlargement?

(b) What scale factor do you use if you want the area to be doubled?

A12 What is the scale factor of an enlargement whose area factor is

(a) 16   (b) 100   (c) 42.25   (d) 40 000   (e) 5

A13 The area of a window is 400 times the area of the rectangle representing it on an architect's drawing.
What is the scale of the architect's drawing?

A14 On a designer's drawing for a watch, the watch face has an area of 105 cm².
The actual watch face has an area of 4.2 cm².

  (a) What is the scale factor of the enlargement from the actual watch to the drawing?

  (b) What is the scale factor of the scaling down from the drawing to the actual watch?

A15 What is the area factor of a scaling down whose scale factor is

  (a) $\frac{1}{4}$ **(b)** 0.6   **(c)** $\frac{3}{4}$ **(d)** 0.2   **(e)** 0.1

A16 The sails of the Astra sailing dinghy have a total area of 12.8 m².

  (a) The manufacturers produce another dinghy called the Comet, which is the Astra design scaled down with a scale factor of 0.85.
  What is the area of the Comet's sails?

  (b) The Meteor is also a scaled-down version of the Astra.
  Its sails have an area of 7.2 m².
  What scale factor is used to scale the Astra down to the Meteor?

A17 **(a)** If you want to scale down a picture so its area is $\frac{1}{25}$ of what it was before, what scale factor should you use?

  (b) What scale factor should you use if you want a picture's area to be $\frac{1}{10}$ of what it was before?

A18 **(a)** Two circles have areas in the ratio 9:4. What is the ratio of their diameters?

  (b) Two similar triangles have areas in the ratio 6.25:1.
  What is the ratio of their heights?

A19 **(a)** Which of these three 'shields' do you think has half its area coloured blue?
  Estimate the fraction coloured blue in the other two shields.

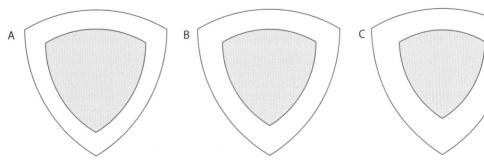

  (b) Each blue part is a reduction of the outline of the shield.
  Take measurements and work out the area factor of each reduction.
  Compare these answers with your estimates.

B Enlargement and volume

B1 **(a)** Calculate the volume of this cuboid.

(b) The cuboid is to be enlarged with scale factor 2. Sketch the enlarged cuboid and mark the new dimensions on it.

(c) Calculate the volume of the enlarged cuboid. By what volume factor has the volume been multiplied as a result of the enlargement?

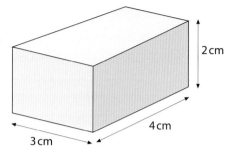

Repeat steps (b) and (c) for

(d) an enlargement of the original cuboid with scale factor 3

(e) an enlargement of the original with scale factor 1.5

(f) a scaling down of the original with scale factor 0.5

(g) a scaling of the original with scale factor k

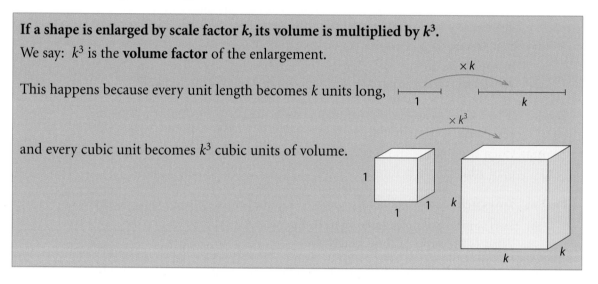

If a shape is enlarged by scale factor k, its volume is multiplied by k^3.

We say: k^3 is the **volume factor** of the enlargement.

This happens because every unit length becomes k units long,

and every cubic unit becomes k^3 cubic units of volume.

B2 A sculptor makes a small-scale clay model of a sculpture she is planning. The model is 40 cm tall. The final sculpture will be 100 cm tall.

(a) What is the scale factor of the enlargement?

(b) What is the volume factor for the enlargement?

(c) The volume of the model is 240 cm³. What will be the volume of the final sculpture?

B3 Find the volume factor for an enlargement whose scale factor is

(a) 4   **(b)** 5   **(c)** 27   **(d)** 10   **(e)** 50

B4 A glass bottle factory makes two types of bottle.
The larger type is an enlargement of the smaller type with scale factor 3.
The smaller type has a volume of $10\,\text{cm}^3$.
What is the volume of the larger type?

B5 Another factory makes two types of bottle.
The larger type is an enlargement of the smaller type with scale factor 1.8.

(a) Calculate the volume factor of the enlargement.

(b) The smaller type of bottle has a volume of $60\,\text{cm}^3$.
Calculate the volume of the larger type to the nearest cm^3.

B6 This carton contains $250\,\text{g}$ of soft cheese.
The manufacturer decides to enlarge the carton.
All the lengths will be increased by 10%.

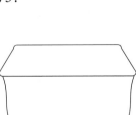

(a) What is the volume factor for the enlargement?

(b) What weight of cheese will the new carton hold?

B7 A model road tanker is made to a scale of $1:10$.

(a) The model tanker holds 75 litres of liquid.
How much does the real tanker hold?

(b) The inside of the model tanker has a surface area of $1.1\,\text{m}^2$.
What is the inside surface area on the real tanker?

B8 An enlarged version of a statue weighs 216 times as much as the original.
Both the original and the enlargement are made of the same metal.
Find the scale factor of the enlargement.

B9 Find the scale factor of an enlargement whose volume factor is

(a) 1000 (b) 343 (c) 8000 (d) 1 000 000 (e) 125 000

B10 A king had an altar of solid gold, in the shape of a cube.
He wanted a new altar with a volume exactly twice that of the existing altar.

The problem was to decide what the scale factor of the enlargement should be.
1.5 would be too much because the volume factor would be 3.375.

Use trial and improvement to find the scale factor needed.

B11 This carton contains ice cream.
The manufacturers want a larger, similar-shaped, carton
that they can label '20% more ice cream'.

(a) What is the volume factor for this enlargement?

(b) Use trial and improvement to find the scale factor needed.

B12 Find the volume factor for an enlargement whose scale factor is

(a) $\frac{1}{2}$ (b) $\frac{1}{3}$ (c) $\frac{3}{4}$ (d) 0.8 (e) 0.1

B13 The young fish in this picture is similar in shape to the adult fish but scaled down by a factor of about 0.4.

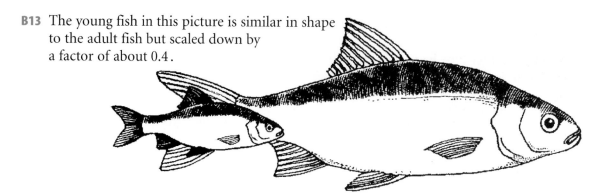

(a) Calculate the volume factor for this reduction.

(b) If the adult fish weighs 800 g, how much would you expect the young fish to weigh?

B14 These are two similar-shaped mugs.
The larger mug holds 324 cm³ of liquid.
What does the smaller one hold?

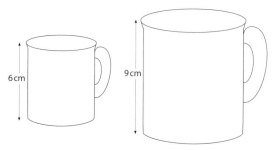

B15 (a) Which of these pictures do you think shows the glass half full?
Estimate the fraction of the glass filled in the other two pictures.

A

B

C

(b) Each 'cone' of liquid can be treated as a similar-shaped reduction of the conical glass itself.

Use these measurements to work out the volume factor for each reduction.
Compare these answers with your estimates.

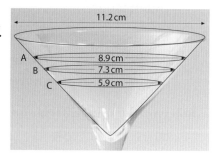

B16 Assume that these four eggs are similar in shape.

   (a) The volume of the jackdaw's egg is $6.00\,cm^3$.
      Calculate the volumes of the other eggs.

   (b) The surface area of the jackdaw's egg is $21.4\,cm^2$.
      Calculate the surface areas of the other eggs.

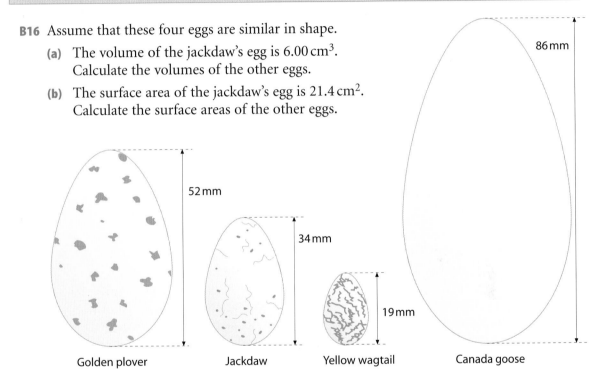

Golden plover   52 mm   Jackdaw   34 mm   Yellow wagtail   19 mm   Canada goose   86 mm

B17 A dolls' house is a reduction (scaled-down copy) of a real house.

   Copy and complete this table of information about the two houses.

	Dolls' house	Real house
Height of front door	6 cm	3 m
Number of windows	4	
Total area of windows	$96\,cm^2$	
Height of chimney		1 m
Capacity of water tank	12 ml	
Number of roof tiles		1600
Area of one roof tile	$0.45\,cm^2$	
Volume of roof space	$3024\,cm^3$	
Percentage of floor carpeted		80%
Total area of carpet		$185\,m^2$

B18 Two spheres have volumes in the ratio $27:343$.
What is the ratio of their diameters?

B19 Two similar cones have surface areas in the ratio $25:9$.

    (a) What is the ratio of their volumes?

    (b) If the volume of the larger cone is $500\,\text{cm}^3$, what is the volume of the smaller cone?

B20 This picture appeared in a magazine in 1979.
The increasing size of the barrels is supposed to represent the increasing price of a barrel of crude oil.

From your own measurements and calculations say whether you think this is a fair representation of the changing price.

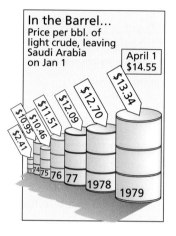

In the Barrel...
Price per bbl. of light crude, leaving Saudi Arabia on Jan 1

April 1 $14.55
$13.34
$12.70
$12.09
$11.51
$10.46
$10.95
$2.41

73 74 75 76 77 1978 1979

On being the right size

These extracts come from an article by the biologist J B S Haldane (1892–1964).

Consider a giant man sixty feet high – about the height of Giant Pope and Giant Pagan in the illustrated *Pilgrim's Progress* of my childhood. These monsters were not only ten times as high as Christian, but ten times as wide and ten times as thick, so that their total weight was a thousand times his, or about eighty to ninety tons. Unfortunately the cross-sections of their bones were only a hundred times those of Christian, so that every square inch of giant bone had to support ten times the weight borne by a square inch of human bone. As the human thigh-bone breaks under about ten times the human weight, Pope and Pagan would have broken their thighs every time they took a step. This was doubtless why they were sitting down in the picture I remember. But it lessens one's respect for Christian and Jack the Giant Killer.

Gravity, a mere nuisance to Christian, was a terror to Pope, Pagan and Despair. To the mouse and any smaller animal it presents practically no dangers. You can drop a mouse down a thousand-yard mine shaft, and, on arriving at the bottom, it gets a slight shock and walks away. A rat would probably be killed, though it can fall safely from the eleventh floor of a building; a man is killed, a horse splashes. For the resistance presented to movement by the air is proportional to the surface of the moving object. Divide an animal's length, breadth and height each by ten; its weight is reduced to a thousandth, but its surface only to a hundredth. So the resistance to falling in the case of the small animal is relatively ten times greater than the driving force.

In work on enlargement and scales you sometimes need to convert the units of measurement.

Examples

A plan of a house is drawn to a scale of $1:50$.
The living room has an area of $15\,m^2$.
What area in cm^2 will this be represented by on the plan?

> With a scale of $1:50$, $2\,cm$ on the plan represents $100\,cm$ in real life.
>
> So a square metre can be represented by a square $2\,cm$ by $2\,cm$. This has an area of $4\,cm^2$.
>
> So $15\,m^2$ is represented by $15 \times 4\,cm^2$, which is $60\,cm^2$.

A map is drawn to a scale of $1:50\,000$.
A lake on the map has an area of $2.6\,cm^2$.
What is the area of the real lake?

> Think of a square $1\,km$ by $1\,km$.
>
> Each edge is $1000\,m$ long, which is $1000 \times 100\,cm$, or $100\,000\,cm$.
>
> So the area of the square is $100\,000 \times 100\,000\,cm^2$, or $10\,000\,000\,000\,cm^2$.

> Scale factor $= 50\,000$
> Area factor $= 50\,000^2 = 2\,500\,000\,000$
> Area of real lake $= 2.6 \times 2\,500\,000\,000\,cm^2$
> $1\,km^2 = 10\,000\,000\,000\,cm^2$
>
> So area of real lake $= \dfrac{2.6 \times 2\,500\,000\,000}{10\,000\,000\,000}\,km^2$
>
> $= 0.65\,km^2$

C1 A plan of a small garden is drawn to a scale of $1:25$.

(a) A pond covers $24\,cm^2$ on the plan.
What is the area in m^2 of the real pond?

(b) The real lawn has an area of $17\,m^2$.
What area in cm^2 will it cover on the plan?

C2 A street plan is drawn to a scale of $1:10\,000$.
A housing estate occupies $60\,cm^2$ on the plan.
What is the area of the real housing estate

(a) in m^2 (b) in km^2

C3 The area of Ullswater lake in Cumbria is $9\,km^2$.
What area in cm^2 would it occupy on a map with

(a) a scale of $1:50\,000$ (b) a scale of $1:25\,000$

C4 The Eiffel Tower is 300 m high.
A model of the Eiffel Tower is 15 cm high and its base area is 25.5 cm^2.
What is the base area in m^2 of the actual tower?

C5 An ornamental pond has width 8 m and contains 50 m^3 of water.
How much water will be contained by a model of the pond with width 20 cm?

C6 A model railway is made to a scale of 1 : 72.
One of its model goods wagons can hold 25 cm^3 of goods.
What volume, in m^3 to 1 d.p., does this represent on a real goods wagon?

C7 This is a model of a water trough.
When full, the surface area of the water in it is 400 cm^2.
The surface area of the water in the real trough is 1.2 m^2 when it is full.
The real trough can hold 0.1 m^3 of water.

How much water can the model hold? Give your answer to
a reasonable degree of accuracy and make your units clear.

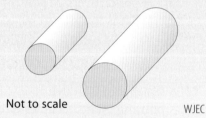

*C8 Ravi has a map of India that has no scale.
He knows that India has an area of about 3 million km^2.
He estimates that India covers 300 cm^2 on this map.

Calculate an estimate of the map scale.

Test yourself

T1 All the dimensions of a design for a suitcase are increased by 20%.

(a) By what percentage has the surface area increased?

(b) By what percentage has the volume increased?

T2 The diagram shows two similar cylinders.
The radius of the smaller cylinder is half the radius
of the larger cylinder.
The volume of the smaller cylinder is 200 cm^3.

Find the volume of the larger cylinder.

Not to scale   WJEC

T3 x ml of paint are needed to paint the surface of a cuboid of height 3 cm.
ax ml of paint are needed to paint the surface of a similar cuboid of height 7.5 cm.

What is the value of a?

T4 Two cones are similar in shape and have surface areas of 60 cm^2 and 135 cm^2.
The height of the smaller cone is 5 cm.
Find the height of the larger cone.

WJEC

12 Algebraic fractions and equations 1

This work will help you

- simplify expressions such as $\dfrac{4(a+1)^2}{8(a+1)}$

- simplify expressions such as $\dfrac{x^2-3x+2}{x^2-4x+4}$ by factorising and cancelling

- simplify multiplications and divisions such as $\dfrac{a}{2} \times \dfrac{b}{a}$ and $\dfrac{y}{x} \div \dfrac{5}{x}$

- solve equations such as $\dfrac{2x+3}{x} = 8$

A Simplifying by cancelling

When simplifying algebraic fractions you can write out expressions in full and 'cancel'.

$$\frac{5a^3b^2}{10ab^5} = \frac{5 \times a \times a \times a \times b \times b}{10 \times a \times b \times b \times b \times b \times b}$$

$$= \frac{\overset{1}{\cancel{5}} \times \cancel{a} \times a \times a \times \cancel{b} \times \cancel{b}}{\underset{2}{\cancel{10}} \times \cancel{a} \times \cancel{b} \times \cancel{b} \times b \times b \times b}$$

$$= \frac{a^2}{2b^3}$$

$$\frac{12(x-3)(x+5)^2}{8(x+5)} = \frac{12(x-3)(x+5)(x+5)}{8(x+5)}$$

$$= \frac{\overset{3}{\cancel{12}}(x-3)\cancel{(x+5)}(x+5)}{\underset{2}{\cancel{8}}\cancel{(x+5)}}$$

$$= \frac{3(x-3)(x+5)}{2}$$

This is equivalent to dividing top and bottom by the same expressions.

$$\frac{5a^3b^2}{10ab^5} \xrightarrow[\div 5]{\div 5} \frac{a^3b^2}{2ab^5} \xrightarrow[\div a]{\div a} \frac{a^2b^2}{2b^5} \xrightarrow[\div b^2]{\div b^2} \frac{a^2}{2b^3}$$

$$\frac{12(x-3)(x+5)^2}{8(x+5)} \xrightarrow[\div 4]{\div 4} \frac{3(x-3)(x+5)^2}{2(x+5)} \xrightarrow[\div (x+5)]{\div (x+5)} \frac{3(x-3)(x+5)}{2}$$

A1 Simplify each of these.

(a) $\dfrac{15x^9}{3x^5}$
(b) $\dfrac{6ab}{12a}$
(c) $\dfrac{3n^2l}{2nl}$
(d) $\dfrac{x^2y^5}{xy^8}$
(e) $\dfrac{4a^2b^7}{10a^5b^3}$

A2 Simplify each of these.

(a) $\dfrac{6(x+3)}{x+3}$
(b) $\dfrac{(x+5)^2}{x+5}$
(c) $\dfrac{5(x-7)^2}{x-7}$
(d) $\dfrac{x-1}{4(x-1)}$

(e) $\dfrac{(a+b)^3}{a+b}$
(f) $\dfrac{a-b}{(a-b)^2}$
(g) $\dfrac{5(x-1)^3}{10(x-1)^2}$
(h) $\dfrac{8(x+7)}{12(x+7)^2}$

A3 Simplify each of these.

(a) $\dfrac{(x+1)(x-3)}{x-3}$

(b) $\dfrac{5(3x-4)(x+5)}{3x-4}$

(c) $\dfrac{(x+1)(x-3)}{(x-3)(x+8)}$

(d) $\dfrac{x(x-1)}{(x-1)^2}$

(e) $\dfrac{(2x+1)^2}{x(2x+1)}$

(f) $\dfrac{x(3x-1)^2}{x(3x-1)}$

B Factorising then simplifying

When simplifying a fraction, first factorise as much as you can.

Examples

$$\frac{2x+8}{3x+12} = \frac{2(x+4)}{3(x+4)}$$
$$= \frac{2}{3}$$

$$\frac{2x-6}{x^2-5x+6} = \frac{2(x-3)}{(x-2)(x-3)}$$
$$= \frac{2}{x-2}$$

$$\frac{2x^2+3x-2}{x^2+x-2} = \frac{(2x-1)(x+2)}{(x+2)(x-1)}$$
$$= \frac{2x-1}{x-1}$$

Cross through common factors like this $\dfrac{(2x-1)(x+2)}{(x+2)(x-1)}$ if it helps you.

B1 Simplify each of these by factorising and cancelling.

(a) $\dfrac{2x+6}{3x+9}$

(b) $\dfrac{6x-3}{12x-6}$

(c) $\dfrac{14-7x}{2-x}$

B2 Ⓐ $\dfrac{3x+4}{x}$ Ⓑ $\dfrac{5x+10}{2x}$ Ⓒ $\dfrac{5x+10}{x+2}$ Ⓓ $\dfrac{2x+11}{2x-1}$

(a) Find the value of each expression above, as an integer or a fraction, when

   (i) $x=2$ (ii) $x=1$ (iii) $x=\,^-4$

(b) One of the expressions has the same value for all these values of x.
Can you explain this?

B3 A student has tried to simplify $\dfrac{2x+1}{x+1}$.

$$\frac{2x+1}{x+1} = \frac{2x+1}{x+1} = 2 \quad \times$$

Explain why this expression cannot be simplified like this.

B4 Simplify each of these by factorising and cancelling.

(a) $\dfrac{5x+10}{x^2+3x+2}$

(b) $\dfrac{x+3}{x^2+8x+15}$

(c) $\dfrac{2x^2+7x+5}{4x+4}$

(d) $\dfrac{x^2+5x}{x^2+7x+10}$

(e) $\dfrac{x^2+3x}{x^2+6x+9}$

(f) $\dfrac{3x^2+19x+20}{2x^2+10x}$

B5 **(a)** Work out the value of $\dfrac{x+4}{x^2+6x+8}$ when $x=2$.

Write your answer as a fraction in its simplest form.

(b) Show that, if x is an integer, then the value of $\dfrac{x+4}{x^2+6x+8}$ can always be written as a unit fraction (a fraction with a numerator of 1).

B6 Simplify these.

(a) $\dfrac{x^2+3x+2}{x^2+4x+3}$ 　　　 **(b)** $\dfrac{x^2+5x+6}{x^2+7x+12}$ 　　　 **(c)** $\dfrac{2x^2+11x+9}{x^2+2x+1}$

B7 Simplify these.

(a) $\dfrac{x^2-2x}{x^2+5x-14}$ 　　　 **(b)** $\dfrac{x^2+x-30}{x^2+6x}$ 　　　 **(c)** $\dfrac{x^2-5x}{x^2-7x+10}$

(d) $\dfrac{x^2-x-2}{x^2+6x+5}$ 　　　 **(e)** $\dfrac{x^2+x-12}{x^2-x-6}$ 　　　 **(f)** $\dfrac{x^2-6x+5}{x^2-8x+15}$

(g) $\dfrac{2x^2+7x+3}{x^2+2x-3}$ 　　　 **(h)** $\dfrac{x^2-2x-15}{2x^2-11x+5}$ 　　　 **(i)** $\dfrac{3x^2-2x-1}{3x^2-17x-6}$

B8 **(a)** Factorise x^2-4.

(b) Hence simplify $\dfrac{x^2+2x}{x^2-4}$.

B9 Simplify these.

(a) $\dfrac{x^2-25}{x^2-5x}$ 　　　 **(b)** $\dfrac{x^2-9}{x^2+2x-15}$ 　　　 **(c)** $\dfrac{x^2-6x-7}{x^2-1}$

(d) $\dfrac{4x^2-9}{4x^2+8x+3}$ 　　　 **(e)** $\dfrac{6x^2-15x}{4x^2-25}$ 　　　 **(f)** $\dfrac{9x^2-4}{15x+10}$

B10 Simplify these.

(a) $\dfrac{2x^2+7x-4}{x^2+2x-8}$ 　　　 **(b)** $\dfrac{x^2-25}{3x^2+14x-5}$ 　　　 **(c)** $\dfrac{x^2+x}{7x^2-7}$

(d) $\dfrac{x^2-7x}{x^2-2x-35}$ 　　　 **(e)** $\dfrac{2x^2-x-1}{x^2+9x-10}$ 　　　 **(f)** $\dfrac{5x-x^2}{50-2x^2}$

B11 **(a)** Factorise $4a^2-b^2$.

(b) Hence simplify $\dfrac{4a^2-b^2}{10a-5b}$.

B12 Simplify these.

(a) $\dfrac{x^2-y^2}{2x+2y}$ 　　　 **(b)** $\dfrac{9p^2-q^2}{6p^2-2pq}$ 　　　 **(c)** $\dfrac{25a^2-4b^2}{15a+6b}$

C Multiplying and dividing

To multiply two algebraic fractions together, you can first multiply the numerators and multiply the denominators, then simplify.

Examples

$$\frac{3a}{5} \times \frac{b}{9a} = \frac{3ab}{45a}$$

$$= \frac{3b}{45} \quad \longleftarrow \quad \boxed{\frac{3ab}{45a}}$$

$$= \frac{b}{15} \quad \longleftarrow \quad \boxed{\frac{3b}{45_{15}}}$$

$$\frac{2(x+3)}{15} \times \frac{10}{x+3} = \frac{20(x+3)}{15(x+3)}$$

$$= \frac{20}{15}$$

$$= \frac{4}{3}$$

$$a \times \frac{4b^2}{a} = \frac{4ab^2}{a}$$

$$= 4b^2$$

$$\frac{\pi}{xyz} \times y = \frac{\pi y}{xyz}$$

$$= \frac{\pi}{xz}$$

An alternative approach is to cancel first and then multiply as usual.

Example

$$\frac{ab}{4} \times \frac{6a}{b} = \frac{ab}{4_2} \times \frac{\overset{3}{6a}}{b} = \frac{3a^2}{2}$$

C1 Simplify each of these.

(a) $\dfrac{a}{2} \times \dfrac{4}{a}$

(b) $\dfrac{3a}{2} \times \dfrac{a}{3}$

(c) $\dfrac{3a}{2} \times \dfrac{5a}{12}$

(d) $\dfrac{a}{5} \times \dfrac{15b}{4}$

(e) $\dfrac{3a}{2} \times \dfrac{1}{a}$

(f) $\dfrac{ab}{2} \times \dfrac{a}{b}$

(g) $\dfrac{ab^2}{2} \times \dfrac{5}{4ab}$

(h) $\dfrac{b}{2a} \times \dfrac{5a^2b}{4ab}$

C2 Simplify each of these.

(a) $a \times \dfrac{b}{a}$

(b) $\dfrac{1}{ab} \times a$

(c) $\dfrac{x}{4\pi yz} \times 2y$

(d) $abc \times \dfrac{7}{ab}$

(e) $(x+1) \times \dfrac{3}{x+1}$

(f) $\dfrac{y}{3(x-4)} \times 6(x-4)$

To divide one fraction by another, multiply the first by the reciprocal of the second.

Examples

$$\frac{3a^2}{4} \div \frac{9}{8a} = \frac{3a^2}{4} \times \frac{8a}{9}$$

$$= \frac{24a^3}{36}$$

$$= \frac{2a^3}{3}$$

$$\frac{3}{a} \div b = \frac{3}{a} \times \frac{1}{b}$$

$$= \frac{3}{ab}$$

C3 Copy and complete this division.

$$\frac{3a}{10} \div \frac{6a^2}{5} = \frac{3a}{10} \times \frac{5}{\blacksquare} = \ldots\ldots$$

C4 Simplify these.

(a) $\dfrac{a}{2} \div \dfrac{4}{a}$
(b) $\dfrac{a}{2} \div \dfrac{a}{3}$
(c) $\dfrac{3a}{10} \div \dfrac{5}{a^2}$
(d) $\dfrac{ab}{3} \div \dfrac{5b}{4a}$

(e) $\dfrac{a^2}{2} \div \dfrac{1}{a}$
(f) $\dfrac{a}{2b^2} \div \dfrac{a}{b}$
(g) $\dfrac{b^2}{2a^2} \div \dfrac{b}{4a}$
(h) $\dfrac{bc}{a} \div \dfrac{abc}{4}$

C5 Simplify these.

(a) $\dfrac{x}{y} \div x$
(b) $\dfrac{y}{x} \div x^2$
(c) $\dfrac{a}{b} \div 3$
(d) $\dfrac{1}{a} \div b$

C6 (a) Factorise $x^2 - 16$.

(b) Hence simplify
(i) $(x + 4) \times \dfrac{x}{x^2 - 16}$
(ii) $\dfrac{2x^2 - 32}{x + 4} \div (x - 4)$

D Solving equations that contain fractions

When solving equations it is usually easiest to multiply to get rid of all fractions first.

Examples

$$\frac{3x + 1}{x} = 11 \qquad [\times x]$$
$$3x + 1 = 11x \qquad [-3x]$$
$$1 = 8x \qquad [\div 8]$$
$$\tfrac{1}{8} = x$$

$$x + 1 = \frac{18}{x - 2} \qquad [\times (x - 2)]$$
$$(x + 1)(x - 2) = 18 \qquad [\text{expand brackets}]$$
$$x^2 - x - 2 = 18 \qquad [-18]$$
$$x^2 - x - 20 = 0 \qquad [\text{factorise}]$$
$$(x - 5)(x + 4) = 0$$
$$x = 5 \text{ or } ^-4$$

D1 Solve each of these equations.

(a) $\dfrac{2x + 3}{x} = 8$
(b) $\dfrac{4x - 3}{5} = x + 1$
(c) $\dfrac{5 - x}{4} = x$

(d) $\dfrac{x + 5}{x + 1} = 2$
(e) $\dfrac{x + 1}{x - 3} = 3$
(f) $\dfrac{2x + 1}{x - 2} = 3$

(g) $\dfrac{2x + 1}{5} = x - 4$
(h) $\dfrac{3x + 1}{4x - 1} = 6$
(i) $\dfrac{1 - 2x}{2x + 1} = 1$

D2 Solve each of these equations.

(a) $\dfrac{2(x - 3)}{x} = 1$
(b) $\dfrac{4(x + 1)}{x} = 2$
(c) $\dfrac{3(2x - 1)}{x - 4} = 3$

D3 Solve each of these equations.

(a) $\dfrac{12}{x+1} = x$

(b) $\dfrac{8}{x} = x - 2$

(c) $\dfrac{x+6}{x} = 2x$

(d) $\dfrac{10}{x} = 3 + x$

(e) $\dfrac{2x-9}{x} = x - 8$

(f) $\dfrac{3(x-1)}{x+7} = 2x + 3$

(g) $\dfrac{10}{x-1} = x - 10$

(h) $\dfrac{16}{x-3} = x + 3$

(i) $\dfrac{4(x+1)}{x+2} = 3x + 2$

Test yourself

T1 Simplify fully $\dfrac{2x^2 + 5x - 3}{x^2 + 2x - 3}$.

AQA

T2 Simplify

(a) $\dfrac{x^2 - 4}{x^2 + 4x}$

(b) $\dfrac{5x^2 - 15x}{x^2 + x - 12}$

T3 Simplify $\dfrac{5x^2 + 14x - 3}{x^2 - 9}$.

AQA

T4 (a) Factorise $9x^2 - 6x + 1$.

(b) Simplify $\dfrac{6x^2 + 7x - 3}{9x^2 - 6x + 1}$.

Edexcel

T5 (a) Factorise $x^2 - 4y^2$.

(b) Simplify $\dfrac{x^2 - 4y^2}{5x + 10y}$.

OCR

T6 Simplify each of these.

(a) $\dfrac{a^2}{12} \times \dfrac{8b}{a}$

(b) $\dfrac{3}{x} \times \dfrac{xyz}{\pi}$

(c) $\dfrac{p}{3q} \times \dfrac{9q^2p}{qp}$

(d) $ac \times \dfrac{5}{abc}$

(e) $\dfrac{a+1}{a-1} \times \dfrac{2}{a+1}$

(f) $\dfrac{x^3}{5} \div \dfrac{1}{x}$

(g) $\dfrac{x^3}{5} \div 2x$

(h) $\dfrac{b}{a} \div ab$

T7 Simplify fully $\dfrac{x^2 - 4}{8} \times \dfrac{4x}{x+2}$.

T8 (a) Solve $\dfrac{40 - x}{3} = 4 + x$.

(b) Simplify fully $\dfrac{4x^2 - 6x}{4x^2 - 9}$.

Edexcel

T9 Solve each of these equations.

(a) $\dfrac{4x+1}{3x} = 2$

(b) $\dfrac{2(x-3)}{x+1} = 6$

(c) $\dfrac{5}{x} = 2x - 3$

(d) $\dfrac{x+5}{x-1} = x - 5$

13 Time series

This work will help you calculate a moving average and use it to detect a trend.

A Trend and moving average

Saveway profits rise steadily

The profits of supermarket giant Saveway show a steady upward trend over a seven-year period, the company reported yesterday.

'One must be careful about predicting the future from the past,' said a company spokesman, 'but we believe that the trend will

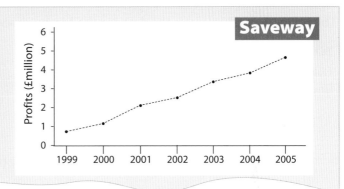

The graph above shows the profits of a supermarket chain.
It shows that the profits have a steady upward **trend**.

The graph below shows how unemployment in a seaside town varies.

- What is the most noticeable feature of this graph?
- Does this graph show a trend?

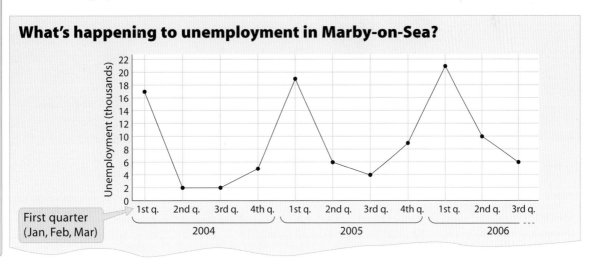

What's happening to unemployment in Marby-on-Sea?

First quarter (Jan, Feb, Mar)

One way to see a trend in the unemployment figures would be to take the mean for each year and see how it changes over time. But we would have to wait for a whole year's figures before we could compare with previous years.

To get a more frequent update we can use a **moving average**. We use overlapping periods of four quarters, like this, and find the mean for each period.

1st	2nd	3rd	4th
	2nd	3rd	4th	1st
		3rd	4th	1st	2nd

This is called a **4-point moving average**.

The following example uses the data for the Marby-on-Sea graph.

Year	2004				2005				2006		
Quarter	1	2	3	4	1	2	3	4	1	2	3
Unemployment (000)	17	2	2	5	19	6	4	9	21	10	6

$$\frac{17 + 2 + 2 + 5}{4} = 6.5$$

$$\frac{2 + 2 + 5 + 19}{4} = 7 \ \ldots \text{ and so on.}$$

We have to decide how to show the moving average on the graph. The rule is to plot it at the centre of the four quarters it covers.

This means plotting it halfway between the middle two quarters.

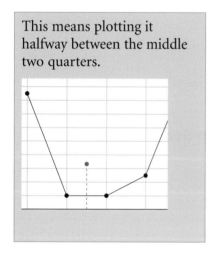

So the graph of the moving average starts like this.

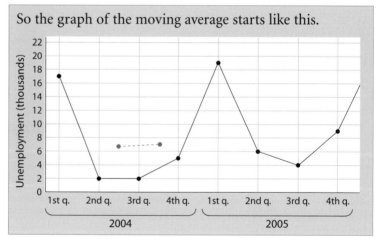

In the table we can show the moving average like this:

Year	2004				2005				2006		
Quarter	1	2	3	4	1	2	3	4	1	2	3
Unemployment (000)	17	2	2	5	19	6	4	9	21	10	6
4-point moving average		6.5	7								

A1 (a) Complete the calculation above of the moving average.

(b) Describe the trend in unemployment.

A short cut

You can calculate the next value of the moving average by adjusting the value before it.

The first moving average calculation is $\dfrac{17 + 2 + 2 + 5}{4}$

The next is $\dfrac{2 + 2 + 5 + 19}{4}$

To get from the total $17 + 2 + 2 + 5$ to the total $2 + 2 + 5 + 19$, we have taken away the 17 and replaced it by the 19.

The total changes by $19 - 17$, or 2.
So the moving average changes by $\frac{2}{4}$ or 0.5.

The first value is 6.5, so the next value will be 7.

A2 This table shows the numbers of visitors to a seaside town.

Year	2005			2006				2007	
Quarter	2	3	4	1	2	3	4	1	2
Visitors (000)	16	23	10	7	15	21	11	3	13

(a) Calculate a 4-point moving average and show it, with the original data, on a graph.

(b) Describe the trend.

A3 This table shows the numbers of visitors to a museum.

Year	2005			2006				2007	
Quarter	2	3	4	1	2	3	4	1	2
Visitors (000)	7	9	14	22	10	10	17	25	11

(a) Calculate a 4-point moving average and show it, with the original data, on a graph.

(b) Describe the trend.

A4 This table shows the number of visitors (in thousands) at a tourist attraction each month.

Month	04/05	05/05	06/05	07/05	08/05	09/05	10/05	11/05	12/05	01/06
Number	18	19	29	33	31	23	10	6	9	5

Month	02/06	03/06	04/06	05/06	06/06	07/06	08/06	09/06	10/06	11/06
Number	7	14	20	22	25	28	27	20	12	7

(a) Choose an appropriate moving average and calculate it.

(b) Describe the trend in the data.

Forecasting

Forecasting the future is always risky. But there are many circumstances where it is necessary, for example to predict how much unemployment benefit will need to be paid. A trend may be used to make a forecast.

The graph of unemployment in Marby-on-Sea is shown below, together with the graph of 4-point moving averages showing the trend.

The graph finishes at the 4th quarter of 2006. The extra lines show a way of forecasting the unemployment figure for the 1st quarter of 2007:

• Extend the trend (the moving average graph), assuming that it continues as before.

• Find the difference between each previous 1st quarter figure and the trend. These differences are called **cyclical variations**. They are +10.4 and +9.8.

• Find the mean cyclical variation. It is $\dfrac{10.4 + 9.8}{2} = 10.1$.

• Add the mean cyclical variation to the extended trend. The forecast is 23.3.

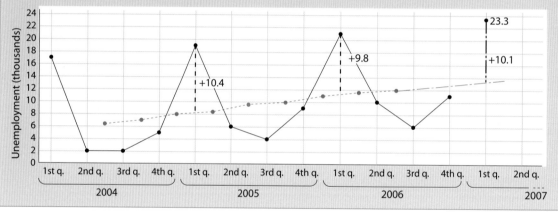

Test yourself

T1 The total rainfall figures, in millimetres, for the past 7 years in Egypt are shown below.

27   24   31   30   28   15   29

Find the five-yearly moving averages.

OCR

T2 This table shows the quarterly profits of a garden centre.

Year	2005				2006				2007	
Quarter	1	2	3	4	1	2	3	4	1	2
Profits (£000)	32	58	75	41	30	63	77	40	36	65

(a) Calculate a 4-point moving average.

(b) Draw a graph showing the original data and the moving average.

(c) Comment on the trend.

Review 2

1 This rule is used to work out the cost, in pounds, of placing a small ad in a local paper.

> Add 2 to the number of lines. Multiply your answer by 3.

The cost of n lines is C pounds.
Write down a formula for C in terms of n.

2 Work out the value of $2a - ab$ when $a = 4$ and $b = {}^-5$.

3 Barry designed this questionnaire to try to find out whether meat-eating is more popular among older people than among younger people in his village.

> 1 How old are you? _____
> 2 How often, on average, do you eat meat in a week? _____

Do you think these questions are satisfactory?
If not, what improvements would you suggest?

4 Expand these.

(a) $(2x - 1)(3x + 2)$ (b) $(2x + 5)^2$ (c) $(3x - 1)(3x + 1)$

5 This diagram shows two villages P and Q.
Q is 53 km east and 13 km north of P.

Calculate the bearing of Q from P.

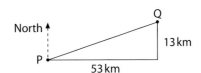

6 Here are the first five terms of a sequence.

$$5, \ 12, \ 19, \ 26, \ 33$$

(a) Find, in terms of n, the nth term of the sequence.

(b) Show that 60 is not a term in this sequence.

7 The numbers of visitors to a museum over 8 years are shown in the table.

Year	2000	2001	2002	2003	2004	2005	2006	2007
Visitors (000s)	19	18	19	17	20	22	19	21

(a) Calculate a 4-year moving average.

(b) Describe the trend in the data.

8 Four points have coordinates A $(0, 4)$, B $(4, 2)$, C $(0, {}^-1)$ and D $(3, 0)$.
Two straight lines are drawn, one going through A and B and one going through C and D.

(a) Find the equation of each line.

(b) Calculate the coordinates of the point where the two lines intersect.

9 V is proportional to $\sqrt{U}$ and $V = 6$ when $U = 4$.
Find an equation for V in terms of U.

10 In this diagram, the circle, whose radius is 5 cm, touches the sides of the regular pentagon.

O is the centre of the circle.

(a) Calculate angle a.

(b) Calculate the length of each side of the regular pentagon.

(c) Calculate the perimeter of the regular pentagon.

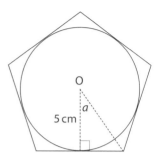

11 Write each of these as a single algebraic fraction.

(a) $\dfrac{a}{6} \times \dfrac{3b}{a}$ (b) $\dfrac{b}{6} \div 2$ (c) $\dfrac{ab^2}{2} \times \dfrac{a}{b}$ (d) $\dfrac{a}{x} \div \dfrac{a^2}{3x}$ (e) $\dfrac{2}{a} \div \dfrac{b}{a}$

12 This cuboid is to be enlarged so that the volume is doubled.

(a) Find the scale factor of the enlargement, correct to three significant figures.

(b) Calculate the dimensions of the enlarged cuboid.

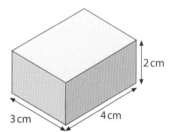

13 Factorise each of these.

(a) $3x^2 + 17x + 10$ (b) $6y^2 + y - 12$ (c) $9m^2 - n^2$

14 In these expressions, the letters a, b, h stand for lengths.
2 and 3 are numbers which have no dimensions.

$$3ha^2 \qquad 2bh \qquad 3b^2 \qquad h\sqrt{a^2 + b^2} \qquad \dfrac{a^2 + b^2}{h} \qquad h(a + b)$$

Write down all the expressions that could represent areas.

15 Solve the equation $2x^2 + 9x - 18 = 0$.

16 y is inversely proportional to the square root of x.
When x is 25, y is 2.5.
Find y when $x = 0.64$.

17 (a) Find an expression for the surface area of this cuboid.
Write the expression in its simplest form.

(b) The surface area of the cuboid is 62 cm².
Form and solve an equation to find the value of x.

(c) Calculate the volume of the cuboid.

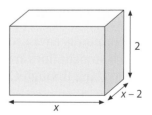

18 Find the equation of the line perpendicular to $y = 2x + 3$, going through $(0, 0)$.

19 This table shows the distribution of weights of a group of 10-year-old boys.

Weight, w kg	Frequency
$20 < w \leq 25$	5
$25 < w \leq 30$	9
$30 < w \leq 35$	17
$35 < w \leq 40$	7
$40 < w \leq 45$	2

(a) Estimate the mean weight, showing your working clearly.

(b) In which class interval is the median height?

Weight, w kg	Cumulative frequency
$20 < w \leq 25$	
$20 < w \leq 30$	
$20 < w \leq 35$	
$20 < w \leq 40$	
$20 < w \leq 45$	

(c) Copy and complete this cumulative frequency table for the data.

(d) Draw a cumulative frequency graph for your table.

(e) Use your graph to estimate the number of these boys who weigh more than 33 kg.

20 The intensity of illumination I (measured in lumens) on a surface is inversely proportional to d^2, where d m is the distance between the light source and the surface.

Given that $I = 40$ when $d = 1.5$, calculate I when $d = 2.5$.

21 Simplify each of these.

(a) $\dfrac{3a + 12}{a + 4}$

(b) $\dfrac{c - 2}{c^2 - 4}$

(c) $\dfrac{5x^2 + 2x - 3}{x^2 - 1}$

(d) $\dfrac{6x^2 - 5x - 4}{4x^2 + 4x + 1}$

22 A map has a scale of $1 : 50\,000$.
Majid estimates the area of Arlington reservoir as $2\,\text{cm}^2$ on the map.
Calculate an estimate of the area of the actual reservoir.

23 Each of these 'step patterns' is made using square tiles.

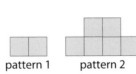 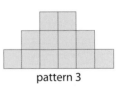

pattern 1   pattern 2   pattern 3

(a) How many tiles would there be in the 10th pattern?

(b) Find a rule for the number of tiles in the nth step pattern.

(c) Show that you could not make a step pattern using exactly 100 tiles.

24 In the following expressions the letters r, s and t all represent lengths.
For each expression, state whether it could represent a length, an area or a volume.

$$r(s + 2t) \qquad \pi(r + s) \qquad r^2 + s^2 \qquad \pi s(s + t) \qquad \pi s^2 t$$

25 Solve each of these equations.

(a) $\dfrac{11 - x}{2} = 1 + 2x$

(b) $\dfrac{2x + 5}{x} = 3x$

(c) $\dfrac{4x + 7}{x + 2} = x + 4$

14 Trigonometric graphs

You need to be familiar with the use of sine, cosine and tangent in right-angled triangles.

This work will help you

- use the sine, cosine and tangent of angles greater than 90° and of negative angles
- work with trigonometric graphs
- relate trigonometric graphs to real-life situations

You need sheet H2–1 and two copies of sheet H2–2. You may find a graph plotter helpful.

A The sine graph

On sheet H2–1, label each point marked on the circle with an angle like this. Continue up to 360°.

Then take the *y*-coordinate of each labelled point and plot it against its angle on sheet H2–2.

Join your points with a smooth curve.

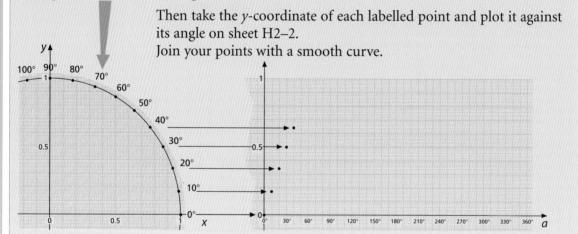

The circle's radius is 1 unit.

So you can see that when the angle (call it *a*) is between 0° and 90° the *y*-coordinate of the point on the circle is sin *a*.

You can think of it this way …   or this way …

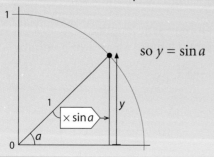

so $y = \sin a$

$$\sin a = \frac{\text{opposite}}{\text{hypotenuse}} = \frac{y}{1}$$

so $y = \sin a$

The sine of an angle outside the range 0° to 90° is also defined as the *y*-coordinate of the corresponding point on the circle.

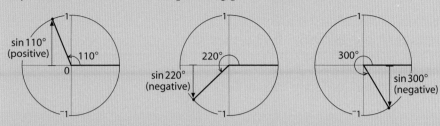

So on sheet H2–2 label the vertical axis of your graph 'sin *a*'.

Starting at (1, 0) and going **anticlockwise** in a circle with radius 1 unit is the standard way to represent the angles for trigonometric functions.

A1 Use your sine graph to get approximate values for these.

(a) sin 65°   (b) sin 105°   (c) sin 153°   (d) sin 212°   (e) sin 285°

A2 Key sin 65° into your calculator to see how close your approximate value was in A1(a). Check your other values the same way.

A3 (a) From your graph, find an angle that has 0.8 as its sine. Can you find more than one angle?

(b) Key sin⁻¹ 0.8 into your calculator (the angle whose sine is 0.8). Does this agree with what you found from your graph?

When you look for sin⁻¹ of a value, there is usually more than one answer between 0° and 360°, but your calculator only gives you one of them.

Making a sketch of a sine graph and using the graph's symmetry can help you find all the angles.

Alternatively, sketching a circle like the one on sheet H2–1 may help.

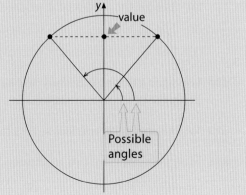

The calculator gives this angle.

Here a second answer is 180° minus the calculator's angle.

Possible angles

A4 What angle between 0° and 360° has exactly the same sine as each of these?

(a) 56°   (b) 112°   (c) 299°   (d) 199°   (e) 11°

(f) 251°   (g) 286°   (h) 82°   (i) 101°   (j) 321°

A5 Find these to the nearest 0.1°, using a calculator. Give all possible answers from 0° to 360°.

(a) $\sin^{-1} 0.7$ (b) $\sin^{-1} 0.2$ (c) $\sin^{-1} 0$ (d) $\sin^{-1} 1$ (e) $\sin^{-1} 0.6$

A6 You are told that $\sin 72° = 0.95$ to 2 d.p.
What angles between 0° and 360° have ⁻0.95 as their sine?

A7 You are told that $\sin 223° = {}^-0.68$ to 2 d.p.
What angles between 0° and 360° have 0.68 as their sine?

> • Where should you mark angles 370°, 380°, 390°, ... on the circle on sheet H2–1?
> • Where should you mark angles ⁻10°, ⁻20°, ⁻30°, ... ?

A8 Read y-coordinates from the circle to get approximate values for these.

(a) $\sin 480°$ (b) $\sin 650°$ (c) $\sin 555°$ (d) $\sin 390°$ (e) $\sin 705°$

(f) $\sin {}^-70°$ (g) $\sin {}^-200°$ (h) $\sin {}^-160°$ (i) $\sin {}^-300°$ (j) $\sin {}^-260°$

A9 Key $\sin 480°$ into your calculator to see how close your approximate value was in A8 (a).
Check your other values the same way.

A10 Complete the graph of $\sin a$ on sheet H2–2 for values of a from ⁻360° to 0°.

A11 What angles between 0° and 360° have **exactly** the same sine as

(a) ⁻20°   (b) ⁻230°   (c) ⁻290°   (d) ⁻95°   (e) ⁻28°

A12 With a calculator find these to the nearest 0.1°. Give all possible answers from ⁻360° to 0°.

(a) $\sin^{-1} 0.6$ (b) $\sin^{-1} {}^-0.4$ (c) $\sin^{-1} 0.1$ (d) $\sin^{-1} {}^-0.25$ (e) $\sin^{-1} 1$

(f) $\sin^{-1} {}^-0.5$ (g) $\sin^{-1} {}^-0.35$ (h) $\sin^{-1} 0.95$ (i) $\sin^{-1} {}^-0.1$ (j) $\sin^{-1} {}^-1$

A13 **Sketch** the graph of $\sin a$, for a between ⁻720° and 720°.

(a) List all the values of a where $\sin a = 0$.

(b) List all the values of a where $\sin a = 1$.

(c) List all the values of a where $\sin a = {}^-1$.

A14 Use your calculator to find one value of $\sin^{-1} 0.3$.
With the help of your sketch, give all the values of $\sin^{-1} 0.3$ between ⁻720° and 720°.

A15 What happens if you key $\sin^{-1} 2$ into your calculator? Why?

A16 Find possible values of x between 0° and 360° for each of these.

(a) $\sin x = 0.7$ (b) $2 \sin x = 1$ (c) $\sin x = {}^-0.3$

(d) $\sin x + \frac{1}{4} = 0$ (e) $4 \sin x = 3$ (f) $5 \sin x = {}^-2$

A17 Toni says: 'I'm thinking of an angle between 0° and 720°. Its sine is greater than 0.6.'
What angle could she be thinking of? Describe all the possibilities.

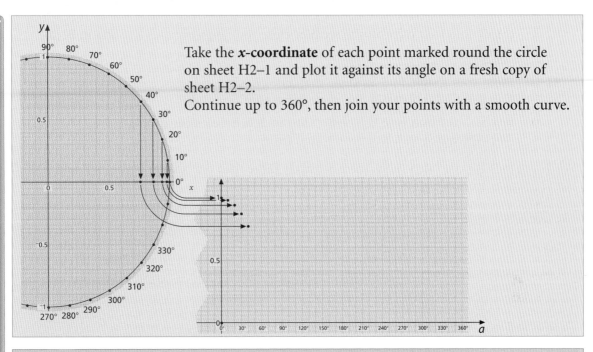

Take the **x-coordinate** of each point marked round the circle on sheet H2–1 and plot it against its angle on a fresh copy of sheet H2–2.
Continue up to 360°, then join your points with a smooth curve.

As with the sine, you can see that when the angle a is between 0° and 90° the x-coordinate of the point on the circle is $\cos a$.

You can think of it this way …

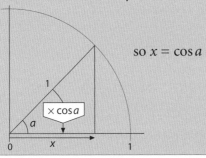

so $x = \cos a$

or this way …

$$\cos a = \frac{\text{adjacent}}{\text{hypotenuse}} = \frac{x}{1}$$

so $x = \cos a$

We define the cosine of an angle outside the range 0° to 90° also as the x-coordinate of the corresponding point on the circle.

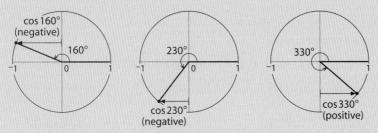

So on your second copy of sheet H2–2 label the vertical axis of your graph '$\cos a$'.

B1 Use your cosine graph to get approximate values for these.

    (a) $\cos 55°$ **(b)** $\cos 95°$ **(c)** $\cos 147°$ **(d)** $\cos 208°$ **(e)** $\cos 305°$

B2 Key $\cos 55°$ into your calculator to see how close your approximate value was in B1(a). Check your other values the same way.

B3 **(a)** From your graph, find an angle that has 0.7 as its cosine. Can you find more than one angle between 0° and 360°?

    (b) Key $\cos^{-1} 0.7$ into your calculator (the angle whose cosine is 0.7). Does this agree with what you found from your graph?

When you look for $\cos^{-1}$ of a value, there is usually more than one answer between 0° and 360°, but your calculator only gives you one of them.

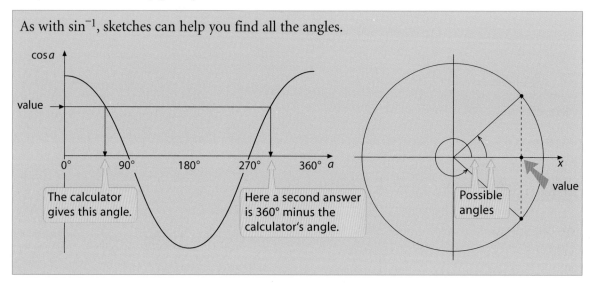

As with $\sin^{-1}$, sketches can help you find all the angles.

The calculator gives this angle.

Here a second answer is 360° minus the calculator's angle.

Possible angles

B4 What angle between 0° and 360° has **exactly** the same cosine as each of these?

    (a) 62°   **(b)** 108°   **(c)** 301°   **(d)** 195°   **(e)** 2°

B5 Extend your cosine graph to show cosines of angles between ⁻360° and 0°. What angles between ⁻360° and 360° have exactly the same cosine as each of these?

    (a) 272°   **(b)** 355°   **(c)** 71°   **(d)** 99°   **(e)** 317°

    (f) ⁻10°   **(g)** ⁻250°   **(h)** ⁻310°   **(i)** ⁻85°   **(j)** ⁻32°

B6 Find these to the nearest 0.1°, using a calculator. Give all possible answers from ⁻360° to 360°.

    (a) $\cos^{-1} 0.6$ **(b)** $\cos^{-1} {}^{-}0.5$ **(c)** $\cos^{-1} 0.1$ **(d)** $\cos^{-1} {}^{-}0.45$ **(e)** $\cos^{-1} 1$

    (f) $\cos^{-1} 0.75$ **(g)** $\cos^{-1} {}^{-}0.2$ **(h)** $\cos^{-1} {}^{-}1$ **(i)** $\cos^{-1} 0.3$ **(j)** $\cos^{-1} 0$

B7 You are told that $\cos 76° = 0.24$ to 2 d.p. What angles between ⁻360° and 360° have ⁻0.24 as their cosine?

B8 You are told that $\cos 100° = {}^-0.17$ to 2 d.p.
What angles between $^-360°$ and $360°$ have 0.17 as their cosine?

B9 Sketch the graph of $\cos a$, for a between $^-720°$ and $720°$.

(a) List all the values of a where $\cos a = 0$.

(b) List all the values of a where $\cos a = 1$.

(c) List all the values of a where $\cos a = {}^-1$.

B10 Use your calculator to find one value of $\cos^{-1} 0.4$.
With the help of your sketch, give all the values of $\cos^{-1} 0.4$ between $^-720°$ and $720°$.

B11 Find possible values of x between $0°$ and $360°$ for each of these.

(a) $\cos x = 0.1$

(b) $7 \cos x = 1$

(c) $\cos x = {}^-0.25$

(d) $\cos x + \frac{1}{5} = 0$

(e) $3 \cos x = 2$

(f) $5 \cos x = {}^-4$

B12 Robert says: 'I'm thinking of an angle between $0°$ and $720°$. Its cosine is less than $^-0.6$.'

What angle could he be thinking of? Describe all the possibilities.

*B13 If $\sin b = {}^-\sin a$ and $\cos b = {}^-\cos a$, what can you say about a and b?

*B14 If $\cos q = \cos p$ and $\sin q = {}^-\sin p$, what can you say about p and q?

C The tangent graph

We can also get the tangent of an angle (call it a) by considering a point moving anticlockwise round a circle of unit radius.

When a is between $0°$ and $90°$, in the normal way:

$$\tan a = \frac{\text{opposite}}{\text{adjacent}} = \frac{y\text{-coordinate of point P}}{x\text{-coordinate of point P}}$$

We also regard the tangent of an angle outside the range $0°$ to $90°$ as

$$\frac{y\text{-coordinate of point P}}{x\text{-coordinate of point P}} \cdot$$

Notice that this is $\frac{\sin a}{\cos a}$.

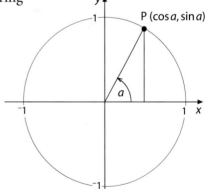

- For what angles between $0°$ and $360°$ is the tangent positive?
- For what angles between $0°$ and $360°$ is it negative?
- For what angles is it zero?
- What happens around $90°$?
- What happens around $270°$?

Here again is part of the graph of the sine function …

… and here is the cosine function.

The tangent function is obtained by dividing sine values by cosine values.

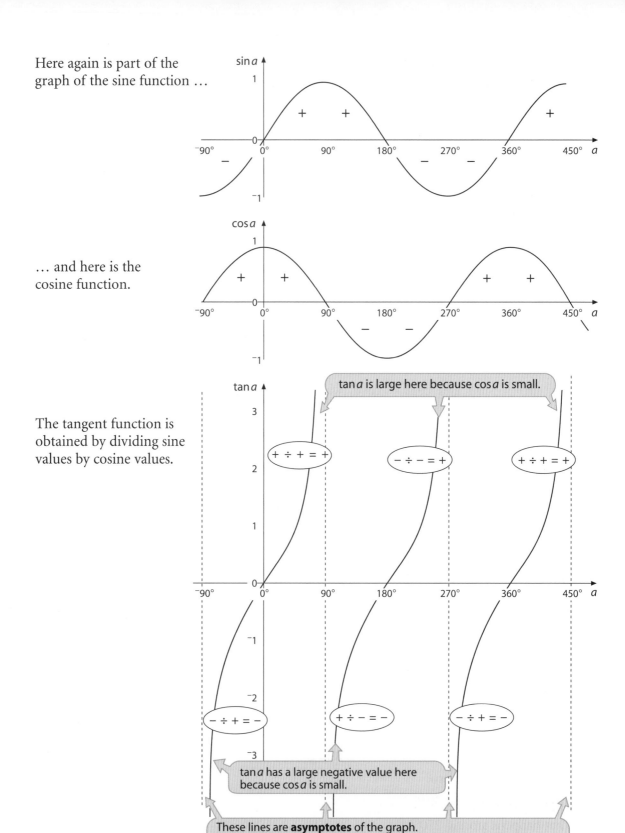

tan*a* is large here because cos*a* is small.

$+ \div + = +$ $- \div - = +$ $+ \div + = +$

$- \div + = -$ $+ \div - = -$ $- \div + = -$

tan*a* has a large negative value here because cos*a* is small.

These lines are **asymptotes** of the graph.
The graph gets closer and closer to them but never touches them.
They divide the graph into disconnected sections.

C1 **(a)** Find $\tan 75°$ on your calculator to 2 d.p.

(b) Find two other angles whose tangent is the same as $\tan 75°$.
Use the tangent graph opposite as a guide.

C2 What angles between $^-90°$ and $450°$ have exactly the same tangent as each of these?

(a) $30°$ **(b)** $440°$ **(c)** $200°$ **(d)** $^-80°$ **(e)** $150°$

(f) $300°$ **(g)** $48°$ **(h)** $399°$ **(i)** $143°$ **(j)** $^-27°$

C3 **(a)** Find $\tan^{-1} 0.9$ on your calculator.

(b) Use the tangent graph opposite as a guide to finding two other
results for $\tan^{-1} 0.9$.

C4 Find these to the nearest $0.1°$, using a calculator.
Give all the possible answers from $^-90°$ to $450°$.

(a) $\tan^{-1} 0.6$ **(b)** $\tan^{-1} 1.7$ **(c)** $\tan^{-1} 45$ **(d)** $\tan^{-1} 0.01$ **(e)** $\tan^{-1} {}^-0.4$

(f) $\tan^{-1} {}^-2.5$ **(g)** $\tan^{-1} {}^-5$ **(h)** $\tan^{-1} {}^-0.1$ **(i)** $\tan^{-1} {}^-0.05$ **(j)** $\tan^{-1} {}^-3.79$

C5 You are told that $\tan 63° = 1.96$ to 2 d.p.
What angles between $0°$ and $360°$ have $^-1.96$ as their tangent?

C6 You are told that $\tan 114° = {}^-2.25$ to 2 d.p.
What angles between $0°$ and $360°$ have 2.25 as their tangent?

C7 Find possible values of x between $0°$ and $360°$ for each of these.

(a) $\tan x = 90$ **(b)** $\tan x = {}^-0.5$ **(c)** $5 \tan x = 8$

(d) $\frac{1}{2} \tan x = {}^-2$ **(e)** $\tan x + \frac{1}{5} = 0$ **(f)** $3 \tan x = {}^-2$

The graphs of $\sin a$ and $\cos a$
are **periodic graphs**.
They 'repeat themselves'
after every $360°$.
We say $360°$ is the
period of each graph.

The graph of $\cos a$ has the same
repeating shape as $\sin a$,
but is shifted $90°$ to the left.

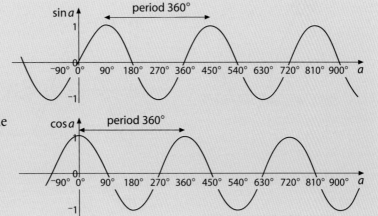

C8 The graph of $\tan a$ is also periodic.
What is the period of the graph of $\tan a$?

D Graphs based on trigonometric functions

 You can use a graph plotter to check answers in this section.

D1 (a) Complete this table for the graph of $y = 3\sin x$.

(b) Draw the graph on graph paper with scales labelled.

(c) How is it different from the graph of $y = \sin x$?

x	0°	45°	90°	360°
$\sin x$	0	0.71	1	
$3\sin x$	0	2.13	3	

D2 (a) Complete this table for the graph of $y = \cos x + 1$.

(b) Sketch the graph, marking key values on the axes.

(c) How is it different from the graph of $y = \cos x$?

x	0°	90°	180°	360°
$\cos x$	1	0		
$\cos x + 1$	2	1		

D3 (a) Make a table for the graph of $y = {}^-\sin x$.

(b) Sketch the graph, marking key values on the axes.

(c) How is it different from the graph of $y = \sin x$?

D4 Sketch these graphs, first working out key points. Mark key values on your sketches.

(a) $y = \sin x - 1$ (Do not confuse this with $\sin(x - 1)$.)

(b) $y = \frac{1}{2}\sin x$ **(c)** $y = {}^-3\cos x$ **(d)** $y = 2\cos x - 1$

D5 Match the graphs below to these equations. Remember to check key points, such as when $x = 0°, 90°, \dots$

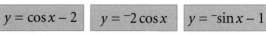

$y = \cos x - 2$ $y = {}^-2\cos x$ $y = {}^-\sin x - 1$

$y = {}^-\cos x + 1$ $y = 2\sin x + 1$ $y = 2\sin x + 2$

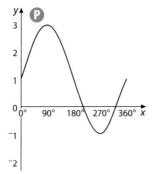

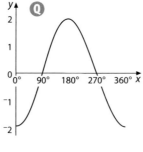

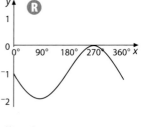

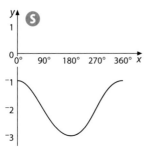

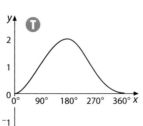

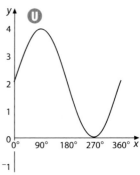

D6

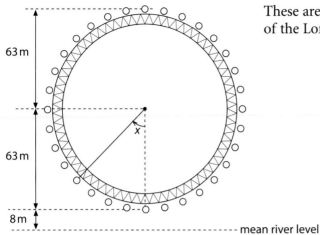

63 m

63 m

8 m

mean river level

These are the dimensions of the London Eye.

This graph shows your height, h metres, above river level after you have travelled through an angle x (starting at the **bottom** of the circle).

(a) What is the equation of this graph? (Test your ideas by trying key points.)

(b) Use your calculator to find your height above river level when you have travelled through

    (i) 100°   (ii) 240°

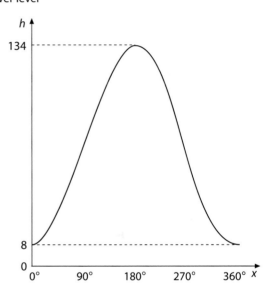

D7 The diagram shows a sketch of part of the curve with equation

$$y = p + q \cos x°$$

where p and q are integers.

(a) Find the values of the integers p and q.

(b) Find the two values of x between 0 and 360 for which

$$p + q \cos x° = 2$$

Edexcel

• What happens when you fill in this table for the graph $y = \sin(4x)$?

• Do you have enough information to sketch the graph?

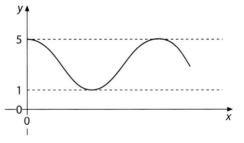

x	0°	90°	180°	270°
$4x$	0°	360°		
$\sin(4x)$	0			

To sketch the graph of $y = \sin(4x)$ it is not enough to mark points every 90°.

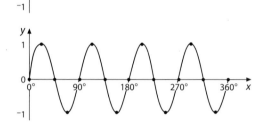

Even marking points every 45° is no use.

Marking every $22\frac{1}{2}°$ gives enough key points, though it is worth checking with more frequent points for part of the graph.

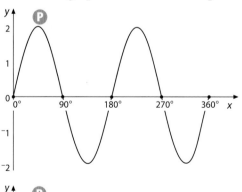

When you have to sketch a graph like $y = \sin(ax)$ or $y = \cos(ax)$, where a is a particular number, you should work out key points every $(90 \div a)°$.

D8 Sketch these graphs, first working out key points.
On each sketch mark x-values where the curve crosses the x-axis and the y-values of the 'peaks' and 'troughs' of the curve.

(a) $y = \cos(3x)$ (b) $y = \sin(2x)$ (c) $y = 3\cos(4x)$ (d) $y = \sin(3x) - 1$

D9 Match the graphs below to these equations.

$$y = \cos(2x) \qquad y = 2\sin(2x)$$

$$y = \sin(2x) - 1 \qquad y = {}^{-}2\cos(2x)$$

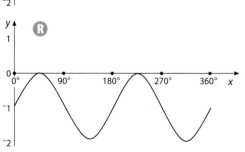

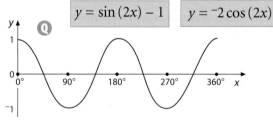

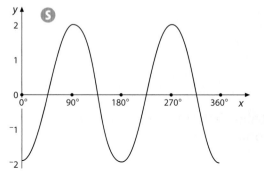

*D10 Sketch these graphs, first working out key points.
Mark key values on your sketches.

    (a) $y = \sin(x + 90°)$ **(b)** $y = 2\sin(x - 60°)$

*D11 This is part of the graph of $y = a\sin(x + b)$.
What are the values of a and b?

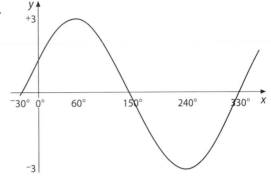

Sine and cosine graphs in the real world

If you hang a weight on a spring, pull down and
let go, the graph of the weight's height against
time is approximately a sine curve.

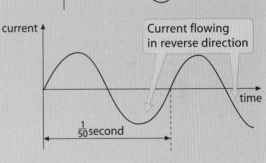

Mains electricity uses alternating current (AC).
The current flows in one direction and then the
other, 50 times a second. We say it has a
frequency of 50 **cycles per second**, or 50 **hertz**.

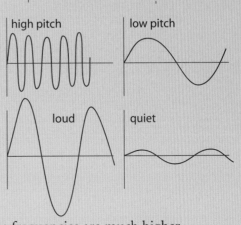

Sounds can be described using sine graphs.
High-pitched sounds (piccolo, triangle) have
high frequencies, while low-pitched sounds
(bass guitar) have low frequencies.

Young people can hear sounds with frequencies
from 20 hertz to about 20 000 hertz.
Dogs and bats can hear higher frequencies
than that.

Radio signals also involve the sine graph idea but the frequencies are much higher.
Local FM radio stations work on about 100 megahertz (100 million cycles per second).

Test yourself

T1 This is the graph of $y = \sin x$.

(a) Sketch the graph and show the locations of the two solutions of the equation
$$\sin x = \tfrac{-1}{2}$$

(b) Work out accurately the two solutions of the equation
$$5 \sin x = 3$$

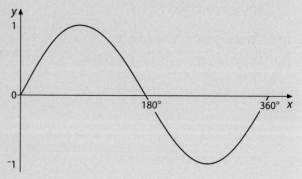

T2 Arrange these into groups with the same value.

| $^{-}\tan 145°$ | $^{-}\tan 35°$ | $\tan 35°$ | $\tan 145°$ | $\tan 215°$ | $\tan 325°$ |

T3 A sketch of the graph of $y = \cos x°$ is drawn for you.

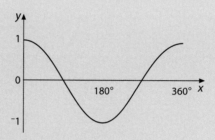

Write down the equation of each of the following graphs.

(a)

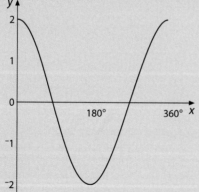

(b)

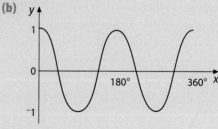

(c)

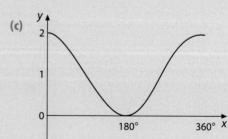

OCR

15 Pyramid, cone and sphere

This work will help you to understand how the formulas for the volume and surface area of a pyramid, cone and sphere are derived and to use them in solving problems.

For section A you need scissors, adhesive and thin card or thick paper.

A Pyramid and cone

Draw accurately a net with these measurements.
Cut, fold and glue it to make a **square-based pyramid**.

This is a **skew pyramid**: it does not have a vertex over the centre of its base.

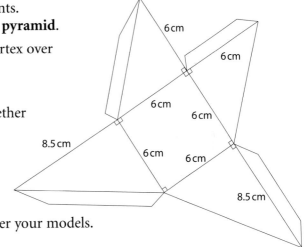

Work with your pyramids in groups of four.

- Can some of these pyramids be fitted together to make a cube?
- How many make a cube?
- What is the volume of the cube?
- What is the volume of one pyramid?

Now make other pyramids by putting together your models.
Record data about them in a table like this.

Pyramid	Volume	Base area	Perpendicular height
One pyramid model			
Pyramid (with a rectangular base) made with two of the models			
Pyramid made with four of the models			

- What do your results suggest about a formula for the volume of a pyramid?

A1 Here is a cube of side a units.
Its centre is joined to each vertex.

Then the cube is split into six identical pyramids (only four are shown).

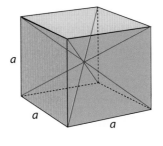
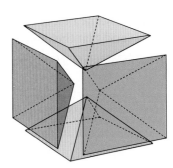

Write an expression for

(a) the volume of one pyramid

(b) its base area

(c) its height

Do these confirm the formula you found from the activity above?

The volume V of a pyramid is $\frac{1}{3} \times$ base area $\times$ height $= \frac{1}{3}Ah$
where A is the area of the base and h is the perpendicular height.

You have seen that the formula works for some pyramids with
a square or rectangular base. In fact it works for any shape base.

It works for a **skew pyramid** …   … and for one with a vertex above
                                                the centre of its base (a **right pyramid**).

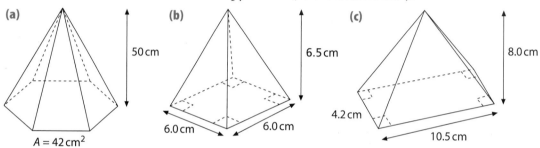

A2 Calculate the volume of each of these pyramids (to the nearest cm³).

(a)
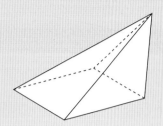
50 cm
$A = 42\,\text{cm}^2$

(b)
6.5 cm
6.0 cm   6.0 cm

(c)
8.0 cm
4.2 cm
10.5 cm

A3 A pyramid-shaped hopper needs to hold $50\,\text{m}^3$ of grain.
It must be 6.0 m high. What must this rectangular area be?

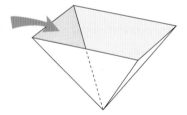

A4 When built, the Great Pyramid of Cheops had a square base 229 m by 229 m.
It was 146 m high.
Assume that 95% of the pyramid was stone (the rest being tunnels and chambers)
and that the density of the stone used was 2.3 tonnes per m³.
Calculate an estimate of the mass of the stone used in the Great Pyramid.

A5 An architect tries out different designs for a spire on a building.
She wants it to be a square-based pyramid.
Design P has a volume of $22.5\,\text{m}^3$.

(a) Design Q has the same base as P but twice the height.
What is the volume of design Q?

(b) Design R has the same height as P but the edges of the base are twice as long.
What is the volume of design R?

A6 A pyramid has a base that is a regular nonagon with sides 6 cm.

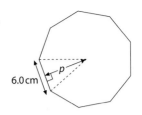

   (a) Use trigonometry to find length p.

   (b) Find the total area of the nonagon-shaped base.

   (c) Given that the pyramid's height is 11 cm, find its volume.

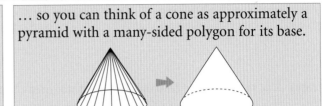

A regular polygon with very many sides starts to look like a circle …	… so you can think of a cone as approximately a pyramid with a many-sided polygon for its base.

A7 A cone has base radius 4.0 cm and perpendicular height 10.0 cm.

   (a) What is the area of its base?

   (b) Treating this cone as you would a pyramid, what is its volume to the nearest cm^3?

A8 Find the volume of a cone with height 8.9 cm and base radius 3.7 cm.

A9 (a) Write an expression for the area of the base of a cone with radius r.

   (b) Using your answer to (a), write an expression for the volume of the cone, given that its height is h.

A10 Find the total area of the four triangular faces of this square-based pyramid.

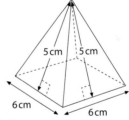

We call the length 5 cm in question A10 the **slant height**.

A11 A pyramid has a regular polygon for its base. Each triangular face has a base length of 2 cm and a slant height of 8 cm.

   (a) What is the area of one of the triangular faces?

   (b) The base is a decagon, so there are 10 triangular faces. What is the total area of all the triangular faces?

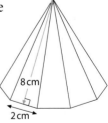

A12 A pyramid has a regular polygon for its base. Each triangular face has a base length of b cm and a slant height of l cm.

   (a) Write an expression for the area of one of the triangular faces.

   (b) The base is an n-sided polygon, so there are n triangular faces. Write an expression for the total area of all the triangular faces.

In question A12 you should have found that the total area of the triangular faces is

$\frac{1}{2} \times n \times b \times l$ or $\frac{1}{2}nbl$

An expression for the perimeter of the polygonal base is

nb (the number of edges multiplied by each triangle's base length)

If you call the perimeter p, you can replace nb by p in the expression for the total area of the triangular faces, giving

area $= \frac{1}{2}pl$

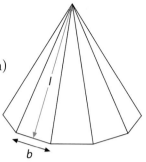

A13 Use this formula to work out the total area (to the nearest cm²) of the triangular faces of these regular polygonal pyramids.

   (a) Base perimeter 20 cm   **(b)** Base perimeter 35 cm   **(c)** Base perimeter 18.8 cm
       Slant height 7 cm   Slant height 12 cm   Slant height 8.4 cm

A14 The total area of the triangular faces of a regular polygonal pyramid is 720 cm².
Its slant height is 18 cm.
Work out the perimeter of its base.

A15 A cone has a base radius of 25.0 cm.

   (a) Work out the perimeter of the base (to the nearest 0.1 cm).

   (b) The slant height is 40.0 cm.
       Treating the cone as if it was a regular polygonal pyramid,
       work out the area of its curved surface, to the nearest cm².

A16 A cone has a base radius r.

   (a) Write an expression (using π) for the perimeter of the base.

   (b) The slant height is l.
       Treating the cone as if it was a regular polygonal pyramid,
       write an expression for the area of its curved surface.

A17 Check the expression you wrote for A16(b) then use it as a formula
to find the area of the curved surface for each of these cones.

   (a) Base radius 5.0 cm   **(b)** Base radius 7.2 cm   **(c)** Base radius 15.9 cm
       Slant height 7.0 cm   Slant height 10.5 cm   Slant height 19.8 cm

A18 The curved surface of a cone has area 110 cm².
The radius of its base is 5.0 cm.
Find its slant height to the nearest 0.1 cm.

A19 The curved surface of a cone has area 370 cm².
Its slant height is 15.0 cm.
Find the radius of its base to the nearest 0.1 cm.

A20 This cone has a base radius of 5 cm and a **perpendicular** height of 12 cm.

    (a) Use Pythagoras's theorem to find the slant height.

    (b) Find the area of the curved surface of the cone.

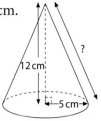

You have seen that the formula for the area of the **curved** surface of a cone is πrl, where r is the radius of the base and l is the slant height.

A21 **(a)** Write the formula for the total surface area of a cone, including its base.

    (b) Use brackets to simplify this formula.

A22 Use the formula from A21(b) to work out the total surface area of these cones.

    (a) Base radius 4.0 cm   **(b)** Base radius 5.4 cm   **(c)** Base radius 3.2 m
         Slant height 11.0 cm   Slant height 8.9 cm   Slant height 8.5 m

---

A **frustum** of a cone looks like this. Its base and its top are both circles and are parallel to one another.

You can think of it as a large cone that has had a smaller cone cut off.

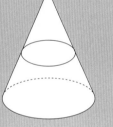

A23 This elephant stand is a frustum of a cone. Find its volume.

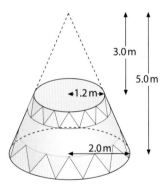

*A24

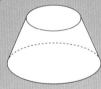

This plastic ice cream tub is a frustum of a cone.

(a) Calculate the volume of ice cream it can contain.

(b) Calculate the total area of the plastic for the tub and the lid. (Ignore the extra plastic needed at the edge of the lid.)

B Sphere

Here is a way to find the formula for the surface area of a sphere.

This sphere has radius r. It has been divided into 20 slices, each $\frac{r}{10}$ thick.

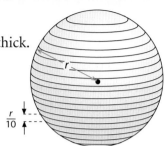

Concentrate on the surface of one of the slices.

The radius of the dotted circle is $r \times \sin x$.
So its circumference is $2\pi r \times \sin x$.

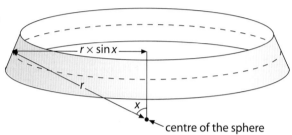

centre of the sphere

The width, w, of the strip is $\frac{r}{10} \div \sin x$.

(Think about why the angle marked here is also x.)

Imagine cutting the curved strip into trapeziums.

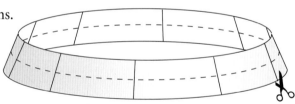

Now imagine laying the trapeziums flat on the table with alternate ones turned upside down. You get approximately a rectangle.

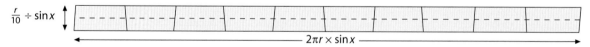

$\frac{r}{10} \div \sin x$

$2\pi r \times \sin x$

Its length is $2\pi r \times \sin x$ (the circumference of the dotted circle).

Its width is $\frac{r}{10} \div \sin x$ (the width of the curved strip).

So its area is $2\pi r \times \sin x \times \frac{r}{10} \div \sin x = \frac{\pi r^2}{5}$.

This approach works for all 20 slices, so the surface area of the sphere is approximately $20 \times \frac{\pi r^2}{5} = 4\pi r^2$.

The result is more accurate the thinner the slices used, and in fact the surface area of a sphere is exactly $4\pi r^2$.

Notice that the surface area of a sphere, $4\pi r^2$, is four times the area of a circle with the same radius. The construction of a tennis ball may help you see why.

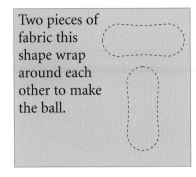

Two pieces of fabric this shape wrap around each other to make the ball.

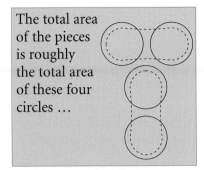

The total area of the pieces is roughly the total area of these four circles …

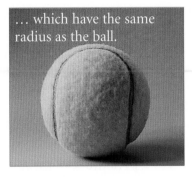

… which have the same radius as the ball.

B1 Calculate the surface area of each of these spheres, to the nearest cm^2.

　(a) Radius 10.0 cm　　　(b) Radius 7.8 cm　　　(c) Radius 15.6 cm

B2 The radius of the Earth is 6300 km.

　(a) Calculate its surface area.

　(b) Given that 70% of the Earth's surface is ocean, what is the area of the Earth's oceans?

B3 A sphere has surface area 412 cm^2. Calculate its radius to the nearest 0.1 cm.

You can think of a sphere as made up of many slender pyramids, each with its vertex at the centre of the sphere and height r, the radius of the sphere.

So the volume of one pyramid is $\frac{1}{3}Ar$, where A the area of its base.

So the total volume of all the pyramids is

$\frac{1}{3} \times$ the total area of the bases of all the pyramids $\times r$

This equals $\frac{1}{3} \times 4\pi r^2 \times r$, because the total area of the bases is the surface area of the sphere.

Simplifying the expression, the volume of a sphere is $\frac{4}{3}\pi r^3$.

B4 Use the formula to find the volume of each of these spheres.

　(a) Radius 5.0 cm　　　(b) Radius 8.8 cm　　　(c) Radius 14.7 cm

B5 A liquid fuel tank is a sphere with a radius of 80 cm.
How many litres of fuel can it contain? (A litre is 1000 cm^3.)

B6 A squash ball has a radius of 2.0 cm. It is sold in a cubical box.
There is no extra space for it to move around in the box.
What percentage of the volume of the box is air?

B7 A tennis ball has radius 3.4 cm.
Some tennis balls are sold in threes in a cylindrical tube.
There is no space for them to move around in the tube.
What percentage of the volume of the tube is air?

*B8 An chemical engineer wants a spherical tank built to contain a million litres of liquid. What radius will the tank need to have?

*B9 A Terry's Chocolate Orange is approximately a sphere of radius 3.2 cm. It separates into 20 pieces like this.

Calculate   **(a)** the volume of one piece   **(b)** the surface area of one piece

---

For a **cylinder** with radius of cross-section r and length l,
     volume = $\pi r^2 l$ area of curved surface = $2\pi rl$ total surface area = $2\pi r(l + r)$

For a **pyramid** with base area A and perpendicular height h,
     volume = $\frac{1}{3}Ah$

For a **cone** with base radius r, perpendicular height h and slant height l,
     volume = $\frac{1}{3}\pi r^2 h$ area of curved surface = πrl total surface area = $\pi r(l + r)$

For a **sphere** with radius r,
     volume = $\frac{4}{3}\pi r^3$ surface area = $4\pi r^2$

Test yourself

T1 A sphere has a radius of 5.4 cm. A cone has a height of 8 cm.
The volume of the sphere is equal to the volume of the cone.

Calculate the radius of the base of the cone.
Give your answer, in centimetres, correct to two significant figures.   *Edexcel*

T2 A metal sphere has a radius of 6 cm.

   (a) Calculate the volume of the sphere. Leave your answer as a multiple of π.

The diagram shows a cylinder of radius 10 cm.
It already contains water to a depth of 15 cm.
The metal sphere is placed in the water.

   (b) Calculate the height, h cm,
       that the water level rises.

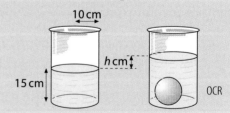

OCR

T3 A party hat is made from card.
The hat is made in two parts: a cone on top of a ring.
The cone has a height of 20 cm and base radius of 7.5 cm.

The ring has an internal radius of 7.5 cm
and an external radius of 10 cm.

Calculate the area of the card used in
making the party hat. Give your answer to
an appropriate degree of accuracy.

Not to scale

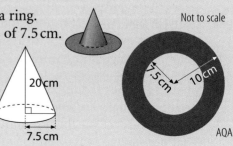

AQA

16 Rearranging a formula

You will revise rearranging a simple formula where the subject appears once.

This work will help you

- rearrange more complex formulas where the subject appears once
- rearrange formulas where the subject appears twice
- form and rearrange your own formulas

A Review: rearranging a simple formula

A1 Make the bold letter the subject of each of these formulas.

(a) $a = 6\mathbf{b} - 3$ (b) $w = 5\mathbf{d} + 10$ (c) $2h = 5\mathbf{j} - 3$ (d) $3e = 21 + 4\mathbf{f}$

A2 Rearrange each of these to make x the subject.

(a) $x + y = 5$ (b) $2y + x = 3$ (c) $2x + 3y = 12$ (d) $6y + 5x = 1$

A3 Rearrange the formula $d = 5 - 3n$ to make n the subject by first adding $3n$ to both sides.

A4 Rearrange each of these to make p the subject.

(a) $q = 8 - p$ (b) $q = 10 - 2p$ (c) $4q - 3p = 24$ (d) $3q = 8 - 7p$

A5 Each equation below is the equation of a straight line.
For each equation,

- (i) rearrange it to make x the subject
- (ii) find where the line crosses the x-axis

(a) $y = 2x + 5$ (b) $y = 10 - x$ (c) $3y + 5x = 11$ (d) $5y = 10 - 4x$

A6 Make the bold letter the subject of each formula.

(a) $t = 12 + \dfrac{\mathbf{s}}{3}$ (b) $h = \dfrac{\mathbf{j} - 2}{5}$ (c) $x = \dfrac{3\mathbf{y}}{2} - 1$ (d) $a = \frac{2}{3}\mathbf{b} - 5$

A7 You are given that $y = 2x + 5z$.

(a) Rearrange the formula to make z the subject.

(b) Find the value of z when $y = 7$ and $x = {}^-\frac{1}{2}$.
Give your answer as a fraction.

A8 Make the bold letter the subject of each formula.

(a) $p = \mathbf{q} - r$ (b) $p = q - \mathbf{r}$ (c) $m = 2n + \mathbf{p}$ (d) $m = 2\mathbf{n} + p$

(e) $u = \dfrac{\mathbf{v} + w}{2}$ (f) $u = \dfrac{\mathbf{v}}{w} - 3$ (g) $u = \mathbf{v}w + x$ (h) $u = 10 - v\mathbf{w}$

B Choosing the first step in a rearrangement

There is often more than one way to change the subject of a formula.

For example, here are two ways to make x the subject of $y = 3(x - 4)$.

$y = 3(x - 4)$

First expand the brackets.

$y = 3x - 12$

Then add 12 to both sides.

$y + 12 = 3x$

Then divide both sides by 3.

$\dfrac{y + 12}{3} = x$

First divide both sides by 3.

Then add 4 to both sides.

$y = 3(x - 4)$

$\dfrac{y}{3} = x - 4$

$\dfrac{y}{3} + 4 = x$

The formulas look different but they are of course equivalent.

We can see this if we manipulate the division to give $\dfrac{y + 12}{3} = \dfrac{y}{3} + \dfrac{12}{3} = \dfrac{y}{3} + 4$.

B1 Make x the subject of each of these formulas.

(a) $y = 5(x - 2)$ (b) $p = 6(x - r)$ (c) $y = 4(z - x)$ (d) $A = 5(2x - 1)$

B2 You are given that $y = \frac{1}{4}x - 3$.

    (a) (i)   Make x the subject of the formula by first adding 3 to both sides.

           (ii)   Make x the subject of the formula by first multiplying both sides by 4.

    (b)   Show that the formulas found in (a) are equivalent.

To choose your first step, look carefully at the letter in the formula that is to be the new subject.

Examples

Make z the subject of $y = x(z + 3)$.

$y = x(z + 3)$

           [divide by x]

$\dfrac{y}{x} = z + 3$

           [subtract 3]

$\dfrac{y}{x} - 3 = z$

or $z = \dfrac{y}{x} - 3$

If you expand the brackets first you get $z = \dfrac{y - 3x}{x}$.

Make x the subject of $y = x(z + 3)$.

$y = x(z + 3)$

           [divide by $(z + 3)$]

$\dfrac{y}{z + 3} = x$

or $x = \dfrac{y}{z + 3}$

Expanding the brackets first does not help here.

B3 Make the bold letter the subject of each of these formulas.

(a) $p = \mathbf{q}(r - 2)$ (b) $p = q(\mathbf{r} - 2)$ (c) $2y = \mathbf{x}(1 - z)$ (d) $2y = x(1 - \mathbf{z})$

B4 You are given that $a = \frac{1}{3}b(c + 5)$.

    Make c the subject of the formula by first multiplying both sides by 3.

When dividing both sides of a formula, divide by the 'largest' expression you can at one time. It usually leads to neater formulas.

Examples

Make b the subject of $p = abc - 5$.

$$p = abc - 5$$
$$p + 5 = abc \qquad \text{[add 5]}$$
$$\frac{p + 5}{ac} = b \qquad \text{[divide by } ac\text{]}$$

Make b the subject of $P = \frac{1}{4}\pi a^2 b$.

$$P = \frac{1}{4}\pi a^2 b$$
$$4P = \pi a^2 b \qquad \text{[multiply by 4]}$$
$$\frac{4P}{\pi a^2} = b \qquad \text{[divide by } \pi a^2\text{]}$$

> It is often a good idea to get rid of fractions as soon as possible.

B5 Make the bold letter the subject of each of these formulas.

(a) $V = lw\mathbf{h}$

(b) $V = l\mathbf{w}h$

(c) $P = 2\mathbf{a}b - 3$

(d) $V = \pi^2 p\mathbf{q}$

(e) $P = \dfrac{\pi x \mathbf{y}}{3}$

(f) $V = \frac{1}{6}\pi x \mathbf{y}$

(g) $R = \dfrac{\pi bc^2 + \mathbf{y}}{2}$

(h) $R = \frac{1}{3}r^2 \mathbf{y} - x^2$

Sometimes the new subject is part of the denominator of a fractional expression.

Examples

Make v the subject of $s = \dfrac{u}{v} + 10$.

$$s = \frac{u}{v} + 10$$
$$s - 10 = \frac{u}{v} \qquad \text{[subtract 10]}$$
$$v(s - 10) = u \qquad \text{[multiply by } v\text{]}$$
$$v = \frac{u}{s - 10} \qquad \text{[divide by } s - 10\text{]}$$

> We say that v is written **in terms of** u and s.

Make r the subject of $a = \dfrac{4\pi}{rt}$.

$$a = \frac{4\pi}{rt}$$
$$rta = 4\pi \qquad \text{[multiply by } rt\text{]}$$
$$r = \frac{4\pi}{ta} \qquad \text{[divide by } ta\text{]}$$

B6 The formula $h = \dfrac{a}{k} + j$ gives h in terms of a, k and j.

Which of the following is a correct rearrangement that gives k in terms of h, a and j?

A $k = a(h - j)$

B $k = ha - j$

C $k = \dfrac{a}{h - j}$

D $k = \dfrac{h - j}{a}$

E $k = ha - ja$

B7 Rearrange each of these formulas to make the bold letter the subject.

(a) $l = \dfrac{2a}{\mathbf{b}}$

(b) $m = \dfrac{a\mathbf{b}}{3c}$

(c) $r = \dfrac{\pi}{x\mathbf{y}z}$

(d) $h = 1 + \dfrac{d^2}{\mathbf{e}}$

B8 Which of the following is a correct rearrangement of $s = w - \dfrac{g}{r}$?

A $r = \dfrac{s - w}{g}$

B $r = \dfrac{w - s}{g}$

C $r = \dfrac{g}{s - w}$

D $r = \dfrac{g}{w - s}$

E $r = gw - s$

B9 Rearrange each of these formulas to make the bold letter the subject.

(a) $s = 1 - \dfrac{l}{t}$

(b) $a = 2b - \dfrac{d}{c}$

(c) $e = \frac{1}{4}d + \dfrac{f}{h}$

(d) $z = ab - \dfrac{2\pi}{r\theta}$

B10 Copy and complete this working to make x the subject of $y = \dfrac{a}{(x-c)}$.

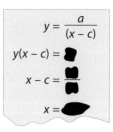

$$y = \frac{a}{(x-c)}$$
$$y(x-c) = \blacksquare$$
$$x - c = \blacksquare$$
$$x = \blacksquare$$

B11 Make the bold letter the subject of each formula.

(a) $a = \dfrac{b}{(c+d)}$

(b) $5x = \dfrac{2z}{6-y}$

(c) $x + 3 = \dfrac{2z}{5+y}$

(d) $w = \dfrac{t+2}{u-3}$

C Simplifying squares and square roots

Examples of simplifying squares

$$(3p^2q)^2 = 3p^2q \times 3p^2q$$
$$= 9p^4q^2$$

$$\left(\frac{2p}{5}\right)^2 = \frac{2p}{5} \times \frac{2p}{5}$$
$$= \frac{4p^2}{25}$$

$$(2\sqrt{a})^2 = 2\sqrt{a} \times 2\sqrt{a}$$
$$= 2 \times 2 \times \sqrt{a} \times \sqrt{a}$$
$$= 4a$$

C1 Multiply out the brackets and simplify each expression.

(a) $(5a)^2$

(b) $(2a^3b)^2$

(c) $(\frac{1}{2}ab)^2$

(d) $\left(\dfrac{3a}{b}\right)^2$

(e) $\left(\dfrac{2a}{5b}\right)^2$

C2 Multiply out the brackets and simplify each expression.

(a) $\left(3\sqrt{p}\right)^2$

(b) $\left(\sqrt{3p}\right)^2$

(c) $\left(\frac{1}{2}\sqrt{ab}\right)^2$

(d) $\left(\dfrac{\sqrt{2}}{a}\right)^2$

(e) $\left(\dfrac{\sqrt{z}}{\sqrt{3}}\right)^2$

Examples of simplifying square roots

$$2x \times 2x = 4x^2$$
$$\text{so } \sqrt{4x^2} = 2x$$

$$\frac{4}{p} \times \frac{4}{p} = \frac{16}{p^2}$$
$$\text{so } \sqrt{\frac{16}{p^2}} = \frac{4}{p}$$

$$\frac{\sqrt{s}}{3} \times \frac{\sqrt{s}}{3} = \frac{s}{9}$$
$$\text{so } \sqrt{\frac{s}{9}} = \frac{\sqrt{s}}{3}$$

C3 Simplify each expression.

(a) $\sqrt{16x^2}$

(b) $\sqrt{25p^4}$

(c) $\sqrt{a^2b^4}$

(d) $\sqrt{\dfrac{a^2}{4}}$

(e) $\sqrt{\dfrac{p}{100}}$

D Formulas involving squares and square roots

The volume V of a cone with base radius r and height h is given by the formula $V = \frac{1}{3}\pi r^2 h$.

We can rearrange the formula to make r the subject.

$V = \frac{1}{3}\pi r^2 h$ [multiply by 3]

$3V = \pi r^2 h$ [divide by πh]

$\dfrac{3V}{\pi h} = r^2$ [take the positive square root]

$\sqrt{\dfrac{3V}{\pi h}} = r$

Here, r is positive as it is the value of the radius.

So use $\sqrt{\dfrac{3V}{\pi h}}$ as it represents the positive square root of $\dfrac{3V}{\pi h}$.

D1 Find the radius (to 3 s.f.) of a cone with a volume of $1000\,\text{cm}^3$ and a height of $10\,\text{cm}$.

D2 The surface area A of a sphere with radius r is given by the formula $A = 4\pi r^2$.

(a) Rearrange the formula to make r the subject.

(b) Work out the radius (to the nearest cm) of a sphere with a volume of $1\,\text{m}^3$.

D3 In each of these formulas h is a length.
Make h the subject of each of these formulas.

(a) $S = \frac{1}{4}h^2 + 3$ (b) $x = \dfrac{9h^2}{r}$ (c) $V = 7\pi h^2 x - 10$ (d) $x = \dfrac{l^2 - h^2}{2r}$

When a formula involves a square root, you need to square both sides to remove it.
It often helps to isolate the square root on one side first.

$y = \frac{1}{4}\sqrt{5x}$ [multiply by 4]

$4y = \sqrt{5x}$ [square]

$16y^2 = 5x$ [divide by 5]

$\dfrac{16y^2}{5} = x$

$P = 3\sqrt{\dfrac{Q}{2R}}$ [divide by 3]

$\dfrac{P}{3} = \sqrt{\dfrac{Q}{2R}}$ [square]

$\dfrac{P^2}{9} = \dfrac{Q}{2R}$ [multiply by $2R$]

$\dfrac{2RP^2}{9} = Q$

D4 Make x the subject of each of these formulas.

(a) $y = \sqrt{x+1}$ (b) $y = \sqrt{x} + 1$ (c) $y = \sqrt{3x}$ (d) $y = 3\sqrt{x}$

(e) $y = \sqrt{\dfrac{x}{2}}$ (f) $y = \dfrac{\sqrt{x}}{2}$ (g) $y = 3\pi\sqrt{x}$ (h) $y = \sqrt{x + 3\pi}$

D5 Make the bold letter the subject of each of these formulas.

(a) $T = \pi\sqrt{\dfrac{\boldsymbol{p}}{q}}$ (b) $a = \sqrt{\dfrac{b}{\boldsymbol{c}}}$ (c) $y = \sqrt{\dfrac{2\boldsymbol{z}}{r}}$ (d) $y = \sqrt{\dfrac{2z}{\boldsymbol{r}}}$

(e) $V = 3\pi\sqrt{\boldsymbol{m}}$ (f) $V = \dfrac{\pi\sqrt{\boldsymbol{g}}}{5h}$ (g) $y = \sqrt{z - 2\boldsymbol{x}}$ (h) $s = 2\pi r\sqrt{\boldsymbol{x} + y^2}$

The equation of a parabola is $y = \frac{1}{2}x^2 - 1$.
Note that x can take any positive or negative value.

$y = \frac{1}{2}x^2 - 1$
         [add 1]
$y + 1 = \frac{1}{2}x^2$
         [multiply by 2]
$2(y + 1) = x^2$
         [take the positive and negative square root]
$x = \pm\sqrt{2(y + 1)}$

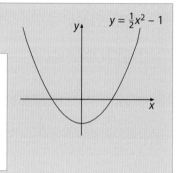

D6 The equation of a parabola is $y = 2x^2 - 50$.

(a) Rearrange the formula to make x the subject.

(b) Where does the graph intersect the x-axis?

D7 In each of these formulas, x, y and z can take positive and negative values. Rearrange each one to make x the subject.

(a) $x^2 + y^2 = 9$ (b) $y = \dfrac{x^2}{3z}$ (c) $\dfrac{y - x^2}{5} = z$ (d) $4x^2 + 9y^2 = 1$

E Formulas where the new subject appears more than once

Sometimes the new subject occurs in more than one place in the original formula. You need to get the new subject in one place only, which usually involves factorising.

Examples

Make c the subject of $a = 4bc - cd^2$.

$a = 4bc - cd^2$
    [factorise]
$a = c(4b - d^2)$
    [divide by $4b - d^2$]
$c = \dfrac{a}{4b - d^2}$

Make r the subject of $a = \dfrac{3r + t}{r - s}$.

$a = \dfrac{3r + t}{r - s}$
    [multiply by $r - s$]
$a(r - s) = 3r + t$
    [expand brackets]
$ar - as = 3r + t$
    [add as and subtract $3r$]
$ar - 3r = t + as$
    [factorise]
$r(a - 3) = t + as$
    [divide by $a - 3$]
$r = \dfrac{t + as}{a - 3}$

E1 Make n the subject of each of these formulas.

(a) $f = 3n + dn$ (b) $3T = \pi n + nk$ (c) $pn - 6 = 3n + s$ (d) $rn = 3(n - e)$

(e) $nv - nu = Ft$ (f) $a + 2n = anp$ (g) $m + n = mnk$ (h) $S = npk + \frac{1}{3}ny^2$

E2 Make v the subject of this formula.

$$3v + 5 = av + b$$

Edexcel

E3 Given that $ay - b = cy - d$, express y in terms of a, b, c and d.

OCR

E4 (a) Factorise $3x^2 + yx^2$.

(b) Rearrange the formula $3x^2 + yx^2 = 7z$ to make x the subject.

E5 Make r the subject of each of these formulas.

(a) $P = 3r + ar + 7$ (b) $H = ax + r - kr$ (c) $A = xr^2 + \pi r^2 - y^2$

E6 Make f the subject of each of these.

(a) $3f = a(f + 2)$ (b) $3(f + u) = q(f - u)$

(c) $k(2f + 1) = 2 - f$ (d) $2(f - 3) = g(1 + f)$

E7 Given that $x(10 - y) = 3(y + z)$ express y in terms of x and z.

E8 Make r the subject of $3(r - 4) = s(7 - 2r)$.

OCR

E9 Rearrange each of these formulas to make k the subject.

(a) $s = \dfrac{3k}{k - 1}$ (b) $t = \dfrac{k + 4}{k}$ (c) $P = \dfrac{3 - k}{k - 1}$ (d) $y = \dfrac{2(k + 2)}{k - 5}$

(e) $h = \dfrac{g + 2k}{n + k}$ (f) $R = \dfrac{2n - 3k}{n + k}$ (g) $Y = \dfrac{n^2 + k}{n + mk}$ (h) $ab = \dfrac{dk}{k - e}$

E10 $t = \dfrac{8(p + q)}{pq}$ $p = 2.71$, $q = {}^-3.97$

(a) Calculate the value of t.
Give your answer to a suitable degree of accuracy.

(b) Make q the subject of the formula $t = \dfrac{8(p + q)}{pq}$.

Edexcel

E11 $R = \dfrac{xyz}{y - z}$

Express z in terms of x, y and R.

E12 Make x the subject of each formula.

(a) $x^2y^2 = x^2 - y^2$ (b) $S = x + \dfrac{xrt}{100}$

(c) $xt^2 - \dfrac{k(t + 1)}{x} = 0$ (d) $m^2 = \dfrac{1}{x^2}(n^2 - x^2)$

F Forming and manipulating formulas

A circle with radius r is enclosed by a square that just touches its edges as shown.
Find a formula for the shaded area A and make r the subject of the formula.

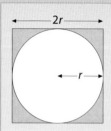

The width of the square is the same as the diameter, which is $2r$.

The area of the square is $(2r)^2 = 4r^2$.

The area of the circle is πr^2.

So the shaded area is given by $A = 4r^2 - \pi r^2$.

Make r the subject:
$$A = 4r^2 - \pi r^2$$
$$A = r^2(4 - \pi) \quad \text{[factorise]}$$
$$\frac{A}{4 - \pi} = r^2 \quad \text{[divide by } 4 - \pi\text{]}$$
$$r = \sqrt{\frac{A}{4 - \pi}} \quad \text{[take the positive square root]}$$

It often helps to draw a sketch and mark in important lengths.

F1 The diagram shows a trapezium.

(a) Show that the area A of the trapezium is given by $A = \frac{3}{2}x^2$.

(b) Rearrange this formula to make x the subject.

(c) Find the value of x for a trapezium of area $20\,\text{cm}^2$.

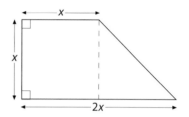

F2 This box is a cuboid with length, width and height as shown.

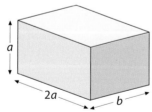

(a) Show that the surface area A of the box is given by the formula $A = 4a^2 + 6ab$.

(b) Rearrange this formula to make b the subject.

(c) Work out the dimensions of a box with surface area $100\,\text{cm}^2$ and a height of $2\,\text{cm}$.

F3 This shape is formed by a semicircle on top of a square.

(a) (i) Show that a formula for the perimeter P of the shape can be written $P = \pi r + 6r$.

(ii) Make r the subject of this formula.

(iii) What is the value of r if the shape has a perimeter of 10 metres?

(b) (i) Find a formula for the area A of the shape.

(ii) Make r the subject of this formula.

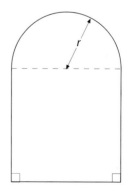

F4 This diagram shows two circles.
The radius of the smaller circle is half the radius of the larger.
The radius of the larger circle is r.

  (a) Find a formula for the shaded area A.

  (b) Rearrange this formula to make r the subject.

F5 The volume V of a sphere with a radius of x is given by the formula $V = \frac{4}{3}\pi x^3$.

  Show that $x = \sqrt[3]{\dfrac{3V}{4\pi}}$.

F6 A cone has radius r and height $3r$.

  (a) Find a formula for the volume V in terms of r.

  (b) Rearrange this formula to make r the subject.

F7 A cylinder has radius r and height h.
A sphere has radius $3r$.

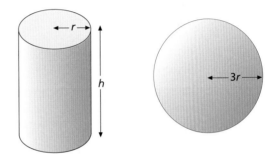

  (a) What is the volume of the cylinder
     in terms of r and h?

  (b) Find an expression for the volume
     of the sphere in terms of r.

  (c) The cylinder and the sphere have
     the same volume.
     Show that $h = 36r$.

F8 The radius of the base of a cylinder is $4x$ cm.
The cylinder contains some water.
The radius of a sphere is $2x$ cm.

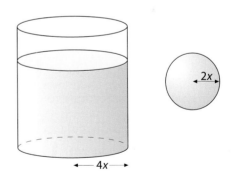

  The sphere is dropped into the cylinder
  and is completely immersed.
  No water is spilled.

  Find, in terms of x, the increase in
  the height of the water in the cylinder.
  Give your answer is its simplest form.

F9 A cylinder has radius x and height $8x$.
A sphere has radius r.

  The total surface area of the cylinder is equal to the surface area of the sphere.

  Show that $x = \dfrac{\sqrt{2}}{3}r$.

Test yourself

T1 Make u the subject of the formula $D = ut + kt^2$.

Edexcel

T2 Rearrange this formula to make d the subject.

$$c = \sqrt{t - 2d}$$

OCR

T3 Rearrange the formula $T = 2\pi\sqrt{\dfrac{L}{G}}$ to make L the subject.

OCR

T4 Make a the subject of the formula $6(a + 2b) = 4a + 7$.

OCR

T5 **(a)** Make r the subject of this formula.

$$V = \tfrac{1}{3}\pi r^2 h$$

(b) Make v the subject of this formula.

$$u + v = uvf$$

OCR

T6 $P = \pi r + 2r + 2a$
$P = 84$
$r = 6.7$

(a) Work out the value of a.
Give your answer to three significant figures.

(b) Make r the subject of the formula $P = \pi r + 2r + 2a$.

Edexcel

T7 **(a)** Make c the subject of the formula $E = mc^2$.

(b) Make m the subject of the formula $E = mgh + \tfrac{1}{2}mv^2$.

AQA

T8 Make r the subject of the formula $r - 3 = \pi(t - 2r)$.

AQA

T9 Make x the subject of the formula $y = \dfrac{3x + 4}{x - 3}$.

AQA

T10 $P = \dfrac{n^2 + a}{n + a}$

Rearrange the formula to make a the subject.

Edexcel

T11 Rearrange this formula to make t the subject.

$$g = \dfrac{3t + 1}{t}$$

OCR

T12 The radius of the base of a cone is x cm
and its height is h cm.
The radius of a sphere is $2x$ cm.
The volume of the cone and the
volume of the sphere are equal.

Express h in terms of x.
Give your answer in its simplest form.

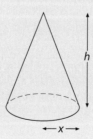 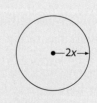

Diagram not
accurately drawn

Edexcel

17 Sampling

This work will help you understand the purpose of sampling and some common methods of sampling:

- random sampling
- systematic sampling
- stratified sampling

You may need sheet H2–3.

A Representative samples

A local council wants to know what people want to do with a reclaimed rubbish tip.

The council can't afford to ask everybody in the area. So they want to select a **representative sample** of the population.

A representative sample should be as much like the whole population as possible. For example, young people might have very different ideas from older people; if there are too many of them in the sample, the sample will not be representative.

An unrepresentative sample is called **biased**.

Below are some suggested ways of choosing a sample of people to ask. For each method say, with reasons

- whether it would give a representative or biased sample
- whether it would be easy to carry out in practice

A Ask the next 300 people who come into the town hall to fill in a questionnaire.

B Open 300 pages of the local residential telephone directory at random. Ring the first number on each page in the early evening.

C Stand in the High Street next Saturday morning and ask every tenth person who comes along.

D Put a page on the internet and ask those in the area who read it to email their opinion.

E Go through the local electoral register (a list of all those entitled to vote) and choose every 50th person to send a questionnaire to.

F Send researchers to every area in the town with instructions to call at every 10th house in every street and ask the person who answers the door.

B Random sampling

Another situation where sampling is used is in estimating
the average weight of a type of animal, for example the
elephants in a large reserve.

To help you learn about sampling and how accurate it can be, a database will be used.
In practice, of course, if you had the database you would not need to sample!

The database on the next page shows the weights of 250 female elephants
living on a reserve. Each elephant has been given an identification number.
(The database is reprinted on sheet H2–3.)

You have to imagine that you can see only the identification numbers and
that you have no idea of the weights. Only after you have selected your sample
will you be able to weigh the elephants in your sample.

> **Random sampling** is a common method of sampling.
> Members of the population are picked at random so that they all have
> the same chance of being included in the sample.

Suppose you want a random sample of 10 elephants from the population of 250.
You could write the numbers 1 to 250 on pieces of paper, jumble up the pieces
and pick out ten.

But it is much easier to use the **random number generator** on a calculator.

- Find out how to generate random numbers on your calculator.
  Most random number generators produce random three-digit numbers.
  They are usually given as decimals, for example: 0.156, 0.065, 0.380, …

As the elephant identification numbers only go up to 250, you ignore
random numbers outside this range. (And if a number is repeated, you
ignore the repeat.)

Increasing the sample size

Questions B1–B6 are for the whole class working together.

B1 Use a random number generator to generate five numbers in the range 001 to 250.

Note down the weights of the elephants with these numbers and
calculate the mean weight of your sample of five.

Weights of 250 female elephants

Elephant	Weight (tonnes)	Elephant	Weight (tonnes)	Elephant	Weight (tonnes)	Elephant	Weight (tonnes)	Elephant	Weight (tonnes)
1	1.33	51	1.33	101	0.97	151	0.90	201	1.04
2	1.31	52	1.45	102	0.47	152	1.59	202	0.54
3	1.35	53	1.26	103	0.58	153	1.26	203	0.66
4	1.40	54	1.25	104	0.61	154	1.37	204	0.68
5	1.34	55	1.34	105	0.63	155	0.95	205	0.71
6	1.37	56	1.47	106	0.71	156	1.13	206	0.79
7	1.36	57	1.01	107	0.79	157	1.30	207	0.86
8	1.39	58	1.42	108	0.83	158	1.39	208	0.90
9	1.27	59	1.34	109	0.91	159	0.77	209	0.99
10	0.62	60	1.02	110	0.96	160	1.31	210	1.03
11	1.05	61	0.92	111	0.99	161	0.73	211	1.06
12	1.24	62	1.62	112	1.01	162	0.93	212	1.08
13	1.55	63	1.28	113	1.05	163	1.32	213	1.12
14	1.23	64	1.39	114	1.06	164	1.25	214	1.14
15	0.90	65	0.97	115	1.06	165	0.55	215	1.14
16	1.32	66	1.16	116	1.16	166	1.30	216	1.23
17	1.25	67	1.33	117	1.20	167	0.65	217	1.27
18	1.14	68	1.42	118	1.20	168	1.14	218	1.28
19	0.95	69	0.79	119	1.25	169	0.52	219	1.32
20	1.35	70	1.33	120	1.25	170	1.28	220	1.32
21	1.47	71	0.75	121	1.26	171	1.27	221	1.33
22	1.28	72	0.95	122	1.26	172	1.30	222	1.34
23	1.28	73	1.34	123	1.29	173	1.35	223	1.36
24	1.37	74	1.28	124	1.29	174	1.29	224	1.37
25	1.49	75	0.57	125	1.30	175	1.33	225	1.37
26	1.03	76	1.33	126	1.32	176	1.31	226	1.39
27	1.44	77	0.67	127	1.32	177	1.34	227	1.39
28	1.37	78	1.16	128	1.33	178	1.22	228	1.40
29	1.05	79	0.54	129	1.34	179	0.57	229	1.41
30	0.94	80	1.31	130	1.35	180	1.00	230	1.42
31	1.64	81	1.29	131	1.35	181	1.19	231	1.43
32	1.30	82	1.33	132	1.37	182	1.50	232	1.44
33	1.42	83	1.38	133	1.37	183	1.19	233	1.44
34	0.99	84	1.32	134	1.37	184	0.85	234	1.44
35	1.18	85	1.35	135	1.37	185	1.27	235	1.44
36	1.35	86	1.34	136	1.37	186	1.20	236	1.45
37	1.44	87	1.37	137	1.37	187	1.10	237	1.45
38	0.81	88	1.25	138	1.38	188	0.90	238	1.45
39	1.36	89	0.60	139	1.38	189	1.30	239	1.46
40	0.77	90	1.03	140	1.38	190	1.42	240	1.46
41	0.97	91	1.22	141	1.39	191	1.24	241	1.46
42	1.36	92	1.53	142	1.40	192	1.23	242	1.48
43	1.30	93	1.21	143	1.41	193	1.32	243	1.49
44	0.59	94	0.88	144	1.43	194	1.45	244	1.51
45	1.35	95	1.30	145	1.46	195	0.99	245	1.53
46	0.70	96	1.23	146	1.46	196	1.39	246	1.53
47	1.19	97	1.12	147	1.49	197	1.32	247	1.56
48	0.57	98	0.93	148	1.51	198	1.00	248	1.58
49	0.45	99	1.33	149	1.57	199	0.90	249	1.64
50	1.23	100	1.45	150	1.66	200	1.59	250	1.73

B2 Make a dot plot of all the estimated mean weights produced by the class with each person using a sample of size 5. It should look something like this:

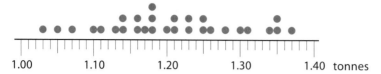

B3 Each person in the class should now select a random sample of 10 elephants and find the mean weight of the sample.
Make a dot plot of the class results, as before.

B4 Now do the same with samples of size 20.

B5 What happens as the sample size is increased?

B6 On the basis of the samples collected, what would you estimate the mean weight of the 250 elephants to be?

With even a relatively small random sample, say 20, the estimate of the mean weight is likely to be close to its actual value. (In this case the actual mean weight is 1.20 tonnes.)

As the sample is increased in size, it is even more likely to give a good estimate.

Sampling frame

To choose a sample from a population, you need a list of all the members of the population. This list is called the **sampling frame**.

For example, when the adults in a town are to be sampled, the register of electors is often used as a sampling frame.

To use random numbers for sampling, each member in the sampling frame has to be given an identification number.

B7 Jason wants to select a random sample of 50 of the students in his year group at school. Suggest how he could do this.

Using random numbers: a warning

It is sometimes suggested that you can get random numbers in the range, say, 0 to 430 by multiplying the calculator's decimal random numbers by 430 and rounding the results. This, however, does not work because some results will be generated more often than others.

For example, the result 208 can come from 0.483 or 0.484, whereas the result 209 can come from 0.485, 0.486 or 0.487. This non-uniformity arises because the 1000 random numbers cannot be shared equally between the results 0 to 430.

C Systematic sampling

If there is no reason to think that the sampling frame has been arranged in any way (for example, in order of weight) then a quicker alternative to random sampling is **systematic sampling**.

This means picking out, for example, every 10th item (or every 5th, for a larger sample).

You can decide where to start by choosing a random number in the range 1 to 10.

> **C1** Choose a starting number and select a systematic sample from the elephant database by picking every 20th item. Estimate the mean weight from your sample.

D Stratified sampling

The organisers of a sports club want to find out members' opinions about a proposed change to the rules.

The club members are 75% men and 25% women, and the organisers think that men and women could have different views about the proposed change.

If they choose a random sample, the proportions of men and women in the sample might not reflect the proportions in the membership as a whole. So the sample might not be representative of members' opinions.

The organisers can get round this problem by using a **stratified sample**. They split the population (the members) into two strata (men, women), and sample each stratum separately.

In this case an obvious approach would be to arrange for the sample to contain men and women in the same proportions as in the club as a whole. This is called **proportional stratified sampling**.*

So if they want a sample of overall size 40, they would select 30 men and 10 women. (The individual men and women could be chosen by random or by systematic sampling.)

In the questions that follow, it is assumed that all stratified sampling is proportional.

---

* There are sometimes good reasons for not using a proportional sample.

Suppose it is known that a population of animals is 60% male and 40% female, but that male weights are much less spread out than female. A relatively small sample of males would give a good estimate of average male weight, but a larger sample of females would be needed to give a good estimate of average female weight. Once the separate estimates are found, they can be combined together in the proportions 60 to 40 to give an overall estimate.

There are 280 girls and 160 boys in a school.

A stratified sample of 30 pupils is to be selected for a survey.

The proportion of girls is $\frac{280}{440} = 0.636\ldots$, so the sample must contain $0.636\ldots \times 30 = $ **19** girls.

D1 Maddy is carrying out a survey on school uniform policy at her school in year 11.
There are 97 males and 115 females in year 11.
Maddy decides to take a stratified sample of 50 students.
How many males and females should she include in her sample?

D2 This table shows the number of students in years 7, 8 and 9 of a school.

Year	7	8	9
Number of students	244	216	180

How many of each year group should be in a stratified sample of 100 students?

D3 This table shows the numbers of male and female students at a college who live on campus and off campus.

	On campus	Off campus
Male	2630	4320
Female	3680	2910

A stratified sample of 200 students is to be selected.
How many of the students in the sample should be

(a) males

(b) females living off campus

Test yourself

T1 A city is divided into four districts: North, South, East and West.
The adult population of each district is given in the table below.

District	North	South	East	West
Population	67 400	58 200	44 900	61 700

A stratified sample of 500 adults is to be selected for a survey about housing in the city.

How many people from each district should be included in the sample?

T2 There are 250 workers in a factory.
The table shows the number of each type of worker in the factory.

Managers	Craftsmen	Labourers	Administrators
25	130	54	41

(a) A stratified sample of size 40 is required.
Calculate the number of each type of worker that should be chosen.

(b) Describe a method to obtain a stratified sample of size 40 from the workers in the factory.

AQA

18 Using graphs to solve equations

This work will help you

- use intersecting graphs to estimate the solutions to equations such as $x^2 + 3x - 1 = x + 5$
- solve an equation such as $x^2 + 2x - 6 = 0$ by rearranging it to one such as $x^2 + 3x - 1 = x + 5$ and using intersecting graphs
- form equations and use graphs to solve problems
- use trial and improvement to find more accurate solutions to problems

You need sheets H2–4, H2–5, H2–6 and H2–7.

A Review: graphs and simple equations

A1 (a) Copy and complete the table below for $y = 2x^2 - 6x$.

x	⁻1	0	1	2	3	4
y		0	⁻4			8

(b) Draw the graph of $y = 2x^2 - 6x$ on a grid like this.

(c) Use your graph to estimate the positive value of x for which $2x^2 - 6x = 5$.

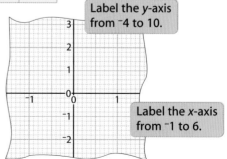

Label the y-axis from ⁻4 to 8.

Label the x-axis from ⁻1 to 4.

A2 (a) Copy and complete the table below for $y = x^2 - 5x + 3$.

x	⁻1	0	1	2	3	4	5	6
y	9		⁻1				3	

(b) On a grid like this, draw the graph of $y = x^2 - 5x + 3$.

Label the y-axis from ⁻4 to 10.

Label the x-axis from ⁻1 to 6.

(c) Use your graph to estimate the values of x for which $y = 4$.

A3 (a) On a suitable set of axes, draw the graph of $x^2 - 2x + 4$ for values of x from ⁻1 to 4.

(b) What is the minimum value of y?

(c) Explain how your graph shows that the equation $x^2 - 2x + 4 = 2$ has no solution.

B Intersection of a linear and a curved graph

This diagram shows the graphs of $y = x^2 - 2x$ and $y = \frac{1}{2}x + 3$.

At the points of intersection the y-values are the same so the corresponding x-values are the solutions to the equation $x^2 - 2x = \frac{1}{2}x + 3$.

Using the graphs we can estimate these solutions to one decimal place as $x = 3.4$ and $x = {}^-0.9$.

We can write the equation in different forms.
For example

$$x^2 - 2x = \tfrac{1}{2}x + 3$$

so $x^2 - 2\tfrac{1}{2}x - 3 = 0$

so $2x^2 - 5x - 6 = 0$

Hence the solutions of the equation $2x^2 - 5x - 6 = 0$ are the same solutions as those of the equation $x^2 - 2x = \frac{1}{2}x + 3$.

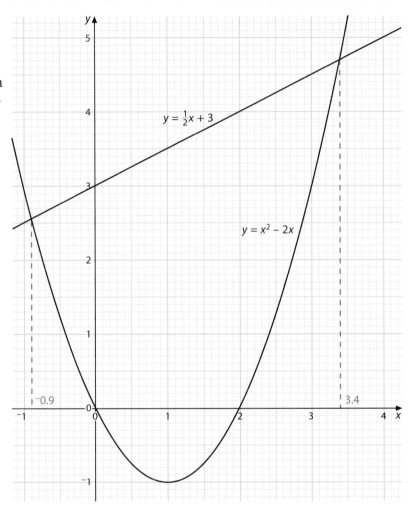

B1 (a) Copy and complete the table below for $y = x^2 - 1$.

x	$^-3$	$^-2$	$^-1$	0	1	2	3
y	8						

(b) On graph paper, draw the graph of $y = x^2 - 1$ for values of x from $^-3$ to 3.

(c) On the same set of axes, draw the graph of $y = 2x$.

(d) Use your graphs to estimate the solutions to the equation $x^2 - 1 = 2x$.

(e) (i) Write the equation in the form $ax^2 + bx + c = 0$.

(ii) Use your answer to (d) and trial and improvement to find the positive solution to this equation, correct to two decimal places.

B2 The curve shown is that of $y = x^3 - 4x^2 + 4$.
The straight line is $y = x + 1$.

(a) Use the graphs to estimate the solutions
to the equation $x^3 - 4x^2 + 4 = x + 1$.

(b) (i) Show that these solutions will satisfy
the equation $x^3 - 4x^2 - x + 3 = 0$.

(ii) Use trial and improvement to find
the largest solution to this equation,
correct to two decimal places.

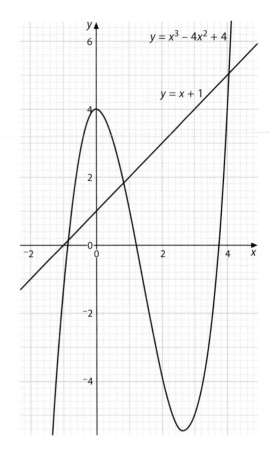

B3 (a) Copy and complete this table of values for the equation $y = \dfrac{3}{x} + 1$.

x	$^-4$	$^-3$	$^-2$	$^-1$	$^-0.5$	$^-0.25$	0.25	0.5	1	2	3	4
$\dfrac{3}{x} + 1$	0.25			$^-2$				7				

(b) Choose suitable scales and draw the graph of $y = \dfrac{3}{x} + 1$ for values of x from $^-4$ to 4.

(c) By drawing a suitable line on the graph estimate the solutions to
the equation $\dfrac{3}{x} + 1 = x$.

(d) Draw the line $y = 1 - x$ on your graph.
Use the line to show that there is no solution to the equation $\dfrac{3}{x} + 1 = 1 - x$.

B4 The graph of $y = x^2 - 2x - 4$ is drawn on sheet H2–4.

(a) (i) By drawing a suitable line on the graph estimate the solutions to
the equation $x^2 - 2x - 4 = 2x - 1$.

(ii) Show that $x^2 - 2x - 4 = 2x - 1$ can be simplified to $x^2 - 4x - 3 = 0$.

(b) (i) By drawing a suitable line on the graph estimate the solutions to
the equation $x^2 - 2x - 4 = 4 - \tfrac{1}{2}x$.

(ii) Show that these solutions also satisfy the equation $2x^2 - 3x - 16 = 0$.

C Deciding which linear graph to draw

The graph of $y = x^2 - x - 1$ is shown on sheet H2–5.

We can use this graph to estimate the solutions to any quadratic equation by first rearranging the equation so that $x^2 - x - 1$ is on one side.

For example, we can use it to solve $x^2 + x - 3 = 0$ as follows.

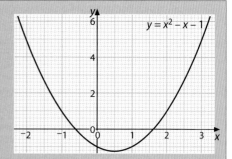

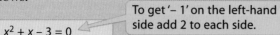

To get '– 1' on the left-hand side add 2 to each side.

To get '– x' on the left-hand side subtract 2x from each side.

So the solutions of this equation can be estimated by reading the x-values of the points where the graphs of $y = x^2 - x - 1$ and $y = 2 - 2x$ intersect.

- Add the line $y = 2 - 2x$ to the graph on sheet H2–5.
  Hence estimate the solutions to the equation $x^2 + x - 3 = 0$ to one decimal place.

- Which line would you draw on the graph of $y = x^2 - x - 1$ to solve each of these equations?

  A $x^2 - 2x - 1 = 0$ **B** $x^2 - 2x - 5 = 0$

  C $x^2 - 3x - 1 = 0$ **D** $x^2 - 3x - 7 = 0$ **E** $x^2 + 2x - 1 = 0$

- Choose two of these equations and estimate their solutions to one decimal place by adding appropriate lines to the graph on sheet H2–5.

- Show that there is no solution to the equation $x^2 - 2x + 3 = 0$.

C1 (a) Which of these are rearrangements of the equation $2x^2 + 2x - 5 = 0$?

A $2x^2 + x + 1 = 6 - x$ **B** $2x^2 + x + 1 = x + 6$ **C** $3x^2 - 5 = x^2 - 2x$

D $2x^2 + 3x - 11 = x - 6$ **E** $2x^2 + x + 1 = 3x + 6$

(b) If you have the graph of $y = 2x^2 + x + 1$, what straight line do you need to draw to estimate the solutions to the equation $2x^2 + 2x - 5 = 0$?

C2 If you have the graph of $y = x^2 - x - 2$, what straight line do you need to draw to estimate the solutions to the equation $x^2 - 5x - 2 = 0$?

C3 If you have the graph of $y = 3x^2 + x + 1$, what straight line do you need to draw to estimate the solutions to the equation $3x^2 + 5x - 1 = 0$?

C4 (a) On graph paper, draw and label axes with $^-3 \leq x \leq 3$ and $^-2 \leq y \leq 12$. On your axes, draw accurately the graph of $y = x^2 - x$.

(b) Use your graph and suitable straight lines to estimate solutions to

    (i) $x^2 = x + 5$ **(ii)** $x^2 + x - 1 = 0$ **(iii)** $x^2 - 4x + 1 = 0$

C5 The graph of $y = x^3 - 2$ is drawn on sheet H2–6.

(a) (i) By drawing a suitable line on the graph estimate the positive solution to the equation $x^3 - x - 2 = 0$.

    (ii) Show that this is the only solution to the equation $x^3 - x - 2 = 0$.

    (iii) Use trial and improvement to find this solution correct to two decimal places.

(b) (i) By drawing a suitable line on the graph estimate the positive solutions to the equation $x^3 - 3x + 1 = 0$.

    (ii) Show that the equation $x^3 - 3x + 1 = 0$ has three solutions.

(c) By drawing a suitable line on the graph estimate all the solutions to the equation $x^3 + x - 3 = 0$.

C6 Part of the graph of $y = \dfrac{2}{x}$ is drawn on sheet H2–6.

(a) By drawing a suitable line on the graph estimate the positive solution to the equation $\dfrac{2}{x} - 4x = 0$.

(b) Show that the positive solution to this equation is equivalent to $\sqrt{\frac{1}{2}}$.

C7 (a) On graph paper, draw an accurate graph of $y = x^2 + x + 1$. Use values of x from $^-3$ to 3.

(b) Which of these are rearrangements of the equation $2x^2 + 3x - 4 = 0$?

Ⓐ $3x^2 + x + 2 = x^2 - 2x + 6$

Ⓑ $3x^2 + x - 4 = x^2 + 2x$

Ⓒ $x^2 + x + 1 = x^2 + 2x - 5$

Ⓓ $x^2 + x + 1 = 3 - \frac{1}{2}x$

(c) (i) What straight line do you need to draw on your graph to estimate the solutions to the equation $2x^2 + 3x - 4 = 0$?

    (ii) Draw this line and estimate the solutions.

C8 If you have the graph of $y = x^2 + x$, what **straight** line do you need to draw to estimate the solutions to the equation $3x^2 + 2x - 3 = 0$?

C9 If you have the graph of $y = 2x^2 - 1$, what straight line do you need to draw to estimate the solutions to the equation $x^2 - 5x + 5 = 0$?

C10 Show that the x-values where the curves $y = \dfrac{1}{x} + 1$ and $y = 7 - x^2$ intersect are solutions to the equation $x^3 - 6x + 1 = 0$.

D Forming equations and using graphs to solve problems

D1 A rectangular pen is to be built against a wall.
The width of the pen is x metres.

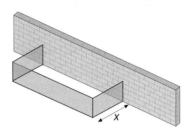

The pen needs to enclose an area of $64\,\text{m}^2$.

(a) Show that the length of fencing needed, L metres, is
given by the formula $L = 2x + \dfrac{64}{x}$.

(b) Draw the graph of L against x for $0 < x \le 20$.

(c) A pen like this is made with 30 metres of fencing.
Use your graph to estimate the two possible values for its width.

(d) Estimate the **minimum** length of fencing needed to make a pen like this.
What is the approximate width of a pen that uses this minimum length of fencing?

D2 A canvas wind-shelter has two square ends, each of side x metres,
and a rectangular back of length l metres.

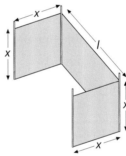

(a) Find an expression for the area of canvas in m^2 in terms of l and x.

(b) The area of canvas is $9\,\text{m}^2$.

  (i) Show that $l = \dfrac{9}{x} - 2x$.

  (ii) Hence show that the enclosed volume, $V\,\text{m}^3$, is given by $V = 9x - 2x^3$.

(c) Plot the graph of V against x for $0 \le x \le 2$.

(d) Use your graph to estimate the values of x that give an enclosed volume of $4\,\text{m}^3$.

(e) **(i)** Estimate the value of x that gives the largest possible volume.

  (ii) From your graph, estimate the largest possible volume.

(f) **(i)** Use trial and improvement or the 'zooming' facility of a graph plotter to find,
correct to 2 d.p., the value of x that gives the largest possible volume.

  (ii) Use this value and the formula for V to calculate the corresponding value of V.
Check the accuracy of your estimate in part (e)(ii).

D3 A piece of paper measures 21 cm by 30 cm.
From each corner, a square of side x cm is cut, as shown in the diagram.

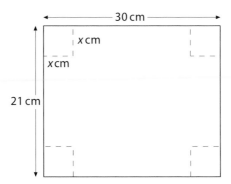

The paper is then folded up to make a box without a lid.

(a) Given that the volume of the box is V cm³, show that $V = x(21 - 2x)(30 - 2x)$.

(b) Draw the graph of V against x for a sensible range of values for x.

(c) Use your graph to estimate the value of x that gives the maximum volume. Estimate this maximum volume.

(d) (i) Use trial and improvement or a graph plotter to find this value of x to 2 d.p.

(ii) Find the value of V for this value of x and compare it with your estimate of the maximum volume in part (c).

D4 A plastic block is to have square ends.

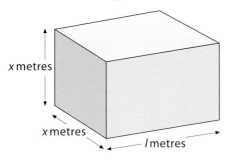

The block is required to have a volume of 100 m³ and a surface area of 200 m².

(a) (i) Write down an expression for the volume of the block, in terms of x and l.

(ii) Show that $l = \dfrac{100}{x^2}$.

(b) Write down an expression for the total surface area of the block, in terms of x and l.

(c) Show that x satisfies the equation $x^3 - 100x + 200 = 0$.

(d) (i) Draw the graph of $y = x^3 - 100x + 200$ for values of x from 0 to 10.

(ii) Hence estimate the dimensions of two different blocks that fit the requirements for volume and surface area.

Test yourself

T1 (a) Copy and complete the table of values for $y = x^2 - 3x + 1$.

x	⁻2	⁻1	0	1	2	3	4
y	11		1	⁻1		1	5

(b) On a grid like this, draw the graph of $y = x^2 - 3x + 1$.

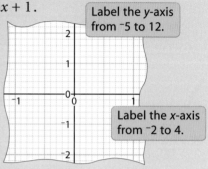

Label the y-axis from ⁻5 to 12.

Label the x-axis from ⁻2 to 4.

(c) Use your graph to find an estimate for the minimum value of y.

(d) Use a graphical method to find estimates of the solutions to the equation

$$x^2 - 3x + 1 = 2x - 4$$

Edexcel

T2 Part of the graph of $y = x^3 + x - 1$ is drawn on sheet H2–7.

(a) Use the graph to estimate the solution of the equation $x^3 + x - 1 = 3$.

(b) By drawing a suitable line on the graph, estimate the solution to the equation

$$x^3 + 3x - 2 = 0$$

T3 A rectangle has a perimeter of 14 cm and an area of 9 cm².

Let the length of the rectangle be x cm.

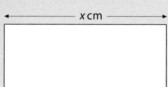

x cm

(a) Show that $x^2 - 7x + 9 = 0$.

(b) On a grid like this, draw the graph of $y = x^2 - 7x + 9$. Use values of x from 0 to 7.

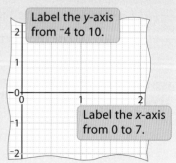

Label the y-axis from ⁻4 to 10.

Label the x-axis from 0 to 7.

(c) Use your graph to estimate the dimensions of the rectangle, correct to 1 d.p.

19 Histograms

This work will help you

- read and draw histograms
- understand frequency density

A Reading a histogram using an 'area scale'

Mili is in charge of a skiing party. She draws this frequency chart of the ages of the people in the party.

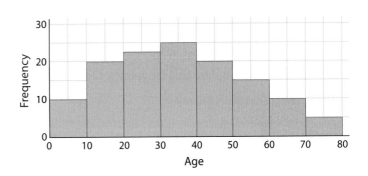

Mili decides to put all the people aged 50 or over into one group.
The total frequency for this new group is 15 + 10 + 5 = 30.

Here is Mili's new frequency chart.

This chart is misleading. It exaggerates the number in the 50–80 age group. This is because our eye is drawn to the **area**, not the height, of the bars.

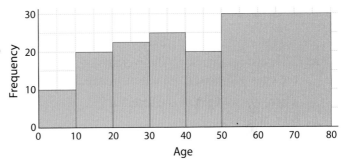

A chart that uses **area** to show frequency is called a **histogram**.

Here is a histogram for the ages of the skiing party. It does not exaggerate the number in the 50–80 group.

We can work out the number of people in each age group by using the 'area scale' printed above the chart.

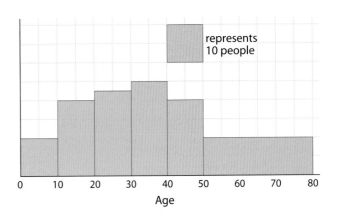

represents 10 people

A1 This histogram shows the distribution of heights in a primary school year group.

Copy and complete this frequency table.

Height, h cm	Frequency
$95 < h \leq 100$	
$100 < h \leq 110$	
$110 < h \leq 115$	
$115 < h \leq 120$	
$120 < h \leq 130$	

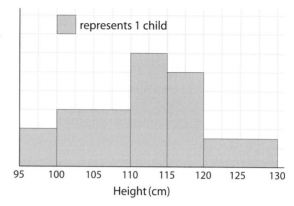

A2 This histogram shows the distribution of weights of a group of babies.

Copy and complete this frequency table.

Weight, w kg	Frequency
$1.0 < w \leq 2.0$	
$2.0 < w \leq 2.5$	
$2.5 < w \leq 3.0$	
$3.0 < w \leq 4.0$	
$4.0 < w \leq 4.5$	

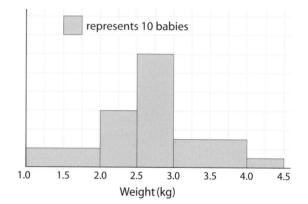

A3 This histogram shows the weights of the eggs collected from a hen-house.

There are 60 eggs in the interval $60 < w \leq 65$.

(a) Work out the number of eggs in the interval $45 < w \leq 55$.

(b) Work out the total number of eggs collected.

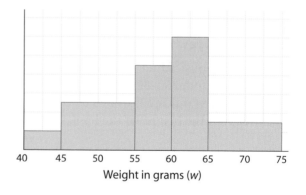

A4 The table below shows the distribution of the prices of flats for sale in a town. ('80k' means 80 000.)

Copy and complete the histogram for the distribution.

Price, £P	Frequency
$70k < P \leq 80k$	40
$80k < P \leq 100k$	120
$100k < P \leq 120k$	200
$120k < P \leq 150k$	120
$150k < P \leq 200k$	50

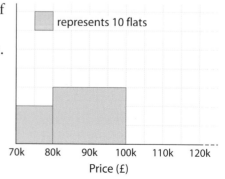

A5 The results of a survey of the lengths of local phone calls are summarised in the table below.

Time, t minutes	Frequency
$0 < t \leq 1$	34
$1 < t \leq 2$	13
$2 < t \leq 5$	12
$5 < t \leq 10$	10
$10 < t \leq 20$	4
$20 < t$	0

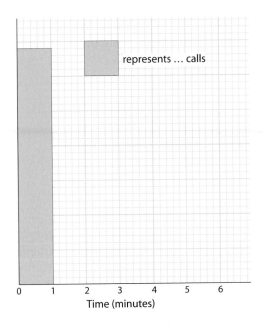

(a) Use mid-interval values to estimate the mean length of a call.

(b) Copy and complete the histogram.

B Frequency density

So far we have not used a vertical scale.

A vertical scale is useful to help work out the frequency represented by a bar.

Here is a histogram of children's heights. The area of the first bar represents 20 children.

The 'length' of this bar is 10 (from 100 to 110). To make the area 20, the height has to be **2**.

This leads to the vertical scale shown. It is called a **frequency density** scale.

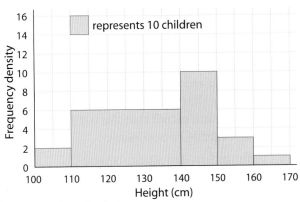

For the bar from 110 to 140 (length 30), the frequency density is 6.
So the number of babies represented by this bar is $30 \times 6 = $ **180**. (Check by counting squares.)

> frequency = length of interval × frequency density

B1 (a) What are the missing numbers on this frequency density scale?

(b) The bar for the interval 70–75 is missing. If there are 30 eggs in this interval, what is the frequency density for this bar?

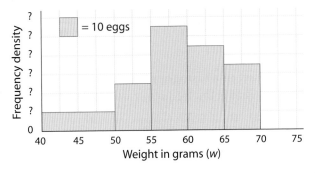

B2 Copy and complete the frequency table below, using the information in the histogram.

Weight, w g	Frequency
$100 < w \leq 150$	
$150 < w \leq 250$	
$250 < w \leq 300$	
$300 < w \leq 450$	

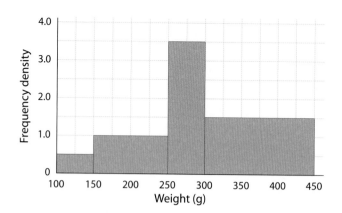

B3 Copy and complete the frequency table below, using the information in the histogram.

Height, h cm	Frequency
$120 < h \leq 130$	
$130 < h \leq 155$	
$155 < h \leq 175$	
$175 < h \leq 190$	

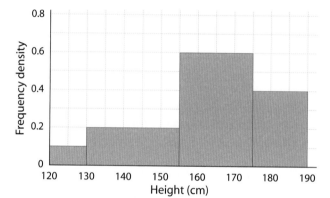

B4 A survey was carried out of the times taken by students to get to school. The distribution is shown in the histogram, except that the bar for the interval 20–35 is missing.

Altogether, 255 students were included in the survey.

What is the frequency density for the interval 20–35?

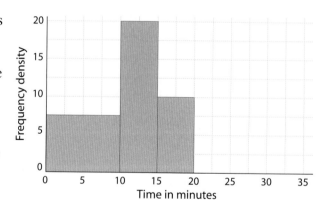

B5 The table below shows the results of a survey of times spent watching TV one evening.

Time, t minutes	$0 < t \leq 30$	$30 < t \leq 60$	$60 < t \leq 150$	$150 < t \leq 300$
Frequency	6	15	54	30

Part of a histogram for this data is shown here. What is the frequency density for the interval

(a) $0 < t \leq 30$

(b) $30 < t \leq 60$

(c) $60 < t \leq 150$

(d) $150 < t \leq 300$

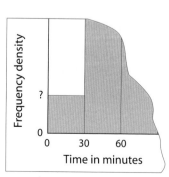

C Drawing a histogram

From the fact that   frequency = length of interval × frequency density

it follows that   frequency density = $\dfrac{\text{frequency}}{\text{length of interval}}$

To draw a histogram from a frequency table,
first calculate the frequency density for each interval.

Example

Draw a histogram to show this data.

> First find the frequency densities.

Weight, w g	Frequency
$100 < w \leq 150$	24
$150 < w \leq 250$	60
$250 < w \leq 300$	15
$300 < w \leq 450$	9

Frequency density
$24 \div 50 = 0.48$
$60 \div 100 = 0.6$
$15 \div 50 = 0.3$
$9 \div 150 = 0.06$

> Then choose convenient graph scales and draw the bars.

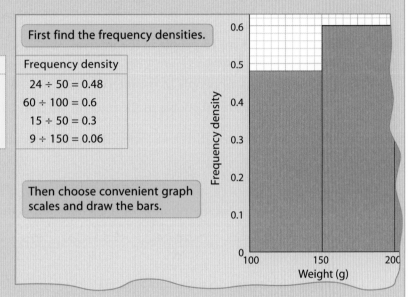

C1 Visitors to a museum spend different amounts of time looking around. This table shows the frequency distribution of the times spent in the museum by visitors on a Saturday in summer.

(a) Calculate the frequency density for each interval.

(b) Draw a histogram for the data.

Time, t minutes	Frequency
$0 < t \leq 30$	24
$30 < t \leq 45$	30
$45 < t \leq 60$	15
$60 < t \leq 90$	12
$90 < t \leq 180$	18

C2 This table shows the distribution of the heights of trees in a wood.

(a) Draw a histogram for the data.

(b) Use the histogram to estimate the number of trees whose heights are between 10 m and 20 m.

Height, h m	Frequency
$0 < h \leq 5$	8
$5 < h \leq 7.5$	12
$7.5 < h \leq 10$	18
$10 < h \leq 15$	7
$15 < h \leq 25$	6

C3 This histogram shows part of the age distribution of the people in a group of care homes.

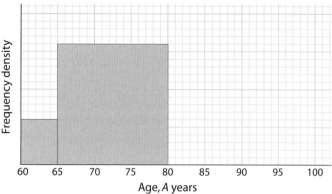

(a) Copy the diagram.
Given that there are 15 people in the interval $60 \leq A < 65$, number the frequency density axis.

(b) Find the number of people in the interval $65 \leq A < 80$.

(c) Given that there are 40 people in the interval $80 \leq A < 100$, complete the histogram.

Test yourself

T1 This table shows the age distribution of the female population of the UK in 2004.

Age, A years	$A < 25$	$25 \leq A < 45$	$45 \leq A < 55$	$55 \leq A < 75$	$75 \leq A < 110$
Frequency (%)	30	28	13	20	9

(a) Draw a histogram to show this information.

(b) Use the histogram to estimate the percentage of the female population aged under 40.

T2 The incomplete table and histogram give some information about the ages of the people who live in a village.

(a) Use the information in the histogram to find the missing frequencies in the table below.

Age (x) in years	Frequency
$0 < x \leq 10$	160
$10 < x \leq 25$	
$25 < x \leq 30$	
$30 < x \leq 40$	100
$40 < x \leq 70$	120

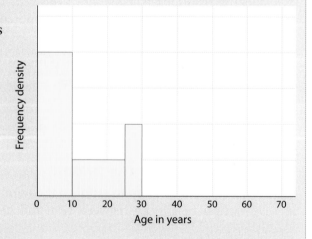

(b) Copy and complete the histogram.

Edexcel

20 Quadratic expressions and equations 2

This work will help you

- solve quadratic equations by using perfect squares and the formula
- solve problems by forming and solving a quadratic equation
- solve simultaneous equations, one linear and one quadratic

A Perfect squares

9 is a perfect square because we can write 9 as 3×3 or 3^2.

$x^2 + 18x + 81$ is a perfect square because we can write it as $(x + 9)^2$.

A1 Expand and simplify these perfect squares.

(a) $(x + 5)^2$ (b) $(x - 4)^2$ (c) $(x - 3)^2$ (d) $(x + 12)^2$

A2 Copy and complete the following identities.

(a) $(x - \blacksquare)^2 = x^2 - 10x + 25$ (b) $(x + \blacksquare)^2 = x^2 + 12x + 36$

(c) $(x + \blacksquare)^2 = x^2 + 8x + \blacksquare$ (d) $(x - \blacksquare)^2 = x^2 - 4x + \blacksquare$

(e) $(x + \blacksquare)^2 = x^2 + 16x + \blacksquare$ (f) $(x - \blacksquare)^2 = x^2 - 14x + \blacksquare$

A3 (a) Which of the following expressions are perfect squares?

A $x^2 + 2x + 1$ **B** $x^2 - 12x + 12$ **C** $x^2 - 12x + 36$

D $x^2 - 18x + 81$ **E** $x^2 + 6x + 9$ **F** $x^2 + 6x + 36$

(b) Write each of the perfect squares in the form $(x + c)^2$.

A4 Expand   (a) $(x + a)^2$ (b) $(x - b)^2$

A5 What number do you need to add to each expression to make it a perfect square?

(a) $x^2 + 4x$ (b) $x^2 + 6x$ (c) $x^2 + 8x$ (d) $x^2 + 2x$

(e) $x^2 - 4x$ (f) $x^2 - 6x$ (g) $x^2 - 2x$ (h) $x^2 - 10x$

A6 What number do you need to add to each expression to make it a perfect square?

(a) $x^2 + 6x + 4$ (b) $x^2 + 4x + 1$ (c) $x^2 + 2x - 5$

(d) $x^2 - 8x + 10$ (e) $x^2 - 10x + 5$ (f) $x^2 - 4x - 3$

A7 What number do you need to subtract from each expression to make it a perfect square?

(a) $x^2 + 6x + 10$ (b) $x^2 + 2x + 5$ (c) $x^2 - 4x + 20$

B Using a perfect square to solve a quadratic equation

A quadratic equation that involves a perfect square can be solved using square roots.

Examples

$(x + 1)^2 = 9$

Remember both the positive and the negative square root.

$x + 1 = \pm\sqrt{9}$

So $x + 1 = {}^-3$　or　$x + 1 = 3$

$x = {}^-3 - 1$ or　$x = 3 - 1$

$x = {}^-4$　or　$x = 2$

$(x - 3)^2 = 7$

$x - 3 = \pm\sqrt{7}$

So $x - 3 = {}^-\sqrt{7}$　or　$x - 3 = \sqrt{7}$

$x = 3 - \sqrt{7}$ or　$x = 3 + \sqrt{7}$

Rounded to three decimal places,

$x = 0.354$ or $x = 5.646$

In these questions, give solutions correct to three decimal places where appropriate.

B1 Solve these equations.

(a) $(x - 5)^2 = 9$　　(b) $(x + 2)^2 = 16$　　(c) $(x - 3)^2 = 7$　　(d) $(x + 1)^2 = 10$

The quadratic equation $x^2 - 6x + 4 = 0$ cannot be solved by factorising.

However, an equation like this can sometimes be solved by adding or subtracting to make the expression on one side a perfect square.

Half of $^-6$ is $^-3$ and $(^-3)^2 = 9$ so we want the perfect square $x^2 - 6x + 9$ on the left-hand side. We need to add 5 to $x^2 - 6x + 4$ to get $x^2 - 6x + 9$. So we need to add 5 to each side.

$x^2 - 6x + 4 = 0$

Factorise the perfect square.

$x^2 - 6x + 9 = 5$

$(x - 3)^2 = 5$

$x - 3 = \pm\sqrt{5}$

So $x = 3 + \sqrt{5}$ or $x = 3 - \sqrt{5}$

Rounded to three decimal places,

$x = 5.236$ or $x = 0.764$

This method of solving a quadratic equation is sometimes called **completing the square**.

B2 (a) What do you need to add to both sides of the equation $x^2 + 6x + 2 = 0$ to make the left-hand side a perfect square?

(b) Hence solve the equation $x^2 + 6x + 2 = 0$.

B3 (a) What do you need to add to both sides of the equation $x^2 + 2x - 4 = 0$ to make the left-hand side a perfect square?

(b) Hence solve the equation $x^2 + 2x - 4 = 0$.

B4 Solve these equations using perfect squares.

    (a) $x^2 + 12x + 8 = 0$ (b) $x^2 + 10x - 5 = 0$ (c) $x^2 + 8x - 7 = 0$

B5 Try to solve $x^2 + 2x + 3 = 0$. What happens?

B6 Solve these equations using perfect squares.

    (a) $x^2 - 4x - 2 = 0$ (b) $x^2 - 12x - 5 = 0$ (c) $x^2 - 6x + 7 = 0$

B7 (a) Expand and simplify $\left(x - \frac{1}{2}\right)^2$.

    (b) Hence solve the equation $x^2 - x - 3 = 0$.

B8 Solve $x^2 + 3x - 2 = 0$.

B9 Copy and complete this working to solve the equation $2x^2 + 8x + 2 = 0$.

$$2x^2 + 8x + 2 = 0$$
$$x^2 + 4x + 1 = 0$$

> If the coefficient of x^2 is not 1 you can divide both sides to make it 1.

B10 Solve these equations.

    (a) $2x^2 + 12x + 4 = 0$ (b) $3x^2 - 24x - 3 = 0$ (c) $5x^2 - 15x + 5 = 0$

C Using a formula to solve a quadratic equation

If a quadratic equation is in the form

$$ax^2 + bx + c = 0$$

it can be shown that $x = \dfrac{-b \pm \sqrt{b^2 - 4ac}}{2a}$.

> This formula can be derived by dividing both sides of the equation $ax^2 + bx + c = 0$ by a and then completing the square. The algebra is quite complicated.

Example

Solve $3x^2 - 8x + 2 = 0$.

$3x^2 - 8x + 2 = 0$

So $a = 3, b = {}^-8$ and $c = 2$

$$\text{giving } x = \frac{{}^-({}^-8) \pm \sqrt{({}^-8)^2 - 4 \times 3 \times 2}}{2 \times 3}$$

$$= \frac{8 \pm \sqrt{40}}{6}$$

$$= 2.387 \text{ or } 0.279 \text{ (to 3 d.p.)}$$

In these questions, give solutions correct to three decimal places where appropriate unless stated otherwise.

C1 Use the formula to solve each equation.

    (a) $x^2 + 5x + 3 = 0$ (b) $x^2 - 3x - 1 = 0$ (c) $x^2 - 11x + 9 = 0$

    (d) $3x^2 + 6x - 2 = 0$ (e) $5 - 10x - 2x^2 = 0$ (f) $5x^2 - 8x + 2 = 0$

C2 Rearrange each equation into the form $ax^2 + bx + c = 0$ and solve it.

(a) $3x^2 + 2x = 7$ (b) $4x - 2x^2 = 1$ (c) $2x + 4 = x^2$

C3 (a) Solve these equations by factorising.

(i) $x^2 + 11x + 30 = 0$ (ii) $3x^2 - 4x + 1 = 0$

(b) Now solve the equations in part (a) by using the formula. Which method do you prefer?

When solving a quadratic equation, first try factorising as it is a more direct method. If you cannot factorise, try using the formula. (You can also try completing the square, but many students find using the formula easier.)

C4 Solve these equations.

(a) $x^2 + 6x - 7 = 0$ (b) $3x^2 + 7x + 1 = 0$ (c) $3x^2 + 10x + 2 = 0$

(d) $6x^2 - 11x = 30$ (e) $5x^2 - 8x = 21$ (f) $2(x^2 - 1) = 5x$

C5 Here is a sketch of the graph of $y = x^2 - 5x - 5$.

(a) Explain why the x-coordinates of the points A and B are found by solving $x^2 - 5x - 5 = 0$.

(b) Find the coordinates of points A and B, giving values correct to one decimal place.

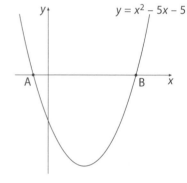

C6 Find the coordinates of the points where the graph of $y = 5x^2 + x - 4$ crosses the x-axis.

C7 (a) Solve $4x^2 - 12x + 9 = 0$.

(b) Use your solution to choose the correct sketch of $y = 4x^2 - 12x + 9$.

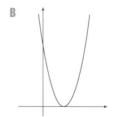

C8 (a) What happens when you use the formula to solve $x^2 - 2x + 5 = 0$?

(b) What does this tell you about the graph of $y = x^2 - 2x + 5$?

D1 The diagram shows a rectangle with
length $x + 4$ and width $x - 1$.
All measurements are given in centimetres.

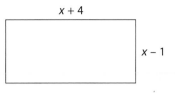

The area of the rectangle is A square centimetres.

(a) Show that $A = x^2 + 3x - 4$.

When $A = 10$, x satisfies the equation $x^2 + 3x - 14 = 0$.

(b) Find the length of the rectangle.
Give your answer correct to two decimal places.

Edexcel

D2 ABC is a right-angled triangle with dimensions as shown.

(a) **(i)** Use Pythagoras's theorem to
write down an equation in x.

(ii) Show that this equation
simplifies to $x^2 - 4x - 8 = 0$.

(b) **(i)** Solve this equation.

(ii) Give the length of the hypotenuse.

D3 The perimeter of this rectangle is $26\,\text{cm}$.
Its area is $35\,\text{cm}^2$.

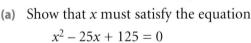

(a) Use the perimeter to find an expression,
in terms of y, for the length of this rectangle.

(b) Form an equation in y and show it can be simplified to $y^2 - 13y + 35 = 0$.

(c) Solve the equation to find the length and width, correct to 2 d.p.

D4 A farmer wants to build a fence to make a rectangular pen.
He is using a wall as one side of the pen, as shown.

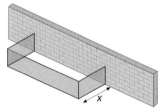

He has 50 metres of fencing and he wants the area of the pen
to be $250\,\text{m}^2$. The width of the pen is x metres.

(a) Show that x must satisfy the equation

$$x^2 - 25x + 125 = 0$$

(b) Solve the equation to find the values of x that give the pen an area of $250\,\text{m}^2$.
Give your answers to an appropriate degree of accuracy.

D5 The base of a triangle is 5 cm longer than its height.
The area of the triangle is $30\,\text{cm}^2$.
Find the length of the base of the triangle correct to three significant figures.

E Simultaneous equations

Example

Find the points of intersection of the curve $y = x^2 - 3x + 3$ and the line $2x - y = 1$.

Rearranging the second equation gives $y = 2x - 1$.
The y-values are equal at the points of intersection so

$$2x - 1 = x^2 - 3x + 3$$
$$x^2 - 5x + 4 = 0$$
$$(x - 4)(x - 1) = 0$$
$$\text{So } x = 4 \text{ or } x = 1$$

When $x = 4$, $y = 2 \times 4 - 1 = 7$ and
when $x = 1$, $y = 2 \times 1 - 1 = 1$.

So the points of intersection are $(1, 1)$ and $(4, 7)$.

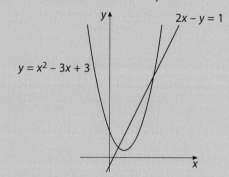

So the solutions to the simultaneous equations
$y = x^2 - 3x + 3$ and $2x - y = 1$ are the
pairs of values $x = 1, y = 1$ and $x = 4, y = 7$.

E1 Solve these pairs of simultaneous equations, correct to 2 d.p. where appropriate.

(a) $y = 5x - 6$
$y = x^2$

(b) $y = x^2 + 7$
$y = 3x + 17$

(c) $y = x^2 - 5$
$y - 2x = 3$

(d) $y = 5x + 7$
$y = 9 - 2x^2$

E2 Find the points of intersection for each pair of graphs.

(a)
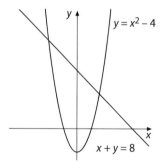

(b)
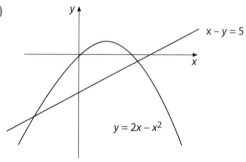

(c)
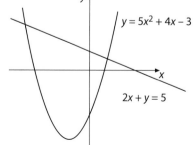

(d)
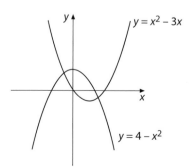

E3 (a) Solve $4x - 8 = x^2 - 4$.

(b) What does your solution show about the line $y = 4x - 8$ and the curve $y = x^2 - 4$?

E4 (a) Show that the line $y = x - 1$ touches the curve $y = 4x^2 + 5x$ at one point only.

(b) Work out the coordinates of this point.

E5 Show that the line $y = x - 3$ does not meet the curve $y = x^2 + 2x + 1$.

Test yourself

T1 (a) What must be added to $x^2 - 12x$ so that it can be written in the form $(x - a)^2$?

(b) Hence solve the equation $x^2 - 12x = 3$ giving your answers correct to 2 d.p.

T2 Solve the equation $x^2 - 10x - 5 = 0$. Give your answers to two decimal places.   AQA

T3 Solve this quadratic equation.

$x^2 - 5x - 8 = 0$

Give your answers correct to three significant figures.   Edexcel

T4 The diagram shows a trapezium.
The measurements on the diagram
are in centimetres.
The lengths of the parallel sides
are x cm and 20 cm.
The height of the trapezium is $2x$ cm
The area of the trapezium is 400 cm².

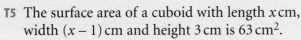

Diagram not accurately drawn

(a) Show that $x^2 + 20x = 400$.

(b) Find the value of x. Give your answer correct to three decimal places.   Edexcel

T5 The surface area of a cuboid with length x cm,
width $(x - 1)$ cm and height 3 cm is 63 cm².

(a) Show that x satisfies the equation $2x^2 + 10x - 69 = 0$.

(b) (i) Solve the equation $2x^2 + 10x - 69 = 0$, giving solutions to two decimal places.

(ii) Hence write down the dimensions of the cuboid.   WJEC

T6 Solve the simultaneous equations

$y = x + 2$
$y = 3x^2$

You must show your working.
Do not use trial and improvement.   AQA

T7 Solve the simultaneous equations $y + x = 7$ and $y = 2x^2 + 12x - 28$.
Give your solutions to 1 d.p.

Review 3

1 (a) Find the lowest common multiple of 12 and 15.

  (b) Evaluate $\frac{7}{12} + \frac{1}{15}$ and write the answer in its simplest form.

2 A shop sells pots of yoghurt for 94p each.
The shop decides to put all its prices up by 7.4%.
What will be the new price of a pot of yoghurt?

3 Rearrange each of these formulas to make q the subject.

  (a) $t = \dfrac{p + rq}{s}$ (b) $p = \dfrac{q^2}{6}$ (c) $s = 2\sqrt{q + b}$ (d) $s = 9q^2$

4 Staff want to survey people who use the public library. Each day for a week they interview 20 people who are in the library between 12 noon and 2 p.m.

  Is the sample of people interviewed likely to be representative of the library users? Explain your answer.

5 Find the equation of the line perpendicular to $2y + 3x = 4$ through point $(3, 1)$.

6 This graph shows Karen's journey to school. She walks to a bus stop, waits for a bus, then a bus takes her the rest of the way to school.

  (a) How far does Karen walk from home to the bus stop?

  (b) At what speed does she walk?

  (c) How long does she wait at the bus stop?

  (d) How far does the bus take her?

  (e) At what speed does the bus go?

  (f) Karen's brother leaves home 12 minutes after she does. At what speed must he run in order to catch the same bus as her?

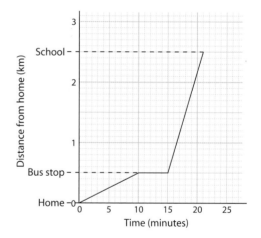

7 Solve these quadratic equations using the formula.

  (a) $x^2 - 4x - 9 = 0$ (b) $2x^2 + 7x - 1 = 0$ (c) $4x^2 - 5 = 2x$

8 The lines PQ and RS are parallel.

  (a) Write down the value of a. Give a reason for your answer.

  (b) Write down the value of c. Give a reason for your answer.

  (c) Work out the value of b.

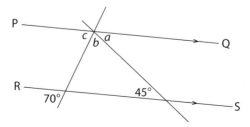

9 (a) Find an approximate value for $\dfrac{29.02 + 6.23}{(2.91)^2}$, showing all your working clearly.

(b) Use a calculator to find the value, correct to three significant figures.

10 Simplify the following.

(a) $\dfrac{a^2b^3}{ab}$ **(b)** $(2a^2b)^4$ **(c)** $4ab^3 \times 2a^2b$ **(d)** $\sqrt{\dfrac{9x^2}{4}}$

11 40 can be expressed as a product of prime factors as $2^n \times 5$.

(a) What is the value of n?

(b) Write 84 as a product of prime factors in the same way.

(c) (i) Find the highest common factor of 40 and 84.

(ii) Find the lowest common multiple of 40 and 84.

12 The bullet train in Japan covers the 120 miles between Hiroshima and Kokura at an average speed of 164 m.p.h.
How long does it take, to the nearest minute?

13 The planet Mars is approximately a sphere of diameter 6786 km.
Calculate the approximate volume of the planet Mars.
Give your answer in standard form correct to three significant figures.

14 This table shows the number of students in years 9, 10 and 11 of a school.

Year	9	10	11
Number of students	157	184	162

How many of each year group should be in a stratified sample of 120 students?

15 Find the value of n in each of these equations.

(a) $2^3 \times 2^n = 2^7$ **(b)** $3^n \times 3^3 = 3^2$ **(c)** $\dfrac{5}{5^n} = 5^{-3}$ **(d)** $(2^n)^3 = 2^{12}$

16 This diagram shows the plan view of a square-based pyramid.
The height of the pyramid is 3 cm.

(a) Draw a full-size **side** view of this pyramid.

(b) Calculate its volume.

5 cm
5 cm

17 Rearrange each of these formulas to make r the subject.

(a) $V = 3r + qr$ **(b)** $P = 5r + \pi r - 2$ **(c)** $A = 9r^2 - \pi r^2$

18 Find all possible values of x between $0°$ and $360°$ for each of these.

(a) $\sin x = 0.5$ **(b)** $\cos x = 0.2$ **(c)** $3 \sin x = 1$

(d) $\tan x = 2$ **(e)** $4 \cos x = {}^-3$ **(f)** $5 \tan x = {}^-1$

19 The frequency of vibration of a stretched string is given by the formula

$$f = \frac{1}{2l}\sqrt{\frac{s}{d}}$$

Rearrange the formula to make s the subject.

20 Given $V = 200 \times (1.06)^n$, find V when $n = 10$.
Give your answer correct to three significant figures.

21 This table shows the distribution of heights of a group of 10-year-old girls.

Height, h cm	Frequency
$120 < h \leq 130$	3
$130 < h \leq 135$	9
$135 < h \leq 140$	12
$140 < h \leq 145$	11
$145 < h \leq 155$	5

(a) Estimate the mean height of these girls.

(b) Draw a histogram for the data.

22 Calculate, correct to 2 d.p., the coordinates of the points where the graph of $y = 2x^2 + 3x - 4$ crosses the x-axis.

23 The total area of land on Earth is about 1.5×10^8 km².
The total area covered by forests is 3.9×10^7 km².
What percentage of land on Earth is covered by forests?

24 Rearrange each of these formulas to make t the subject.

(a) $b = \dfrac{a}{a+t}$ (b) $b = \dfrac{a+t}{t}$ (c) $b = \dfrac{at}{a+t}$ (d) $b = \dfrac{a+t}{a-t}$

25 An **open** cardboard box of height h cm has a square base of side x cm.

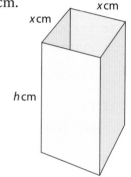

(a) Write down an expression in terms of x and h for the total area of cardboard.

(b) The area of cardboard is 50 cm².
Show that $h = \dfrac{50 - x^2}{4x}$.

(c) Show that if V cm³ is the volume of the box,
then $V = \dfrac{x\left(50 - x^2\right)}{4}$.

(d) Draw a graph of V against x for values of x from 0 to 7.

(e) Use your graph to estimate the value of x for which V is a maximum and hence the maximum volume of the box.

26 This is a cylinder of modelling clay.
The clay is reformed to make a sphere.
Find the radius of the sphere, giving your answer to an appropriate degree of accuracy.

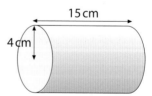

27 (a) Sketch the graph of $y = \cos \dfrac{x}{2}$ for $0° \leq x \leq 360°$.

(b) What is the period of the graph of $y = \cos \dfrac{x}{2}$?

(c) Use your sketch to help you find all the solutions to $\cos \dfrac{x}{2} = 0.5$ between $0°$ and $360°$.

28 Convert the speed $90\,\text{km/h}$ into m/s.

29 The diagram shows a triangle.
The lengths of the base and the height are $x\,\text{cm}$ and $(x-2)\,\text{cm}$.
The area of the triangle is $30\,\text{cm}^2$.

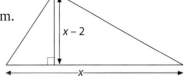

(a) Show that $x^2 - 2x - 60 = 0$.

(b) Calculate the value of x, correct to 2 d.p.

30 The diagram shows a sketch of the graph of
$$y = x^3 - 2x^2$$

(a) Give the equation of the straight line that crosses the curve at the points whose x-coordinates are the solutions of the equation
$$x^3 - 2x^2 - x + 1 = 0$$

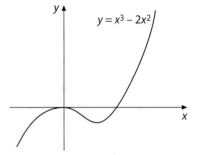

(b) Draw an accurate graph of $y = x^3 - 2x^2$ and add the graph of the straight line.
Hence find the approximate values of the solutions of $x^3 - 2x^2 - x + 1 = 0$.

(c) Use trial and improvement to find the solution between 2 and 3, correct to 2 d.p.

31 (a) Show that the curved surface area of this cone is given by the formula
$$A = \pi r \sqrt{r^2 + h^2}$$

(b) Rearrange the formula to make h the subject.

(c) When $A = 360\,\text{cm}^2$ and $r = 5.0\,\text{cm}$, calculate h to an appropriate degree of accuracy and use this value to work out the volume of the cone.

32 Solve these pairs of simultaneous equations.

(a) $y = 3x^2$
$y = 2x + 1$

(b) $y = 2x^2 - 4$
$2x + y = 20$

(c) $y = x^2 + 2$
$2x + 3y = 7$

33 This shape is the sector of a circle.
It has an area of $100\,\text{cm}^2$.
Find, to the nearest degree, the angle θ.

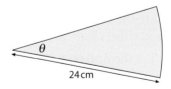

34 (a) Write $0.000\,035\,7$ in standard form.

(b) Work out $(3 \times 10^6) \times (5 \times 10^2)$, giving the result in standard form.

(c) Work out $\dfrac{4 \times 10^3}{5 \times 10^5}$, giving the result in standard form.

21 Working with rounded quantities

This work will help you

- find the lower and upper bounds for a rounded quantity, including a decimal
- find the lower and upper bounds of the result of a calculation involving rounded quantities

A Lower and upper bounds

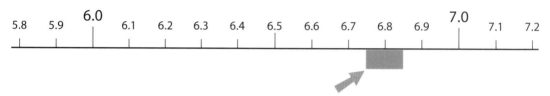

All the numbers for which 6.8 is the nearest tenth lie in this interval.

The lower bound of the interval is 6.75.
The upper bound of the interval is 6.85.

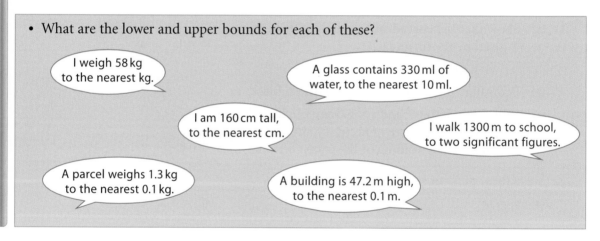

- What are the lower and upper bounds for each of these?

  I weigh 58 kg to the nearest kg.

  A glass contains 330 ml of water, to the nearest 10 ml.

  I am 160 cm tall, to the nearest cm.

  I walk 1300 m to school, to two significant figures.

  A parcel weighs 1.3 kg to the nearest 0.1 kg.

  A building is 47.2 m high, to the nearest 0.1 m.

A1 What are the lower and upper bounds of the interval containing all the numbers for which

    (a) 6.1 is the nearest tenth   **(b)** 7.0 is the nearest tenth

A2 The length of a bolt is given as 5.7 cm to two significant figures.
What are the lower and upper bounds of its actual length?

A3 The weight of a truck is 3400 kg to two significant figures.
What are the lower and upper bounds of the weight of the truck?

A4 What are the lower and upper bounds of all the numbers which give
3.28 when rounded to the nearest hundredth?

A5 Write down the lower and upper bounds for each of these.

  (a) The height of a post is 3.46 m correct to three significant figures.

  (b) The weight of a sack is 3.8 kg correct to two significant figures.

  (c) The capacity of a tank is 1530 litres correct to the nearest 10 litres.

  (d) The length of a path, to the nearest tenth of a kilometre, is 4.0 km.

  (e) The length of a pipe is 4.58 m correct to the nearest cm.

A6 The population of a town is given as 74 200, correct to the nearest hundred. What is

  (a) the maximum possible population   (b) the minimum possible population

A7 The resistance of an electrical component is given as 3.50 ohm, correct to 2 d.p. What are the upper and lower bounds of the actual resistance?

B Calculating with rounded quantities

- What is the maximum possible total length of three rods like these?

  | 3.6 m to the nearest 0.1 m | 3.6 m to the nearest 0.1 m | 3.6 m to the nearest 0.1 m |

- What is their minimum possible total length?

- What can you say about …

  (a) the total length of these rods?

  | 3.6 m to the nearest 0.1 m | 2.3 m to the nearest 0.1 m |

  (b) the perimeter of this rectangle?

  2.8 m to the nearest 0.1 m

  1.3 m to the nearest 0.1 m

  (c) the area of the rectangle?

  (d) the difference in length between these two rods?

  | 7.4 m to the nearest 0.1 m |
  | 4.2 m to the nearest 0.1 m |

  (e) the average speed of this plane?

  Distance travelled: 4284 km, to the nearest km
  Time taken: 8 hours, to the nearest hour

B1 Find the upper and lower bounds of the total weight of four bottles,
each weighing 325 g to the nearest gram.

B2 Find the upper and lower bounds of the total length of five rods,
each of length 3.9 m to two significant figures.

B3 A torch contains three batteries.
The torch itself, without batteries, weighs 86 g correct to the nearest gram.
Each battery weighs 54 g correct to the nearest gram.
Find the greatest and least possible total weights of the torch and batteries.

B4 The sides of a triangle are of length 12 cm, 17 cm and 9 cm, each correct to
the nearest centimetre.
Find the upper and lower bounds for the perimeter of the triangle.

B5 The dimensions of a cuboid, to the nearest 0.1 cm, are 7.6 cm, 9.5 cm and 12.0 cm.
Find the maximum and minimum possible values of the volume of the cuboid.

B6 In this right-angled triangle, side a is 13 cm to two significant figures
and angle θ is 43° to two significant figures.

Calculate upper and lower bounds for the height h.
Give each answer to four significant figures.

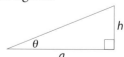

C Subtracting

Example

Saul weighed 85 kg before training and 81 kg afterwards.
Both weights are to the nearest kilogram.
Find the lower and upper bounds of his weight loss.

Before training: lower bound 84.5 kg, upper bound 85.5 kg

After training: lower bound 80.5 kg, upper bound 81.5 kg

The sketch below shows these intervals.

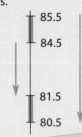

The loss would be smallest if he
went from the lowest starting weight
to the highest finishing weight.

So the lower bound of his weight loss
is 84.5 – 81.5 = **3 kg**.

The loss would be biggest if he went
from the highest starting weight to the
lowest finishing weight.

So the upper bound of his weight loss
is 85.5 – 80.5 = **5 kg**.

C1 A beaker of water weighed 426 g to the nearest gram.
After the water had been poured out, the beaker weighed 173 g to the nearest gram.
Find the lower and upper bounds of the weight of the water.

C2 A piece weighing 260 g, to two significant figures, is cut from a cheese
weighing 840 g, to two significant figures.
Find the lower and upper bounds of the weight of cheese that remains.

C3 A cable is 50 m long correct to the nearest metre.
Barrie cuts off a piece which is 15.0 m long correct to the nearest 10 cm.
Calculate the maximum length of the remaining cable.   OCR

C4 (a) Plastic bricks are made in the form of cubes.
The length of each brick is 11.3 cm, measured correct to the nearest mm.
Write down the least and greatest values of the length of a brick.

(b) The length of a shelf between two walls is 91 cm,
measured correct to the nearest cm.
Explain, showing all your calculations, why it is
not always possible to place eight bricks on the shelf.

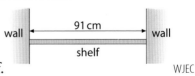

WJEC

C5 Hitesh has a reel of wire.
The wire on the reel is of length 900 cm to the nearest centimetre.

Hitesh cuts off 20 pieces of wire.
Each piece is of length 35 cm to the nearest centimetre.

Calculate the minimum and maximum possible values of
the length that is left on the reel.

Example

A runner covers 75 m (to the nearest metre) in 7 seconds (to the nearest second).
Find the lower and upper bounds for the runner's average speed.

> The lower and upper bounds for the distance are 74.5 m and 75.5 m.
> The lower and upper bounds for the time are 6.5 seconds and 7.5 seconds.
>
> The speed would be lowest if the runner covered the shortest distance in the longest time.
>
> So the lower bound of the average speed is $\frac{74.5}{7.5}$ = **9.933... m/s**.
>
> The speed would be highest if the runner covered the longest distance in the shortest time.
>
> So the upper bound of the average speed is $\frac{75.5}{6.5}$ = **11.615... m/s**.

D1 A pump delivers 3260 litres of water (to the nearest 10 litres) in 17 minutes (to the nearest minute).

Find the upper and lower bounds of the rate, in litres per minute, at which the pump is working. (Give your answers to four significant figures.)

D2 Kirstie measures the mass and volume of a piece of metal.
The mass is 141 g to the nearest gram; the volume is 18 cm^3 to the nearest cm^3.

Find the upper and lower bounds of the density of the metal in g/cm^3.
(Give your answers to four significant figures.)

D3 The magnification of a lens is given by the formula $m = \dfrac{v}{u}$.

In an experiment, u is measured as 8.5 cm and v is measured as 14.0 cm, both correct to the nearest 0.1 cm.

Find the least possible value of m.
You must show full details of your calculation

OCR

D4 The length of a rectangle is a centimetres.
Correct to two decimal places, $a = 6.37$.

(a) For this value of a, write down

    (i) the upper bound   (ii) the lower bound

Correct to one significant figure, the area of the same rectangle is 20 cm^2.

(b) Calculate the upper bound for the width of the rectangle.
Write down all the figures on your calculator display.

A diagonal of the rectangle makes an angle of $\theta°$ with one of the sides of length a cm.

(c) Calculate the upper bound for the value of $\tan \theta°$.
Write down all the figures on your calculator display.

Edexcel

Test yourself

T1 Fiona drives to work.

Each day she drives 49 miles to the nearest mile.

Calculate the least possible distance she drives in five working days. OCR

T2 A crane has a cable with a breaking strain of 5300 kg measured to two significant figures. It is used to lift crates which weigh 100 kg measured to the nearest 10 kg.

What is the greatest number of crates that can be lifted at one time so that the cable does not break? AQA

T3 A can of drink weighs 342 g to the nearest gram.

(a) What are the minimum and maximum weights of the can?

(b) The cans are sold in packs of 12.

What are the minimum and maximum weights of a pack of cans? AQA

T4 **(a)** The numbers in this calculation are given to three significant figures.

Find the least possible value of $\dfrac{12.3}{15.6 - 7.20}$.

You must show all your working.

(b) The maximum safe load of a lift is 1500 kg, to the nearest 50 kg. The lift is loaded with boxes weighing 141 kg and 150 kg, both weights given to the nearest kilogram.

Can the lift safely carry 3 boxes weighing 141 kg each and 7 boxes weighing 150 kg each?
You must show all your working. AQA

T5 The time period, T seconds, of a pendulum is calculated using the formula

$$T = 6.283 \times \sqrt{\dfrac{L}{g}}$$

where L metres is the length of the pendulum and $g\,\text{m/s}^2$ is the acceleration due to gravity.

$L = 1.36$ correct to two decimal places.
$g = 9.8$ correct to one decimal place.

Find the difference between the lower bound of T and the upper bound of T. Edexcel

T6 The radius, r, of this cone is 5.8 cm correct to two significant figures.
The volume, V, of this cone is 415 cm^3 correct to three significant figures.

Use the formula $h = \dfrac{3V}{\pi r^2}$ to find the minimum possible height of the cone.

Show your calculation clearly.

OCR

22 Using exact values

You will revise

- finding the circumference and area of a circle
- using Pythagoras's theorem

This work will help you write exact answers using terms like $\sqrt{10}$ (surds) and π, instead of changing them to approximate decimals.

A Showing π in a result

These shapes are drawn on a grid of centimetre squares.

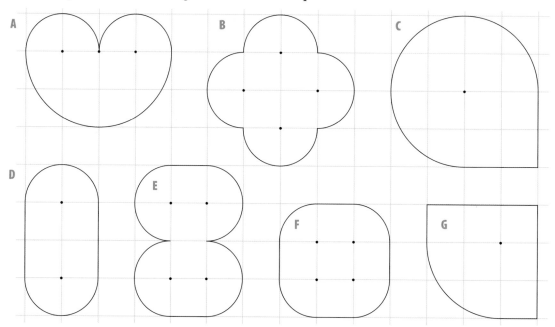

Shape A is made of two semicircles with radius 1 cm and one semicircle with radius 2 cm. Their centres are marked with dots.

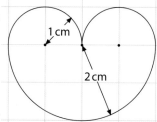

The length in centimetres of the large semicircle is

$$\tfrac{1}{2} \times 2\pi r = \tfrac{1}{2} \times 2 \times \pi \times 2 = 2\pi$$

Trying to work 2π out gives a decimal that starts as 6.283 185 307… But the decimal doesn't end or recur. It isn't equal to an exact fraction. So the only way to write this length in centimetres **exactly** is 2π.

A1 (a) Find the exact length of one small semicircle in shape A.

(b) Find the exact value of the whole perimeter of shape A.

A2 Find the exact perimeter of each of the other shapes above.

A3 (a) Find the area of one small semicircle in shape A on the opposite page. Give the exact answer, with π left in it.

(b) Find the exact area of the large semicircle in shape A.

(c) Find the exact value of the whole area of shape A.

A4 Find the exact area of all the other shapes on the opposite page.

A5 (a) What is the area of the square with the black outline?

(b) What is the exact area of the quarter circle?

(c) Write an exact expression for the area of the blue shape.

(d) Write an exact expression for the perimeter of the blue shape.

A6 For each of these shapes, find　(i) the exact area　(ii) the exact perimeter

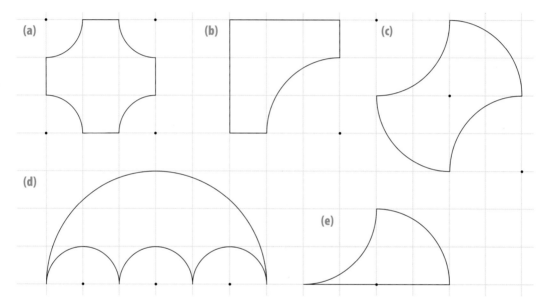

(a)

(b)

(c)

(d)

(e)

A7 Find the perimeter of this shape, keeping π in your answer.

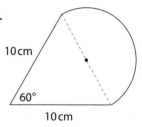

10 cm

60°

10 cm

*A8 Sketch shapes with these values.

	Perimeter (cm)	Area (cm²)
(a)	2π	2
(b)	2π	$4 - \pi$
(c)	4π	$\pi + 4$

B Showing a surd in a result

This is a right-angled triangle.

Using Pythagoras's theorem, the length in centimetres of its hypotenuse is $\sqrt{29}$.

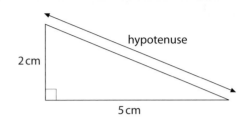

Trying to work this out gives a decimal that starts as 5.385 164 807…
But the decimal doesn't end or recur.
So the only way to write this length in centimetres **exactly** is $\sqrt{29}$.

B1 Find the length of each hypotenuse, leaving each answer as an exact value.

(a)
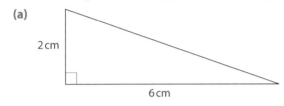

(b)
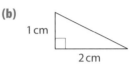

This triangle is drawn on centimetre squares.
In centimetres, the exact length of its hypotenuse is $\sqrt{10}$.
So its perimeter is $1 + 3 + \sqrt{10}$, which you can leave as the exact value $4 + \sqrt{10}$.

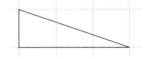

B2 This triangle is on centimetres squares.

(a) How long is AB exactly?

(b) How long is AC exactly?

(c) What is the exact perimeter of the triangle?

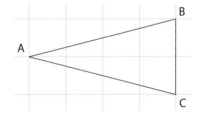

An expression that contains an exact square root, like $4 + \sqrt{10}$, is called a **surd**.
The answers to B1 and B2 are also surds.

Pythagoras spiral

How long exactly is the hypotenuse of the first triangle?

Show that the hypotenuse of the second triangle is $\sqrt{3}$ units long.

How long exactly is the hypotenuse of the fourth triangle?

If triangles continue to be added in the same way, how long exactly will be the hypotenuse of the nth triangle?

Which triangle will have a hypotenuse exactly 3 units long?

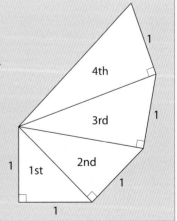

B3 Shapes P to U are drawn on a grid of centimetre squares.
By working out exact perimeters (showing your answers as surds),
sort them into pairs with the same perimeter.

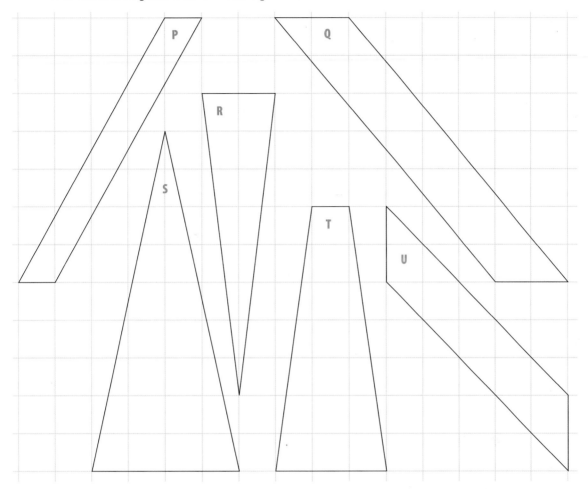

B4 Use Pythagoras to find the missing side in each of these.
They are not drawn accurately.
Leave each answer as an exact value.

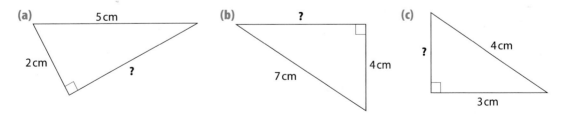

B5 Give the perimeter of each of the triangles in B4, showing your answers as surds.

B6 Calculate the area of each of the triangles in B4, showing your answers as exact values.

B7 The length of the hypotenuse of this right-angled triangle is $\sqrt{2}$.

So the sine of 45° is exactly $\dfrac{1}{\sqrt{2}}$.

As an approximate check, make sure you can get 0.707… for $1 \div \sqrt{2}$ on a calculator, and that the calculator also gives 0.707… for sin 45°.

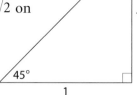

(a) Use the triangle to give an exact value for cos 45°.
Do an approximate calculator check for your answer.

(b) Give exact values for   **(i)** sin 135°   **(ii)** cos 135°

B8 This equilateral triangle has sides 2 units long.
M is the mid-point of side BC.

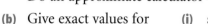

(a) Sketch the triangle replacing the question marks by values.

(b) How long is the line AM exactly (left as a surd)?
Mark this on your sketch.

(c) Use the diagram to give these exactly.

    (i) sin 60°   **(ii)** cos 60°   **(iii)** tan 60°

    (iv) sin 30°   **(v)** cos 30°   **(vi)** tan 30°

    Do a calculator check as in B7 for these answers.

(d) Give these exactly.

    (i) sin 120°   **(ii)** cos 120°   **(iii)** tan 120°   **(iv)** sin 150°   **(v)** cos 150°   **(vi)** tan 150°

(e) Calculate the area of the equilateral triangle, leaving any surds in your answer.

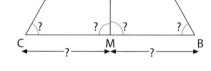

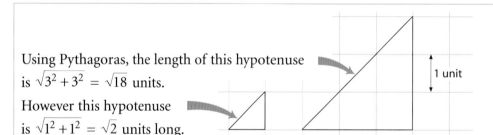

Using Pythagoras, the length of this hypotenuse is $\sqrt{3^2 + 3^2} = \sqrt{18}$ units.

However this hypotenuse is $\sqrt{1^2 + 1^2} = \sqrt{2}$ units long.

The large triangle is an enlargement with scale factor 3 of the small one, so $\sqrt{18}$ must be equal to $3\sqrt{2}$.

We can also show that $3\sqrt{2}$ is the square root of 18 by squaring it to get 18:

$(3\sqrt{2})^2 = (3\sqrt{2}) \times (3\sqrt{2}) = 3 \times \sqrt{2} \times 3 \times \sqrt{2} = 3 \times 3 \times \sqrt{2} \times \sqrt{2} = 9 \times 2 = 18$

We can also start with $\sqrt{18}$ and get $3\sqrt{2}$ like this: $\sqrt{18} = \sqrt{9 \times 2} = \sqrt{9} \times \sqrt{2} = 3\sqrt{2}$.

Another example is: $\sqrt{20} = \sqrt{4 \times 5} = \sqrt{4} \times \sqrt{5} = 2\sqrt{5}$.

B9 Use this triangle and a suitable enlargement of it to show that $\sqrt{20} = 2\sqrt{5}$.

B10 Find a suitable triangle and an enlargement of it to show that $\sqrt{160} = 4\sqrt{10}$.

C Mixed questions

C1 These shapes are drawn on a centimetre squared grid.
Find their areas and perimeters, giving exact values.

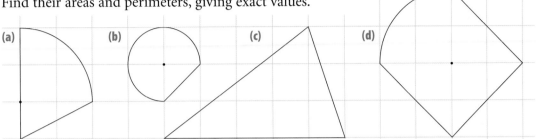

(a)   (b)   (c)   (d)

C2 The pink area is formed by two circles with the same centre.
Find the pink area exactly, in terms of a.

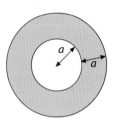

C3 Calculate the surface area of this cone, including the base.
Give your answer in terms of π.

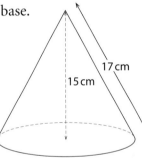

17 cm

15 cm

C4 Find the area of the shaded semicircle in terms of π.

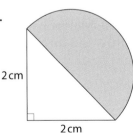

2 cm

2 cm

C5 A circle has an area of 10 square units. Find its radius in terms of π.

C6 In this right-angled triangle, $\cos a = \frac{3}{4}$.

(a) Make a sketch of the triangle and label all its sides with
possible exact lengths.

(b) Write as surds   (i) $\sin a$ (ii) $\tan a$

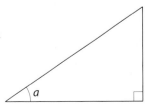

a

D Exact relationships between variables

Exact expressions for quantities can be used to find relationships between variables.

Example

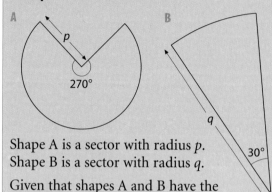

Shape A is a sector with radius p.
Shape B is a sector with radius q.

Given that shapes A and B have the same area, express q in terms of p.

Area of shape A $= \frac{3}{4}\pi p^2$

Area of shape B $= \frac{1}{12}\pi q^2$

Since the areas of the two shapes are equal,
$$\frac{3}{4}\pi p^2 = \frac{1}{12}\pi q^2$$
Multiplying both sides by 12,
$$9\pi p^2 = \pi q^2$$
Dividing both sides by π,
$$9p^2 = q^2$$
Taking the positive square root of both sides,
$$3p = q, \text{ so } q = 3p$$

D1 (a) A circle of radius r fits exactly inside a square of side $2r$.
Exactly what fraction of the square does the circle occupy?

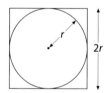

(b) A square fits exactly inside a circle of radius r.
Exactly what fraction of the circle does the square occupy?

D2 The cone and cylinder have the same radius, r, and the same volume.
How are the heights a and b related?

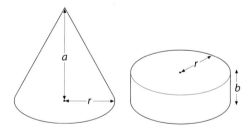

D3 A sphere has a surface area of 25π square units.

(a) What is its radius?　　　　　**(b)** What is its volume, exactly?

D4 A solid sphere of radius r fits inside a cylindrical space that has radius r and height $2r$.
Exactly what fraction of the cylinder's volume does the sphere occupy?

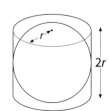

D5 A cylinder has radius y and height $5y$.

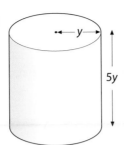

A sphere has radius r.

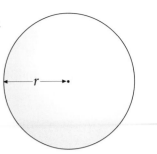

The total surface area of the cylinder is equal to the surface area of the sphere.

(a) Show that $r^2 = 3y^2$.

(b) Find the value of y when $r = 6$, giving your answer in the form $a\sqrt{b}$.

Test yourself

T1 Find the missing lengths, leaving your answers as exact values.

(a)

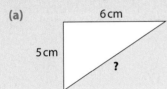

(b)

12 cm
?
11 cm

T2 These shapes are drawn on centimetre squares with centres of arcs shown by dots.
Find their areas and perimeters, giving exact values.

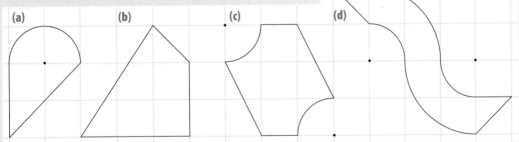

(a)   **(b)**   **(c)**   **(d)**

T3 Given that $\tan x = 3$, write exact values for $\sin x$ and $\cos x$.

T4 A semicircle of radius 3 cm has the same area as a circle of radius a cm.
Find the exact value of a.

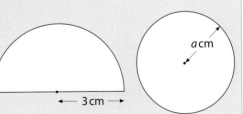

a cm

3 cm

T5 A cone has height 12 cm and volume 196 cm³.
Find, in terms of π, the diameter of its base.

23 Fractional indices

This work will help you understand and evaluate expressions that use fractional indices.

A Review: positive and negative indices

Rules and definitions

$$a^m \times a^n = a^{m+n} \qquad \frac{a^m}{a^n} = a^{m-n} \qquad (a^m)^n = a^{mn} \qquad a^0 = 1 \qquad a^{-n} = \frac{1}{a^n}$$

A1 Write each of these as a single power of 5.

(a) $5^3 \times 5^4$　　(b) 5×5^5　　(c) $\frac{5^7}{5^3}$　　(d) $(5^4)^3$　　(e) $(5^{-4})^2$

A2 Evaluate each of these as an integer or a fraction.

(a) 8^{-1}　　(b) 3^3　　(c) 3^{-3}　　(d) $\left(\frac{2}{3}\right)^3$　　(e) $\left(\frac{1}{2}\right)^{-3}$

A3 Write each of these as a single power of 2.

(a) 8　　(b) $\frac{1}{8}$　　(c) $\frac{1}{32}$　　(d) $\left(\frac{1}{2}\right)^4$　　(e) $\left(\frac{1}{4}\right)^3$

A4 Find the value of n in each of these equations.

(a) $3^n = 9$　　(b) $2^n = 64$　　(c) $6^n = 1$　　(d) $7^n = \frac{1}{7}$

(e) $4^n = \frac{1}{16}$　　(f) $\left(\frac{1}{3}\right)^n = \frac{1}{27}$　　(g) $3^{n+1} = 81$　　(h) $2^{3n} = 64$

B Roots

$\sqrt{a}$ is the positive square root of a.　　For example, $\sqrt{9} = 3$ because $3^2 = 9$.
$\sqrt[3]{a}$ is the cube root of a.　　For example, $\sqrt[3]{125} = 5$ because $5^3 = 125$.

B1 Evaluate each of these as an integer or a fraction.

(a) $\sqrt[3]{64}$　　(b) $\sqrt{\frac{1}{4}}$　　(c) $\sqrt[3]{1}$　　(d) $\sqrt[3]{\frac{1}{8}}$　　(e) $\sqrt[3]{\frac{8}{27}}$

The notation and ideas extend to fourth roots, fifth roots, and so on.
$\sqrt[4]{a}$ is the positive fourth root of a.　　For example, $\sqrt[4]{81} = 3$ because $3^4 = 81$.
$\sqrt[5]{a}$ is the fifth root of a.　　For example, $\sqrt[5]{32} = 2$ because $2^5 = 32$.

B2 Evaluate each of these as an integer or a fraction.

(a) $\sqrt[4]{16}$　　(b) $\sqrt[4]{1}$　　(c) $\sqrt[4]{\frac{1}{81}}$　　(d) $\sqrt[5]{243}$　　(e) $\sqrt[5]{\frac{1}{32}}$

$\sqrt[n]{a}$ is the nth root of a: if $a = x^n$ then $x = \sqrt[n]{a}$.

For example, the sixth root of 729 is 3 because $3^6 = 729$.

This is written as $\sqrt[6]{729} = 3$.

B3 Evaluate $\sqrt[6]{\frac{1}{729}}$ as a fraction.

B4 What is the value of $\sqrt[7]{128}$?

C Fractional indices of the form 1/*n* or ⁻1/*n*

Waterweed is growing in a lake.
The area covered by the weed doubles
during the course of each year.
It covers $1\,\text{km}^2$ when measurement starts.

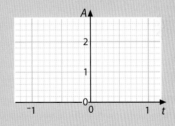

Time (years)

0   1   2   3

$1\,\text{km}^2$ $2\,\text{km}^2$ $4\,\text{km}^2$ $8\,\text{km}^2$

The growth is shown in the table below.
The table can be extended backwards to show
the area at time ⁻1 (one year before 0), ⁻2, ⁻3, and so on.

Time, t years	⁻3	⁻2	⁻1	0	1	2	3
Area, $A\,\text{km}^2$				1	2	4	8

- Copy and complete the table to show the values of A when $t = $ ⁻1, ⁻2 and ⁻3.

- What is the formula connecting A and t?

- Plot the values from the table on graph paper.
  Suitable scales are shown here.

- Suppose the area grows continuously.
  Draw a smooth curve through the plotted points.

- Assume that the formula connecting A and t is true
  for all values of t, including fractions.
  What value does the graph give for $2^{\frac{1}{2}}$?

- Use the rules of indices to copy and complete $2^{\frac{1}{2}} \times 2^{\frac{1}{2}} = 2^{\blacksquare}$.
  What do you think $2^{\frac{1}{2}}$ means?

- What value does the graph give for $2^{-\frac{1}{2}}$?
  What do you think $2^{-\frac{1}{2}}$ means?

- What value does the graph give for $2^{\frac{1}{4}}$?
  What do you think $2^{\frac{1}{4}}$ means?

$a^{\frac{1}{2}}$ must be $\sqrt{a}$ by the rules of indices: $a^{\frac{1}{2}} \times a^{\frac{1}{2}} = a^{\frac{1}{2}+\frac{1}{2}} = a^1 = a$ so $a^{\frac{1}{2}} = \sqrt{a}$.

Also $a^{-\frac{1}{2}} = \dfrac{1}{a^{\frac{1}{2}}} = \dfrac{1}{\sqrt{a}}$.

C1 Evaluate each of these as an integer or a fraction.

    (a) $9^{\frac{1}{2}}$ **(b)** $25^{\frac{1}{2}}$ **(c)** $\left(\frac{1}{16}\right)^{\frac{1}{2}}$ **(d)** $100^{-\frac{1}{2}}$ **(e)** $\left(\frac{1}{9}\right)^{-\frac{1}{2}}$

C2 (a) Use the rules of indices to simplify $5^{\frac{1}{3}} \times 5^{\frac{1}{3}} \times 5^{\frac{1}{3}}$.

    (b) What does $5^{\frac{1}{3}}$ mean?

C3 (a) Use the rules of indices to simplify $81^{\frac{1}{4}} \times 81^{\frac{1}{4}} \times 81^{\frac{1}{4}} \times 81^{\frac{1}{4}}$.

    (b) What does $81^{\frac{1}{4}}$ mean?

$a^{\frac{1}{n}}$ must be $\sqrt[n]{a}$ by the rules of indices: $\left(a^{\frac{1}{n}}\right)^n = a^{\frac{1}{n} \times n} = a^1 = a$ so $a^{\frac{1}{n}} = \sqrt[n]{a}$.

Also $a^{-\frac{1}{n}} = \dfrac{1}{a^{\frac{1}{n}}} = \dfrac{1}{\sqrt[n]{a}}$.

C4 (a) Write $\sqrt{3}$ as a power of 3.   **(b)** Write $\sqrt[4]{5}$ as a power of 5.

C5 (a) Find the value of each of these.

    (i) $27^{\frac{1}{3}}$ **(ii)** $125^{\frac{1}{3}}$ **(iii)** $1000^{\frac{1}{3}}$

    (b) What is the value of each of these as a fraction?

    (i) $27^{-\frac{1}{3}}$ **(ii)** $125^{-\frac{1}{3}}$ **(iii)** $8^{-\frac{1}{3}}$

C6 What is the value of each of these as an integer or a fraction?

    (a) $16^{\frac{1}{4}}$ **(b)** $16^{-\frac{1}{4}}$ **(c)** $32^{\frac{1}{5}}$ **(d)** $32^{-\frac{1}{5}}$ **(e)** $625^{\frac{1}{4}}$

    (f) $1000^{-\frac{1}{3}}$ **(g)** $\left(\frac{1}{8}\right)^{\frac{1}{3}}$ **(h)** $\left(\frac{1}{81}\right)^{\frac{1}{4}}$ **(i)** $\left(\frac{1}{25}\right)^{-\frac{1}{2}}$ **(j)** $\left(\frac{1}{32}\right)^{-\frac{1}{5}}$

C7 Simplify each of these as an integer or a fraction.

    (a) $7^{-1} \times 49^{\frac{1}{2}}$ **(b)** $144^{\frac{1}{2}} \times 3^{-2}$ **(c)** $36^{-\frac{1}{2}} \times 4^2$ **(d)** $\left(36^{\frac{1}{2}}\right)^3 \times 144^{-\frac{1}{2}}$

C8 Solve each of these equations.

    (a) $9^n = 3$ **(b)** $8^n = 2$ **(c)** $27^n = \frac{1}{3}$ **(d)** $\left(\frac{1}{9}\right)^n = \frac{1}{3}$ **(e)** $\left(\frac{1}{9}\right)^n = 3$

C9 Write each of these as a power of 64.

    (a) 8   **(b)** 2   **(c)** 1   **(d)** $\frac{1}{8}$ **(e)** $\frac{1}{4}$

C10 Write $\frac{1}{3}$ as a power of 81.

*C11 Write 27 as a power of 81.

D Fractional indices of the form p/q or $^-p/q$

⊠ **D1** (a) Copy and complete: $27^{\frac{2}{3}} = (27^{\blacksquare})^2 = \blacksquare^2$.　　　(b) Hence evaluate $27^{\frac{2}{3}}$ as an integer.

In general, $a^{\frac{p}{q}} = \left(a^{\frac{1}{q}}\right)^p = \left(\sqrt[q]{a}\right)^p$.

Examples

Find the value of $125^{\frac{2}{3}}$.

$$125^{\frac{2}{3}} = \left(125^{\frac{1}{3}}\right)^2 = \left(\sqrt[3]{125}\right)^2 = 5^2 = 25$$

Find the value of $32^{-\frac{3}{5}}$.

$$32^{-\frac{3}{5}} = \frac{1}{32^{\frac{3}{5}}} = \frac{1}{\left(32^{\frac{1}{5}}\right)^3} = \frac{1}{\left(\sqrt[5]{32}\right)^3} = \frac{1}{2^3} = \frac{1}{8}$$

⊠ **D2** Find the value of each of these.

(a) $8^{\frac{2}{3}}$ 　　(b) $9^{\frac{3}{2}}$ 　　(c) $16^{\frac{3}{4}}$ 　　(d) $1000^{\frac{2}{3}}$ 　　(e) $25^{\frac{3}{2}}$

(f) $27^{-\frac{2}{3}}$ 　　(g) $16^{-\frac{3}{2}}$ 　　(h) $9^{-\frac{3}{2}}$ 　　(i) $64^{-\frac{2}{3}}$ 　　(j) $16^{-\frac{3}{4}}$

(k) $\left(\frac{1}{8}\right)^{\frac{2}{3}}$ 　　(l) $\left(\frac{1}{16}\right)^{\frac{3}{2}}$ 　　(m) $\left(\frac{4}{9}\right)^{\frac{3}{2}}$ 　　(n) $\left(\frac{1}{81}\right)^{-\frac{3}{4}}$ 　　(o) $\left(\frac{8}{125}\right)^{-\frac{2}{3}}$

You can use the rules of indices to write some expressions as single powers.

Examples

Write $\dfrac{4}{\sqrt[3]{2}}$ as a power of 2.

$$\frac{4}{\sqrt[3]{2}} = \frac{2^2}{2^{\frac{1}{3}}} = 2^{2-\frac{1}{3}} = 2^{1\frac{2}{3}} = 2^{\frac{5}{3}}$$

> We usually write indices that are mixed numbers as 'top-heavy' fractions. Here, we write $1\frac{2}{3}$ as $\frac{5}{3}$.

Write $\sqrt{27}$ as a power of 3.

$$\sqrt{27} = \sqrt{3^3} = (3^3)^{\frac{1}{2}} = 3^{3 \times \frac{1}{2}} = 3^{\frac{3}{2}}$$

D3 Copy and complete: $8\sqrt{2} = 2^{\blacksquare} \times 2^{\frac{1}{2}} = 2^{\blacksquare}$.

D4 Write each of these as a power of 2.

(a) $4\sqrt{2}$ 　　(b) $4\sqrt[3]{2}$ 　　(c) $(\sqrt{2})^3$ 　　(d) $\dfrac{16}{\sqrt{2}}$ 　　(e) $\dfrac{\sqrt{2}}{4}$

(f) $(\sqrt[3]{2})^{-2}$ 　　(g) $\dfrac{\sqrt[3]{2}}{4}$ 　　(h) $\left(\dfrac{1}{\sqrt[3]{2}}\right)^{-2}$ 　　(i) $\dfrac{(\sqrt[3]{2})^2}{2}$ 　　(j) $\dfrac{\sqrt{2}}{\sqrt[3]{2}}$

D5 Write each of these as a power of 2.

(a) $\sqrt{8}$ 　　(b) $\sqrt{32}$ 　　(c) $\sqrt[3]{16}$ 　　(d) $\sqrt[4]{8}$ 　　(e) $\dfrac{1}{\sqrt[5]{4}}$

D6 Find the value of n in each statement.

(a) $9\sqrt{27} = 3^n$ 　　(b) $5\sqrt{n} = 5^{\frac{3}{2}}$ 　　(c) $2\sqrt{n} = 2^{\frac{7}{2}}$ 　　(d) $4\sqrt{n} = 2^{-\frac{1}{2}}$

D7 Solve each of these equations.

(a) $4^x = 32$ 　　(b) $8^x = 16$ 　　(c) $4^n = \sqrt{2}$ 　　(d) $8^k = \frac{1}{4}$ 　　(e) $27^y = 81^{\frac{1}{2}}$

E Powers and roots on a calculator

- The key for calculating powers may be labelled x^y or $\wedge$.

  To work out $5^{0.3}$ you do $\boxed{5}$ $\boxed{x^y}$ $\boxed{0}$ $\boxed{\cdot}$ $\boxed{3}$ or $\boxed{5}$ $\boxed{\wedge}$ $\boxed{0}$ $\boxed{\cdot}$ $\boxed{3}$

- $\sqrt[5]{7}$ as a power is $7^{\frac{1}{5}}$.

  So you use the power key to find $\sqrt[5]{7}$ like this: $\boxed{7}$ $\boxed{x^y}$ $\boxed{(}$ $\boxed{1}$ $\boxed{\div}$ $\boxed{5}$ $\boxed{)}$

  Alternatively, your calculator may have a key labelled $\boxed{x^{\frac{1}{y}}}$ or $\boxed{\sqrt[x]{}}$.

E1 Use a calculator to find the following, to four significant figures.

   (a) $15^{0.5}$ (b) $2^{\frac{1}{5}}$ (c) $\sqrt[4]{10}$ (d) $3.5^{2.8}$ (e) $0.8^{\frac{3}{4}}$

E2 The Indian mathematician Ramanujan discovered that $\left(\frac{2143}{22}\right)^{\frac{1}{4}}$ is a good approximation for π. How close is it to your calculator value of π?

E3 Solve these equations.
Give each result to four significant figures.

   (a) $x^4 = 20$ (b) $x^{10} = 100$ (c) $x^7 = 250$ (d) $2x^8 = 100$ (e) $x^{0.2} = 4.5$

Test yourself

T1 (a) Find the value of $64^{\frac{1}{3}}$.   (b) Find the value of $8x^0$.   AQA

T2 Simplify each of the following.   (a) $16^{\frac{3}{4}}$ (b) $9^{-\frac{1}{2}}$ WJEC

T3 Work out the value of $16^{\frac{3}{2}}$.

T4 (a) Write down the value of 11^0.
   (b) Find the value of $8^{\frac{2}{3}}$.
   (c) Simplify $6^{-2} \times 144^{0.5}$.   AQA

T5 Find the value of $\left(\frac{27}{125}\right)^{-\frac{1}{3}}$.   Edexcel

T6 (a) Find the value of
      (i) 64^0 (ii) $64^{\frac{1}{2}}$ (iii) $64^{-\frac{2}{3}}$
   (b) $3 \times \sqrt{27} = 3^n$. Find the value of n.   Edexcel

T7 (a) (i) Evaluate $13z^0$.   (ii) Evaluate $(13z)^0$.
   (b) If $3^x = \frac{1}{27}$, find the value of x.
   (c) If $4^y = 64^{\frac{1}{2}}$, find the value of y.   AQA

24 Exponential growth and decay

This work will help you understand exponential growth and decay.

In section A you need a graphic calculator or a graph plotting facility on a computer.

A Exponential growth

The population, P, of a colony of animals is increasing by 35% every year. When the population is first counted it is 500.

After 1 year P is 500×1.35, after 2 years it is $500 \times 1.35 \times 1.35$, and so on.

The equation for P in terms of t is $P = 500 \times 1.35^t$, where t is the time in years since the population was first counted.

A function of t in which t appears as a power is called an **exponential function**. ('Exponent' is another word for 'power'.)

This is the graph of P against t.

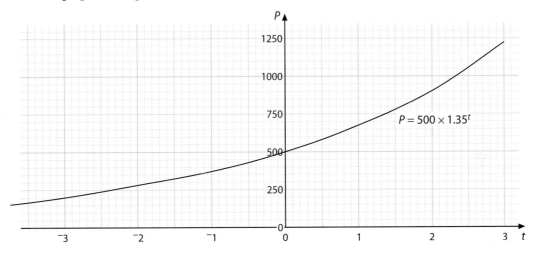

A1 (a) Use the equation $P = 500 \times 1.35^t$ to calculate the value of P when $t = 2.5$. Use the graph above to check this result.

(b) Calculate P when $t = {}^-1.8$ and check that your result agrees with the graph.

A2 The area, $A\,\mathrm{m}^2$, of a mouldy patch on a wall is given by the formula $A = 6.5 \times 1.05^t$, where t is the time in weeks since the first measurement.

(a) What was the area of the patch when first measured?

(b) By what percentage does the area increase each week?

(c) Calculate, to two significant figures, the area after $4\frac{1}{2}$ weeks.

(d) Calculate, to two significant figures, A when $t = {}^-2$. What does this result tell you?

A3 The population, P, of a city is predicted to rise by 9% each year during the next five years. The population now is 247 000.

(a) Write down the formula for the value of P after t years.

(b) Copy and complete this table.

Time, t years	0	1	2	3	4	5
Population, P	247 000					

(c) Draw a graph of P against t.

(d) From the graph, estimate the value of t for which $P = 300\,000$.

(e) Substitute this value of t into the formula for P and check that it is approximately correct.

A4 The population of a colony of micro-organisms grows at a rate of 15% per hour. The population is measured as 2600 to start with.

(a) Write down an expression for the population after t hours.

(b) Calculate the population $3\frac{1}{2}$ hours after the first measurement.

A5 A sum of money invested on March 1st 1995 has increased by 4.5% each year. On March 1st 2005 the investment was worth £13 200.24. Calculate, to the nearest pound, how much was invested in 1995.

OCR

A6 The population of a country grows at a rate of 2% each year. Show that it will double in 35 years.

A7 (a) Use a graph plotter to investigate graphs that have equations of the form $y = k^x$ for positive values of k. Include fractional values of k such as $k = \frac{1}{2}$.

(b) What does the value of k tell you about the graph?

(c) What is the y-intercept of each graph? Prove that all these graphs have the same y-intercept.

(d) What happens when you try a negative value for k? Can you explain this?

(e) What do you think graphs of the form $y = k^{-x}$ will look like?

B Exponential decay

When a quantity grows exponentially, it is multiplied by the same number in equal periods of time. The multiplier is greater than 1.

When the multiplier is less than 1, we get **exponential decay**.

For example, suppose a population of insects decreases by 6% every year.

The population is multiplied by 0.94 every year. In t years it is multiplied by 0.94^t.

B1 The population of a town is 24 300 now. The population decreases by 4% every year.

(a) Calculate, to three significant figures, the population 4 years from now.

(b) If P is the population after t years, write down the equation connecting P and t.

(c) Assuming the population has been decreasing at the same rate in the past, calculate the population 2 years ago.

B2 Which of these sketch graphs shows exponential decay? Give reasons for your choice.

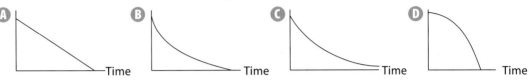

B3 It has been observed that the population of a particular snail is dropping by 8% each year.

At the start of the observation the snail population was 10 000.

(a) Copy and complete this table for the population.

Time, t years	0	1	2	3	4	5	6
Population, P	10 000						

(b) Draw the graph of P against t.

(c) From the graph, how long will it be before the snail population has fallen by 30%?

(d) Calculate how many snails there were 2 years before the observation started.

(e) What is the equation connecting P and t?

B4 At the start of 2005, the population of a village was 4500.
After t years, the population, P, of the village is given by $P = 4500 \times 0.95^t$.

(a) By what percentage does the population change each year?

(b) In which year will the population be half of that in 2005?

Test yourself

T1 (a) Draw a graph of $y = 2^x$ for values of x from $^-3$ to 3.

(b) Use your graph to estimate the positive solution to the equation
$2^x - x = 3$, correct to one decimal place. OCR

T2 Bill invests £500 on 1st January 2004 at a compound interest rate of R% per annum. The value, £V, of this investment after n years is given by the formula

$V = 500 \times (1.045)^n$

(a) Write down the value of R.

(b) Use your calculator to find the value of Bill's investment after 20 years. Edexcel

25 Angle properties of a circle

This work will help you understand

- **what is meant by proving a statement**

- **the relationships between angles connected with a circle, and how they are proved**

You need an angle measurer in section B.

A Angles of a triangle

It is a well-known fact that the angles of a triangle add up to 180°.

But how can we be sure that this is true for all triangles?
We could draw some triangles and measure their angles accurately.
But we could never draw every possible triangle.
And in any case, we can never be absolutely accurate in measuring.

In mathematics, we try to **prove** that statements are true.
Proving a statement means showing that it follows from other statements
which are already known to be true.

For example, suppose these three statements are known to be true:

> It is impossible to get from London to Birmingham in less than an hour.
> Stanley's offices in Birmingham were broken into between 5:15 p.m. and 5:45 p.m.
> Pete was in London at 5 p.m.

- Does it follow that Pete did not break into Stanley's offices?

Proving that the angles of a triangle add up to 180°

We shall assume for the moment that these three statements are known to be true.
They are labelled **a** (for 'assumption').

a Angles on a straight line add up to 180°.	**a** Corresponding angles made with parallel lines are equal.	**a** Alternate angles made with parallel lines are equal.

This diagram shows a triangle ABC.

Side AC has been extended to D.
Line CE has been drawn parallel to AB.

- Which other angle is equal to *x*, and why?

- Which other angle is equal to *y*, and why?

- Explain why the three angles of triangle ABC add up to 180°.

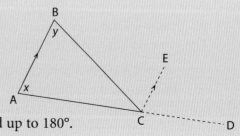

The proof on the previous page depends on drawing – or 'constructing' –
extra lines on the original diagram.
Finding a suitable construction is often the key to proving a statement.

If one side of a triangle is extended, the angle formed
is called an **exterior angle** of the triangle.

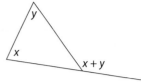

In the diagram at the foot of the previous page, the
exterior angle BCD is proved to be equal to $x + y$.

This property of a triangle is usually stated as follows (the **p** shows it has been proved):

   p **An exterior angle of a triangle is equal to the sum of the other two interior angles.**

We shall assume for the moment that this statement is also known to be true:

   a In an isosceles triangle, the angles opposite the equal sides are equal.

(In fact you will meet a proof of this in chapter 29.)

A1 Find the value of each letter.
Explain your method in each case.

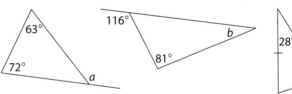

A2 Use the fact that the angles of a triangle add up to 180° to prove that
the angles of a quadrilateral add up to 360°.

B Angles in a circle

Draw a circle, radius about 5 cm.

Mark two points A, B on it and join them
to the centre, O.

Mark a point P on the circle. Join A and B to P.

• Measure angles AOB and APB.

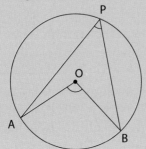

Choose different positions for A and B
and repeat.

Include cases where angle AOB is reflex.

• Collect everyone's results together.
  What do you notice?

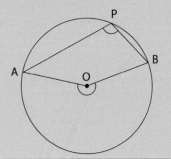

B1 It may help to sketch this diagram and write in each value you find. Line PO has been drawn and extended to C.

(a) What kind of triangle are triangles POA and POB?

(b) What is the size of angle OAP?

(c) Use the exterior angle property with triangle OAP to find the size of angle AOC.

(d) What is the size of angle OBP?

(e) What is the size of angle BOC?

(f) What is the size of angle AOB?
Do you notice any connection between angles APB and AOB?

B2 Repeat B1 but with angle OPA = 40° and angle OPB = 45°.
How is angle APB related to angle AOB now?

B3 (a) Write an expression for angle OAP here.

(b) Write an expression for angle AOC.

(c) What can you say about angle BOC?

(d) Explain why angle AOB is twice angle APB.

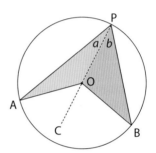

In B3 you proved this fact:

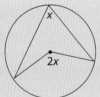

p Angle at centre = twice angle at circumference

In this proof it was assumed that

a All radii of a circle are equal.

This is, of course, how a circle is defined.

B4 Find the angles marked with letters.

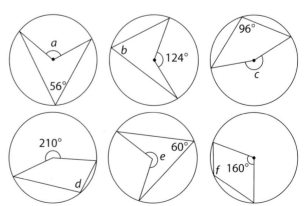

B5 In this diagram AOB is a diameter of the circle.

    (a) What is the size of the marked angle AOB?

    (b) Explain why angle APB is a right angle.

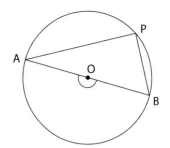

In B5 you proved this:

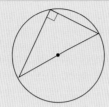

p The angle in a semicircle is a right angle.

B6 In the diagram here, imagine that A and B are fixed, but that P moves on the circle between A and B.

P$_1$ and P$_2$ are two possible positions of P.

Explain why angles AP$_1$B and AP$_2$B are equal.

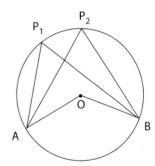

In B6 you proved this:

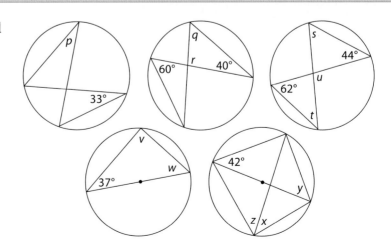

p Angles in same segment are equal.
(The shaded part is called a **segment** of the circle.)

B7 Find the angles marked with letters.

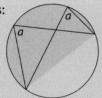

C Angles of a cyclic quadrilateral

Quadrilateral ABCD, whose vertices are all on a circle, is called a **cyclic quadrilateral** ('cyclic quad' for short).

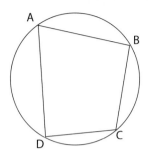

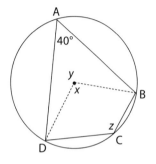

C1 In the diagram on the left, vertices B and D of the cyclic quad have been joined to the centre of the circle, making angles x and y at the centre.

(a) Work out angles x, y and z giving the reasons.

(b) Suppose angle BAD were 50° instead of 40°. Work out x, y and z in this case.

(c) Now repeat for when angle BAD is 60°.

(d) Do you notice any connection between angles BAD and BCD?

C2 In this diagram, vertices B and D of the cyclic quad have been joined to the centre of the circle, making angles x and y at the centre.

(a) State the relationship between angles x and a.

(b) State the relationship between angles y and b.

(c) State the relationship between angles x and y.

(d) From what you have stated, deduce the relationship between angles a and b.

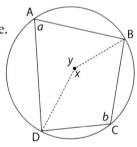

In C2 you proved this:

p Opposite angles a, b of a cyclic quadrilateral add up to 180°.

C3 Here side DC has been extended.
The angle marked e is an exterior angle of the cyclic quad.

From the result you got in C2, deduce the relationship between angles e and a.

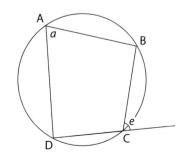

In C3 you proved this:

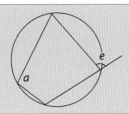

p Exterior angle *e* of a cyclic quadrilateral = opposite interior angle *a*

C4 Calculate angles *a*, *b*, *c*, …

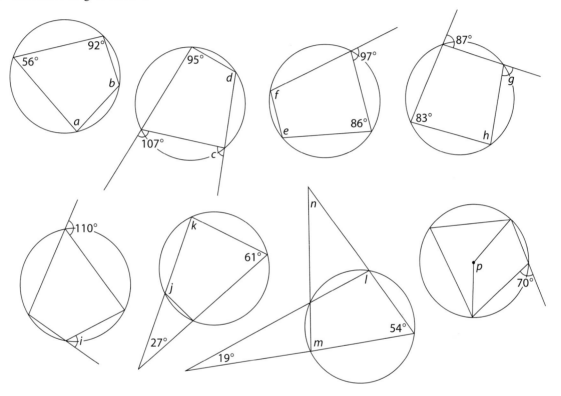

C5 Two sides of this cyclic quad are parallel, so it is a trapezium.

(a) Use your knowledge of angles with parallel lines to find the size of angle BCD.

(b) Use the fact that this is a cyclic quad to find the size of angle ADC.

(c) What is the size of angle DAB?

(d) What special property does this trapezium have?

(e) Explain why every cyclic quad that is a trapezium will have this special property.

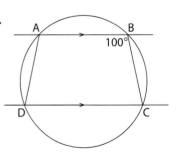

C6 A kite is drawn that is a cyclic quad.
What can you say about its two equal angles?

Example

Calculate the obtuse angle POQ, giving the reason for each step of working.

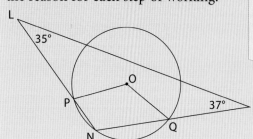

angle PNQ = 180° – 35° – 37° (angle sum of triangle LNM)
    = 108°
reflex angle POQ = 216° (twice angle at circumference)
obtuse angle POQ = 360° – 216° (angles round a point)
    = 144°

C7 In each of the following, give the reason for each step of working.

(a) Calculate angle ADB.

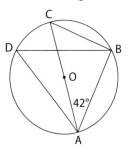

(b) Calculate angle BAC.

(c) Calculate angles LNM and LOM.

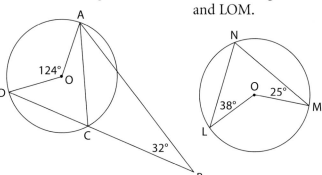

(d) Calculate *a*, *b* and *c*.

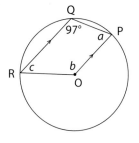

(e) Calculate *l*.

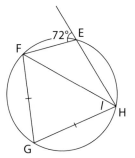

(f) Calculate *h*.

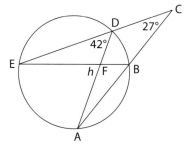

C8 (a) Find angle BEF, giving reasons for your answer.

(b) Explain why lines CD and EF are parallel, no matter what the size of angle BCG.

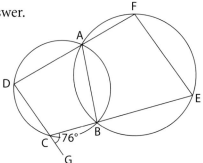

D Tangent to a circle

A **tangent** is a line that touches a circle at one point only.

We will assume that this statement is known to be true:

    a A tangent is perpendicular to the radius at the point of contact.

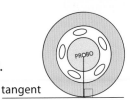

Think of a wheel touching horizontal ground.
The centre of the wheel is vertically above the point of contact,
so the radius is at right angles to the horizontal tangent.

If the entire diagram is rotated it will make no difference
to the fact that the angle is a right angle.

tangent

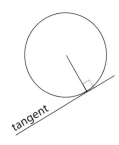

tangent

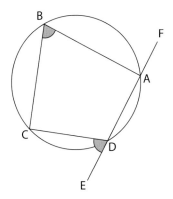

This diagram shows a cyclic quad ABCD.
Side AD has been extended in both directions to make line EF.

Exterior angle CDE is equal to opposite interior angle CBA.

Imagine that point D moves
along the circle towards A.

The orange angles stay equal.

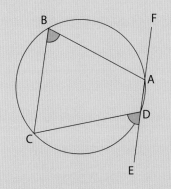

When D coincides with A, line EF will be the tangent at A.

The orange angle CAE is the angle between the tangent
and the chord CA.

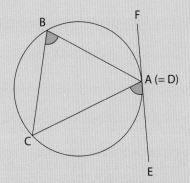

The orange angle CBA is called the angle in the
'alternate segment' (the segment on the other side of
the chord from the orange angle CAE).

The result on the previous page is usually stated as

The angle between tangent and chord is equal to the angle in the alternate segment.

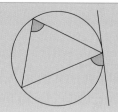

D1 Each of these question parts involves a tangent to a circle.
In each case, give the reason for each step of working.

(a) Find angle LKN.

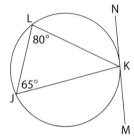

(b) Find angle QPR.

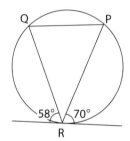

(c) Find angle ADE.

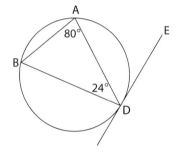

(d) Find angle QRS.

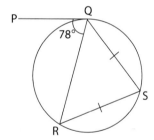

(e) Find angle DEB.

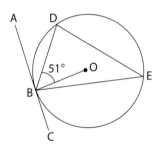

(f) Find angle TQU.

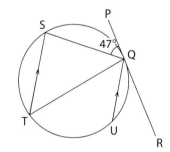

(g) Find angles BDF and DFE.

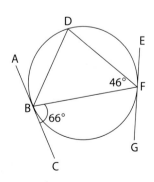

(h) Find angle QSR.

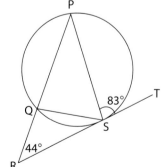

(i) Find angle STU.

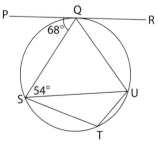

D2 Proving the 'alternate segment' statement

In this diagram, TA is the tangent to the circle at A,
AB is a chord, and angle ACB is in the 'alternate segment'
to angle TAB.

Extra lines have been drawn from A and B to the centre O.

Let x be the size of angle TAB.

We need to prove that angle ACB = x.

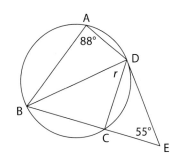

(a) Explain why the angles marked y are equal.

(b) Explain why $x + y = 90°$.

(c) Find an expression for angle AOB in terms of y, giving the reason.

(d) Find an expression for angle ACB in terms of y, giving the reason.

(e) Hence explain why angle ACB = x.

A geometry program can be set up to demonstrate equal angles in the same
segment, the properties of cyclic quadrilaterals and the alternate segment
property, as the user moves points around a circle.

This is a good way of demonstrating these properties – and spotting other
relationships that seem to be true – but it is not the same as proving them.

E Mixed questions

E1 Find the value of each letter.

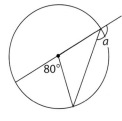   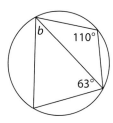   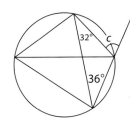   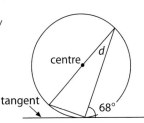

*E2 Find the value of each letter.

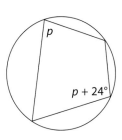   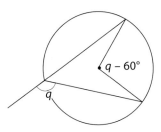

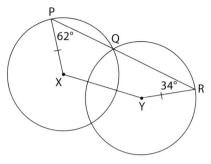

*E3 X and Y are the centres of two circles of equal radius.
PQR is a straight line.
Q is a point on both circles.

Calculate angles PXY and RYX, showing your method.

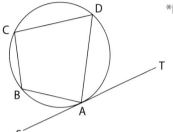

*E4 A, B, C, D are four points on a circle.
The line SAT is the tangent to the circle at A.

Explain why

    angle SAB + angle TAD = angle BCD

In this chapter you have seen statements that are not obvious (like the one about the angle in the alternate segment) **deduced** (proved) in a series of steps from assumptions that many people would accept as obviously true (such as that corresponding angles made with parallel lines are equal).

There is often a question whether the number of assumed facts can be reduced by starting 'further back' with an even simpler set of assumptions. For example, see whether you can remove the need to assume the alternate angles property by deducing it from the corresponding angles property and the fact that angles on a straight line add up to 180°.

The assumed facts in a deductive system are called **axioms**.
A statement that can be proved from the axioms is called a **theorem**.

There is more about proof in chapters 29 and 30; chapter 29 includes some further circle properties.

Test yourself

T1 A, B and C are points on the circumference of a circle, with centre O.

  (a) Find angle AOC.

  (b) Give a reason for your answer.

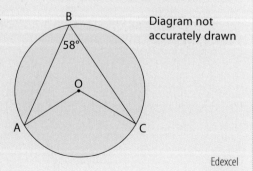

Diagram not accurately drawn

Edexcel

T2 Find the value of each letter.

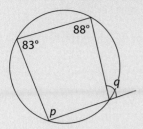 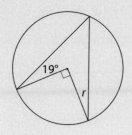 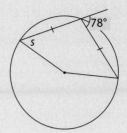

T3 Each of these diagrams includes a tangent to the circle.

Find the angles *e*, *f* and *g*, giving reasons for your answers.

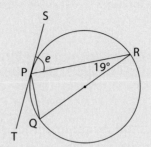 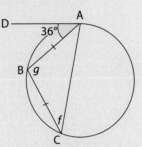

T4 A, B, C and D are four points on the circumference of a circle.

TA is the tangent to the circle at A.

Angle DAT = 30°.
Angle ADC = 132°.

(a) (i) Calculate the size of angle ABC.

    (ii) Explain your method.

(b) (i) Calculate the size of angle CBD.

    (ii) Explain your method.

(c) Explain why AC cannot be a diameter of the circle.

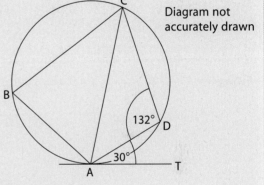

Diagram not accurately drawn

Edexcel

T5 A, B, C and D are four points on the circumference of a circle centre O. AC is a straight line passing through the centre of the circle.

The tangent PT meets the circle at D.

Given that angle AOD = 62°, find each of the following angles. Give reasons for your answers.

(a) Angle ABD   (b) Angle ADC

(c) Angle CAD   (d) Angle CDP

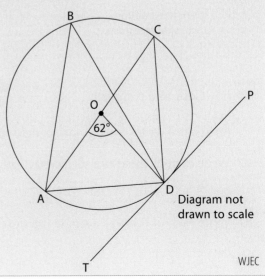

Diagram not drawn to scale

WJEC

26 Algebraic fractions and equations 2

You should know how to solve a quadratic equation by factorising or by using the formula.

This work will help you

- add and subtract algebraic fractions

- solve equations such as $\dfrac{x}{x+1} - \dfrac{3}{x-2} = 2$

- change the subject of formulas that involve algebraic fractions

A Adding and subtracting algebraic fractions

When adding or subtracting fractions we look for a suitable common denominator. For example, a suitable common denominator for $\frac{1}{6}$ and $\frac{3}{4}$ is 12 because 12 is divisible by 6 and 4.

So $\quad \dfrac{1}{6} + \dfrac{3}{4} = \dfrac{2}{12} + \dfrac{9}{12} = \dfrac{11}{12}$

We do the same when adding or subtracting algebraic fractions to obtain a single fraction.

Examples

$\dfrac{a}{3} + \dfrac{a}{5}$

$= \dfrac{5a}{15} + \dfrac{3a}{15}$

$= \dfrac{8a}{15}$

$\dfrac{3a}{2} - \dfrac{a}{6}$

$= \dfrac{9a}{6} - \dfrac{a}{6}$

$= \dfrac{8a}{6}$

$= \dfrac{4a}{3}$

Write any fraction in its simplest form.

$\dfrac{a}{6} + \dfrac{2b}{9}$

$= \dfrac{3a}{18} + \dfrac{4b}{18}$

$= \dfrac{3a + 4b}{18}$

$\dfrac{a+1}{3} - \dfrac{a-1}{8}$

$= \dfrac{8(a+1)}{24} - \dfrac{3(a-1)}{24}$

$= \dfrac{(8a+8) - (3a-3)}{24}$

$= \dfrac{8a + 8 - 3a + 3}{24}$

$= \dfrac{5a + 11}{24}$

A1 (a) Copy and complete: (i) $\dfrac{b}{6} = \dfrac{\blacksquare}{24}$ (ii) $\dfrac{5b}{8} = \dfrac{\blacksquare}{24}$

(b) Hence write $\dfrac{b}{6} + \dfrac{5b}{8}$ as a single fraction.

A2 Write each of these as a single fraction.

(a) $\dfrac{a}{2} + \dfrac{a}{4}$ (b) $\dfrac{a}{3} - \dfrac{a}{4}$ (c) $\dfrac{3a}{2} + \dfrac{a}{6}$ (d) $\dfrac{5a}{2} - \dfrac{3a}{7}$

A3 Write each of these as a single fraction.

(a) $\dfrac{a}{2} + \dfrac{b}{4}$ (b) $\dfrac{x}{3} - \dfrac{y}{5}$ (c) $\dfrac{3a}{4} + \dfrac{5b}{16}$ (d) $\dfrac{2p}{5} - \dfrac{3q}{2}$

A4 Write each of these as a single fraction.

(a) $\dfrac{a+2}{2} + \dfrac{a}{4}$ (b) $\dfrac{2a-1}{3} - \dfrac{a}{4}$ (c) $\dfrac{3a+1}{2} - \dfrac{3a}{4}$ (d) $\dfrac{a+3}{3} + \dfrac{a}{6}$

A5 (a) Copy and complete: $2 = \dfrac{\blacksquare}{5}$.

(b) Hence write $2 + \dfrac{3a}{5}$ as a single fraction.

A6 Write each of these as a single fraction.

(a) $3 + \dfrac{a}{4}$ (b) $1 + \dfrac{2a-1}{4}$ (c) $2 + \dfrac{5a-6}{3}$ (d) $5 - \dfrac{a-6}{2}$

A7 Write each of these as a single fraction.

(a) $\dfrac{a+2}{2} + \dfrac{2a-1}{4}$ (b) $\dfrac{a-3}{3} + \dfrac{a+1}{6}$ (c) $\dfrac{2a+1}{2} - \dfrac{3a+1}{3}$ (d) $\dfrac{3a+1}{6} - \dfrac{2a-1}{9}$

A8 Write $5 + \dfrac{a+5}{6} + \dfrac{a+2}{3}$ as a single fraction.

With algebraic denominators, you need to look for a 'common multiple' of the denominators.

For example, a suitable common denominator for $\dfrac{1}{2a} + \dfrac{3}{a^2}$ is $2a^2$ because $2a \times a = 2a^2$ and $a^2 \times 2 = 2a^2$.

Examples

$\dfrac{1}{5} + \dfrac{3a}{a}$

$= \dfrac{a}{5a} + \dfrac{15}{5a}$

$= \dfrac{a+15}{5a}$

$\dfrac{1}{2a} + \dfrac{3}{a^2}$

$= \dfrac{a}{2a^2} + \dfrac{6}{2a^2}$

$= \dfrac{a+6}{2a^2}$

$\dfrac{3}{2a} + \dfrac{a}{b}$

$= \dfrac{3b}{2ab} + \dfrac{2a^2}{2ab}$

$= \dfrac{3b + 2a^2}{2ab}$

$\dfrac{1}{2a} - \dfrac{a+1}{4b}$

$= \dfrac{2b}{4ab} - \dfrac{a(a+1)}{4ab}$

$= \dfrac{2b - (a^2 + a)}{4ab}$

$= \dfrac{2b - a^2 - a}{4ab}$

A9 Write each of these as a single fraction.

(a) $\dfrac{1}{a} + \dfrac{1}{2a}$ (b) $\dfrac{3}{4a} - \dfrac{2}{3a}$ (c) $\dfrac{1}{a^2} - \dfrac{3}{a}$ (d) $\dfrac{1}{6a} - \dfrac{2}{3a}$

(e) $\dfrac{1}{2a} + \dfrac{1}{3b}$ (f) $\dfrac{1}{a} - \dfrac{1}{b}$ (g) $\dfrac{5a}{4} + \dfrac{1}{8a}$ (h) $\dfrac{2a+1}{a} - \dfrac{a+4}{2}$

A10 Find four pairs of equivalent expressions.

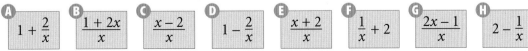

A $1 + \dfrac{2}{x}$ **B** $\dfrac{1+2x}{x}$ **C** $\dfrac{x-2}{x}$ **D** $1 - \dfrac{2}{x}$ **E** $\dfrac{x+2}{x}$ **F** $\dfrac{1}{x} + 2$ **G** $\dfrac{2x-1}{x}$ **H** $2 - \dfrac{1}{x}$

B More complex denominators

Examples

$$\frac{x}{x+1} + \frac{4}{x}$$

> The simplest common denominator here is the product $x(x+1)$.

$$= \frac{x^2}{x(x+1)} + \frac{4(x+1)}{x(x+1)}$$

$$= \frac{x^2 + 4x + 4}{x(x+1)}$$

> Factorising the perfect square here makes the final expression neater.

$$= \frac{(x+2)^2}{x(x+1)}$$

$$\frac{1}{x+1} - \frac{x-4}{x^2-1}$$

> Factorise any denominator where possible.

$$= \frac{1}{x+1} - \frac{x-4}{(x+1)(x-1)}$$

> Factorising here makes it clear that $(x+1)(x-1)$ is the simplest common denominator.

$$= \frac{x-1}{(x+1)(x-1)} - \frac{x-4}{(x+1)(x-1)}$$

$$= \frac{x-1-(x-4)}{(x+1)(x-1)}$$

$$= \frac{x-1-x+4}{(x+1)(x-1)}$$

$$= \frac{3}{(x+1)(x-1)} \text{ or } \frac{3}{x^2-1}$$

B1 Write each of these as a single fraction in its simplest form.

(a) $\dfrac{1}{x} + \dfrac{1}{x+3}$ 　　(b) $\dfrac{2}{3x} - \dfrac{5}{x+1}$ 　　(c) $\dfrac{1}{x+5} + \dfrac{1}{3x-2}$ 　　(d) $\dfrac{3}{x+6} - \dfrac{1}{x+2}$

B2 Write each of these as a single fraction in its simplest form.

(a) $\dfrac{x}{x-2} + \dfrac{1}{x+5}$ 　　(b) $\dfrac{2x}{x-3} - \dfrac{3}{2x+1}$ 　　(c) $2 + \dfrac{1}{x+5}$ 　　(d) $\dfrac{x}{x+1} - \dfrac{5}{x+5}$

B3 Prove that $\dfrac{x}{x+1} + \dfrac{1}{x-1} = \dfrac{x^2+1}{x^2-1}$.

B4 Write each of these as a single fraction in its simplest form.

(a) $\dfrac{x+1}{x+2} + \dfrac{1}{x}$ 　　(b) $\dfrac{x+2}{x} - \dfrac{x}{2x-1}$ 　　(c) $\dfrac{x+3}{x-2} - \dfrac{1}{x+2}$ 　　(d) $\dfrac{x-5}{x+3} - \dfrac{x}{x-1}$

B5 Prove that $\dfrac{x}{x-1} - \dfrac{4}{x} = \dfrac{(x-2)^2}{x(x-1)}$.

B6 Write each of these as a single fraction in its simplest form.

(a) $\dfrac{3}{1-x} + \dfrac{5}{(1-x)^2}$ 　　(b) $\dfrac{x+1}{x^2-4} + \dfrac{5}{x+2}$ 　　(c) $\dfrac{x}{3x-9} - \dfrac{x}{x^2-9}$

B7 A rectangle has a width of x cm and an area of $20\,\text{cm}^2$.

Show that the perimeter is equivalent to $\dfrac{2(x^2+20)}{x}$.

B8 Reese cycles 20 miles at a speed of x m.p.h and then 30 miles at a speed of $(x+5)$ m.p.h.

Show that the total time taken is $\dfrac{50(x+2)}{x(x+5)}$.

C Solving equations containing fractions

When solving equations it is usually easiest to multiply to remove any fractions first.
Multiply by a common multiple of all the denominators to remove all the fractions
in one step.

Examples

$$\frac{x}{x+3} + \frac{2}{x} = 1$$

$$\frac{x \times x(x+3)}{x+3} + \frac{2 \times x(x+3)}{x} = 1 \times x(x+3) \qquad [\times x(x+3)]$$

$$x^2 + 2(x+3) = x(x+3) \qquad \text{[cancel]}$$

$$x^2 + 2x + 6 = x^2 + 3x \qquad \text{[expand brackets]}$$

$$2x + 6 = 3x \qquad [-x^2]$$

$$6 = x \qquad [-2x]$$

$$\frac{4}{x-6} - \frac{9}{x+2} = 3$$

$$\frac{4(x-6)(x+2)}{x-6} - \frac{9(x-6)(x+2)}{x+2} = 3(x-6)(x+2) \qquad [\times (x-6)(x+2)]$$

$$4(x+2) - 9(x-6) = 3(x-6)(x+2) \qquad \text{[cancel]}$$

$$4x + 8 - 9x + 54 = 3x^2 - 12x - 36 \qquad \text{[expand brackets]}$$

$$0 = 3x^2 - 7x - 98 \qquad \text{[collect terms]}$$

$$0 = (3x+14)(x-7) \qquad \text{[factorise]}$$

$$x = \frac{-14}{3} \text{ or } 7$$

C1 Solve each of these equations.

(a) $\dfrac{x-1}{5} + \dfrac{x+1}{6} = 4$ (b) $\dfrac{5x+3}{4} - \dfrac{x}{2} = 6$ (c) $\dfrac{x+1}{3} + \dfrac{x-2}{4} = x - 6$

C2 Solve each of these equations.

(a) $\dfrac{2}{x} - \dfrac{3}{2x} = 2$ (b) $\dfrac{x}{x+3} + \dfrac{2}{x-1} = 1$ (c) $\dfrac{3x}{x-1} - \dfrac{5}{x} = 3$

(d) $\dfrac{x}{x+1} - \dfrac{3}{x-2} = 1$ (e) $\dfrac{6x}{3x+1} + \dfrac{2}{x-1} = 2$ (f) $\dfrac{3}{x-2} + \dfrac{2}{x+2} = \dfrac{4}{x^2-4}$

C3 Solve each of these equations.

(a) $\dfrac{x}{5x-18} = \dfrac{3}{x}$ (b) $\dfrac{4}{x-2} + \dfrac{2x}{x+1} = 3$ (c) $\dfrac{5}{x+3} - \dfrac{2x}{x-4} = 3$

(d) $\dfrac{4}{x} + 4x = 10$ (e) $\dfrac{x}{x-6} + \dfrac{1}{x} = 0$ (f) $\dfrac{x}{4+x} - 2x = 3$

C4 Solve these equations, giving each solution correct to two decimal places.

(a) $\dfrac{1}{x-3} + \dfrac{2}{x-1} = \dfrac{1}{3}$ (b) $\dfrac{x+3}{x+2} = \dfrac{3x+1}{x+4}$ (c) $\dfrac{x-4}{x^2-16} - \dfrac{1}{x-5} = 2$

C5 I drive 100 miles at x m.p.h. and then 60 miles at $(x + 10)$ m.p.h.

(a) Write down an expression in x for the total time taken.

(b) The total time I take is exactly 3 hours.
Form an equation in x and show that it simplifies to $3x^2 - 130x - 1000 = 0$.

(c) Solve this equation and thus work out my two speeds.

*C6 I always cycle uphill at 3 km/h less than I go on the flat.
I always cycle downhill at 3 km/h more than I go on the flat.
My route to work is 1 km uphill and 1 km downhill.
It takes me a quarter of an hour to cycle.
What is my speed on the flat?

*C7 A pile of apples has a total weight of 640 grams.
One apple that weighs 98 grams is added to the pile.
This increases the mean weight of an apple by 2 grams.
How many apples could be in the original pile?

D Rearranging formulas containing fractions

Rearranging a formula containing fractions is very like solving an equation.

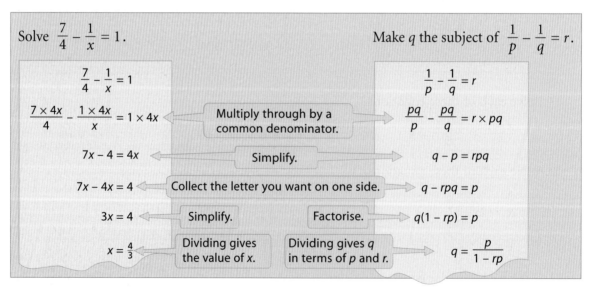

Solve $\dfrac{7}{4} - \dfrac{1}{x} = 1$.

$$\dfrac{7}{4} - \dfrac{1}{x} = 1$$

$$\dfrac{7 \times 4x}{4} - \dfrac{1 \times 4x}{x} = 1 \times 4x$$ ← Multiply through by a common denominator.

$$7x - 4 = 4x$$ ← Simplify.

$$7x - 4x = 4$$ ← Collect the letter you want on one side.

$$3x = 4$$ ← Simplify.

$$x = \dfrac{4}{3}$$ ← Dividing gives the value of x.

Make q the subject of $\dfrac{1}{p} - \dfrac{1}{q} = r$.

$$\dfrac{1}{p} - \dfrac{1}{q} = r$$

$$\dfrac{pq}{p} - \dfrac{pq}{q} = r \times pq$$

$$q - p = rpq$$

$$q - rpq = p$$ Factorise.

$$q(1 - rp) = p$$ Dividing gives q in terms of p and r.

$$q = \dfrac{p}{1 - rp}$$

D1 Rearrange $\dfrac{1}{p} - \dfrac{1}{q} = r$ to make p the subject.

D2 Rearrange each formula to make x the subject.

(a) $\dfrac{x}{a} - \dfrac{y}{b} = 1$

(b) $\dfrac{1}{x} + \dfrac{3}{y} = 5$

(c) $z = \dfrac{1}{x} - \dfrac{1}{y}$

(d) $\dfrac{1}{3y} + \dfrac{z}{4x} = 2$

(e) $y = \dfrac{1}{x^2} - \dfrac{4}{z}$

(f) $\dfrac{1}{x^2} + \dfrac{1}{y^2} = 3$

D3 Given that $\dfrac{1}{f} = \dfrac{1}{u} + \dfrac{1}{v}$ show that $f = \dfrac{uv}{v+u}$.

D4 The harmonic mean h of two numbers x and y is defined by the formula $\dfrac{1}{h} = \dfrac{1}{2x} + \dfrac{1}{2y}$.
Rearrange the formula to make x the subject.

Test yourself

T1 Write each of these as a single fraction in its simplest form.

(a) $\dfrac{1}{3x} + \dfrac{2}{5x}$

(b) $\dfrac{4}{x-1} - \dfrac{3}{2x+1}$

(c) $\dfrac{x}{x-3} - \dfrac{x}{x+2}$

(d) $\dfrac{x}{x-1} + x$

T2 (a) Anne drives 15 miles at a steady speed of 20 m.p.h. and then 30 miles at a steady speed of 60 m.p.h.
Work out the total time for her journey.

(b) (i) Jamie cycles 12 miles at a steady speed of x m.p.h. and then 25 miles at a steady speed of $(x + 4)$ m.p.h.
Write down an expression, in terms of x, for the total time that Jamie takes.

(ii) The total time that Jamie takes is 2 hours.
Form an equation in x and show that it simplifies to $2x^2 - 29x - 48 = 0$.

(iii) Solve the equation $2x^2 - 29x - 48 = 0$ to find the speed x m.p.h.   OCR

T3 Solve algebraically $\dfrac{2x}{2x-5} - \dfrac{1}{x-4} = 1$.   OCR

T4 Solve $\dfrac{2}{x+1} + \dfrac{3}{x-1} = \dfrac{5}{x^2-1}$.   Edexcel

T5 Solve $\dfrac{x}{x-3} = \dfrac{16}{x}$.

T6 Solve the equation $\dfrac{1}{x+1} + \dfrac{5x}{x-2} = 3$.   AQA

T7 (a) Solve $\dfrac{3}{x} + \dfrac{3}{2x} = 2$.

(b) Using your answer to part (a), or otherwise, solve $\dfrac{3}{(y-1)^2} + \dfrac{3}{2(y-1)^2} = 2$.   Edexcel

T8 Make P the subject of the formula $Q = \dfrac{2}{3P} + \dfrac{1}{R}$.

27 Vectors

This work will help you

- use vector notation
- express a vector in terms of a combination of other vectors
- use vectors to solve problems and prove statements

A Vector notation

A **vector** describes a movement from one position to another. On this diagram **a** and **b** are vectors.

We can describe them in columns: $\mathbf{a} = \begin{bmatrix} 1 \\ 2 \end{bmatrix}$ and $\mathbf{b} = \begin{bmatrix} 2 \\ -3 \end{bmatrix}$

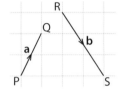

We can also identify a vector using the letters for its starting point and finishing point.

Here we can write $\overrightarrow{PQ} = \mathbf{a}$ and $\overrightarrow{RS} = \mathbf{b}$.

A1 Which vector on the right is equivalent to **a**?

A2 Which vector is equivalent to **b**?

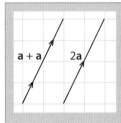

A movement of **a** followed by a second movement of **a** gives you this vector **a** + **a** or more briefly 2**a**.

Notice that $2\mathbf{a} = \begin{bmatrix} 2 \\ 4 \end{bmatrix}$ which has twice the values of $\begin{bmatrix} 1 \\ 2 \end{bmatrix}$.

A3 Which vector on the right is equivalent to

 (a) 2**a** (b) 3**a** (c) 2**b**

If you reverse the vector **a** you get this vector.

We write this as ⁻**a** because it 'undoes' **a**.

Notice that $^-\mathbf{a} = \begin{bmatrix} -1 \\ -2 \end{bmatrix}$.

A4 Which vector on the right is equivalent to ⁻**a**?

A5 Which is equivalent to (a) ⁻2**a** (b) ⁻3**a**

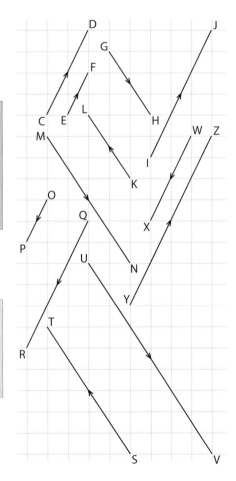

A6 Every vector on the diagram opposite can be described in terms of either **a** or **b**.
Write each of these vectors on the diagram in terms of either **a** or **b**.

(a) $\overrightarrow{YZ}$ (b) $\overrightarrow{UV}$ (c) $\overrightarrow{KL}$ (d) $\overrightarrow{ST}$

A7 (a) What do you notice about all the vectors that can be described in terms of **a**?

(b) What do you notice about all the vectors that can be described in terms of **b**?

A8 This diagram shows vectors **c** and **d**.

On squared paper draw and label vectors equivalent to

(a) 2**c**   (b) 3**d**   (c) ⁻**c**

(d) ⁻**d**   (e) ⁻2**c**   (f) ⁻4**d**

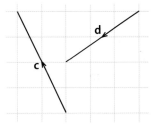

A9 $\mathbf{e} = \begin{bmatrix} 4 \\ 1 \end{bmatrix}$ and $\mathbf{f} = \begin{bmatrix} -3 \\ 2 \end{bmatrix}$

(a) Write each of these as a column vector.

(i) 2**e**   (ii) 3**f**   (iii) ⁻**e**   (iv) ⁻2**f**

(b) Write each of these in terms of **e** or **f**.

(i) $\begin{bmatrix} 12 \\ 3 \end{bmatrix}$ (ii) $\begin{bmatrix} -6 \\ 4 \end{bmatrix}$ (iii) $\begin{bmatrix} 3 \\ -2 \end{bmatrix}$ (iv) $\begin{bmatrix} -16 \\ -4 \end{bmatrix}$

A10 Vectors **s** and **t** are shown on a grid of congruent parallelograms.

(a) $\overrightarrow{PK} = \mathbf{s}$. Give another vector equivalent to **s**.

(b) Write these vectors in terms of **s** or **t**.

(i) $\overrightarrow{LG}$ (ii) $\overrightarrow{TE}$ (iii) $\overrightarrow{FJ}$ (iv) $\overrightarrow{BG}$

(v) $\overrightarrow{LK}$ (vi) $\overrightarrow{GI}$ (vii) $\overrightarrow{TR}$ (viii) $\overrightarrow{DS}$

B Adding vectors

Vector **a** followed by vector **b** is equivalent to the single vector **a** + **b**.
a + **b** is sometimes called the **resultant** of vectors **a** and **b**.

$$\mathbf{a} + \mathbf{b} = \begin{bmatrix} 2 \\ 5 \end{bmatrix} + \begin{bmatrix} 3 \\ -4 \end{bmatrix} = \begin{bmatrix} 5 \\ 1 \end{bmatrix}$$

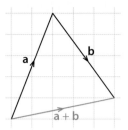

B1 $\mathbf{c} = \begin{bmatrix} 1 \\ 6 \end{bmatrix}$, $\mathbf{d} = \begin{bmatrix} -2 \\ 3 \end{bmatrix}$, $\mathbf{e} = \begin{bmatrix} -1 \\ -4 \end{bmatrix}$

What single column vector is equivalent to

(a) **c** + **d**   (b) **c** + **e**   (c) **d** + **e**   (d) **c** + **d** + **e**

Draw a diagram to check your answer each time.

B2 Vectors **x** and **y** are shown on this grid.

(a) Draw a diagram to show vector

(i) **x** + **y**   (ii) **y** + **x**

(b) Is it true that **x** + **y** = **y** + **x**?

(c) Is it true that **x** + **y** = **y** + **x** for **any** two vectors **x** and **y**?

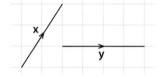

B3 $\mathbf{f} = \begin{bmatrix} 1 \\ 4 \end{bmatrix}$ and $\mathbf{g} = \begin{bmatrix} -4 \\ 2 \end{bmatrix}$

(a) On squared paper draw the resultant vector of each of these.

(i) **f** + **g**   (ii) 3**f** + **g**   (iii) **f** + 2**g**   (iv) 2**f** + 2**g**

(b) Write the resultant of each of these as a column vector.

(i) 2**f** + **g**   (ii) 4**f** + **g**   (iii) 2**f** + 3**g**   (iv) 5**f** + 2**g**

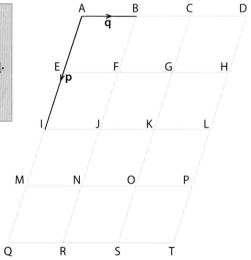

On this grid of congruent parallelograms,
$\overrightarrow{AI} = \mathbf{p}$ and $\overrightarrow{AB} = \mathbf{q}$.

We can write vectors on this grid in terms of **p** and **q**.

For example $\overrightarrow{JT} = \overrightarrow{JR} + \overrightarrow{RT}$.
$= \mathbf{p} + 2\mathbf{q}$.

B4 (a) Copy and complete: $\overrightarrow{AR} = \blacksquare + \overrightarrow{QR}$.

(b) Hence write $\overrightarrow{AR}$ in terms of **p** and **q**.

B5 Which of these vectors are equivalent
to **p** + 3**q**?
$\overrightarrow{MH} \quad \overrightarrow{AL} \quad \overrightarrow{BL} \quad \overrightarrow{AH} \quad \overrightarrow{IT} \quad \overrightarrow{EP}$

B6 Write these vectors in terms of **p** and **q**.

(a) $\overrightarrow{CL}$ (b) $\overrightarrow{FP}$ (c) $\overrightarrow{AT}$ (d) $\overrightarrow{BT}$

Vectors **m** and **n** are shown in this diagram.
$\overrightarrow{AB} = \mathbf{n}$ so $\overrightarrow{BA} = ^-\mathbf{n}$.

We can see that

$$\overrightarrow{BC} = \overrightarrow{BA} + \overrightarrow{AC}$$
$$= ^-\mathbf{n} + \mathbf{m}$$

This can be written as $\overrightarrow{BC} = \mathbf{m} + ^-\mathbf{n}$

or $\overrightarrow{BC} = \mathbf{m} - \mathbf{n}$

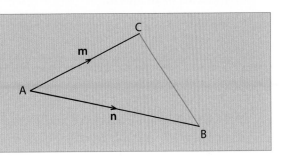

We can show the resultant of a vector subtraction like this.

Vectors **a** and **b** are shown on this grid.

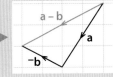

$\mathbf{a} - \mathbf{b} = \mathbf{a} + ^-\mathbf{b}$ so
$\mathbf{a} - \mathbf{b}$ can be found by
adding vectors **a** and $^-\mathbf{b}$.

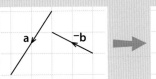 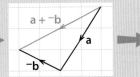 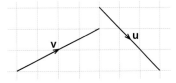

C1 Vectors **v** and **u** are shown on this grid.
Draw diagrams to show

(a) $\mathbf{v} - \mathbf{u}$ (b) $\mathbf{u} - \mathbf{v}$

C2 This diagram shows two vectors **j** and **k**.

(a) Which of these vectors are equivalent to $^-\mathbf{k}$?
$\overrightarrow{EF}$ $\overrightarrow{CB}$ $\overrightarrow{HD}$ $\overrightarrow{ED}$

(b) (i) Copy and complete: $\overrightarrow{HD} = \overrightarrow{HE} + \blacksquare$.

    (ii) Hence write $\overrightarrow{HD}$ in terms of **j** and **k**.

(c) Express these vectors in terms of **j** and **k**.

    (i) $\overrightarrow{IE}$ (ii) $\overrightarrow{CF}$

(d) Which of these vectors are equivalent to $^-2\mathbf{j}$?
$\overrightarrow{CH}$ $\overrightarrow{GB}$ $\overrightarrow{BG}$ $\overrightarrow{IB}$

(e) (i) Copy and complete: $\overrightarrow{HA} = \overrightarrow{HC} + \blacksquare$.

    (ii) Hence write $\overrightarrow{HA}$ in terms of **j** and **k**.

(f) Show that $\overrightarrow{HB} = 2\mathbf{j} - \mathbf{k}$.

(g) Express $\overrightarrow{EG}$ in terms of **j** and **k**.

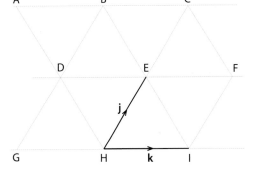

C3 For this parallelogram, express these vectors in terms of **m** and **n**.

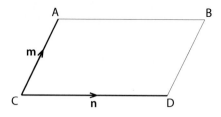

(a) $\overrightarrow{AD}$

(b) $\overrightarrow{DA}$

(c) $\overrightarrow{CB}$

(d) $\overrightarrow{BC}$

C4 In this diagram lengths AB and BC are equal. Lengths AD and DE are also equal.

$\overrightarrow{AB} = \mathbf{u}$ and $\overrightarrow{AD} = \mathbf{v}$

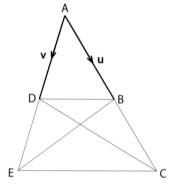

(a) Which of these vectors is equivalent to 2**v**?

$\overrightarrow{AD}$ $\overrightarrow{AC}$ $\overrightarrow{AE}$ $\overrightarrow{DC}$

(b) Express these vectors in terms of **u** and **v**.

(i) $\overrightarrow{AC}$

(ii) $\overrightarrow{BD}$

(iii) $\overrightarrow{DB}$

(iv) $\overrightarrow{BE}$

(v) $\overrightarrow{DC}$

(vi) $\overrightarrow{EC}$

C5 ABCDEF is a regular hexagon.

$\overrightarrow{OA} = \mathbf{m}$ and $\overrightarrow{OF} = \mathbf{n}$

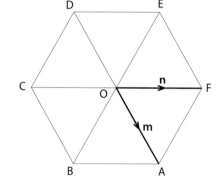

(a) Express these vectors in terms of **m** and **n**.

(i) $\overrightarrow{DA}$

(ii) $\overrightarrow{AB}$

(iii) $\overrightarrow{FC}$

(iv) $\overrightarrow{OE}$

(v) $\overrightarrow{DC}$

(vi) $\overrightarrow{FD}$

(b) (i) Copy and complete: $\overrightarrow{CE} = \blacksquare + \overrightarrow{FE}$.

(ii) Hence write $\overrightarrow{CE}$ in terms of **m** and **n**.

(c) Express these vectors in terms of **m** and **n**.

(i) $\overrightarrow{DB}$

(ii) $\overrightarrow{FB}$

(iii) $\overrightarrow{AE}$

C6 PQRS is a rectangle.

$\overrightarrow{RQ} = \mathbf{x}$ and $\overrightarrow{MQ} = \mathbf{y}$

Express these vectors in terms of **x** and **y**.

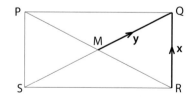

(a) $\overrightarrow{RM}$

(b) $\overrightarrow{SQ}$

(c) $\overrightarrow{PQ}$

C7 A, B and C are three points.

Describe in words as fully as possible the situations described by each of these.

(a) $\overrightarrow{AB} = \overrightarrow{BC}$

(b) $\overrightarrow{AB} = 2\overrightarrow{BC}$

(c) $\overrightarrow{AC} = 2\overrightarrow{AB}$

(d) $\overrightarrow{AB} = {}^{-}\overrightarrow{BC}$

D Fractions of a vector

Sometimes we need to use fractional multiples of a vector.

For example, $\frac{1}{2}\mathbf{a}$ is the vector in the same direction as $\mathbf{a}$ but half its length.

Here we have $\mathbf{a} = \begin{bmatrix} 6 \\ 3 \end{bmatrix}$.

The vectors $\mathbf{a}$, $\frac{1}{2}\mathbf{a}$ and $\frac{-2}{3}\mathbf{a}$ are shown on this grid.

As column vectors $\frac{1}{2}\mathbf{a} = \begin{bmatrix} 3 \\ 1\frac{1}{2} \end{bmatrix}$ and $\frac{-2}{3}\mathbf{a} = \begin{bmatrix} -4 \\ -2 \end{bmatrix}$.

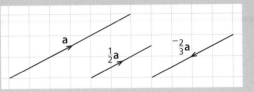

D1 This diagram shows vectors $\mathbf{g}$ and $\mathbf{h}$.

On squared paper draw and label vectors

(a) $\frac{1}{3}\mathbf{h}$ (b) $\frac{1}{2}\mathbf{g}$ (c) $\frac{3}{4}\mathbf{g}$

(d) $1\frac{1}{3}\mathbf{h}$ (e) $\frac{-2}{3}\mathbf{h}$ (f) $-2\frac{1}{2}\mathbf{g}$

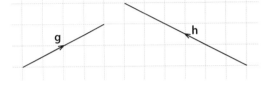

D2 Vectors $\mathbf{p}$ and $\mathbf{q}$ are shown on a grid of congruent parallelograms.

(a) Write these vectors in terms of $\mathbf{p}$ or $\mathbf{q}$.

(i) $\overrightarrow{AI}$ (ii) $\overrightarrow{KL}$ (iii) $\overrightarrow{JF}$

(b) Write these vectors in terms of $\mathbf{p}$ and $\mathbf{q}$.

(i) $\overrightarrow{CP}$ (ii) $\overrightarrow{AG}$ (iii) $\overrightarrow{BL}$

(iv) $\overrightarrow{GL}$ (v) $\overrightarrow{DO}$ (vi) $\overrightarrow{KF}$

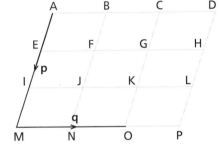

D3 This shows points O, A and B and the vectors $\mathbf{a}$ and $\mathbf{b}$.

Copy the diagram on to triangular dotty paper.
Mark points C, D, E and F to give these vectors.

(a) $\overrightarrow{OC} = \mathbf{a} + \frac{1}{2}\mathbf{b}$ (b) $\overrightarrow{OD} = \frac{3}{4}\mathbf{b} - \frac{1}{2}\mathbf{a}$

(c) $\overrightarrow{BE} = \frac{1}{2}\mathbf{a} + \frac{1}{2}\mathbf{b}$ (d) $\overrightarrow{CF} = 2\mathbf{a} - \frac{1}{4}\mathbf{b}$

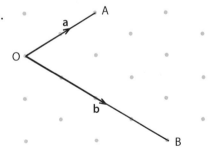

D4 WXYZ is a parallelogram.
U is the mid-point of WX.
V is the point on YX for which $YV:VX = 1:2$.
$\overrightarrow{ZY} = \mathbf{a}$ and $\overrightarrow{ZW} = \mathbf{b}$.

Write down, in terms of $\mathbf{a}$ and $\mathbf{b}$, expressions for

(a) $\overrightarrow{WU}$ (b) $\overrightarrow{ZU}$ (c) $\overrightarrow{YV}$

(d) $\overrightarrow{ZV}$ (e) $\overrightarrow{VX}$ (f) $\overrightarrow{VW}$

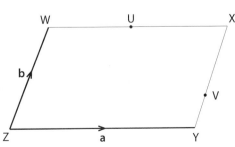

E Vector algebra

This diagram shows $\mathbf{b} + \mathbf{a} + \mathbf{b}$ and $2\mathbf{b} + \mathbf{a}$.

- What does this show about the vectors $\mathbf{b} + \mathbf{a} + \mathbf{b}$ and $2\mathbf{b} + \mathbf{a}$?

Draw diagrams to show whether these statements are true or false.

- $\mathbf{a} + \mathbf{b} + \mathbf{a} + 2\mathbf{b} = 2\mathbf{a} + 3\mathbf{b}$
- $2\mathbf{a} + \frac{1}{2}\mathbf{b} - \mathbf{a} + \frac{1}{2}\mathbf{b} = \mathbf{a} + \mathbf{b}$
- $\mathbf{a} + 2\mathbf{b} = 2\mathbf{a} + \mathbf{b}$
- $2(\mathbf{a} + \mathbf{b}) = 2\mathbf{a} + 2\mathbf{b}$
- $\mathbf{a} - \mathbf{b} = \mathbf{b} - \mathbf{a}$
- $\frac{1}{2}(2\mathbf{a} + \mathbf{b}) = \mathbf{a} + \frac{1}{2}\mathbf{b}$

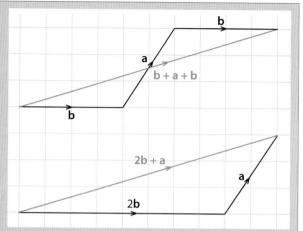

The algebra of combining vectors like this works in the same way as the algebra of numbers.

E1 Write each vector expression in a simpler form.

(a) $2\mathbf{a} + 3\mathbf{b} + \mathbf{a} + 2\mathbf{b}$ (b) $\mathbf{a} + 6\mathbf{b} + \mathbf{a} - 5\mathbf{b}$ (c) $\mathbf{a} - \mathbf{b} + 3\mathbf{a} + 5\mathbf{b}$

(d) $2\mathbf{a} - 4\mathbf{b} - \mathbf{a} + \mathbf{b}$ (e) $\frac{1}{2}\mathbf{a} + \frac{1}{3}\mathbf{b} + \frac{1}{2}\mathbf{a} + \frac{1}{3}\mathbf{b}$ (f) $\frac{1}{2}\mathbf{a} + \frac{2}{3}\mathbf{b} + \frac{1}{3}\mathbf{a} - \frac{1}{2}\mathbf{b}$

E2 Write each of these without brackets, in its simplest form.

(a) $3(2\mathbf{a} - \mathbf{b})$ (b) $\frac{1}{2}(\mathbf{a} + 2\mathbf{b})$ (c) $4\mathbf{a} + 2(\mathbf{b} - \mathbf{a})$

E3 In triangle OAB, point M is a point such that $\overrightarrow{AM} = \frac{1}{3}\overrightarrow{AB}$.
Write these as simply as possible in terms of $\mathbf{a}$ and $\mathbf{b}$.

(a) $\overrightarrow{AB}$ (b) $\overrightarrow{AM}$ (c) $\overrightarrow{OM}$

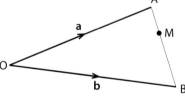

E4 ABCD is a trapezium.
$\overrightarrow{DC} = 2\overrightarrow{AB}$

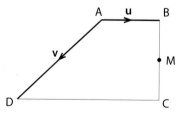

(a) Write these as simply as possible in terms of $\mathbf{u}$ and $\mathbf{v}$.

(i) $\overrightarrow{DC}$ (ii) $\overrightarrow{BD}$ (iii) $\overrightarrow{AC}$ (iv) $\overrightarrow{BC}$

(b) M is the point halfway along BC.
Write these as simply as possible in terms of $\mathbf{u}$ and $\mathbf{v}$.

(i) $\overrightarrow{BM}$ (ii) $\overrightarrow{AM}$ (iii) $\overrightarrow{DM}$

E5 OPQ is a triangle.

T is the point on PQ for which $PT:TQ = 2:1$.

$\overrightarrow{OP} = \mathbf{a}$ and $\overrightarrow{OQ} = \mathbf{b}$.

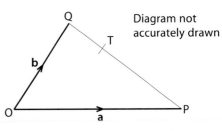

Diagram not accurately drawn

(a) Write down, in terms of $\mathbf{a}$ and $\mathbf{b}$, an expression for $\overrightarrow{PQ}$.

(b) Express $\overrightarrow{OT}$ in terms of $\mathbf{a}$ and $\mathbf{b}$.
Give your answer in its simplest form.

Edexcel

E6

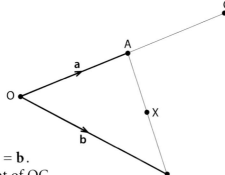

$\overrightarrow{OA} = \mathbf{a}$ and $\overrightarrow{OB} = \mathbf{b}$.

A is the mid-point of OC.

X is the mid-point of AB.

Find $\overrightarrow{XC}$, in terms of $\mathbf{a}$ and $\mathbf{b}$, in its simplest form.

OCR

E7 Triangle OAB is drawn on a grid of equilateral triangles.

$\overrightarrow{OA} = \mathbf{a}$ and $\overrightarrow{OB} = \mathbf{b}$.

(a) Write these as simply as possible in terms of $\mathbf{a}$ and $\mathbf{b}$.

(i) $\overrightarrow{AB}$ (ii) $\overrightarrow{BA}$ (iii) $\overrightarrow{OP}$

(iv) $\overrightarrow{BP}$ (v) $\overrightarrow{AP}$

(b) M is the mid-point of $\overrightarrow{AB}$.
Write these as simply as possible in terms of $\mathbf{a}$ and $\mathbf{b}$.

(i) $\overrightarrow{MB}$ (ii) $\overrightarrow{MP}$

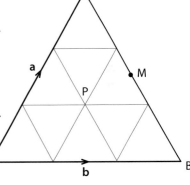

E8 In this diagram $\overrightarrow{OA} = 2\mathbf{p} - \mathbf{q}$ and $\overrightarrow{AB} = \mathbf{p} + \mathbf{q}$.

(a) Write the vector $\overrightarrow{OB}$ in terms of $\mathbf{p}$ and $\mathbf{q}$.
Write this in its simplest form.

(b) From the diagram write $\overrightarrow{OB}$ in the form $\begin{bmatrix} m \\ n \end{bmatrix}$,
where m and n are whole numbers.

(c) Use your answers to (a) and (b) to write $\mathbf{p}$ as a column vector.

(d) Write $\mathbf{q}$ as a column vector.

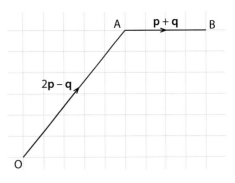

F Proof by vectors

- If $\overrightarrow{AB} = \overrightarrow{CD}$, then the line segments AB, CD are parallel and equal in length.
- If $\overrightarrow{AB} = k\overrightarrow{CD}$ (where k is a number), then the line segment AB is parallel to CD and the length AB is k times the length CD.

   For example, if you have shown that $\overrightarrow{CD} = \mathbf{p} - \mathbf{q}$ and that $\overrightarrow{AB} = 3(\mathbf{p} - \mathbf{q})$, it follows that CD is parallel to AB, and $3CD = AB$.
- If $\overrightarrow{AC} = k\overrightarrow{AB}$ (where k is a number), then points A, B and C lie in a straight line.

Investigation

- Draw any quadrilateral.
  Join up the mid-points of the sides to make a new quadrilateral.
  What type of quadrilateral do you get?

- Try this with a number of different quadrilaterals.
  Do you always get the same type of quadrilateral by joining mid-points?

The result can be proved by using vectors.

Here is a quadrilateral PQRS.

K, L, M and N are the mid-points of the sides.

Define these four vectors:

$$\mathbf{a} = \overrightarrow{PQ} \quad \mathbf{b} = \overrightarrow{QR} \quad \mathbf{c} = \overrightarrow{PS} \quad \mathbf{d} = \overrightarrow{SR}$$

We have $\overrightarrow{QS} = \overrightarrow{QP} + \overrightarrow{PS}$, so $\overrightarrow{QS} = {}^{-}\mathbf{a} + \mathbf{c} = \mathbf{c} - \mathbf{a}$.

Also $\overrightarrow{QS} = \overrightarrow{QR} + \overrightarrow{RS}$, so $\overrightarrow{QS} = \mathbf{b} + {}^{-}\mathbf{d} = \mathbf{b} - \mathbf{d}$.

So it follows that $\mathbf{c} - \mathbf{a} = \mathbf{b} - \mathbf{d}$.

$\overrightarrow{KN} = \overrightarrow{KP} + \overrightarrow{PN}$, so $\overrightarrow{KN} = {}^{-}\frac{1}{2}\mathbf{a} + \frac{1}{2}\mathbf{c} = \frac{1}{2}(\mathbf{c} - \mathbf{a})$.

$\overrightarrow{LM} = \overrightarrow{LR} + \overrightarrow{RM}$, so $\overrightarrow{LM} = \frac{1}{2}\mathbf{b} + {}^{-}\frac{1}{2}\mathbf{d} = \frac{1}{2}(\mathbf{b} - \mathbf{d})$.

From the fact that $\mathbf{c} - \mathbf{a} = \mathbf{b} - \mathbf{d}$ it follows that $\overrightarrow{KN} = \overrightarrow{LM}$.

So the line segments KN and LM are parallel and equal in length.

- Find expressions for $\overrightarrow{KL}$ and $\overrightarrow{NM}$ in terms of $\mathbf{a}, \mathbf{b}, \mathbf{c}, \mathbf{d}$ and show that $\overrightarrow{KL} = \overrightarrow{NM}$.

The quadrilateral KLMN has both pairs of opposite sides parallel, so it is a parallelogram.

- Show that, if diagonals QS and PR intersect at right angles, then KLMN is a rectangle.

F1 In this diagram C is $\frac{2}{3}$ of the way along OA and D is $\frac{2}{3}$ of the way along OB.

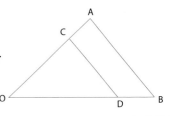

(a) Given that $\overrightarrow{OA} = \mathbf{a}$ and $\overrightarrow{OB} = \mathbf{b}$, find expressions for $\overrightarrow{AB}$ and $\overrightarrow{CD}$ in terms of $\mathbf{a}$ and $\mathbf{b}$.

(b) What does this tell you about the lines AB and CD?

F2 This diagram shows a triangle ABC.
Points X, Y and Z are the mid-points of AB, BC and CA respectively.
$\overrightarrow{AX} = \mathbf{a}$ and $\overrightarrow{AZ} = \mathbf{b}$.

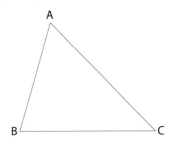

(a) Sketch triangle ABC.
Mark points X, Y and Z and vectors $\mathbf{a}$ and $\mathbf{b}$ on your sketch.

(b) (i) Express $\overrightarrow{ZX}$ and $\overrightarrow{CB}$ terms of $\mathbf{a}$ and $\mathbf{b}$.

(ii) Hence write down **two** facts about the relationship between lines ZX and CB.

(c) Express, in terms of $\mathbf{a}$ and $\mathbf{b}$, the vector $\overrightarrow{AY}$.

F3 In triangle RST, A and B are the mid-points of RS and RT respectively.
$\overrightarrow{RS} = \mathbf{x}$ and $\overrightarrow{RT} = \mathbf{y}$.

Find in terms of $\mathbf{x}$ and $\mathbf{y}$

(a) $\overrightarrow{ST}$

(b) $\overrightarrow{RA}$

(c) $\overrightarrow{AB}$

(d) What conclusions can you draw about the lines AB and ST?   OCR

F4 In this diagram $\overrightarrow{OA} = \mathbf{a}$ and $\overrightarrow{OB} = \mathbf{b}$.
Also $\overrightarrow{AC} = 2\mathbf{a}$ and $\overrightarrow{AD} = 3\mathbf{b} - \mathbf{a}$.

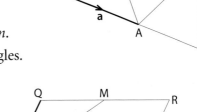

(a) Write $\overrightarrow{AB}$ in terms of $\mathbf{a}$ and $\mathbf{b}$.

(b) $\overrightarrow{OD} = n\mathbf{b}$ where n is a whole number. Find n.

(c) Prove that OAB and OCD are similar triangles.

F5 PQRS is a parallelogram.
M is the mid-point of QR.
X is the point on MP such that $MX = \frac{1}{3}MP$.
$\overrightarrow{PQ} = 3\mathbf{a}$ and $\overrightarrow{PS} = 3\mathbf{b}$.

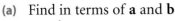

(a) Find in terms of $\mathbf{a}$ and $\mathbf{b}$

(i) $\overrightarrow{PX}$ (ii) $\overrightarrow{SX}$

(b) Prove that points S, X and Q all lie on a straight line.

F6 ABCD is a parallelogram.

M is the mid-point of the line AC.

N is a point $\frac{2}{3}$ of the way along the line AD.

$\overrightarrow{AB} = \mathbf{u}$ and $\overrightarrow{AD} = 3\mathbf{v}$.

AB is extended to a new point O so that BO = AB.

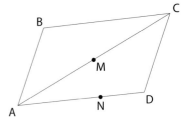

(a) Write $\overrightarrow{AM}$ in terms of $\mathbf{u}$ and $\mathbf{v}$.

Hence write $\overrightarrow{NM}$ in terms of $\mathbf{u}$ and $\mathbf{v}$.

(b) Write $\overrightarrow{NO}$ in terms of $\mathbf{u}$ and $\mathbf{v}$.

(c) Prove that N, M and O lie on a straight line.

(d) Prove that NM is a quarter of the length of NO.

F7 In the diagram OACD, OADB and ODEB are parallelograms.

$\overrightarrow{OA} = \mathbf{a}$ and $\overrightarrow{OB} = \mathbf{b}$

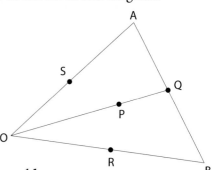

(a) Express, in terms of $\mathbf{a}$ and $\mathbf{b}$, the following vectors.
Give your answers in their simplest form.

(i) $\overrightarrow{OD}$ (ii) $\overrightarrow{OC}$ (iii) $\overrightarrow{AB}$

(b) The point F is such that OCFE is a parallelogram.
Write the vector $\overrightarrow{CF}$ in terms of $\mathbf{a}$ and $\mathbf{b}$.

(c) What geometrical relationship is there between the points O, D and F?
Justify your answer.

AQA

F8 OJKL is a parallelogram with $\overrightarrow{OJ} = \mathbf{x}$ and $\overrightarrow{OL} = \mathbf{y}$.
M is the mid-point of OK.

Use vectors to prove that M is also the mid-point of JL.

F9 A triangle OAB has mid-points on its sides Q, R and S as shown in this diagram.

$\overrightarrow{OA} = \mathbf{a}$ and $\overrightarrow{OB} = \mathbf{b}$.

P is a point $\frac{2}{3}$ of the way along OQ.

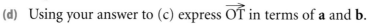

(a) Express $\overrightarrow{OQ}$ in terms of $\mathbf{a}$ and $\mathbf{b}$.
Hence express $\overrightarrow{OP}$ in terms of $\mathbf{a}$ and $\mathbf{b}$.

(b) Express $\overrightarrow{AR}$ in terms of $\mathbf{a}$ and $\mathbf{b}$.

(c) T is a point $\frac{2}{3}$ along AR.
Express $\overrightarrow{AT}$ in terms of $\mathbf{a}$ and $\mathbf{b}$.

(d) Using your answer to (c) express $\overrightarrow{OT}$ in terms of $\mathbf{a}$ and $\mathbf{b}$.

(e) What does this tell you about the points P and T?

(f) If X is a point $\frac{2}{3}$ along BS, what do you think the vector $\overrightarrow{OX}$ will be
in terms of $\mathbf{a}$ and $\mathbf{b}$? Prove your result.

Test yourself

T1 ORS is a triangle.
   T is the point on RS such that $RT = \frac{1}{4}RS$.
   $\overrightarrow{OR} = \mathbf{r}$ and $\overrightarrow{OS} = \mathbf{s}$.

   (a) Find, in terms of $\mathbf{r}$ and $\mathbf{s}$,
      (i) $\overrightarrow{SR}$ (ii) $\overrightarrow{ST}$

   (b) Find $\overrightarrow{OT}$ in terms of $\mathbf{r}$ and $\mathbf{s}$.
      Give your answer in its simplest form.

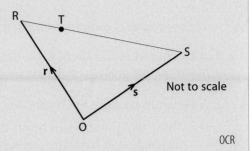

Not to scale

OCR

T2 ABCDEF is a regular hexagon with centre O.
   $\overrightarrow{OA} = \mathbf{a}$ and $\overrightarrow{AB} = \mathbf{b}$

   (a) Find expressions, in terms of $\mathbf{a}$ and $\mathbf{b}$, for
      (i) $\overrightarrow{OB}$ (ii) $\overrightarrow{AC}$ (iii) $\overrightarrow{EC}$

   (b) The positions of points P and Q are
      given by the vectors

   $$\overrightarrow{OP} = \mathbf{a} - \mathbf{b} \qquad \overrightarrow{OQ} = \mathbf{a} + 2\mathbf{b}$$

   (i) Copy the diagram.
      Draw and label the positions of points P and Q on the diagram.

   (ii) Hence, or otherwise, deduce an expression for $\overrightarrow{PQ}$.

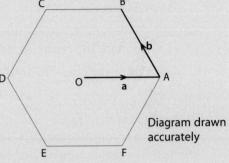

Diagram drawn
accurately

AQA

T3 OAB is a triangle where M is the mid-point of OB.
   P and Q are points on AB such that $AP = PQ = QB$.
   $\overrightarrow{OA} = \mathbf{a}$ and $\overrightarrow{OB} = 2\mathbf{b}$

   (a) Find, in terms of $\mathbf{a}$ and $\mathbf{b}$, expressions for
      (i) $\overrightarrow{BA}$ (ii) $\overrightarrow{MQ}$ (iii) $\overrightarrow{OP}$

   (b) What can you deduce about quadrilateral OMQP?
      Gave a reason for your answer.

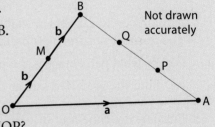

Not drawn
accurately

AQA

T4 OABC is a parallelogram.
   P is the point on AC such that $AP = \frac{2}{3}AC$.
   $\overrightarrow{OA} = 6\mathbf{a}$ and $\overrightarrow{OC} = 6\mathbf{c}$.

   (a) Find the vector $\overrightarrow{OP}$.
      Give your answer in terms of $\mathbf{a}$ and $\mathbf{c}$.

   The mid-point of CB is M.

   (b) Prove that OPM is a straight line.

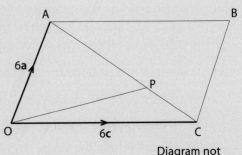

Diagram not
accurately drawn

Edexcel

Review 4

You need a pair of compasses for question 2.

1 A cardboard box is 28 cm high, to the nearest centimetre.
What are the greatest and least possible heights of a pile of five of these boxes?

2 A sketch of triangle ABC is shown.

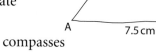

(a) Show that point B will be on the circumference of
the circle that has diameter AC.

(b) Use a ruler and compasses to construct an accurate
copy of triangle ABC.

(c) (i) Without measuring, use a straight-edge and compasses
to mark the centre of the circle that has diameter AC.

(ii) Draw the circle on your diagram.

3 The diagram shows a cuboid.
Vertex O is at the origin.
Vertex G has coordinates $(2, 3, 1)$.
Write down the coordinates of each
vertex of the cuboid.

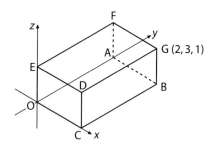

4 A colony of 26 gannets is established on an island.
The number of gannets is predicted to be $26 \times (1.195)^n$ after n years.

(a) By what percentage is the population expected to increase per year?

(b) Find the predicted size of the colony after 20 years.

5 Evaluate the cube root of $\dfrac{180}{\pi}$, correct to three significant figures.

6 Copy the diagram, showing triangles A and B.

(a) Triangle B is an enlargement of triangle A.
Write down the scale factor and find the
coordinates of the centre of the enlargement.

(b) Triangle A is translated by $\begin{bmatrix} -2 \\ -2 \end{bmatrix}$ and then

rotated through 90° clockwise about $(0, {}^-2)$.

(i) Draw and label the final image C.

(ii) Describe fully the single transformation
that maps A on to C.

(c) Reflect C in the line $y = {}^-2$ and label the image D.

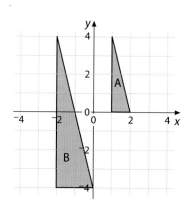

7 In this diagram points A, B, C and D lie on a circle centre O. Find these angles, giving reasons for your answers.

(a) ABC   (b) ADC   (c) OCA   (d) OAB

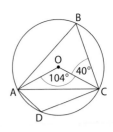

8 Write each of these as a single algebraic fraction.

(a) $\dfrac{2}{a} + \dfrac{a}{4}$ (b) $\dfrac{x+5}{3} + \dfrac{x-2}{2}$ (c) $\dfrac{1}{p+1} - \dfrac{2}{2p+1}$ (d) $\dfrac{y}{y+1} + \dfrac{2y+1}{y-1}$

9 A, B, C and D are four points on the circumference of a circle.
DE is the tangent to the circle at D.

Given that angle CDE = 35° and angle BDC = 70°, calculate each of the following angles. Give reasons for your answers.

(a) Angle BCD   (b) Angle BAD

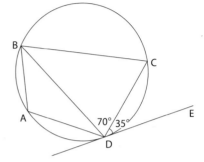

10 A small generator has a power output of 1250 watts, to the nearest ten watts. The generator's design is made more efficient, with the result that it now has a power output of 1480 watts to the nearest ten watts.

(a) Calculate the maximum possible increase in the power output.

(b) Calculate the maximum possible percentage increase in the power output, to the nearest 0.1%.

11 Points M, N and P are the mid-points of the edges of triangle OAB as shown.

$\overrightarrow{OM} = \mathbf{m}$ and $\overrightarrow{OP} = \mathbf{p}$

Express each of these vectors in terms of $\mathbf{m}$ and $\mathbf{p}$.

(a) $\overrightarrow{AB}$ (b) $\overrightarrow{BN}$ (c) $\overrightarrow{ON}$

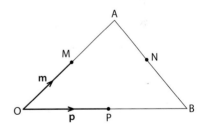

12 (a) Find, as an integer or fraction, the exact value of each of these.

(i) $25^{\frac{1}{2}}$ (ii) $8^{\frac{1}{3}}$ (iii) $\left(\dfrac{25}{16}\right)^{-\frac{1}{2}}$

(b) Find the value of t if

(i) $2^t = \dfrac{1}{16}$ (ii) $9^t = 3$ (iii) $4^t = \dfrac{1}{2}$ (iv) $27^t = 9$

13 Solve these equations, giving solutions correct to 2 d.p. where appropriate.

(a) $\dfrac{x+5}{3} + \dfrac{x-1}{2} = 7$ (b) $\dfrac{x-4}{2} - \dfrac{x+3}{5} = 1$ (c) $\dfrac{3}{x} + \dfrac{x+3}{3} = x$

(d) $\dfrac{3x-4}{x-1} = \dfrac{x+4}{x+1}$ (e) $\dfrac{3x-1}{x+2} - \dfrac{2(x-3)}{x-1} = 1$ (f) $\dfrac{x}{x-3} + \dfrac{2}{x+1} = 4$

14 Point $(3, 2)$ is on the circumference of a circle with centre $(0, 0)$.
Calculate, as exact values, the radius, the area and the circumference of this circle.

15 AB is a diameter of this circle.
AB = 12 cm and BC = 7 cm.

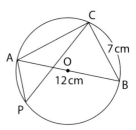

(a) Calculate the length of AC correct to 1 d.p.

(b) Use trigonometry to calculate angle CAB to the nearest degree.

(c) Hence find the size of angle APC.

16 (a) Find, as an integer or fraction, the exact value of each of these.

    (i) $3^{-2} \times 16^{\frac{1}{4}}$ (ii) $\left(2^{\frac{1}{3}}\right)^6$ (iii) $36^{0.5} \times 27^{-\frac{1}{3}}$

(b) Write $25\sqrt{5}$ as a power of 5.

(c) Find the integer N where $\dfrac{N}{\sqrt{3}} = 3^{\frac{3}{2}}$.

17 OACB is a parallelogram.
$\overrightarrow{OA} = \mathbf{a}$ and $\overrightarrow{OB} = \mathbf{b}$.

D is the mid-point of OA.
E is the mid-point of AC.

Point F is on BC such that $BF = \frac{1}{6}BC$.

Point G is on BC such that $BG = \frac{5}{6}BC$.

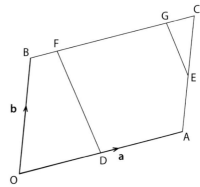

(a) Write, in terms of $\mathbf{a}$ and $\mathbf{b}$,

    (i) $\overrightarrow{EC}$ (ii) $\overrightarrow{CG}$

    (iii) $\overrightarrow{EG}$ (iv) $\overrightarrow{DF}$

(b) What do your results for $\overrightarrow{EG}$ and $\overrightarrow{DF}$ tell you about line segments EG and DF?

18 A car travels 18 miles in 21 minutes.
The distance is correct to the nearest mile and the time to the nearest minute.
Calculate, correct to 2 d.p., the minimum average speed of the car in m.p.h.

19 Shape OAB is the sector of a circle.
The length of arc AB is 20 cm.
Find the length of OA as an exact value.

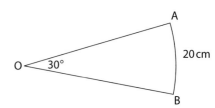

20 A journey of d miles is travelled at the average speed of a_1 miles per hour.
The average speed of the return journey is a_2 miles per hour.
The total time taken is t hours.

(a) Find a formula for t in terms of d, a_1 and a_2.

(b) Rearrange the formula to make d the subject.

28 Circles and equations

You should know how to solve simultaneous equations such as $y = 3x^2$ and $y = 5x + 1$.

This work will help you

- find the equation of a circle with centre $(0, 0)$
- sketch the graph of $x^2 + y^2 = k$ where k is a constant
- solve simultaneous equations such as $x^2 + y^2 = 4$ and $y = 3x + 1$, interpreting the solutions as the points of intersection of a circle and a straight line

A Equation of a circle

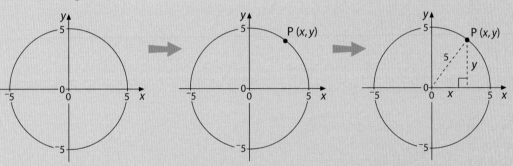

This circle has centre $(0, 0)$ and radius 5. What is its equation?

Let P (x, y) be a point on the circle.

We can draw a right-angled triangle.

Using Pythagoras, $x^2 + y^2 = 5^2$

So the equation is $x^2 + y^2 = 25$.

- In the same way, find the equation of the circle that has centre $(0, 0)$ and radius 12.

A1 Show that $(3, 4)$ is a point on the circle with equation $x^2 + y^2 = 25$.

A2 (a) Which of these circles has the equation $x^2 + y^2 = 4$?

Ⓐ
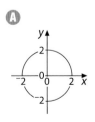

Ⓑ
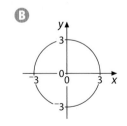

Ⓒ
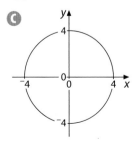

(b) Write down the equations of the other two circles.

A circle with centre $(0, 0)$ and radius r has the equation $x^2 + y^2 = r^2$.

A3 **(a)** Sketch the circle with equation $x^2 + y^2 = 49$.

    (b) Show that any straight line that passes through the point $(3, 2)$ must cut the circle with equation $x^2 + y^2 = 49$ in two places.

A4 **(a)** Give the coordinates of the points where the circle $x^2 + y^2 = 100$ cuts the x-axis.

    (b) Which of these points are on the circle $x^2 + y^2 = 100$?

$$(0, {}^-10) \quad ({}^-6, {}^-8) \quad (20, 30) \quad \left(1, {}^-\sqrt{99}\right) \quad \left({}^-5, \sqrt{75}\right)$$

A5 Write down the radius of each of these circles.

    (a) $x^2 + y^2 = 64$ **(b)** $x^2 + y^2 = 400$ **(c)** $x^2 + y^2 = 11$

A6 Write down the equations of the circles with centre $(0, 0)$ and the following radii.

    (a) 6 **(b)** 1 **(c)** $\frac{1}{2}$ **(d)** $\sqrt{7}$ **(e)** $\sqrt{18}$

B Intersection of a line and a circle

To find the coordinates of the points where the line $y = 3x - 1$ meets the circle $x^2 + y^2 = 5$, we need to solve the simultaneous equations

$$y = 3x - 1$$
$$x^2 + y^2 = 5$$

Substituting $y = 3x - 1$ into $x^2 + y^2 = 5$ gives

$$x^2 + (3x - 1)^2 = 5$$
$$x^2 + 9x^2 - 6x + 1 = 5$$
$$10x^2 - 6x - 4 = 0$$
$$5x^2 - 3x - 2 = 0$$
$$(5x + 2)(x - 1) = 0$$
$$\text{So } x = {}^-\tfrac{2}{5} \text{ or } x = 1$$

Substitution gives an equation that does not involve y so this method is sometimes called **eliminating** y.

$x = {}^-\frac{2}{5}$ gives $y = 3 \times {}^-\frac{2}{5} - 1 = {}^-2\frac{1}{5}$

$x = 1$ gives $y = 3 \times 1 - 1 = 2$

So the solutions are $x = {}^-\frac{2}{5}$, $y = {}^-2\frac{1}{5}$ and $x = 1$, $y = 2$.

Hence the coordinates are $\left({}^-\frac{2}{5}, {}^-2\frac{1}{5}\right)$ and $(1, 2)$.

B1 The diagram shows a sketch of the circle $x^2 + y^2 = 17$ and the line $y = x + 5$.

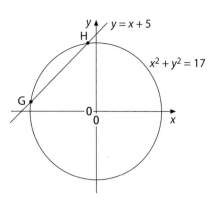

(a) By eliminating y, show that the x-coordinates of G and H satisfy the equation $x^2 + 5x + 4 = 0$.

(b) Hence find the coordinates of G and H.

B2 (a) Sketch the circle with equation $x^2 + y^2 = 9$.

(b) Add a sketch of the line with equation $y = 2x - 3$ to your diagram.

(c) Find the coordinates of the points where the line $y = 2x - 3$ meets the circle $x^2 + y^2 = 9$.

B3 The straight line with equation $y = x + 6$ meets the circle with equation $x^2 + y^2 = 50$ at two points P and Q.
By solving two simultaneous equations, find the coordinates of P and Q.

B4 This diagram shows the circle $x^2 + y^2 = 4$ and the line $y = x + 1$.

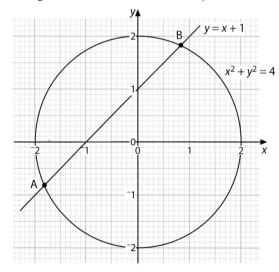

(a) Use the graph to estimate the coordinates of points A and B, correct to 1 d.p.

(b) Find the coordinates of A and B, correct to 2 d.p.

B5 The straight line $y = 2x + 1$ meets the circle $x^2 + y^2 = 7$ at two points P and Q. Find the coordinates of P and Q, correct to 2 d.p.

B6 (a) Try to solve the simultaneous equations

$$x^2 + y^2 = 4$$
$$y = x - 3$$

(b) What does this tell you about the line $y = x - 3$ and the circle $x^2 + y^2 = 4$? Confirm your answer by sketching the line and circle on the same set of axes.

B7 (a) Solve the simultaneous equations

$$x^2 + y^2 = 5$$
$$y = 5 - 2x$$

(b) What does this tell you about the line $y = 5 - 2x$ and the circle $x^2 + y^2 = 5$?

B8 Solve these pairs of simultaneous equations.

(a) $x^2 + y^2 = 25$ **(b)** $y = 7 - 3x$ **(c)** $6x^2 + y^2 = 22$
  $y = x - 1$ $x^2 + y^2 = 5$ $x = 2y + 5$

B9 The diagram shows a sketch of a circle with centre $(0, 0)$ and the line $x + y = 5$.

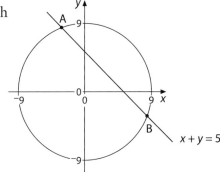

(a) What is the equation of the circle?

(b) Rearrange the equation $x + y = 5$ to make y the subject.

(c) Find the coordinates of the points A and B, correct to 2 d.p.

B10 Solve these pairs of simultaneous equations.

(a) $x^2 + y^2 = 10$ **(b)** $x^2 + y^2 = 5$ **(c)** $x - 3y = 2$
  $x + y = 4$ $x - y = 1$ $x^2 + y^2 = 2$

Test yourself

T1 (a) Sketch the graph of $x^2 + y^2 = 121$.

(b) What are the coordinates of the points where the graph cuts the y-axis?

T2 What is the equation of a circle with centre $(0, 0)$ and radius 3?

T3 The diagram shows the circle $x^2 + y^2 = 2$ and the line $y = 2x - 1$.
The line and the circle intersect at the points A and B.

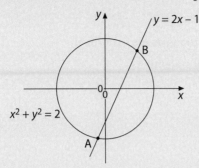

Not drawn accurately

(a) Show that the x-coordinates of A and B satisfy the equation $5x^2 - 4x - 1 = 0$.

(b) Hence find the coordinates of A and B.   AQA

T4 (a) Show that the radius of the circle $x^2 + y^2 = 50$ is between 7 and 8.

(b) (i) Expand and simplify $\left(5\sqrt{2}\right)^2$.

(ii) Sketch the circle $x^2 + y^2 = 50$ showing the exact values of the intercepts.

(c) Use algebra to solve these simultaneous equations.

$x^2 + y^2 = 50$
$y = x - 6$

T5 The straight line with equation $y = 3x - 1$ intersects the circle with equation $x^2 + y^2 = 40$ at two points A and B.

Solve these equations simultaneously to find the coordinates of A and B.   OCR

T6 Bill said that the line $y = 6$ cuts the curve $x^2 + y^2 = 25$ at two points.

(a) By eliminating y, show that Bill is incorrect.

(b) By eliminating y, find the solution to the simultaneous equations

$x^2 + y^2 = 25$
$y = 2x - 2$ Edexcel

T7 Solve the simultaneous equations

$x^2 + y^2 = 29$
$y - x = 3$ Edexcel

T8 (a) (i) Without sketching, show that the point $(3, 4)$ is inside the circle $x^2 + y^2 = 27$.

(ii) Hence show that the line $x + y = 7$ cuts the circle at two points.

(b) Find the coordinates of the points where $x + y = 7$ cuts $x^2 + y^2 = 27$.
Give values correct to two decimal places.

29 Congruent triangles

This work will help you

- decide from given information whether two triangles are congruent
- use congruent triangles to prove geometrical statements

A 'Fixing' a triangle

- You are told that the angles of a triangle are 40°, 60° and 80°.
  Is this information enough to fix both the size and shape of the triangle?
  (Imagine you are trying to use the information to draw the triangle.)

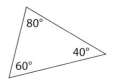

- Is the information in each sketch below enough to fix the size and shape of the triangle?
  (Again, imagine you are trying to use the information to draw each triangle,
  using a ruler, angle measurer and compasses as appropriate.)

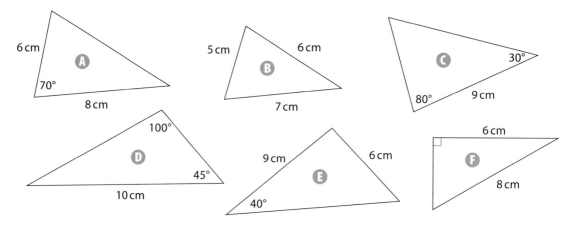

There are four sets of information that 'fix' a triangle:

- Three sides are known (SSS).
- Two sides and the angle between them are known (SAS).
- Two angles and the side between them are known (ASA).
- There is a right angle, and the hypotenuse and one other side are known (RHS).

At first sight, triangle D does not have one of the four sets of information
listed above. However, once you have calculated its third angle it is clear
that it has the information ASA.

Triangle E on the opposite page may appear to be fixed by the values given, yet SSA is not listed as a set of information that fixes a triangle.

Think about it this way.
If the side 9 cm long is drawn at 40° to a base, you would use compasses set at 6 cm to find the position of the third vertex. What will happen?

Congruent triangles

Objects that are the same shape and size as one another are called **congruent**.

Suppose we have two triangles and the lengths of the sides of one of them are the same as the lengths of the sides of the other.
Since they are both 'fixed' by the same set of information (SSS), they are the same shape and size and are therefore congruent.

In the same way, any two triangles are congruent if they share the same SAS, ASA or RHS information.

A1 The sketches below are deliberately distorted, so you can't tell by looking whether any of the triangles are congruent to each other.

Use the information about sides and and angles to find as many pairs of congruent triangles as you can. Give the reason (SSS, …) in each case.

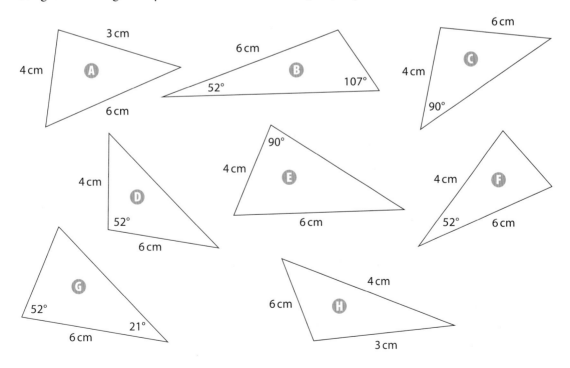

B Proving that two triangles are congruent

For the work in this chapter, these facts about angles can be assumed to be true.

- Vertically opposite angles are equal.
- Corresponding angles (made with parallel lines) are equal.
- Alternate angles (made with parallel lines) are equal.

These facts about a circle can be assumed to be true.

- All radii are equal. (This comes from the definition of a circle.)
- A tangent is perpendicular to the radius at the point of contact.

To prove that two triangles are congruent, you have to use one of these four reasons.

SSS   SAS   ASA   RHS

Example

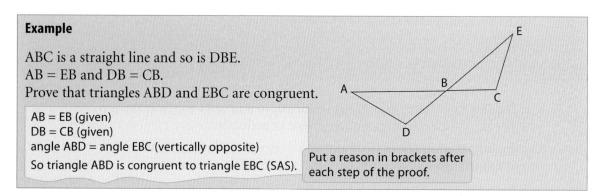

ABC is a straight line and so is DBE.
AB = EB and DB = CB.
Prove that triangles ABD and EBC are congruent.

> AB = EB (given)
> DB = CB (given)
> angle ABD = angle EBC (vertically opposite)
> So triangle ABD is congruent to triangle EBC (SAS).

Put a reason in brackets after each step of the proof.

B1 O is the centre of the circle and M is the mid-point of the chord AB.

  (a) Prove that the triangles OAM and OBM are congruent.

  (b) What can you deduce about angles OMA and OMB?

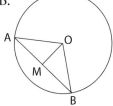

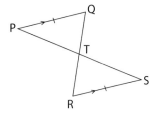

B2 In the diagram on the left, PQ is equal and parallel to RS. The lines PS and QR cross at T.

Prove that triangles PTQ and STR are congruent.

B3 JKL is an equilateral triangle and KM = LN. MKLN is a straight line.

Prove that triangles JKM and JLN are congruent.

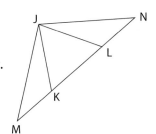

c Proving by congruent triangles

Congruent triangles are used in this way to help prove geometrical statements.

- First find a pair of triangles that you think may be congruent.
  You may need to draw an extra line ('construction line') to make the triangles.

- State which sides and angles are equal, giving a reason in each case.

- Use what you know about these triangles to prove they are congruent.
  Give the reason (SSS, …).

- Then use the fact that all the corresponding pairs of sides and angles must be equal.

Example

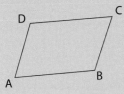

ABCD is a parallelogram.
Prove that AB = CD.

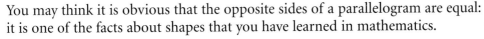

The definition of a parallelogram tells us
that AB is parallel to DC
and AD is parallel to BC.
Draw the line AC to make two triangles.

In the triangles ABC and CDA,
AC = CA (common side)
angle BAC = angle DCA (alternate)
angle ACB = angle CAD (alternate)

So triangle ABC is congruent to triangle CDA (ASA).
So AB = CD.

You may think it is obvious that the opposite sides of a parallelogram are equal:
it is one of the facts about shapes that you have learned in mathematics.

However, the mathematical study of space and shapes (geometry) has not been
about getting to know facts, but about showing they can be deduced in a sequence
starting from a small number of self-evident facts or axioms (see chapter 25).

The person best known for working in this way is the Greek
mathematician Euclid, who lived around 300 BCE. The use of
congruent triangles is a key component in Euclid's geometric proofs.
See what you can find out about Euclid on the web.

Until the 1960s, school geometry mostly followed Euclid's approach.
But then transformations, vectors and so on were introduced to give students
an idea of more recent approaches to geometry. As a result, the idea of
arranging provable facts (theorems) in a sequence has mostly disappeared
from school mathematics. So students who are asked to prove a statement
in geometry are now sometimes unsure what facts they are allowed to
assume for their proof.

C1 ABC is an isosceles triangle, with AB equal to AC.
M is the mid-point of BC.

Explain why triangle ABM is congruent to triangle ACM.

From this it follows that angle ABM = angle ACM.

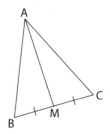

> In C1 you have proved that in an isosceles triangle
> the angles opposite the equal sides are equal.
> This was a fact assumed in chapter 25.

C2 PQRS is a quadrilateral in which PQ = PS and QR = SR (a kite).

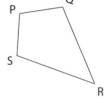

(a) Draw the diagram and join PR.
Prove that triangles PQR and PSR are congruent.

(b) It now follows that angle PQR is equal to another angle.
Which angle?

C3 *l* is a straight line and X is a point on it.
XA is perpendicular to *l*.
The lines AP and AQ are equal in length.

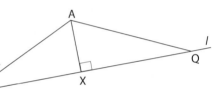

(a) Explain why triangles XAP and XAQ are congruent.

(b) It follows that two other lengths are equal.
Which are they?

C4 The two lines *p* and *q* cross at V.
VA = VB.
AK is drawn parallel to BL.

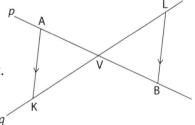

(a) Explain why triangles VAK and VBL are congruent.

(b) What further deductions can you make
about lines and angles in the diagram?

C5 The lines PQ and PR are equal in length.
Line *b* bisects angle QPR.
S is a point on *b*.

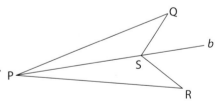

(a) Explain why triangles PQS and PRS are congruent.

(b) What further deductions can you make
about lines and angles in the diagram?

C6 AX and AY are tangents touching a circle at X and Y.
O is the centre of the circle.

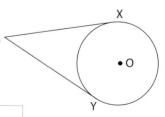

(a) Explain why triangles AOX and AOY are congruent.

(b) What can you deduce about the lengths AX and AY?

> In C6 you have proved that tangents to a circle from an
> external point to the points of contact are equal in length.

C7 A and B are the centres of two circles that intersect at P and Q.

By using congruent triangles, prove that angle APB = angle AQB.

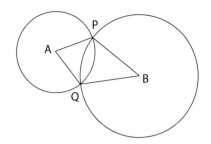

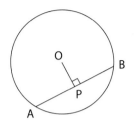

C8 O is the centre of a circle and AB is a chord. P is on AB and OP is perpendicular to AB.

Prove by congruent triangles that P is the mid-point of AB.

> In C8 you have proved that the perpendicular from the centre of a circle to a chord bisects the chord.

D Justifying ruler-and-compasses constructions

Congruent triangles can be used to prove that ruler-and-compasses constructions are correct.

For example, the construction for bisecting an angle is as follows.

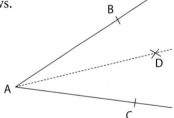

- With centre at the vertex A of the angle, draw arcs with the same radius, cutting the arms of the angle at B and C.

- With centre B draw an arc.
  With centre C and the same radius draw an arc to cut the previous arc at D.

- AD bisects the angle BAC.

D1 Copy and complete this proof of the angle bisection construction.

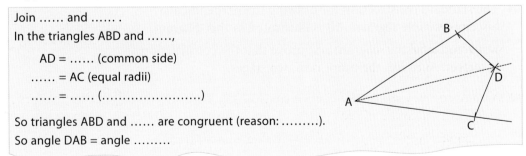

Join ...... and ....
In the triangles ABD and ......,

  AD = ... (common side)
  ...... = AC (equal radii)
  ...... = ... (......................)

So triangles ABD and ...... are congruent (reason: ....).
So angle DAB = angle ....

D2 A construction for drawing a perpendicular to a line *l* from a point P on it is as follows.

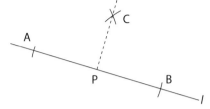

- With centre P, draw arcs with the same radius to cut the line *l* at A and B.

- With centre A, draw an arc.
  With centre B, draw an arc with the same radius to cut the previous arc at C.

- Draw PC.

  (a) Use congruent triangles to prove that angle APC = angle BPC.

  (b) Explain why it follows that each of these angles is a right angle.

D3 A construction for drawing a perpendicular from a point P to a line *l* (when P is not on *l*) is as follows.

- With centre P, draw arcs with the same radius to cut the line *l* at A and B.

- With centre A, draw an arc.
  With centre B, draw an arc with the same radius to cut the previous arc at D.

- Draw PD.

The proof of this construction is in two stages.
The point where PD cuts the line has been labelled E.

(a) First stage

  (i) Prove that triangles APD and BPD are congruent.

  (ii) Deduce that angle APD = angle BPD.

(b) Second stage

  (i) Prove that triangles PEA and PEB are congruent.

  (ii) Deduce that angles PEA and PEB are equal, and that each is a right angle.

D4 The standard construction for drawing the perpendicular bisector of a line segment AB is illustrated in this diagram.

Draw and label the diagram and prove that the construction is correct. As in D3, the proof is in two stages.

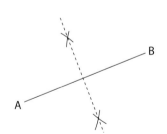

Test yourself

T1 O is the centre of a circle.
AB and CD are two chords of equal length.

   (a) Draw a diagram for this information.

   (b) Prove by using congruent triangles that angle AOB = angle COD.

T2

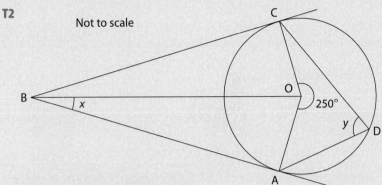

Not to scale

O is the centre of the circle.
A, C and D are points on the circle.
The tangents at A and C meet at B.

   (a) Show that AB = CB by proving that triangles OAB and OCB are congruent.

   (b) **(i)** Calculate angle *x*.

   (ii) Calculate angle *y*, giving your reasons.

OCR

T3 In this triangle, angle ABC = angle ACB.
Line BQ bisects angle ABC.
Line CP bisects angle ACB.

Prove that PB = QC.

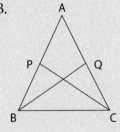

T4 ABCD and BEFG are squares.

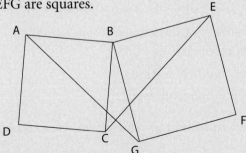

   (a) Explain why angle ABG = angle CBE.

   (b) Show that AG = CE by proving that triangles ABG and CBE are congruent.

30 Proof

This work will help you

- use a counterexample to prove a general statement is false
- use algebra to prove a general statement is true

A Proving a statement is false with a counterexample

- Can you prove that each of these people is wrong?

I think that the sum of two multiples of 3 is always odd.

I think that the expression $n^2 + 23n + 23$ will give a prime number for any positive integer value of n.

I think the expression $\dfrac{10}{x + y}$ is equivalent to $\dfrac{10}{x} + \dfrac{10}{y}$.

Showing a statement is true in **many** cases is not enough to prove it is true in **all** cases.

For example, showing that '$n^2 + 23n + 23$ is prime' is true for many integers n is not enough to show it is true for all integers n.

Showing a statement is false in **one** case is enough to prove it is false.

For example, we can show that 'all multiples of 5 end in a 5' is false by pointing out that 20 is a multiple of 5 but does not end in 5.

This is showing a statement is false by finding a **counterexample**.

A1 State which of these statements is false and use a counterexample to show it is false.

A The sum of two odd numbers is even.

B The sum of two even numbers is even.

C The product of two odd numbers is even.

D The product of two even numbers is even.

A2 Sophie says, 'For any whole number n, the value of $6n - 1$ is always a prime number'.
Sophie is wrong.
Give an example to show that Sophie is wrong.

Edexcel

A3 Jagdeep says, 'The square root of a number is always smaller than the number itself.'
Is he correct? Give an example to support your answer.

A4 Show that each statement below is false.

    (a) $3n + 1$ is odd for all integers n.   **(b)** $2n$ is even for **all** values of n (not just integers).

    (c) $2^n \geq 1$ for all values of n.   **(d)** $2n^2 + 11$ is prime for all integers n.

A5 Show that the statement '$(x + y)^2 = x^2 + y^2$ for all values of x and y' is false.

A6 Show that each statement below is false.

    (a) If $k^2 > 0$ then $k > 0$.   **(b)** If k is even then $\dfrac{k}{2}$ is even.

    (c) If p is prime then $p + 2$ is prime.   **(d)** If $a < 1$ and $b < 1$ then $ab < 1$.

B Algebraic proof

To prove a statement is true in general (not just in some cases), you often need to use algebra.

Example

Prove that the product of any two odd numbers is odd. Any odd number can be written in the form $2k + 1$ where k is an integer.

If m and n are integers then $2n + 1$ and $2m + 1$ are odd numbers.

The product is $(2n + 1)(2m + 1) = 4mn + 2m + 2n + 1$

$$= 2(2mn + m + n) + 1, \text{ which is odd}$$

So the product of two odd numbers is odd.

$2mn + m + n$ is an integer so $2(2mn + m + n) + 1$ is of the form $2k + 1$ where k is an integer.

B1 Use algebra to prove that the product of an odd and an even number is even.

Basic relationships between odd and even numbers are usually taken to be self-evident.

For example, 'the sum of two odd numbers is even' can be proved algebraically but is usually just stated as self-evidently true.

B2 X is an odd number and Y is an even number.
Which of these statements are true?

    A $X + Y + 1$ is odd.   B $X^2 + Y^2$ is odd.

    C $Y(X + 1)$ is even.   D $X(X + 1)$ is even.

    E $2X$ is even.   F $XY + 1$ is odd.

B3 P is an odd number.
Q is an even number.

    (a) Explain why $P + Q - 1$ is always an even number.

    (b) Alex says that $P + Q - 1$ cannot be a prime number.
          Explain why Alex is wrong.

          AQA

Prove that the sum of any five consecutive numbers is a multiple of 5.

Five consecutive numbers are n, $n + 1$, $n + 2$, $n + 3$ and $n + 4$ where n is an integer.
The sum is $n + (n + 1) + (n + 2) + (n + 3) + (n + 4) = 5n + 10$
$\qquad\qquad\qquad\qquad\qquad\qquad\qquad\qquad\qquad\qquad = 5(n + 2)$, which is a multiple of 5.
So the sum of any five consecutive numbers is a multiple of 5.

B4 Prove that the sum of any seven consecutive numbers is divisible by 7.

Prove that, for any three consecutive odd numbers,
the square of the middle number is 4 more than the product of the other two.

Three consecutive odd numbers can be written $2n + 1$, $2n + 3$ and $2n + 5$ where n is an integer.
The square of the middle number is $\qquad\qquad\qquad (2n + 3)^2 = 4n^2 + 12n + 9$
The product of the other two numbers is $\quad (2n + 1)(2n + 5) = 4n^2 + 12n + 5$
which is 4 less than the expression above.
This proves that, for any three consecutive odd numbers,
the square of the middle number is 4 more than the product of the other two.

B5 (a) Prove that the sum of any two consecutive even numbers cannot be a multiple of 4.

(b) Prove that the sum of any two consecutive odd numbers is a multiple of 4.

B6 Choose any three consecutive numbers.
Multiply the first and last number and add 1.
Square the middle number.

Try this with a few sets of numbers. What do you notice? Prove it.

B7 Prove that, for any four consecutive numbers, the product of the middle two numbers is always 2 more than the product of the first and last numbers.

B8 (a) If k^2 is a square number, which of these expressions gives the next square number?

$k^2 + 1$ $\qquad$ $k^2 + 3$ $\qquad$ $(k + 2)^2$ $\qquad$ $(k + 1)^2$ $\qquad$ $2k^2$

(b) Prove that the difference between two consecutive square numbers is always odd.

B9 Prove that the sum of the squares of any three consecutive numbers is always one less than a multiple of 3.

B10 For any three consecutive numbers,

(a) Explain why at least one of the numbers must be even.

(b) Explain why one of the numbers must be a multiple of 3.

(c) Hence explain why the product of the three numbers must be a multiple of 6.

*B11 (a) Factorise $p^2 - q^2$.

    (b) Here is a sequence of numbers. 0, 3, 8, 15, 24, 35, 48, …
       Write down an expression for the nth term of this sequence.

    (c) Show algebraically that the product of **any** two consecutive terms of the sequence
           0, 3, 8, 15, 24, 35, 48, …
       can be written as the product of four consecutive integers.

*B12 Prove that there is only one prime number of the form $k^2 - 1$ where k is a whole number.

*B13 Choose a triangle number, multiply it by 8 and add 1.
      Prove that the result will always be an **odd** square number.

Test yourself

T1 (a) k is an even number.
     Jo says that $\frac{1}{2}k + 1$ is always even.
     Give an example to show that Jo is wrong.

    (b) The letters a and b represent prime numbers.
     Give an example to show that $a + b$ is **not** always an even number.   AQA

T2 p is an odd number.
    Explain why $p^2 + 1$ is always an even number.   AQA

T3 Explain why the product of two consecutive multiples of 3 is always an even number.

T4 Show that the sum of **any** three consecutive integers is always a multiple of 3.   AQA

T5 Prove that $(n + 1)^2 - (n - 1)^2$ is a multiple of 4, for all positive integer values of n.   Edexcel

T6 Prove that for any three consecutive numbers, the difference between
    the squares of the first and last numbers is 4 times the middle number.

T7 (a) n is a positive integer.
      (i) Explain why $n(n + 1)$ must be an even number.
      (ii) Explain why $2n + 1$ must be an odd number.

    (b) Expand and simplify $(2n + 1)^2$.

    (c) Prove that the square of any odd number is always 1 more than a multiple of 8.   AQA

T8 (a) Show that $(2a - 1)^2 - (2b - 1)^2 = 4(a - b)(a + b - 1)$.

    (b) Prove that the difference between the squares of any two odd numbers is
     a multiple of 8.
     (You may assume that any odd number can be written in the form $2r - 1$,
     where r is an integer).   Edexcel

31 Extending trigonometry to any triangle

You will revise

- **using sine, cosine and tangent in a right-angled triangle**
- **using Pythagoras's theorem**

Where enough information has been given to 'fix' a triangle, this work will help you

- **find other lengths or angles in the triangle**
- **find the area of the triangle**

You need an angle measurer and compasses.

A Revision: trigonometry and Pythagoras

A1 Find the missing lengths (to the nearest 0.1 cm).

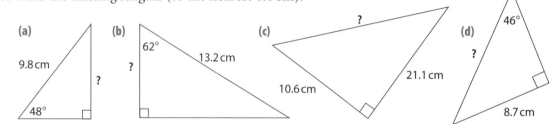

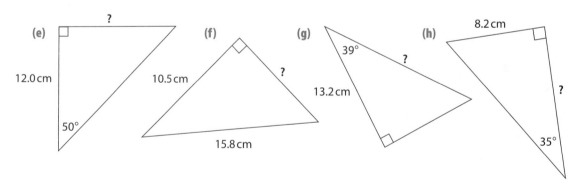

A2 Find the missing angles (to the nearest degree).

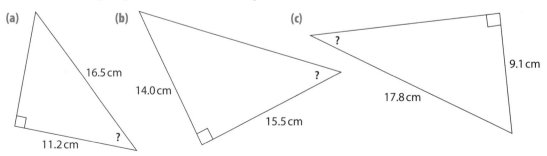

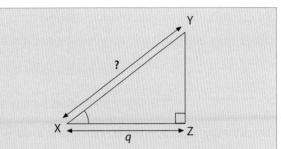

Length BC can be written as an **expression**:

$p \sin A$ (p times the sine of the angle at A)

Length XY can be written as an expression:

$\dfrac{q}{\cos X}$ (q divided by the cosine of the angle at X)

A3 Write an expression for each of the lengths marked x.

(a)

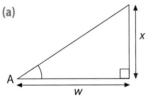

(b)

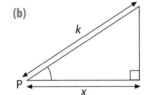

(c)

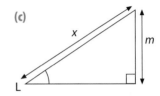

(d)

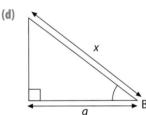

(e)

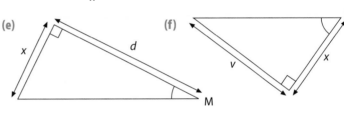

(f)

B The sine rule: finding a side

B1 In this triangle, a perpendicular has been drawn from C on to AB.
Let the length of the perpendicular be h.

(a) Use $\sin 40°$ to find the value of h to 3 d.p.

(b) Use $\sin 65°$ and your answer to (a) to find BC to 1 d.p.

(c) Check by drawing the triangle accurately from the
values given in the diagram, and measuring BC.
(Work out angle ACB before you start to draw).

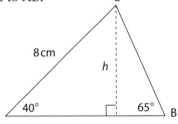

B2 In this triangle, a is the length of the side opposite angle A
and b is the length of the side opposite angle B.

(a) Write an expression for h in terms of length b and
$\sin A$ (the sine of the angle at A).

(b) Write an expression for h in terms of
length a and $\sin B$.

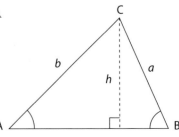

In question B2, you should have found these two expressions for h: $a\sin B$, $b\sin A$.

Since they both equal h, they must equal each other: $a\sin B = b\sin A$

Dividing both sides by $\sin B$, we get $a = \dfrac{b\sin A}{\sin B}$

Dividing both sides by $\sin A$, we get $\dfrac{a}{\sin A} = \dfrac{b}{\sin B}$

By drawing a perpendicular from A to side BC, you can prove that $\dfrac{b}{\sin B} = \dfrac{c}{\sin C}$.

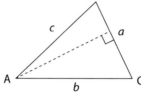

The formula $\dfrac{a}{\sin A} = \dfrac{b}{\sin B} = \dfrac{c}{\sin C}$ is known as the **sine rule**.

Notice how the sides and vertices of a triangle are lettered: side a is opposite vertex A, and so on.

You can use the sine rule to solve some triangle problems.

Example

Find the missing length.

Copy and label the diagram with a opposite A, and so on.

Write the part of the sine rule that you need.

$$\dfrac{a}{\sin A} = \dfrac{c}{\sin C}$$

Substitute the angles and side.

$$\dfrac{9.0}{\sin 70°} = \dfrac{c}{\sin 35°}$$

Make the missing length the subject.

$$c = \dfrac{9.0\sin 35°}{\sin 70°}$$

Find the answer on a calculator and give it to a suitable degree of accuracy.

$$c = 5.5\,\text{cm (to 1 d.p.)}$$

If letters other than A, B, C are given as vertices of the triangle, you can adapt the sine rule.

For example, $\dfrac{p}{\sin P} = \dfrac{q}{\sin Q} = \dfrac{r}{\sin R}$

where p is the length of side QR and so on.

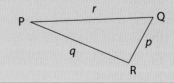

B3 Find each missing length to 1 d.p.
Check that each answer makes sense for the values given in the question.

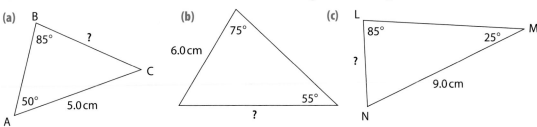

(a) B, 85°, ?, C, 50°, 5.0 cm, A

(b) 75°, 6.0 cm, 55°, ?

(c) L, 85°, 25°, M, ?, 9.0 cm, N

B4

(a) Calculate this angle.

(b) Use the sine rule to find the length of this side.

(c) Use the sine rule to find the length of this side.

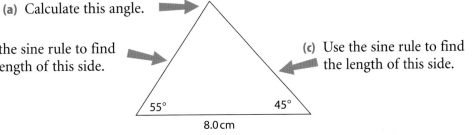

55°   45°
8.0 cm

B5 Find the lengths marked with letters.

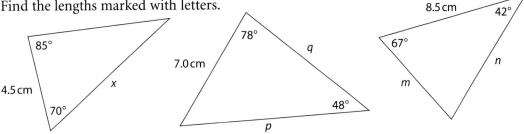

85°, 4.5 cm, 70°, x

78°, 7.0 cm, q, 48°, p

8.5 cm, 42°, 67°, m, n

The proof of the sine rule given earlier assumed that all the angles of the triangle were acute.

It is also possible to prove the sine rule when one of the angles is obtuse.

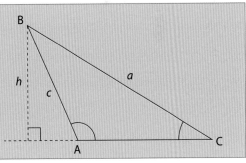

B, h, c, a, A, C

B6 Find the missing lengths.

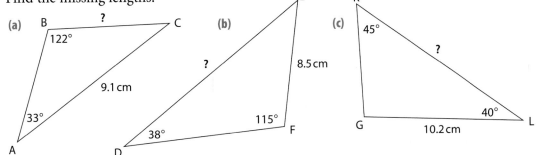

(a) B, ?, C, 122°, 9.1 cm, 33°, A

(b) E, ?, 8.5 cm, 115°, F, 38°, D

(c) K, 45°, ?, G, 10.2 cm, 40°, L

B7 The line MN represents the vertical mast of a radio transmitter.
Points P, Q and N are on level ground.
From P, the angle of elevation of the top of the mast is 28°.
The angle of elevation from Q is 35°.
The distance between P and Q is 50 m.

Find

(a) QM   **(b)** the height of the mast, MN

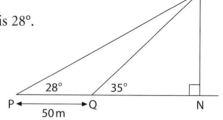

C The sine rule: finding an angle

When you try to find an angle with the sine rule, you need to use $\sin^{-1}$ on your calculator.

But remember there are usually **two** angles that have a particular sine.

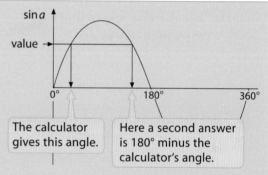

The calculator gives this angle.

Here a second answer is 180° minus the calculator's angle.

Example

Find the angle at A.

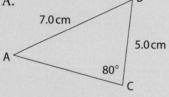

Remember there are **two** angles between 0° and 180° with this sine.

When you have obtained your answer, check that it makes sense by looking back at the diagram.

$$\frac{a}{\sin A} = \frac{c}{\sin C}$$

$$\frac{5.0}{\sin A} = \frac{7.0}{\sin 80°}$$

$$\sin A = \frac{5.0 \sin 80°}{7.0}$$

$\sin A = 0.7034...$ (calculator result)

So A = 45° or 135° to the nearest degree

But if A was 135°, the sum of the angles of the triangle would be greater than 180°, because $80 + 135 = 215$.

So A = 45°

C1 For each of these …

- Find the sine of the missing angle.
- Give two angles that have that sine.
- Explain which angle is possible in this case.

(a) **(b)**

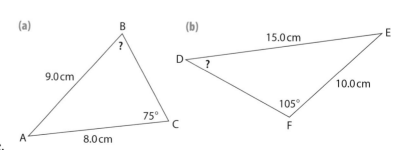

C2 (a) In this triangle …

- Find the sine of the missing angle.

- Give two angles that have that sine.

- What happens when you check to see which angle is possible?

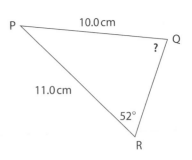

(b) Try drawing the triangle from the information given in the diagram.
Use this to explain what you found in part (a).

C3 (a) Find the sine of the missing angle here.
What angles have this sine?

(b) Try drawing the triangle from the information given in the diagram.
Use this to explain what you found in part (a).

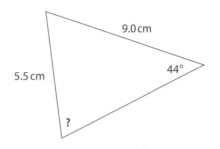

D The cosine rule

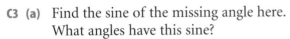

D1 In this triangle, a perpendicular has been drawn from B on to AC, which it meets at point P.
Let length BP be h.
Let length AP be x.

(a) Use a cosine to work out x to 3 d.p.

(b) Use Pythagoras to find h to 3 d.p.

(c) Use your answer to (a) to find length PC to 3 d.p.

(d) Use Pythagoras with your answers to (b) and (c) to find BC to 1 d.p.

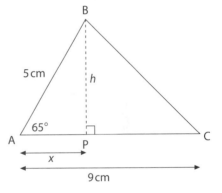

D2 In this triangle, lengths are given as variables.

(a) Write length PC in terms of b and x.

(b) Use Pythagoras and your answer to (a) to express h^2 in terms of a, b and x.

(c) Use Pythagoras to express h^2 in terms of c and x.

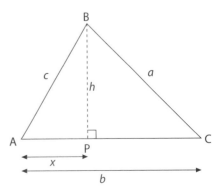

In question D2 you should have found these two expressions for h^2:
$$a^2 - (b-x)^2, \quad c^2 - x^2$$

Since they both equal h^2, they must equal each other.
$$a^2 - (b-x)^2 = c^2 - x^2$$

D3 Make a^2 the subject of the formula.
Expand the brackets and simplify the right-hand side.

D4 Look back at the diagram for D2.
Write an expression for x in terms of c and angle A.

If you replace x in your answer to D3 by the expression you wrote for D4, you should get
$$a^2 = b^2 + c^2 - 2bc\cos A$$

This formula is known as the **cosine rule**.

D5 Substitute the values from question D1 into this formula.
From a^2 work out a.
Does this give you the same answer as in D1(d) ?

The cosine rule refers to all three sides of the triangle but only one angle.
So it is useful to have two other versions of it when solving triangle problems:
$$b^2 = a^2 + c^2 - 2ac\cos B$$
$$c^2 = a^2 + b^2 - 2ab\cos C$$

The angle used in the proof above is acute, but the cosine rule also works when the angle it refers to is obtuse.

Example

Find the length BC.

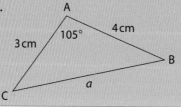

$a^2 = b^2 + c^2 - 2bc\cos A$
$a^2 = 3^2 + 4^2 - 2 \times 3 \times 4 \times \cos 105°$
$a^2 = 31.2116...$ (calculator result)
$a = \sqrt{31.2116...} = 5.6$ to 1 d.p.
So the length of BC is 5.6 cm.

D6 Work out the missing length in each of these.

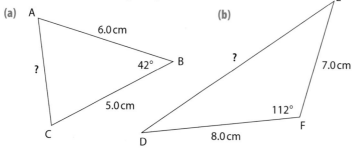

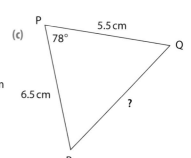

D7 The hour hand of a clock is 4.5 cm long.
The minute hand is 6.2 cm long.

Calculate the distance between the tips of
the hands at 7 o'clock.

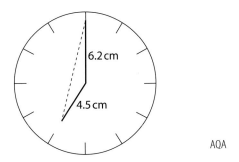

AQA

D8 Two ships, A and B, leave port at 1300 hours.
Ship A travels at a constant speed of 18 km per hour
on a bearing of 070°.
Ship B travels at a constant speed of 25 km per hour
on a bearing of 152°.

Calculate the distance between A and B at 1400 hours.

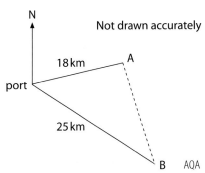

Not drawn accurately

AQA

Example

Find the angle at B.

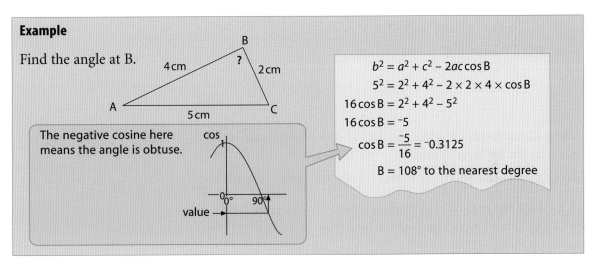

The negative cosine here
means the angle is obtuse.

$$b^2 = a^2 + c^2 - 2ac \cos B$$
$$5^2 = 2^2 + 4^2 - 2 \times 2 \times 4 \times \cos B$$
$$16 \cos B = 2^2 + 4^2 - 5^2$$
$$16 \cos B = {}^-5$$
$$\cos B = \frac{{}^-5}{16} = {}^-0.3125$$
$$B = 108° \text{ to the nearest degree}$$

D9 Use the cosine rule to find the missing angles, to the nearest degree.

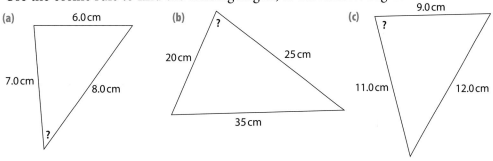

(a) 6.0 cm, 7.0 cm, 8.0 cm, ?

(b) 20 cm, 25 cm, 35 cm, ?

(c) 9.0 cm, 11.0 cm, 12.0 cm, ?

D10 Rework the example on the opposite page but with angle A changed to 90°.
Comment on the result.

E The sine formula for the area of a triangle

E1 Calculate the area of this triangle.

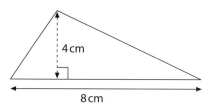

4 cm

8 cm

E2 (a) Use $\sin 70°$ to find h to 3 d.p.

(b) Calculate the area of triangle ABC to the nearest cm^2.

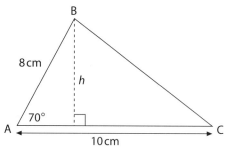

B

8 cm

h

70°

A

10 cm

C

E3 In this triangle, lengths are given as variables.

(a) Write an expression for h in terms of c and angle A.

(b) Write an expression for the area of triangle ABC.

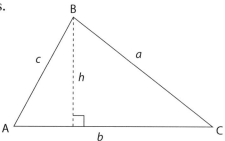

B

c

a

h

A

b

C

Using the standard lettering, the area of any triangle can be given by the formula $\frac{1}{2}ac\sin B$.

This formula can also be written as $\frac{1}{2}ab\sin C$ and $\frac{1}{2}bc\sin A$.

E4 Find the area of each triangle to the nearest cm^2.

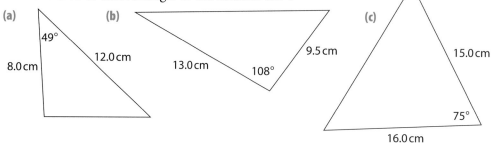

(a)

49°

8.0 cm

12.0 cm

(b)

13.0 cm

108°

9.5 cm

(c)

15.0 cm

75°

16.0 cm

E5 In triangle ABC, $AB = 11\,cm$, $BC = 9\,cm$ and $CA = 10\,cm$. Find the area of triangle ABC.

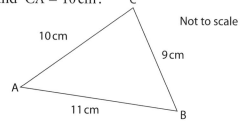

C

Not to scale

10 cm

9 cm

A

11 cm

B

AQA

F1 Each of these triangles represents a problem to be solved.
'G' shows where a length or angle is given.
'?' shows a length or angle that you have to find.

In each case, say whether you should use the sine rule or the cosine rule.
If two different triangles might be drawn from the information given, say so.

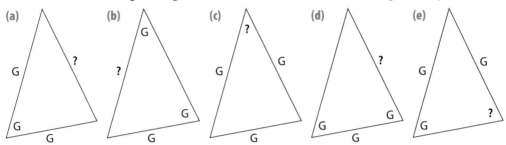

F2 (a) Calculate the area of triangle PQS.

(b) Calculate the length of QS.

(c) Calculate the size of angle QRS.

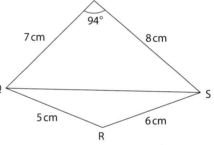

F3 In this diagram LMN is a straight line.
Calculate the length of KN.

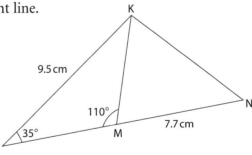

F4 Two coastguard stations, P and Q, are 32 kilometres apart.
Q is due south of P.
A boat, B, is on a bearing of 145° from P and 040° from Q.
Calculate the distance QB.

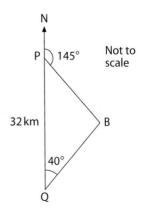

OCR

F5 In triangle ABC,
AC = 8 cm,
CB = 15 cm,
angle ACB = 70°.

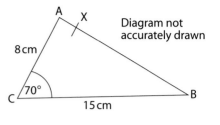

Diagram not accurately drawn

(a) Calculate the area of triangle ABC.
Give your answer correct to three significant figures.

X is the point on AB such that angle CXB = 90°.

(b) Calculate the length of CX.
Give your answer correct to three significant figures.

Edexcel

F6 The area of this triangle is 32 cm².

(a) Find the obtuse angle at C.

(b) Find the length of AB.

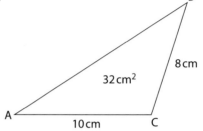

F7 PQ represents a vertical phone antenna.
QR represents the vertical mast that it is mounted on.
RS represents horizontal ground.

(a) Calculate the height PQ of the antenna,
in metres to 3 s.f.

(b) Calculate the height QR of the mast,
in metres to 3 s.f.

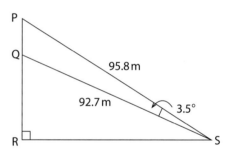

Test yourself

T1 The distance AC is 10.3 m. The distance CD is 16.0 m.
Angle BAC = 47°, angle ACD = 69° and
angle ABC is a right angle.

(a) Calculate the distance BC.

(b) Calculate the distance AD.

(c) Calculate the area of triangle ACD.

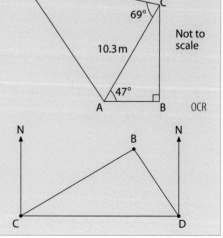

Not to scale

OCR

T2 Coastguard station C is 48 km due west of
coastguard station D.

Boat B is 39 km away from C, on a bearing of 065°.

What is the boat's bearing and distance from D?

32 Transforming graphs

You should know how to

- draw and interpret a range of graphs, including simple trigonometric graphs
- solve a quadratic equation such as $(x + 4)^2 = 3$

This work will help you

- find and use the completed-square form of a quadratic expression
- transform graphs and find their equations
- use function notation
- sketch graphs of $y = af(x)$, $f(ax)$, $^-f(x)$, $f(^-x)$, $f(x) + a$ and $f(x + a)$ given the graph of $y = f(x)$

You need sheet H2–8.

A Working with quadratic expressions in the form $(x + a)^2 + b$

T

- What is the value of $(x - 1)^2 + 6$ when $x = 4$?
- Try other values of x.
- What is the minimum value of $(x - 1)^2 + 6$?
  What value of x gives the minimum?

A1 (a) What is the value of $(x - 6)^2$ when

   (i) $x = 8$ (ii) $x = 10$ (iii) $x = 3$ (iv) $x = ^-1$ (v) $x = 6$

(b) What is the minimum value of $(x - 6)^2$?

(c) What is the minimum value of

   (i) $(x - 6)^2 + 7$ (ii) $(x - 6)^2 + 1$ (iii) $(x - 6)^2 - 5$

A2 Write down the minimum value of each expression and the value of x that gives the minimum.

   (a) $(x - 4)^2 + 3$ (b) $(x + 2)^2 + 5$ (c) $(x - 3)^2 - 6$ (d) $(x + 1)^2$

A3 (a) (i) Expand $(x + 3)^2$.

   (ii) Hence, show that $(x + 3)^2 - 5$ is equivalent to $x^2 + 6x + 4$.

(b) Hence, write down the minimum value of $x^2 + 6x + 4$.

A4 (a) Which expression below is equivalent to $x^2 - 10x + 26$?

   $(x - 10)^2 + 16$ $(x - 5)^2 + 26$ $(x - 10)^2 - 74$ $(x - 5)^2 + 1$

(b) Hence find the minimum value of the expression $x^2 - 10x + 26$.

$(x-1)^2 + 3$ is a quadratic expression so the graph of $y = (x-1)^2 + 3$ is a parabola.

When $x = 1$, $(x-1)^2 + 3 = 0^2 + 3 = 3$ and this is the minimum value.

So the minimum point on the parabola has coordinates $(1, 3)$ and we can sketch the graph as shown.

When $x = 0$,
$y = (^-1)^2 + 3$
$= 1 + 3$
$= 4$

So the graph cuts the y-axis at $(0, 4)$.

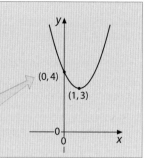

A5 These equations match the graphs below. Match each one with its appropriate graph.

A $y = (x-2)^2 + 1$

B $y = (x+2)^2$

C $y = (x-1)^2 + 2$

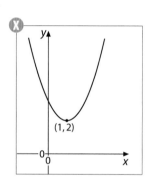

$(1, 2)$

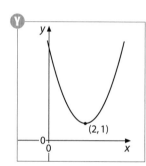

$(2, 1)$

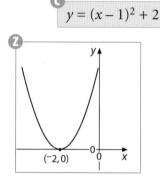

$(^-2, 0)$

A6 (a) Which equation below matches the graph on the right?

$y = (x-2)^2 + 4$

$y = (x+4)^2 + 2$

$y = (x+2)^2 + 4$

$y = (x-4)^2 + 2$

$y = (x+4)^2 - 2$

$y = (x-2)^2 - 4$

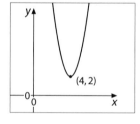

$(4, 2)$

(b) Where will the graph cut the y-axis?

A7 Sketch the graph of $y = (x+4)^2 + 1$, showing its minimum point clearly.

A8 Copy and complete the working to solve the equation $(x-3)^2 - 16 = 0$.

$(x-3)^2 - 16 = 0$
$(x-3)^2 = \blacksquare$
$x - 3 = \pm \blacktriangledown$
$x = \blacksquare$
So the solutions are $x = \bullet$ and $x = \bullet$

A9 Solve these equations.

(a) $(x-4)^2 - 9 = 0$ **(b)** $(x-2)^2 - 16 = 0$ **(c)** $(x+3)^2 - 25 = 0$

A10 (a) Show that the graph of $y = (x-5)^2 + 1$ does not cut the x-axis.

(b) Where does the graph of $y = (x-5)^2 - 1$ cut the x-axis?

B Completing the square

Writing an expression such as $x^2 - 6x + 10$
in the form $(x + a)^2 + b$
where a and b are positive or negative constants is called **completing the square.**

It can be useful to do this when looking for a minimum value, sketching a graph or solving an equation.

In the expression $x^2 - 6x + 10$, the coefficient of x is $^-6$.

Half of $^-6$ is $^-3$ so the expression that we want begins $(x - 3)^2$.

$$(x - 3)^2 = x^2 - 6x + 9$$

We want an expression equivalent to $x^2 + 6x + 10$ so we need to add 1 to each side to obtain

$$(x - 3)^2 + 1 = x^2 - 6x + 10.$$

So $x^2 - 6x + 10$ is equivalent to $(x - 3)^2 + 1$.

This is called writing $x^2 - 6x + 10$ in **completed-square form.**

B1 Which of these expressions are in completed-square form?

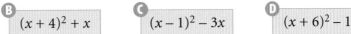

A $(x - 3)^2 + 5$ **B** $(x + 4)^2 + x$ **C** $(x - 1)^2 - 3x$ **D** $(x + 6)^2 - 1$

B2 Copy and complete each identity to write each quadratic in completed-square form.

(a) $x^2 + 4x + 5 = (x + \blacksquare)^2 + \blacksquare$ (b) $x^2 - 8x + 19 = (x - \blacksquare)^2 + \blacksquare$

(c) $x^2 + 10x + 11 = (x + \blacksquare)^2 - \blacksquare$ (d) $x^2 - 6x + 2 = (x - \blacksquare)^2 - \blacksquare$

B3 Write each expression below in completed-square form.
Hence work out the minimum value of each expression.

(a) $x^2 + 6x + 15$ (b) $x^2 + 2x + 5$ (c) $x^2 + 8x + 20$

(d) $x^2 + 4x + 1$ (e) $x^2 + 10x + 8$ (f) $x^2 + 12x + 4$

B4 Write each expression below in completed-square form.
Hence work out the minimum value of each expression.

(a) $x^2 - 4x + 7$ (b) $x^2 - 2x + 5$ (c) $x^2 - 6x + 14$

(d) $x^2 - 4x + 3$ (e) $x^2 - 10x + 8$ (f) $x^2 - 14x + 40$

B5 Write $x^2 - 8x + 21$ in the form $(x - a)^2 + b$, where a and b are constants.
What are the values of a and b?

B6 Write $x^2 + 6x + 2$ in the form $(x + p)^2 - q$, where p and q are constants.
What are the values of p and q?

B7 Copy and complete each identity.

(a) $x^2 + 6x - 1 = (x + \blacksquare)^2 - \blacksquare$ (b) $x^2 - 8x - 3 = (x - \blacksquare)^2 - \blacksquare$

(c) $x^2 + 8x = (x + \blacksquare)^2 - \blacksquare$ (d) $x^2 - 14x = (x - \blacksquare)^2 - \blacksquare$

B8 The expression $x^2 + 8x + 11$ can be written in the form $(x + p)^2 + q$, where p and q are constants. Find the value of p and show that $q = {}^-5$.

B9 Write each expression below in the form $(x + a)^2 + b$, where a and b are constants. Write down the value of a and b each time.

   (a) $x^2 + 4x + 2$ **(b)** $x^2 + 2x - 3$ **(c)** $x^2 + 8x - 3$

   (d) $x^2 - 6x + 13$ **(e)** $x^2 - 2x - 5$ **(f)** $x^2 - 10x - 5$

B10 The expression $x^2 - 12x + 20$ can be written in the form $(x - a)^2 + b$, where a and b are integers.

   (a) Calculate the values of a and b.

   (b) Hence find the minimum point on the graph of $y = x^2 - 12x + 20$.

   (c) Sketch the graph of $y = x^2 - 12x + 20$, showing the minimum point and y-intercept.

B11 **(a)** Write $y = x^2 - 4x - 3$ in completed-square form.

   (b) Sketch the graph of $y = x^2 - 4x - 3$, showing the minimum point and y-intercept.

B12 **(a)** Write $x^2 + 4x - 5$ in completed-square form.

   (b) **(i)** Show that the equation $x^2 + 4x - 5 = 0$ can be written as $(x + 2)^2 = 9$.

   (ii) Hence solve $x^2 + 4x - 5 = 0$.

B13 **(a)** Write $x^2 - 6x + 7$ in completed-square form.

   (b) Hence solve the equation $x^2 - 6x + 7 = 0$, giving your answers to 2 d.p.

B14 **(a)** Expand $(3x + 2)^2$.

   (b) Write the expression $9x^2 + 12x + 5$ in the form $(ax + b)^2 + c$, where a, b and c are constants.

B15 Copy and complete each identity.

   (a) $x^2 + 3x + 2 = (x + \blacksquare)^2 - \blacksquare$ **(b)** $x^2 - 5x + 7 = (x - \blacksquare)^2 + \blacksquare$

C Transforming quadratic graphs

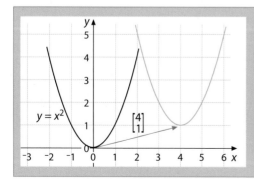

$y = x^2$

$\begin{bmatrix} 4 \\ 1 \end{bmatrix}$

The blue curve is the image of $y = x^2$ after a translation by $\begin{bmatrix} 4 \\ 1 \end{bmatrix}$.

The minimum point on the blue curve is $(4, 1)$.

Hence the equation of the image of $y = x^2$ can be written as

$$y = (x - 4)^2 + 1$$

C1 Each of the following sketches shows the graph of $y = x^2$ after a translation. Find the equation of each curve.

(a) 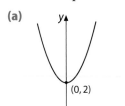 (b) 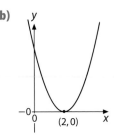 (c) 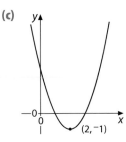 (d)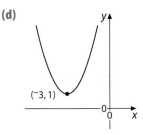

C2 The graph of $y = x^2$ is translated 4 units to the left. What is the equation of the transformed curve?

C3 What translation will map the graph of $y = x^2$ on to the graph of $y = (x + 5)^2 + 1$?

C4 The graph of $y = x^2$ is translated by $\begin{bmatrix} 3 \\ -4 \end{bmatrix}$. What is the equation of the image?

C5 What is the equation of the image of $y = x^2$ after

(a) reflection in the x-axis

(b) reflection in the y-axis

Stretching in the y-direction

To stretch a shape from the x-axis by a factor of 2 in the y-direction, multiply all y-coordinate values by 2.

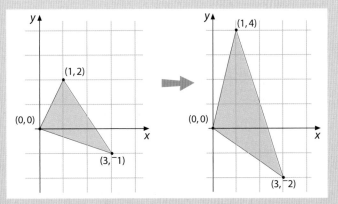

In general, to stretch a shape from the x-axis by a factor of a in the y-direction, multiply all y-coordinate values by a.

C6 (a) Write down the coordinates of five points on the graph of $y = x^2$.

(b) Multiply each y-value by 2 to find the image of each point under a stretch by a factor of 2 in the y-direction.

(c) On the same set of axes, draw and label graphs of $y = x^2$ and its image after a stretch by a factor of 2 in the y-direction.

(d) What is the equation of the transformed curve?

C7 Describe the transformation that maps $y = x^2$ to $y = 3x^2$.

C8 **(a)** Write down the coordinates of three points on the graph of $y = x^2$.

(b) Multiply each y-value by $\frac{1}{2}$ to find the image of each point after a stretch by a factor of $\frac{1}{2}$ in the y-direction.

(c) On the same set of axes, draw and label graphs of $y = x^2$ and its image after a stretch by a factor of $\frac{1}{2}$ in the y-direction.

(d) What is the equation of the transformed curve?

Stretching in the *x*-direction

To stretch a shape from the y-axis by a factor of $\frac{1}{2}$ in the x-direction, multiply all x-coordinate values by $\frac{1}{2}$.

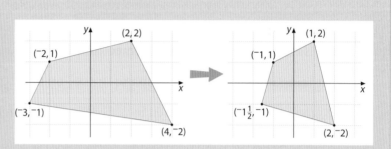

In general, to stretch a shape from the y-axis by a factor of a in the x-direction, multiply all x-coordinate values by a.

C9 **(a)** Write down the coordinates of five points on the graph of $y = x^2$.

(b) Multiply each x-value by 2 to find the image of each point after a stretch by a factor of 2 in the x-direction.

(c) On the same set of axes, draw and label graphs of $y = x^2$ and its image after a stretch by a factor of 2 in the x-direction.

(d) Which of these is the equation of the transformed curve?

A $y = 2x^2$ **B** $y = \frac{1}{2}x^2$ **C** $y = 4x^2$ **D** $y = \frac{1}{4}x^2$

C10 **(a)** On the same set of axes, draw and label graphs of $y = x^2$ and its image after a stretch by a factor of $\frac{1}{2}$ in the x-direction.

(b) Which of these is the equation of the transformed curve?

A $y = 2x^2$ **B** $y = \frac{1}{2}x^2$ **C** $y = 4x^2$ **D** $y = \frac{1}{4}x^2$

C11 Find the equation, in its simplest form, of the image of $y = x^2$ after a stretch by a factor of $\frac{1}{3}$ in the x-direction.

C12 Sketch the image of $y = x^2$ after a reflection in the x-axis followed by a translation of 5 units vertically. Label the transformed curve with its equation.

C13 What is the equation of the image of $y = x^2$ after a stretch by a factor of 4 in the y-direction followed by a translation of $\begin{bmatrix} 0 \\ 3 \end{bmatrix}$?

D Transforming graphs in general

The equation of a graph often gives y in terms of x.

For example, we usually write $y = x + 5$ rather than the equivalent $x = y - 5$.

This makes it straightforward to deal with a transformation that alters the y-coordinates.

Examples

- To translate the graph of $y = x^2$ by $\begin{bmatrix} 0 \\ 2 \end{bmatrix}$ we add 2 to each y-coordinate.

  Hence the equation of the image is $y = x^2 + 2$.

- To stretch $y = x^3$ by a factor of 4 in the y-direction we multiply each y-coordinate by 4.

  Hence the equation of the image is $y = 4x^3$.

- To reflect $y = \cos x$ in the x-axis we multiply each y-coordinate by $^-1$.

  Hence the equation of the image is $y = {}^-\cos x$.

D1 Each graph below is the image of $y = \sin x$ after a transformation.
Write an equation for each graph.

(a)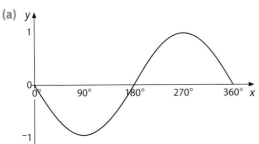

(b)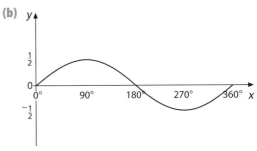

D2 The graph of $y = x^3$ is translated by $\begin{bmatrix} 0 \\ -4 \end{bmatrix}$. What is the equation of the image?

D3 Each graph below is the image of $y = \cos x$ after a transformation.
Write an equation for each graph.

(a)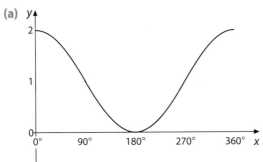

(b)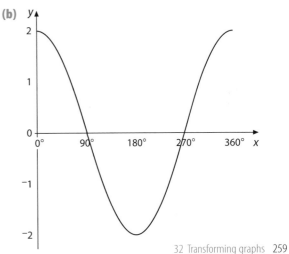

If we transform a graph with an equation in the form $y = \ldots$ by using a rule to transform the **x-coordinates** then we need a different approach.

We could start by writing x in terms of y.
For example, rearrange $y = x^2$ to give $x = \pm\sqrt{y}$.

To translate the graph of $y = x^2$ by $\begin{bmatrix} 2 \\ 0 \end{bmatrix}$ we add 2 to each x-coordinate.

Hence the equation of the image is $x = \pm\sqrt{y} + 2$.

Rearranging gives $x - 2 = \pm\sqrt{y}$ and $y = (x - 2)^2$.
Here, the equation of the image can be found by replacing the x in $y = x^2$ by $x - 2$.
This idea works for any graph translated horizontally.

> If we translate a graph by $\begin{bmatrix} a \\ 0 \end{bmatrix}$ the equation of the image is found by replacing x by $x - a$.

- What is the equation of $y = x^3$ after a translation of $\begin{bmatrix} -5 \\ 0 \end{bmatrix}$?

D4 Write down the equation of $y = \cos x$ after a translation of $\begin{bmatrix} 90° \\ 0 \end{bmatrix}$.

D5 Write down the equation of each graph below after a translation of $\begin{bmatrix} -3 \\ 0 \end{bmatrix}$.

    (a) $y = x^2$ (b) $y = \sin x$ (c) $y = \dfrac{1}{x}$

D6 Sketch the graph of $y = \sin(x - 30°)$.

To stretch the graph of $y = x^2$ by a factor of 2 in the x-direction we double each x-coordinate.
We know that $x = \pm\sqrt{y}$ and so the equation of the image is $x = \pm 2\sqrt{y}$.

Rearranging gives $\frac{1}{2}x = \pm\sqrt{y}$ and $y = \left(\frac{1}{2}x\right)^2$.
Here, the equation of the image can be found by replacing the x in $y = x^2$ by $\frac{1}{2}x$.
This idea works for any graph stretched horizontally.

> If we stretch a graph by a factor of a in the x-direction the equation of the image is found by replacing x by $\dfrac{1}{a}x$ or $\dfrac{x}{a}$.

- What is the equation of $y = x^2$ after a stretch by a factor of 5 in the x-direction?

D7 Write down the equation $y = \cos x$ after a stretch by a factor of 2 in the x-direction.

D8 Find the equation of each graph below after a stretch by a factor of 3 in the x-direction.

    (a) $y = x^3$ (b) $y = x^2 + 1$ (c) $y = 3x$

To stretch the graph of $y = x^2$ by a factor of $\frac{1}{2}$ in the x-direction we multiply each x-coordinate by $\frac{1}{2}$.

We know that $x = \pm\sqrt{y}$ and so the equation of the image is $x = \pm\frac{1}{2}\sqrt{y}$.

Rearranging gives $2x = \pm\sqrt{y}$ and $y = (2x)^2$.

Here, the equation of the image can be found by replacing the x in $y = x^2$ by 2x.

This idea works for any graph stretched by a fractional factor horizontally.

> If we stretch a graph by a factor of $\dfrac{1}{a}$ in the x-direction the equation of the image is found by replacing x by ax.

- What is the equation of $y = x^3$ after a stretch by a factor of $\frac{1}{3}$ in the x-direction?

D9 Write down the equation of $y = \sin x$ after a stretch by a factor of $\frac{1}{4}$ in the x-direction.

D10 Find the equation of each graph below after a stretch by a factor of $\frac{1}{2}$ in the x-direction.

(a) $y = x^2$ (b) $y = x^3 - 1$ (c) $y = \dfrac{1}{x}$

D11 This graph is the image of $y = \sin x$ after a transformation.
Find the equation of the graph.

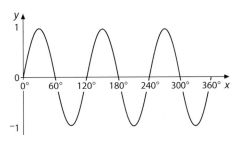

To reflect the graph of $y = x^3$ in the y-axis we change the sign of each x-coordinate.

The equation rearranges to give $x = \sqrt[3]{y}$.

Hence the equation of the image is $x = -\sqrt[3]{y}$.

Rearranging gives $^{-}x = \sqrt[3]{y}$ and $y = (^{-}x)^3$.

Here, the equation of the image can be found by replacing the x in $y = x^3$ by ^{-}x.

> If we reflect any graph in the y-axis the equation of the image is found by replacing x by ^{-}x.

- What is the equation of $y = \sin x$ after a reflection in the y-axis?

D12 Write down the equation of each graph below after a reflection in the y-axis.

(a) $y = x^2$ (b) $y = \cos x$ (c) $y = 2x^3$

*D13 Show that $\sin(^{-}x) = ^{-}\sin x$ for all x.

E Function notation

A **function** is another name for a rule.

We often use a letter to label a function.
For example, we could use f to mean 'square and add 1'.

We write this as $f(x) = x^2 + 1$.

We say 'f of $x = x^2 + 1$'.

$f(2)$ means the value of $x^2 + 1$ when $x = 2$.
So $f(2) = 2^2 + 1 = 5$.

E1 When $f(x) = 2x - 3$, evaluate   (a) $f(2)$ (b) $f(5)$ (c) $f(0)$

E2 When $g(t) = t^2 - 9$, evaluate   (a) $g(4)$ (b) $g(^-4)$ (c) $g(0)$

E3 When $k(x) = \cos x$, evaluate   (a) $k(0°)$ (b) $k(180°)$ (c) $k(^-90°)$

Writing one rule in terms of another

$f(x) = x^2$ is a function.

Let $y = f(x) + 2$.   For example, when $x = 3$, $y = f(3) + 2$
$$= 3^2 + 2$$
$$= 11$$

The rule for y in terms of x is $y = x^2 + 2$.

Let $y = f(x + 2)$.   For example, when $x = 3$, $y = f(3 + 2)$
$$= f(5)$$
$$= 5^2$$
$$= 25$$

The rule for y in terms of x is $y = (x + 2)^2$.

E4 (a)   When $f(x) = x^2$, evaluate
  (i) $f(^-4)$ (ii) $f(0)$

(b)   Given that $y = f(x + 5)$, find the value of y when
  (i) $x = ^-5$ (ii) $x = 2$

(c)   Which of these gives the rule for y in terms of x?
  A $y = x^2 + 5$ B $y = (x + 5)^2$ C $y = x^2 - 5$ D $y = (x - 5)^2$

E5 $f(x) = x^2$ and $y = 2f(x)$

(a)   Find the value of y when
  (i) $x = 4$ (ii) $x = ^-1$ (iii) $x = 5$

(b)   Write the rule for y in terms of x.

E6 $f(x) = \sin x$ and $y = f(2x)$

    (a) Evaluate $f(90°)$.

    (b) Find the value of y when   **(i)** $x = 45°$ **(ii)** $x = 15°$

    (c) Write the rule for y in terms of x.

E7 Given that $f(x) = x^2 + 1$, write each of the following rules for y in terms of x.
Expand any brackets and write each rule in its simplest form.

    (a) $y = f(x) + 2$ **(b)** $y = f(x - 3)$ **(c)** $y = f(2x)$

E8 $f(x) = x^2$ and $y = f(x + 2)$

    (a) Find the value of y when   **(i)** $x = 3$ **(ii)** $x = {}^-2$

    (b) Write the rule for y in terms of x.

    (c) On the same set of axes, sketch the graphs of $y = f(x)$ and $y = f(x + 2)$.

F Transforming functions

The equation $y = f(x - 2)$ can be obtained from $y = f(x)$ by replacing x with $x - 2$.

So translating the graph of $y = f(x)$ by $\begin{bmatrix} 2 \\ 0 \end{bmatrix}$ will give the graph of $y = f(x - 2)$.

Part of the graph of $y = f(x)$ is shown.

• Sketch the graph of $y = f(x - 2)$.

Describe the graphs of these equations.

• $y = f(x) + 2$ • $y = 2f(x)$
• $y = \frac{1}{2}f(x)$ • $y = {}^-f(x)$
• $y = f(x + 2)$ • $y = f(2x)$
• $y = f(\frac{1}{2}x)$ • $y = f({}^-x)$

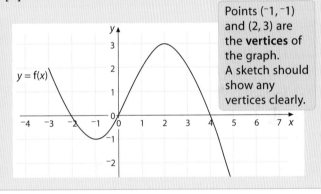

Points $({}^-1, {}^-1)$ and $(2, 3)$ are the **vertices** of the graph.
A sketch should show any vertices clearly.

F1 The graph of $y = f(x)$ is shown on the grid.

    (a) What transformation will map the graph of $y = f(x)$ to the graph of $y = f(x) + 1$?

    (b) **(i)** What transformation will map the graph of $y = f(x)$ to the graph of $y = f(x + 1)$?

        (ii) Sketch the graph of $y = f(x + 1)$.

    (c) Sketch the graphs of

        (i) $y = f(2x)$ **(ii)** $y = 2f(x)$

        (iii) $y = {}^-f(x)$ **(iv)** $y = f({}^-x)$

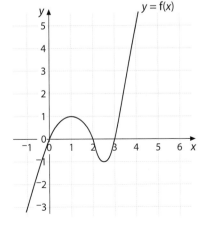

F2 This is the sketch of the curve with equation $y = f(x)$.

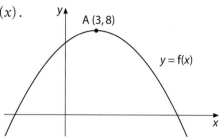

The maximum point of the curve is A (3, 8).

Write down the coordinates of the maximum point for each of the curves having the following equations.

(a) $y = f(x) + 2$ **(b)** $y = f(x - 3)$ **(c)** $y = f(^-x)$ **(d)** $y = f(3x)$ Edexcel

F3 The graph of the function $y = f(x)$ is shown on the grid.

The point P $(^-1, 5)$ lies on the curve.

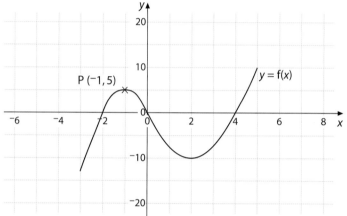

Draw three grids like the one in the diagram.

On each of the grids draw the graph of the transformed function. In each case write down the coordinates of the transformed point P.

(a) $y = f(x + 3)$ **(b)** $y = 2f(x)$ **(c)** $y = ^-f(x)$ AQA

F4 This question is on sheet H2–8.

F5 This is a sketch of the curve with equation $y = f(x)$. It passes through the origin O.
The only vertex of the curve is at A $(2, ^-4)$.

(a) Write down the coordinates of the vertex of the curve with equation

    (i) $y = f(x - 3)$

    (ii) $y = f(x) - 5$

    (iii) $y = ^-f(x)$

    (iv) $y = f(2x)$

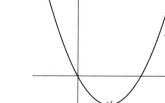

The curve with equation $y = x^2$ has been translated to give the curve $y = f(x)$.

(b) Find f(x) in terms of x.   Edexcel

F6 $f(x) = x^2 - 8x + 17$

This is the sketch of the curve with equation $y = f(x)$.
P is the minimum point.

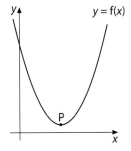

(a) Find the coordinates of P.

(b) Write down the coordinates of the minimum point for each of the curves having the following equations.

    (i) $y = 3f(x)$ (ii) $y = f(x + 1)$ (iii) $y = f(4x)$ (iv) $y = f\left(\dfrac{x}{4}\right)$

(c) Where does the graph of $y = f(x - 2)$ cross the y-axis?

Transforming functions: a summary

From the function $y = f(x)$,

- $y = f(x) + a$ is a translation by $\begin{bmatrix} 0 \\ a \end{bmatrix}$.

- $y = f(x + a)$ is a translation by $\begin{bmatrix} {}^-a \\ 0 \end{bmatrix}$.

- $y = af(x)$ is a stretch in the y-direction (leaving the x-axis unchanged) by a factor of a.

- $y = f(ax)$ is a stretch in the x-direction (leaving the y-axis unchanged) by a factor of $\dfrac{1}{a}$.

- $y = f\left(\dfrac{x}{a}\right)$ is a stretch in the x-direction (leaving the y-axis unchanged) by a factor of a.

- $y = {}^-f(x)$ is a reflection in the x-axis.

- $y = f({}^-x)$ is a reflection in the y-axis.

Test yourself

T1 The expression $x^2 - 4x - 21$ can be written in the form $(x - a)^2 - b$.

    (a) Find the values of a and b.

    (b) Hence find the minimum value of the expression and the value of x at which it occurs.

                                                                            OCR

T2 (a) Find values of p and q such that $x^2 + 6x - 7 = (x + p)^2 + q$.

    (b) Hence solve the equation $x^2 + 6x - 7 = 0$.

T3 Sketch the graph of $y = (x - 2)^3$ showing clearly the coordinates of the x- and y-intercepts.

T4 What is the equation of the image of $y = x^2$ after a translation of $\begin{bmatrix} {}^-2 \\ 3 \end{bmatrix}$?

T5 The diagrams, which are not drawn to scale, show the graph of $y = x^2$ and four other graphs A, B, C and D.

A, B, C and D represent four different transformations of $y = x^2$.

Find the equation of each of the graphs A, B, C and D.

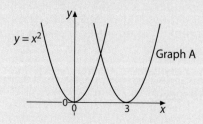

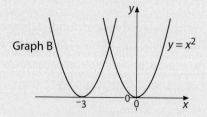

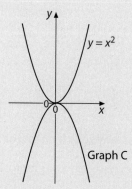

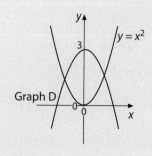

AQA

T6 This diagram shows the graph of $y = f(x)$.

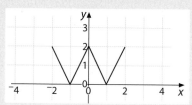

The two graphs below are transformations of $y = f(x)$.

Choose the correct equation for each graph.

$y = f(x + 2)$ $y = f\left(\dfrac{x}{2}\right)$ $y = f(x - 2)$ $y = \frac{1}{2}f(x)$

$y = f(2x)$ $y = f(x) - 2$ $y = 2f(x)$ $y = f(x) + 2$

(a) 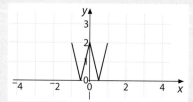   **(b)**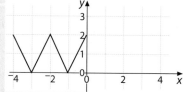

OCR

T7 The graph of $y = \sin x$ for $0° \leq x \leq 360°$ is shown on the grid below.

The point P (90, 1) lies on the curve.

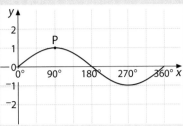

Draw two grids like the one in the diagram.

On each of the grids draw the graph of the transformed function.
In each case write down the coordinates of the transformed point P.

(a) $y = \sin(x - 45°)$ \qquad\qquad (b) $y = 2\sin x$ \qquad\qquad\qquad AQA

T8 The expression $x^2 - 6x + 14$ can be written in the form $(x - p)^2 + q$, for all values of x.

(a) Find the value of

(i) p \qquad\qquad\qquad (ii) q

The equation of a curve is $y = f(x)$, where $f(x) = x^2 - 6x + 14$.
Here is a sketch of the graph of $y = f(x)$.

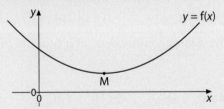

(b) Write down the coordinates of the minimum point, M, of the curve.

Here is a sketch of the graph of $y = f(x) - k$, where k is a positive constant.
The graph touches the x-axis.

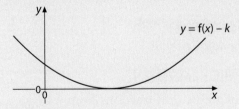

(c) Find the value of k.

(d) For the graph of $y = f(x - 1)$,

(i) write down the coordinates of the minimum point,

(ii) find the coordinates of the point where the curve crosses the y-axis. \qquad Edexcel

T9 What transformation maps the graph of $y = \sin x$ on to the graph of $y = \sin 2x$?

33 Rational and irrational numbers

This work will help you

- write recurring decimals as fractions
- learn about rational and irrational numbers
- manipulate irrational numbers in surd form

A Review: fractions to decimals

Rational numbers are numbers that can be written in the form $\frac{a}{b}$ (a and b are integers). Their decimal equivalents either **terminate** or **recur**.

$$\frac{7}{8} = 7 \div 8 = 0.875$$

$$\begin{array}{r} 0.875 \\ 8\overline{)7.000} \end{array}$$

$$\frac{5}{12} = 5 \div 12 = 0.41666... = 0.41\dot{6}$$

$$\begin{array}{r} 0.41666... \\ 12\overline{)5.00000...} \end{array}$$

$$\frac{3}{11} = 3 \div 11 = 0.272727... = 0.\dot{2}\dot{7}$$

$$\begin{array}{r} 0.2727... \\ 11\overline{)3.0000...} \end{array}$$

In dot notation, a dot is written above the first and last digit of the recurring group.

$$0.4444... = 0.\dot{4} \qquad 0.2454545... = 0.2\dot{4}\dot{5} \qquad 0.7184184184... = 0.7\dot{1}8\dot{4}$$

- Use remainders to explain why the decimal equivalent of a fraction always either terminates or recurs.

A1 Write these fractions as decimals. **(a)** $\frac{3}{5}$ **(b)** $\frac{7}{25}$ **(c)** $\frac{39}{50}$ **(d)** $\frac{5}{8}$ **(e)** $\frac{9}{40}$

A2 Write each of these recurring decimals using dot notation.

(a) $0.33333...$ **(b)** $0.232323...$ **(c)** $0.233333...$ **(d)** $0.321321321...$ **(e)** $0.3212121...$

A3 Write these fractions as decimals. **(a)** $\frac{5}{6}$ **(b)** $\frac{2}{11}$ **(c)** $\frac{1}{7}$ **(d)** $\frac{6}{11}$ **(e)** $\frac{7}{30}$

A4 (a) Write the following fractions as decimals. $\quad \frac{1}{9} \quad \frac{3}{9} \quad \frac{5}{9} \quad \frac{7}{9}$

(b) What do you think is the value of $0.\dot{9}$?

A5 Unit fractions are fractions with numerator 1.

(a) List the decimal values of all the unit fractions from $\frac{1}{2}$ to $\frac{1}{20}$. Which of these fractions are equivalent to terminating decimals?

(b) Can you find a rule for deciding whether a fraction is equivalent to a terminating or a recurring decimal?

(c) Use the rule to decide which fractions below are equivalent to terminating decimals.
$$\frac{9}{20} \quad \frac{7}{8} \quad \frac{1}{21} \quad \frac{3}{47} \quad \frac{1}{25} \quad \frac{4}{30} \quad \frac{1}{80} \quad \frac{3}{64}$$

A6 The number $0.252252225222252222225...$ continues to follow the pattern. Can you write this number using recurring decimal notation? Explain your answer.

B Recurring decimals to fractions

Terminating decimals can be converted to fractions by thinking about place values.

$$0.45 = \frac{45}{100} = \frac{9}{20}$$

$$0.384 = \frac{384}{1000} = \frac{48}{125}$$

Recurring decimals need a different approach.

Let f stand for $0.\dot{5}$.
Multiply by 10.
Subtract.

$f = 0.5555...$
$10f = 5.5555...$
$9f = 5$
$f = \frac{5}{9}$

Let g stand for $0.9\dot{6}\dot{3}$.
Get the non-recurring part before the decimal point, by multiplying by 10.
Multiply both sides by 100 to get the 6s and 3s aligned.
Subtract $10g$ from $1000g$.

$g = 0.96363...$
$10g = 9.6363...$
$1000g = 963.6363...$
$990g = 954$
$g = \frac{954}{990} = \frac{53}{55}$

B1 Write the following decimals as fractions in their simplest form.

(a) 0.7
(b) 0.85
(c) 0.03
(d) 0.924
(e) 0.025

B2 Write the following decimals as fractions in their simplest form.

(a) 0.888 888...
(b) 0.151 515...
(c) 0.272 727...
(d) 0.147 147...

(e) $0.\dot{2}$
(f) $0.\dot{3}\dot{6}$
(g) $0.\dot{0}0\dot{3}$
(h) $0.\dot{3}2\dot{6}$

B3 (a) Copy and complete the working on the right.

(b) Hence write 0.155 5... as a fraction in its lowest terms.

$f = 0.155\,555\,5...$
$10f =$
$100f =$
So $90f =$

B4 Write these as fractions in their lowest terms.

(a) 0.177 7777...
(b) 0.044 4444...
(c) 0.254 444 444...
(d) 0.312 121 212...

(e) $0.0\dot{3}$
(f) $0.4\dot{2}\dot{7}$
(g) $0.0\dot{1}\dot{6}$
(h) $0.98\dot{9}\dot{7}$

B5 (a) Write $0.\dot{5}$ as a fraction.
(b) Hence write $0.0\dot{5}$ as a fraction.

B6 (a) Write 0.333 33... as a fraction.
(b) Write $0.\dot{1}$ as a fraction.
(c) Hence write 0.433 33... as a fraction.

B7 (a) Write 0.666... as a fraction.
(b) Write 0.4 as a fraction.
(c) Hence write 0.266 6... as a fraction.

*B8 The sum of the reciprocals of two consecutive numbers is 0.366 666 66...
Find the numbers.

C Irrational numbers

Rational numbers can be written in the form $\frac{a}{b}$ (a and b are integers).

Irrational numbers cannot be written in this form.
Their decimal equivalents never terminate or recur.

Some examples of irrational numbers are $\sqrt{2}$, π, $\sqrt{3}$, $\sqrt[3]{12}$.

• Which of these numbers are irrational?

| $\sqrt{5}$ | $2\frac{1}{2}$ | $\frac{4}{3}$ | $\sqrt{2\frac{1}{4}}$ | $\sqrt[3]{\frac{1}{8}}$ | $\frac{15}{9}$ | $\sqrt{5}+1$ | $\sqrt{49}$ | $2\sqrt{10}$ | π^2 | $\sqrt[3]{9}$ | $\pi+1$ | $\left(\sqrt{5}\right)^2$ |

Any number that involves an irrational root, such as $\sqrt{7}$, $3\sqrt{2}$ or $\sqrt{5}+1$, is said to be in **surd** form.

 It is difficult to prove that numbers like $\sqrt{2}$ are irrational, and it is not required here.
You could search the internet for a proof and see if you can follow it.

C1 Which of these numbers are irrational?

| $\sqrt{8}$ | $\sqrt{16}$ | $4\sqrt{7}$ | $\frac{\pi}{2}$ | $1.\dot{7}$ | 5.1879 | $\sqrt{125}$ | $\sqrt[3]{25}$ | $\sqrt{3}+4$ | π^2+1 |

C2 Sort these into four matching pairs of equivalent numbers.

| $\sqrt{5}+\sqrt{5}$ | $6\sqrt{5}-2\sqrt{5}$ | $2(\sqrt{5}+2)$ | $2\sqrt{5}$ | $(2\sqrt{5})^2$ | $2\sqrt{5}+4$ | 20 | $4\sqrt{5}$ |

C3 Simplify these.

(a) $\sqrt{7}+\sqrt{7}$ (b) $\left(\sqrt{7}\right)^2$ (c) $5\sqrt{7}-2\sqrt{7}$

(d) $3\left(\sqrt{7}+2\right)$ (e) $\left(2+\sqrt{7}\right)+\left(5-\sqrt{7}\right)$ (f) $\left(3\sqrt{7}+6\right)-\left(\sqrt{7}-2\right)$

C4 Which of these numbers are between 2 and 3?

| $\pi-1$ | $\sqrt{5}$ | $\sqrt{3}$ | $\sqrt{8}$ | $\sqrt{11}$ | $\sqrt{12}-1$ | $\sqrt{17}-1$ |

C5 Write down an irrational number between

(a) 4 and 5   (b) 5 and 6   (c) 0 and 1   (d) 10 and 11

C6 Is the number $0.747\,744\,777\,444\,777\,744\,447\,777\,744\,444\ldots$ rational or irrational? Explain your answer carefully.

C7 (a) For each of these decimals, state with reasons whether it is a rational or an irrational number.

     (i) 0.1 (ii) $0.121\,121\,112\,111\,12\ldots$ (iii) $0.\dot{1}2\dot{3}$

(b) Write, where possible, the decimals in (a) as fractions in their simplest form.   OCR

C8 Write down the **exact** lengths of the sides of squares with these areas.

(a) $10\,\text{cm}^2$ (b) $3\,\text{cm}^2$ (c) $16\,\text{m}^2$ (d) $101\,\text{mm}^2$ (e) $81\,\text{cm}^2$

C9 Find the exact length of AC, where ABCD is a square.

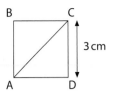

*C10 The sloping line in this diagram has a gradient of $\sqrt{3}$.

Prove that, no matter how far it is extended, it will never go through an intersection of two grid lines.

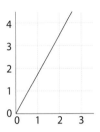

*C11 Two tiny insects move at the same speed.

One walks round and round the perimeter of a square; the other walks backwards and forwards across a diagonal of the same square.

They start together at one corner of the square.
Prove that their positions never coincide again.

*C12 Prove this statement.

'There is no square number that is double another square number.'

D Simplifying expressions containing square roots

- Simplify these expressions.   (a) $\left(\sqrt{a}\times\sqrt{b}\right)^2$ (b) $\left(\sqrt{ab}\right)^2$

  What can you say about $\sqrt{a}\times\sqrt{b}$ and $\sqrt{ab}$?
- Try to sort these into matching pairs of equivalent numbers.

  Which is the odd one out?

A $\sqrt{4}\times\sqrt{9}$ B $3\sqrt{2}$ C $\sqrt{4}\times\sqrt{6}$ D $\sqrt{8}+\sqrt{10}$

E $\sqrt{20}$ F $\sqrt{2}\times\sqrt{5}$ G $\sqrt{10}$ H $\sqrt{18}$ I $\sqrt{24}$ J $2\sqrt{5}$ K $\sqrt{36}$

D1 Write each of these in the form $\sqrt{n}$, where n is an integer.

(a) $\sqrt{3}\times\sqrt{5}$ (b) $\sqrt{2}\times\sqrt{7}$ (c) $\sqrt{3}\times\sqrt{8}$ (d) $\sqrt{5}\times\sqrt{10}$

D2 Simplify these.

(a) $\sqrt{5}\times\sqrt{5}$ (b) $\left(\sqrt{3}\right)^2$ (c) $\sqrt{2}\times\sqrt{8}$ (d) $\sqrt{5}\times\sqrt{20}$

D3 Simplify these.

(a) $2\sqrt{3} \times \sqrt{3}$ (b) $3\sqrt{7} \times 2\sqrt{7}$ (c) $3\sqrt{2} \times \sqrt{5}$ (d) $2\sqrt{5} \times 4\sqrt{2}$

D4 Work out the value of the letter in each statement.

(a) $\sqrt{3} \times \sqrt{a} = \sqrt{33}$ (b) $\sqrt{21} = \sqrt{b} \times \sqrt{7}$ (c) $\sqrt{30} = \sqrt{3} \times \sqrt{c}$

A root can sometimes be written in the form $p\sqrt{q}$, where p and q are both integers.

Examples

$\sqrt{28}$
$= \sqrt{4 \times 7}$
$= \sqrt{4} \times \sqrt{7}$
$= 2 \times \sqrt{7} = 2\sqrt{7}$

$\sqrt{10} \times \sqrt{20}$
$= \sqrt{10 \times 20}$
$= \sqrt{100 \times 2}$
$= \sqrt{100} \times \sqrt{2}$
$= 10 \times \sqrt{2} = 10\sqrt{2}$

D5 Write each number below in the form $p\sqrt{q}$, where q is the smallest integer possible.

(a) $\sqrt{27}$ (b) $\sqrt{50}$ (c) $\sqrt{80}$ (d) $\sqrt{98}$ (e) $\sqrt{300}$

D6 Write each of these in the form $p\sqrt{q}$, where q is the smallest integer possible.

(a) $3\sqrt{8}$ (b) $2\sqrt{32}$ (c) $2\sqrt{45}$ (d) $3\sqrt{72}$ (e) $5\sqrt{80}$

D7 Jake thinks that $\sqrt{9} + \sqrt{9} = \sqrt{18}$.
How would you convince him that he is wrong?

D8 Write each of these in the form $p\sqrt{q}$, where q is the smallest integer possible.

(a) $\sqrt{2} \times \sqrt{10}$ (b) $\sqrt{3} \times \sqrt{18}$ (c) $\sqrt{15} \times \sqrt{5}$ (d) $\sqrt{18} \times \sqrt{2}$

D9 (a) Write $\sqrt{12}$ in the form $a\sqrt{b}$, where a and b are both prime numbers.

(b) Hence simplify $\sqrt{12} + 5\sqrt{3}$.

D10 Simplify $4\sqrt{12} - \sqrt{3}$, giving your answer in the form $p\sqrt{q}$.   OCR

D11 Simplify these.

(a) $\sqrt{8} + \sqrt{2}$ (b) $\sqrt{27} - \sqrt{12}$ (c) $\sqrt{20} + 4\sqrt{5}$ (d) $\sqrt{200} - \sqrt{32}$

D12 (a) Write $\sqrt{75}$ in the form $a\sqrt{b}$, where b is a prime number.

(b) Hence simplify $\dfrac{\sqrt{75}}{5}$.

D13 (a) Write $\sqrt{108}$ in the form $a\sqrt{b}$, where b is a prime number.

(b) Hence simplify $\dfrac{\sqrt{108}}{2}$.

D14 Simplify these.

(a) $\dfrac{\sqrt{12}}{2}$ (b) $\dfrac{\sqrt{18}}{\sqrt{2}}$ (c) $\dfrac{5}{\sqrt{5}}$ (d) $\dfrac{\sqrt{72}}{3}$ (e) $\dfrac{\sqrt{200}}{5}$

E Multiplying out brackets containing square roots

After multiplying out brackets, collect like terms and simplify where possible.

Examples

$$\sqrt{2}(5 + \sqrt{18})$$
$$= (\sqrt{2} \times 5) + (\sqrt{2} \times \sqrt{18})$$
$$= 5\sqrt{2} + \sqrt{36}$$
$$= 5\sqrt{2} + 6$$

$$(\sqrt{3} + 4)(\sqrt{3} - 1)$$
$$= (\sqrt{3} \times \sqrt{3}) - (\sqrt{3} \times 1) + (4 \times \sqrt{3}) - (4 \times 1)$$
$$= 3 - \sqrt{3} + 4\sqrt{3} - 4$$
$$= 3\sqrt{3} - 1$$

E1 Multiply out the brackets and simplify where possible.

(a) $\sqrt{3}(4 + \sqrt{2})$ (b) $\sqrt{2}(\sqrt{5} + \sqrt{2})$ (c) $\sqrt{5}(\sqrt{20} + 1)$ (d) $\sqrt{2}(\sqrt{8} + \sqrt{32})$

E2 Multiply out the brackets and simplify where possible.

(a) $(3 + \sqrt{2})(2 + \sqrt{2})$ (b) $(\sqrt{5} - 4)(1 + \sqrt{5})$ (c) $(5 + \sqrt{3})(5 - \sqrt{3})$

(d) $(1 - \sqrt{7})(5 - \sqrt{7})$ (e) $(2 + \sqrt{5})^2$ (f) $(1 - \sqrt{3})^2$

E3 Two rectangles, A and B, are equal in area.

Calculate the length of rectangle B.
Give your answer in the form $p\sqrt{3}$.

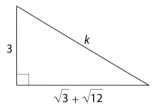

AQA

E4 Multiply out the brackets and simplify where possible.

(a) $(1 + \sqrt{2})(2 + \sqrt{3})$ (b) $(6 - \sqrt{3})(1 + \sqrt{5})$ (c) $(\sqrt{5} + \sqrt{3})(\sqrt{5} - \sqrt{3})$

(d) $(\sqrt{2} + \sqrt{18})^2$ (e) $(\sqrt{5} - \sqrt{3})^2$ (f) $(\sqrt{50} - \sqrt{2})^2$

E5 k is an integer.

Find the value of k.

Edexcel

E6 (a) Expand and simplify $(1 + \sqrt{5})^2$.

(b) Hence, or otherwise, show that $x = 1 + \sqrt{5}$ is a solution to the equation $x^2 - 2x - 4 = 0$.

E7 (a) Write $\sqrt{48}$ in the form $a\sqrt{b}$, where b is prime.

(b) Write $(\sqrt{24} - \sqrt{2})^2$ in the form $p - q\sqrt{3}$.

E8 Write $(\sqrt{5} + \sqrt{10})^2$ in the form $p + q\sqrt{2}$.

E9 Write $(\sqrt{15} + \sqrt{3})^2$ in the form $p + q\sqrt{r}$, where r is as small as possible.

F Further simplifying with square roots

- Simplify these expressions. **(a)** $\left(\dfrac{\sqrt{a}}{\sqrt{b}}\right)^2$ **(b)** $\left(\sqrt{\dfrac{a}{b}}\right)^2$

  What can you say about $\dfrac{\sqrt{a}}{\sqrt{b}}$ and $\sqrt{\dfrac{a}{b}}$?

- Sort these expressions into matching pairs of equivalent numbers.

A	**B**	**C**	**D**	**E**	**F**	**G**	**H**
$\sqrt{5}$	$\dfrac{\sqrt{12}}{\sqrt{4}}$	$2\sqrt{2}$	$\dfrac{\sqrt{36}}{\sqrt{3}}$	$\dfrac{\sqrt{20}}{\sqrt{4}}$	$\sqrt{3}$	$\dfrac{\sqrt{16}}{\sqrt{2}}$	$2\sqrt{3}$

F1 Simplify   **(a)** $\dfrac{\sqrt{12}}{\sqrt{2}}$ **(b)** $\dfrac{\sqrt{8}}{\sqrt{2}}$ **(c)** $\dfrac{\sqrt{15}}{\sqrt{3}}$

F2 Evaluate   **(a)** $\sqrt{\dfrac{9}{25}}$ **(b)** $\sqrt{\dfrac{81}{144}}$ **(c)** $\sqrt{\dfrac{16}{121}}$

F3 Write $\sqrt{\dfrac{3}{16}}$ in the form $\dfrac{\sqrt{a}}{b}$, where a and b are integers.

F4 Write $\sqrt{\dfrac{25}{2}}$ in the form $\dfrac{a}{\sqrt{b}}$, where a and b are integers.

Sometimes it is useful to write an expression with an integer denominator.
This is called **rationalising the denominator**.

Example

$$\dfrac{\sqrt{7}}{\sqrt{2}} = \dfrac{\sqrt{7}\times\sqrt{2}}{\sqrt{2}\times\sqrt{2}}$$

Multiplying both the numerator and denominator by $\sqrt{2}$ does not change the value of the expression.

$$= \dfrac{\sqrt{14}}{2}$$

F5 For each expression, rationalise the denominator and write the result in its simplest form.

   (a) $\dfrac{7}{\sqrt{5}}$ **(b)** $\dfrac{1}{\sqrt{3}}$ **(c)** $\dfrac{6}{\sqrt{2}}$ **(d)** $\dfrac{7}{\sqrt{7}}$ **(e)** $\dfrac{\sqrt{5}}{\sqrt{2}}$ **(f)** $\dfrac{\sqrt{10}}{\sqrt{3}}$

F6 Write $\dfrac{9}{\sqrt{3}}$ in the form $p\sqrt{q}$.

F7 Rationalise each denominator.   **(a)** $\dfrac{3+\sqrt{5}}{\sqrt{5}}$ **(b)** $\dfrac{\sqrt{2}+6}{\sqrt{2}}$ **(c)** $\dfrac{\sqrt{3}-4}{\sqrt{3}}$

F8 Show that $\dfrac{1}{\sqrt{2}} + \dfrac{\sqrt{2}}{6} = \dfrac{2\sqrt{2}}{3}$.

F9 Simplify $\dfrac{\sqrt{18}\times\sqrt{75}}{\sqrt{50}}$.

Simplifying roots

For all values of a and b it is true that $\sqrt{a}\,\sqrt{b} = \sqrt{ab}$, for example:

$$\sqrt{2} \times \sqrt{18} = \sqrt{36} = 6 \qquad\qquad \sqrt{75} = \sqrt{25} \times \sqrt{3} = 5\sqrt{3}$$

For all values of a and b it is true that $\dfrac{\sqrt{a}}{\sqrt{b}} = \sqrt{\dfrac{a}{b}}$, for example:

$$\frac{\sqrt{18}}{\sqrt{2}} = \sqrt{\frac{18}{2}} = \sqrt{9} = 3 \qquad\qquad \sqrt{\frac{2}{25}} = \frac{\sqrt{2}}{\sqrt{25}} = \frac{\sqrt{2}}{5}$$

G Surd solutions to quadratic equations

Example

Solve the equation $x^2 + 10x + 7 = 0$, giving the solution in the form $x = p \pm q\sqrt{r}$, where r is a positive integer and as small as possible.

First method

Complete the square by writing
$x^2 + 10x$ as $(x^2 + 10x + 5^2) - 5^2$,
which is $(x + 5)^2 - 25$.

So $(x + 5)^2 - 25 + 7 = 0$

$$(x + 5)^2 = 18$$
$$x + 5 = \pm\sqrt{18}$$
$$= \pm\sqrt{9 \times 2}$$
$$= \pm 3\sqrt{2}$$

So $\qquad\qquad\qquad x = {}^-5 \pm 3\sqrt{2}$

Second method

Using the quadratic formula with $a = 1, b = 10$ and $c = 7$,

we get $\quad x = \dfrac{{}^-10 \pm \sqrt{100 - 28}}{2}$

so $\qquad x = \dfrac{{}^-10 \pm \sqrt{72}}{2}$

$$= \frac{{}^-10 \pm \sqrt{36 \times 2}}{2}$$

$$= \frac{{}^-10 \pm 6\sqrt{2}}{2}$$

$$= {}^-5 \pm 3\sqrt{2}$$

G1 Solve the equation $x^2 - 8x + 3 = 0$, giving the solution in the form $x = p \pm \sqrt{q}$.

G2 Solve each of these equations, giving the solution in the form $x = p \pm \sqrt{q}$.

(a) $x^2 - 4x + 2 = 0$ (b) $x^2 - 6x + 3 = 0$ (c) $x^2 - 2x - 2 = 0$ (d) $x^2 + 8x + 3 = 0$

G3 (a) Write the expression $x^2 - 6x + 2$ in the form $(x - p)^2 - q$.

(b) Hence solve the equation $x^2 - 6x + 2 = 0$, giving the solution in the form $x = a \pm \sqrt{b}$.

G4 (a) Write the expression $x^2 + 12x + 4$ in the form $(x + p)^2 - q$.

(b) Hence solve the equation $x^2 + 12x + 4 = 0$, giving the solution in the form $x = a \pm b\sqrt{c}$, where c is as small as possible.

G5 Solve each of these equations by completing the square, giving the solution in surd form.

(a) $x^2 + 4x + 1 = 0$ (b) $x^2 + 6x + 4 = 0$ (c) $x^2 - 10x + 2 = 0$ (d) $x^2 - 3x - 1 = 0$

G6 Use the quadratic formula to solve the equation $2x^2 - 8x + 3 = 0$, giving the solution in the form $x = a \pm b\sqrt{c}$.

G7 Use the quadratic formula to solve each of these equations, giving the solution in the form $x = a \pm b\sqrt{c}$.

(a) $2x^2 - 4x + 1 = 0$ (b) $2x^2 - 3x - 3 = 0$ (c) $3x^2 - 4x - 1 = 0$

*G8 (a) Write the expression $2x^2 + 8x + 5$ in the form $p(x + q)^2 - r$.

(b) Hence show that the solution of the equation $2x^2 + 8x + 5 = 0$ can be written in the form $x = {}^-2 \pm \frac{1}{2}\sqrt{6}$.

H Mixed questions

H1 A square has area $24\,\text{cm}^2$. What is the exact length of one edge in the form $p\sqrt{q}$, where p and q are integers?

H2 The shaded areas in each diagram are squares.
Find the area and perimeter of each white rectangle in surd form, simplifying your answers as far as you can.

(a)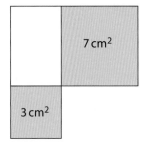

(b)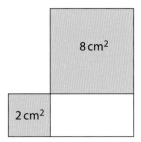

H3 (a) Express $0.\overset{..}{4}\overset{}{2}$ as a fraction in its simplest form.

(b) Hence, or otherwise, express $0.7\overset{..}{4}\overset{..}{2}$ as a fraction.
Write this fraction in its simplest form.

AQA

H4 Solve the equation $x^2 - 4x + 1 = 0$, giving your solutions in the form $a \pm \sqrt{b}$.

H5 (a) Simplify $\sqrt{72} - \sqrt{32}$, giving your answer in the form $p\sqrt{q}$.

(b) Show that $\dfrac{\sqrt{72} - \sqrt{32}}{\sqrt{18} + \sqrt{8}} = \dfrac{2}{5}$.

H6 The table shows three pairs of expressions.

For each expression in column A, state whether or not it is exactly equal to the corresponding expression in column B, justifying your answer.

	A	B
(a)	$\sqrt{2} \times \sqrt{6}$	$2\sqrt{3}$
(b)	$\sqrt{2^2 + 1^2}$	$2.236\,067\,977\,49$
(c)	$\sqrt{\dfrac{144}{121}}$	$1.\overset{..}{0}\overset{..}{9}$

OCR

H7 $p = 2 + \sqrt{3}$ $q = 2 - \sqrt{3}$

    (a) **(i)** Work out $p - q$.

         (ii) State whether $p - q$ is rational or irrational.

    (b) **(i)** Work out pq.

         (ii) State whether pq is rational or irrational.   Edexcel

Test yourself

T1 **(a)** Which of these fractions can be written as recurring decimals?

            $\frac{1}{5}$ $\frac{1}{6}$ $\frac{5}{8}$ $\frac{2}{3}$

    (b) Express $\frac{2}{9}$ as a recurring decimal.

    (c) Prove that $0.15\dot{4}$ is equal to $\frac{17}{110}$.   AQA

T2 **(a)** Express $0.\dot{4}\dot{5}$ as a fraction. Simplify your answer.

    (b) **(i)** Simplify $\left(\sqrt{7} + \sqrt{5} \right)^2$.

         (ii) State whether your answer to (i) is rational or irrational.   OCR

T3 **(a)** You are given that $\sqrt{12} + \sqrt{27} = a\sqrt{3}$ where a is an integer.
        Find the value of a.

    (b) Find the value of $(m + p)^2$ when $m = \sqrt{2}$ and $p = \sqrt{8}$.   AQA

T4 Prove that the recurring decimal $1.207\,207\,207\ldots$ is equal to the fraction $1\frac{23}{111}$.   AQA

T5 **(a)** Express the following in the form $p\sqrt{q}$, where p and q are integers.

$$\frac{4}{\sqrt{2}}$$

    (b) Simplify the following. Give your answer in the form $a + b\sqrt{2}$,
        where a and b are integers.

$$\left(1 + \sqrt{2} \right)\left(3 - \sqrt{2} \right)$$ OCR

T6 Show clearly that $\dfrac{3}{\sqrt{6}} + \dfrac{\sqrt{6}}{3} = \dfrac{5}{\sqrt{6}}$.   OCR

T7 Rationalise the denominator of $\dfrac{2 + \sqrt{3}}{\sqrt{3}}$.

Simplify your answer fully.   AQA

T8 Work out $\dfrac{\left(5 + \sqrt{3} \right)\left(5 - \sqrt{3} \right)}{\sqrt{22}}$.

Give your answer in its simplest form.   Edexcel

T9 Solve the equation $x^2 - 6x - 3 = 0$.
Give your answers in the form $p \pm q\sqrt{3}$ where p and q are integers.   AQA

34 Pythagoras and trigonometry in three dimensions

This work will help you use Pythagoras and trigonometry to solve three-dimensional problems, including those that involve three-dimensional coordinates.

You need sheet H2–9, scissors, adhesive, an angle measurer and compasses.

A Solving problems using a grid

Cut out the grid on sheet H2–9.
Fold and stick it with the gridlines on the inside.

The grid consists of centimetre squares.

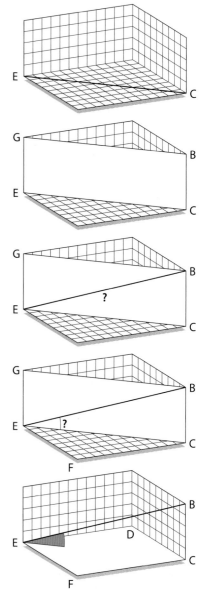

A1 (a) Use Pythagoras to calculate the length of a straight line from E to C.

Using this result, draw and cut out the rectangle GBCE. Label its vertices and check that it fits on your grid. (We can refer to it as the **plane** GBCE.)

(b) Draw the line EB on your rectangle GBCE. Use Pythagoras to find its length. Check by measuring. Keep a record of the calculated length to 1 d.p.

(c) Mark the angle BEC on your rectangle. Use trigonometry to find this angle. Check by measuring.

If rectangle EDCF represents horizontal ground, angle BEC is the **angle of elevation** of B from the point E.

It is also the **angle between the line EB and the plane EDCF**.

A2 Use the same approach as in A1 to find the following, checking by measuring as you go.

    (a) The length and width of the plane ABHI

    (b) The length of line AH

    (c) The angle IAH

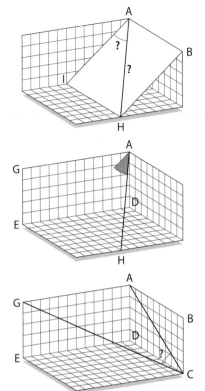

The angle you calculated in A2(c) is the angle between the line AH and the plane GADE

A3 (a) What rectangle (plane) would you use to find the angle GCA?

    (b) Instead of cutting out the rectangle, make a labelled sketch of it.
Calculate angle GCA, showing your working.

    (c) Copy and complete:
Angle GCA is the angle between line CG and the plane _____.

A4 What plane (rectangle) contains lines GH and HA?

A5 What plane contains lines JB and IB?

The following questions refer to your grid.
Try to do them without cutting out a plane.
But always make a labelled sketch of the plane you are using.

A6 Calculate

    (a) the length of HG

    (b) the angle of elevation of G from H

A7 Calculate the angle FHG.

A8 Calculate the angle between EB and the plane GADE.

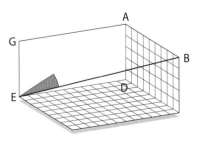

A9 Find   **(a)** the length of HJ   **(b)** the angle FJC   **(c)** the area of triangle FJC

A10 **(a)** Use Pythagoras to find the lengths of these lines to 3 d.p.

       (i) AC   **(ii)** CI   **(iii)** IA

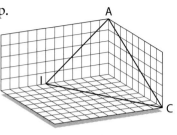

    (b) Use the lengths you have found to construct the triangle ACI on plain paper, using compasses. Write the correct letter inside each vertex. Cut out the triangle and check that it fits on your grid.

You have met the cosine rule, $a^2 = b^2 + c^2 - 2bc\cos A$.

    (c) Use your answers to (a) and the cosine rule to find these angles to the nearest degree.

       (i) IAC   **(ii)** ACI   **(iii)** CIA

    Check your answers by measuring the angles.

A11 Referring to your grid, sketch triangle GIF.

    Work out   **(a)** the lengths of its sides to 3 d.p.   **(b)** its angles

---

In three-dimensional problems you may sometimes need the sine rule,

$$\frac{a}{\sin A} = \frac{b}{\sin B} = \frac{c}{\sin C},$$ and the formula for the area of a triangle, $\frac{1}{2}ab\sin C$.

B Solving problems without a grid

Example

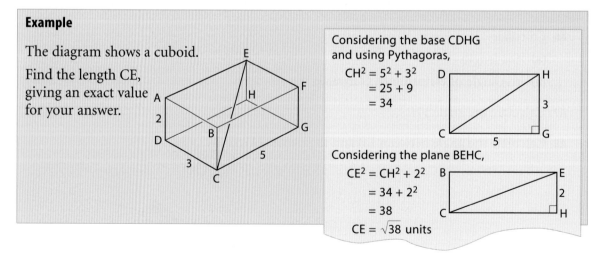

The diagram shows a cuboid.

Find the length CE, giving an exact value for your answer.

Considering the base CDHG and using Pythagoras,

$$CH^2 = 5^2 + 3^2$$
$$= 25 + 9$$
$$= 34$$

Considering the plane BEHC,

$$CE^2 = CH^2 + 2^2$$
$$= 34 + 2^2$$
$$= 38$$

$$CE = \sqrt{38} \text{ units}$$

B1 Find the exact value of the length CE above by first finding an expression for DE², then considering the plane DEFC.

B2 If, in the example on the previous page, AD was 4 units, DC was 7 units and CG was 10 units, what would be the exact value of CE?

B3 Let the length, breadth and height of the cuboid in the example be l, b and h. Use the approach shown to obtain an expression for the length CE.

B4 The diagram shows a cube with edge length 12 cm.

P is $\frac{1}{3}$ of the way along EH.

Q is $\frac{2}{3}$ of the way along BC.

Find the length of PQ, giving an exact value for your answer.

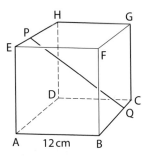

*B5 The diagonal of a cube, shown in the diagram, is 6 units long. What is the edge length of the cube, given as an exact value?

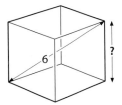

B6 The diagram shows a triangular prism. Calculate the following.

(a) Angle EAD to the nearest degree

(b) EF to 3 d.p.

(c) DF to 3 d.p.

(d) The volume of the prism to 1 d.p.

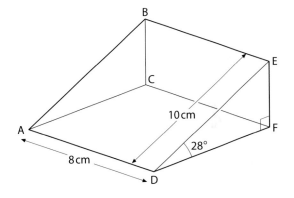

B7 The diagram shows a vertical flagpole QF, which stands at the corner of a horizontal rectangular field PQRS.

(a) Calculate the length PQ.

(b) Calculate the angle of elevation of the top of the flagpole from S.

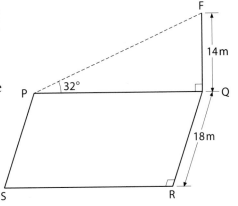

B8 By sketching and labelling a suitable plane in each case, calculate the marked angles, to the nearest degree.

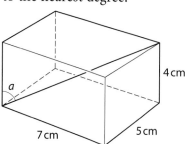
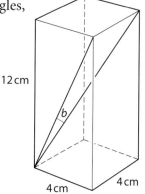
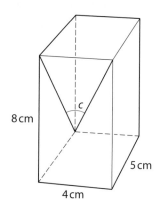

B9 Peter and Queenie are surveying on a horizontal plane PQT, using PQ as a base line.

TM is a vertical television mast of height 70 m.
Angle PTQ = 134°.
The angles of elevation of M from P and Q are 32° and 35° respectively.

(a) Show that the distance from P to Q is approximately 195 m.

(b) Calculate the size of angle TPQ.

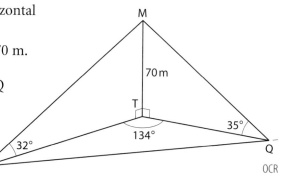

OCR

B10 In these cuboids, sketch a copy of the diagram, mark the angle asked for, then calculate the angle to the nearest degree.

(a)

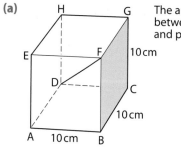

The angle between line FD and plane BFGC

(b)

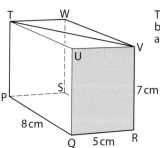

The angle between line TV and plane QRVU

(c)

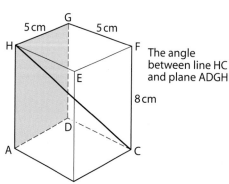

The angle between line HC and plane ADGH

(d)

The angle between line VX and plane UVZY

B11 This inn sign is supported by two wires, AB and AC.

(a) Calculate the length of each of the wires, showing your method.

(b) Calculate the angle that each wire makes with the wall.

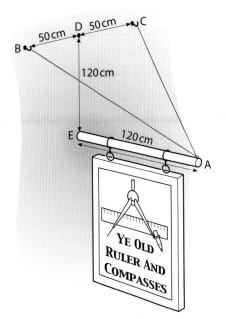

B12 The diagram shows a **right** square-based pyramid (one with its top vertex directly over the centre of the base).

(a) Find the length of PR, a diagonal of the base, to 3 d.p., and hence the length PC.

(b) Draw a sketch of triangle PTR and use it to calculate

(i) the length of the slant edge PT to 1 d.p.

(ii) the angle between PT and the base to the nearest degree

(c) M is the mid-point of SR.
Use Pythagoras to find TM, and hence find the area of triangle STR.

B13 Work to 4 s.f. throughout this question, then give your answer to part (f) to 2 s.f.

PQRS is a regular tetrahedron.
Each of its six edges is 2 units long.
M is the mid-point of the edge QR.

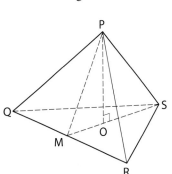

(a) Find the length SM.

(b) What is the length of the line PM?

(c) Find the angle PMS.

(d) Hence find the area of the triangle PMS.

(e) Use your answer to find the perpendicular height PO.

(f) Given that the volume of any pyramid is $\frac{1}{3}$ × base area × perpendicular height, find the volume of this tetrahedron.

*B14 OABV is a triangular-based pyramid with vertex V directly above vertex O.

AB = 7 cm, angle VAB = 50° and angle VBA = 64°.
The angle between line AV and plane OAB is 20°.

(a) Calculate the height, OV.

(b) Calculate the angle between BV and the plane OAB.

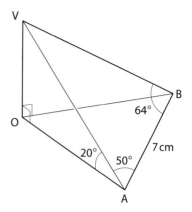

*B15 The diagram shows a right square-based pyramid.
Calculate its volume.

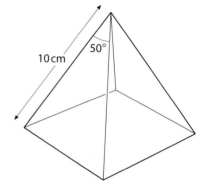

C Using coordinates in three dimensions

C1 The point A (3, 2, 4) is shown.
What is the length, to 2 d.p., of the line segment from the origin O (0, 0, 0) to point A?

(Imagine O and A are opposite vertices of the cuboid shown dotted, and use the approach at the beginning of section B.)

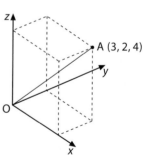

C2 Find the length, to 2 d.p., of the line segment from the origin to each of the points K (5, 2, 3), L (4, 3, 10), M (6, 2, 7), N (7, 6, 6).

C3 (a) Find, as an exact value, the length of the line segment from the origin to each of the points P (5, 7, 5), Q (3, 3, 9), R (1, 7, 7), S (3, 9, 3).

(b) Explain why these four points all lie on the surface of a sphere. Describe the position and size of the sphere.

C4 Find the length, to 2 d.p., of the line segment from A (1, 2, 4) to B (4, 6, 9). (Think of, or sketch, a cuboid with edges parallel to the axes, with A and B as opposite vertices.)

C5 The cubes in this model have an edge length of 1 unit.

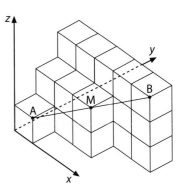

(a) Write the coordinates of points A, M and B.

(b) Explain why line segment AM is the same length as MB and goes in the same direction as MB (making M the mid-point of the line segment AB).

(c) How is the x-coordinate of M related to the x-coordinates of A and of B? Is what you find true for the y-coordinate and z-coordinate of M?

Mid-point of a line segment in three dimensions

The x-coordinate of the mid-point is the mean of the x-coordinates of the end-points.
The y-coordinate and z-coordinate of the mid-point are obtained the same way.

C6 Find the mid-point of each of these line segments.

(a) From $(1, 3, 6)$ to $(3, 7, 2)$

(b) From $(9, 4, ^-1)$ to $(3, 7, 3)$

*C7 The three points A, B, C have the coordinates shown in the diagram.

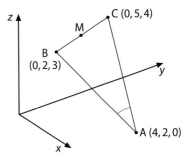

(a) Give the coordinates of M, the mid-point of BC.

(b) Calculate the lengths AB, BC, CA, giving your answers as exact values.

(c) Calculate the angle CAB.

(d) Find the area of the triangle ABC, to 1 d.p.

Test yourself

T1 The diagram shows a triangular prism with the plane PQRS horizontal.
Calculate the following.

(a) The angle of elevation of U from S

(b) The length of PU

(c) The angle between PU and the plane PQRS

T2 The diagram shows a pyramid ABCDE. The base, ABCD, is a rectangle and E is vertically above the mid-point of the base.

AB = 8 cm, BC = 6 cm and the height of the pyramid is 12 cm.

Calculate the length of CE.

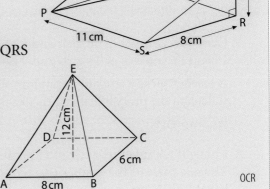

OCR

Review 5

You need a pair of compasses.

1 This container is a prism.

  (a) Calculate the capacity of the container in m^3.

  (b) What is this capacity in litres?

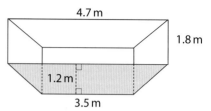

2 p is an odd number and q is an even number.
Decide whether each of these statements is true or false.

  (a) $p^2 + q$ is always an integer.

  (b) $p^2 + q$ is always odd.

  (c) $p^2 + q$ is always a prime number.

3 Solve the inequality $^-6 < 2x + 3 \leq 11$.

4 Simon planted some bulbs and grew 50 tulips.
He grew red, yellow and pink tulips in the ratio $4:5:1$.
How many red tulips did he grow?

5 A circle has centre $(0, 0)$ and radius 10.

  (a) Write down the equation of the circle.

  (b) By solving a pair of simultaneous equations, find the coordinates of the
points where the circle intersects the line $y = x + 2$.

6 Draw the square ABCD whose sides are 6 cm.

  (a) Draw the locus of all the points inside the square that are
nearer to AB than to AD, and more than 2 cm from C.

  (b) **(i)** Find the area that this locus occupies as an exact value.

      (ii) Show that the fraction of the area of the square that
this locus occupies is $\dfrac{36 - \pi}{72}$.

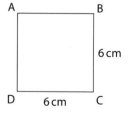

7 Class 11X consists of 18 girls and 12 boys.
Class 11Y consists of 15 girls and 9 boys.

A teacher picks a student at random from each of the two classes.
Calculate the probability that the teacher picks

  (a) two girls   **(b)** one student of each sex

8 I bought a jumper in a sale at 11% off.
The sale price of the jumper was £32.04.
What was the price of the jumper before the sale?

9 Rationalise the denominator and simplify $\dfrac{14}{\sqrt{7}}$.

10 This is a sketch of the graph of $y = \sin x$.
Sketch each of the following graphs.

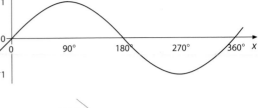

(a) $y = 2\sin x$

(b) $y = \sin 2x$

(c) $y = 1 + \sin x$

11 A, B and C are three points on the
circumference of a circle, centre O.
PA and PB are tangents to the circle.
Angle POB = 57°.

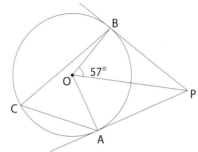

(a) Prove that shape OBPA is a kite.

(b) Calculate the size of angle BPO.
Give reasons for your answer.

(b) Calculate the size of angle ACB.
Give reasons for your answer.

12 Here is a simple rule for working out the squares of $1\tfrac{1}{2}, 2\tfrac{1}{2}, 3\tfrac{1}{2}, 4\tfrac{1}{2}, \ldots$
Example: $\left(5\tfrac{1}{2}\right)^2$ Work out $5 \times$ the next number after 5, and then add $\tfrac{1}{4}$.
$$\text{So } \left(5\tfrac{1}{2}\right)^2 = (5 \times 6) + \tfrac{1}{4} = 30\tfrac{1}{4}.$$
Multiply out $\left(n + \tfrac{1}{2}\right)^2$ and prove that the rule works.

13 What is the exact value of the perimeter of a square with a diagonal of 10 cm?
Give your answer in the form $a\sqrt{b}$ where b is prime.

14 This is a sketch of the graph of the
function $y = \mathrm{f}(x)$.
The graph has a maximum point at $(^-2, 1)$
and a minimum point at $(4, ^-1)$.

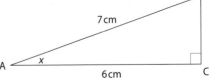

What are the coordinates of the maximum
and minimum points of the graphs with
the following equations?

(a) $y = \mathrm{f}(x) + 2$ (b) $y = \mathrm{f}(x + 1)$

(c) $y = 2\mathrm{f}(x)$ (d) $y = \mathrm{f}(2x)$

15 Triangle ABC is right-angled at C.
AB = 7 cm and AC = 6 cm.

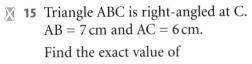

Find the exact value of

(a) $\cos x$ (b) $\tan x$

16 The equation $x^3 + 5x = 50$ has a solution between 3 and 4.
Use trial and improvement to find this solution, correct to 1 d.p.

17 Quadrilateral ABCD is a kite.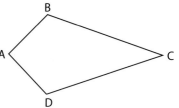

    (a) Show that triangles ABC and ADC are congruent.

    Point B is on the circumference of a circle with centre A.
    BC is a tangent to the circle.

    (b) What is the size of angle ABC?

    (c) **(i)** Show that a circle exists that has points A, B, C and D on its circumference.

        (ii) Describe the position of the centre of this circle.

18 The expression $x^2 + 10x - 3$ can be written in the form $(x + a)^2 + b$.

    (a) Find the values of a and b.

    (b) Find the minimum value of the expression $x^2 + 10x - 3$ and
    the value of x for which it is a minimum.

19 The function $f(x)$ is defined for
values of x in the interval $^-3 \leq x \leq 3$.
The graph of $y = f(x)$ is shown on
the right.

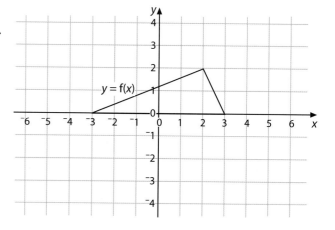

On similar grids, draw each
of these graphs.

    (a) $y = 2f(x)$

    (b) $y = ^-\frac{1}{2}f(x)$

    (c) $y = f(^-x)$

    (d) $y = f(2x)$

    (e) $y = f\left(\frac{1}{2}x\right)$

20 **(a)** Simplify as far as possible the expression $3\sqrt{5} \times 2\sqrt{20}$.

    (b) Write $\left(\sqrt{3} + \sqrt{6}\right)^2$ in the form $a + b\sqrt{c}$,
    where a, b and c are positive integers and c is as small as possible.

21 A and B are two points on level ground.
B is 5.8 km east of A.

The point C is on a bearing of 076° from A
and on a bearing of 033° from B.

    (a) Find the size of angle ACB.

    (b) Calculate the distance AC, to an
    appropriate degree of accuracy.

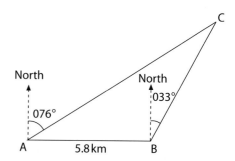

22 Solve the simultaneous equations $y = 3x + 2$
                                    $x^2 + y^2 = 2$

23 Prove that the sum of three consecutive numbers is always
three times the middle number.

24 **(a)** Write $\frac{9}{11}$ as a recurring decimal.

   (b) Prove that $0.\overset{\bullet}{1}\overset{\bullet}{2} = \frac{4}{33}$.

   (c) Write the following recurring decimals in fractional form.

   (i) $0.\overset{\bullet}{4}$ **(ii)** $0.\overset{\bullet}{2}\overset{\bullet}{7}$ **(iii)** $0.0\overset{\bullet}{2}\overset{\bullet}{7}$

25 AB and CD are parallel lines.
AD and BC meet at point X.
AB = 10 cm, XD = 4.2 cm and CD = 6 cm.
Angle BAD = 42°.

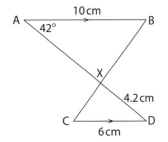

   (a) Show that ABX and DCX are similar triangles.

   (b) Find the length of AX.

   (c) Find the area of triangle CDX.

26 Solve the equation $x^2 - 2x - 1 = 0$, giving solutions in the form $a \pm \sqrt{b}$.

27 The diagram shows a sketch of a parallelogram PQRS.

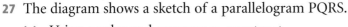

   (a) Using a ruler and compasses, construct
the parallelogram PQRS.

   (b) Calculate the size of the angle PQS.

   (c) **(i)** Using a straight edge and compasses, construct
the perpendicular from point R to the line QS.

   (ii) **Calculate** the length of this perpendicular from R to the line QS.

28 **(a)** Find the exact value of $\left(1 - \frac{9}{25}\right)^{-\frac{3}{2}}$.

   (b) Express $\dfrac{8\sqrt{5}}{\sqrt{2}}$ in the form $a\sqrt{b}$, where a and b are integers, and b is
as small as possible.

29 The diagram shows a cuboid ABCDEFGH.

Calculate

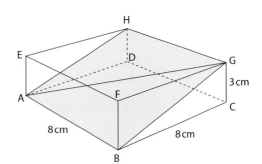

   (a) the angle between plane ABGH
and base ABCD

   (b) the length of diagonal AG

   (c) the angle between AG and base ABCD

*30 The distance between two ports is 165 miles.
The passenger ferry between them travels 8 m.p.h. faster than the cargo ferry
and takes 2 hours less for the journey.

By forming and solving an equation, calculate the speed of each ferry.

Answers

1 Graphing inequalities

A Inequalities on a grid (p 8)

A1 B, E

A2 (a) D   (b) E

A3 (a) D

(b) The required points are grey.

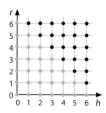

A4 The required points are grey.

(a)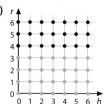

(b)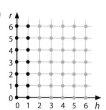

(c)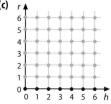

(d)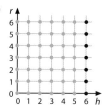

(e)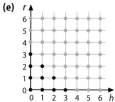

B Regions with vertical and horizontal boundaries (p 10)

B1 (a) K   (b) H   (c) J

B2 (a) $x \leq 4$ (b) $y \geq 2$ (c) $y \leq 0$ (d) $x \geq {}^{-}1$

B3 (a)

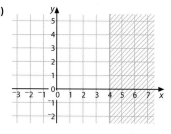

(b)

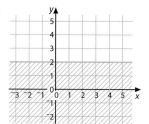

(c)

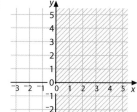

(d)

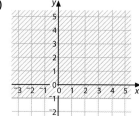

B4 (a)–(f) (i)

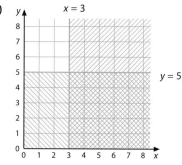

(f) (ii) Any three points with $x \geq 3$ and $y \leq 5$

B5 (a) A

(b) Any two points with $x \leq 2$ and $y \geq 1$

B6 $x \leq 6$, $y \leq 2$, $y \geq {}^{-}1$

B7 (a) V: $0 \leq y \leq 2$

(b) U: $0 \leq x \leq 2$

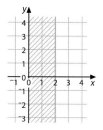

W: $^-1 \le x \le 7$

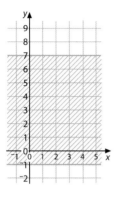

X: $^-1 \le y \le 7$

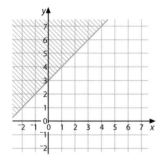

C Sloping boundary lines (p 12)

C1 A, with explanation

C2 (a) $y \le x + 1$ **(b)** $y \ge 2x$ **(c)** $y + x \le 3$

C3 (a), (b)

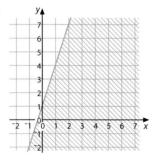

(c) Any two points that satisfy $y \ge x + 3$

C4 (a)

(b)

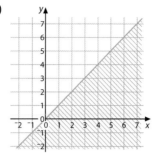

(c)

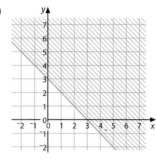

(d)

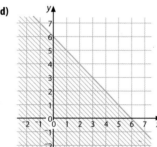

(e)

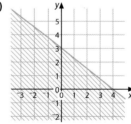

C5 (a) $y = x,\ y \ge x$

(b) $y = 2x + 1,\ y \ge 2x + 1$

(c) $x + y = 4,\ x + y \le 4$ or $y = 4 - x,\ y \le 4 - x$

C6 (a) $a + b \le 30$ **(b)**

C7 (a) $3n + 5m$ **(b)** $3n + 5m \le 60$

(c)

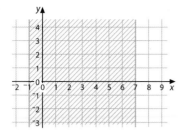

D Overlapping regions (p 14)

D1 (a) A, three points in A **(b)** $y \geq 1$, $x \leq 5$, $y \leq x + 1$

D2 (a) $y \leq 5$, $x \geq 0$, $y \geq 2x + 2$

    (b) $x \geq 0$, $x \leq 4$, $y \geq x$

D3 (a)

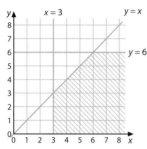

    (b) Two points that satisfy all three inequalities
$x \geq 3$, $y \leq 6$ and $y \leq x$

D4 (a)

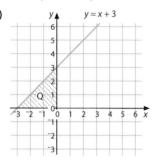

    (b) $(0, 3)$, $(^-1, 2)$, $(0, 2)$, $(^-2, 1)$, $(^-1, 1)$, $(0, 1)$, $(^-3, 0)$,
$(^-2, 0)$, $(^-1, 0)$, $(0, 0)$

D5

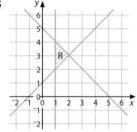

D6 $x \leq 4$, $y \leq x + 2$, $y \leq 5$

D7 (a) $y \geq 1$, $y \leq x + 1$, $x + y \leq 5$

    (b) $x \geq 3$, $y \leq 4$, $y \leq x - 1$

D8

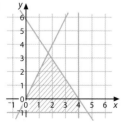

E Boundaries: included or not included (p 16)

E1 (a) $y > 2x + 3$ **(b)** $x + y > 4$

E2 (a) **(b)** $p = 0$, $q = 1$

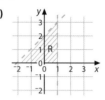

E3 (a)

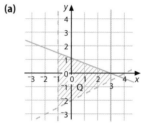

    (b) $(2, 0)$, $(3, 0)$, $(1, \frac{-1}{2})$, $(2, \frac{1}{3})$

    (c) Trapezium

E4 (a), (b)

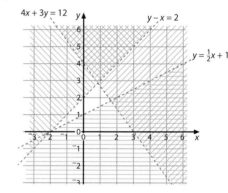

    (c) $4x + 3y \leq 12$, $y - x \leq 2$, $y \geq \frac{1}{2}x + 1$

Test yourself (p 17)

In all these, the required region can instead be shown as an **unshaded** region.

T1 (a)

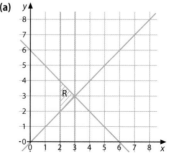

    (b) $(2, 2)$, $(2, 3)$, $(2, 4)$, $(3, 3)$

T2

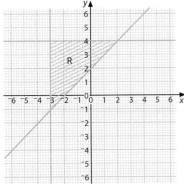

T3

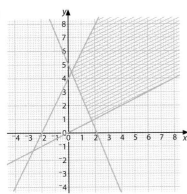

T4

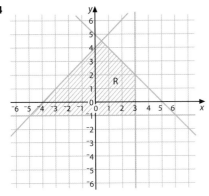

T5 $y \leq \frac{1}{2}x$, $x \leq 6$, $y \geq 0$

T6 (a) $^-1, 0, 1$

(b)

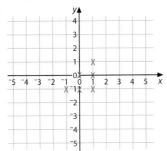

2 Enlargement and similarity

A Enlargement and scale factor (p 18)

A1 $a = 7.5$, $b = 10.0$, $c = 13.5$, $d = 7.0$

A2 5

A3 (a) 1.2   **(b)** $a = 5.4$, $b = 6.0$

A4 (a) 0.8   **(b)** $a = 3.6$, $b = 5.5$

A5 (a) $\frac{5}{6}$ **(b)** $a = 20$, $b = 30$, $c = 30$

A6 (a) $\frac{11}{8}$ **(b)** $a = 55$, $b = 88$, $c = 48$

A7 No, because they do not have the same set of angles at their vertices

B Similar triangles (p 20)

B1 A is similar to C; B is similar to D.

B2 (a) XY   **(b)** YA   **(c)** AX

B3 (a) PJ   **(b)** JU   **(c)** UP

B4 (a) The marked angles are the same in both triangles. Since the sum of the angles is 180° in both triangles, the unmarked angles must be the same.

    (b) 1.2

    (c) $a = 7.5$, $b = 9.6$

B5 $a = 13$, $b = 7.7$

B6 $\frac{x}{y} = \frac{3}{4}$ or 0.75

Triangles A and D are similar to the blue triangle.

B7 (a) 2.4

    (b) $a = 12$, $b = 7.2$, $c = 10.8$, $d = 7.5$, $e = 10$

B8 16.25 m

B9 (a) $\angle$ABC = $\angle$ADE (corresponding angles)
$\angle$ACB = $\angle$AED (corresponding angles)
$\angle$A is common to both triangles.
Hence the triangles have equal angles.
So triangles ABC and ADE are similar.

    (b) 1.5

    (c) 8 cm

    (d) 18 cm

B10 (a) $\angle$P = $\angle$T (alternate angles)
$\angle$Q = $\angle$S (alternate angles)
$\angle$PRQ = $\angle$TRS (vertically opposite angles)
Hence the triangles have equal angles.
So triangles PQR and TSR are similar.

    (b) 10.5 cm

    (c) 7.5 cm

B11 (a) 24 cm   **(b)** 40.5 cm

B12 (a) ∠JMK = ∠KLM (given)
∠JKM = ∠KML (alternate angles)
Hence the triangles have equal angles.
So triangles JKM and KML are similar.
(b) 4.9 cm

B13 33.2 cm

C Map scale (p 24)

C1 20 mm by 44 mm

C2 (a) 1 : 25   (b) 1.05 m

C3 (a) 1.25 km   (b) 60 cm

D Repeated enlargement (p 24)

D1 (a) 30 cm   (b) 3
(c) It is the product of the separate scale factors.

D2 4.2

D3 2.4

D4 (a) 130%
(b) Reduce on a setting of 50% then reduce the result on a setting of 72%, or reduce on a setting of 60% then reduce the result on a setting of 60%.

E Enlargement with a negative scale factor (p 25)

E1 (a), (b)

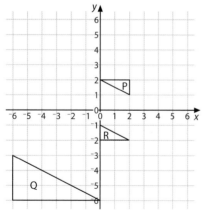

(c) An enlargement with scale factor 3, centre (3, 0)

Test yourself (p 26)

T1 (a) 1.3   (b) $a = 7.8, b = 4$

T2 8.25 cm

T3 (a) 5.4 cm   (b) 8 cm

T4 (a) 1 : 20   (b) 42 mm

T5 8.4

T6 Enlargement with scale factor $^-2$, centre (0, 1)

3 The reciprocal function

A Review: reciprocals (p 27)

A1 $\frac{1}{3}$

A2 (a) 4   (b) 6   (c) $\frac{3}{2}$ (d) $\frac{4}{3}$ (e) $\frac{5}{9}$

A3 (a) $\frac{9}{4}$ (b) $\frac{4}{9}$

A4 (a) $\frac{3}{10}$ (b) $\frac{10}{3}$

A5 (a) 4   (b) 10   (c) 100
(d) $\frac{10}{6}$ or $\frac{5}{3}$ (e) $\frac{10}{17}$

A6 32

A7 The reciprocal of 7

A8 The reciprocal of 0.0001

A9 (a) $x = \frac{1}{5}$ (b) $x = \frac{9}{2}$ (c) $x = \frac{10}{9}$

A10 0.5

A11 (a) 0.125   (b) 0.0625   (c) 1.25
(d) 12.5   (e) 0.156 25   (f) $^-0.04$

A12 (a) 24.8   (b) 4.50

B Graphs of reciprocal functions (p 28)

B1 (a)

x	$^-4$	$^-3$	$^-2$	$^-1$	$^-0.5$	$^-0.25$
$y = \frac{1}{x}$	$^-0.25$	$^-0.33$	$^-0.5$	$^-1$	$^-2$	$^-4$

0.25	0.5	1	2	3	4
4	2	1	0.5	0.33	0.25

(b)

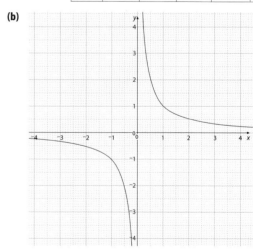

(c) (i) 0.1   (ii) 0.001   (iii) 0.000 01   (iv) 0.000 000 1
(d) The value of y gets smaller and smaller, staying positive but getting closer and closer to 0.
(e) (i) 10   (ii) 10 000   (iii) 1 000 000 (iv) 100 000 000
(f) The value of y gets larger and larger without limit.

(g) The **size** of the value of y gets smaller and smaller (though the numbers actually get higher), staying negative but getting closer and closer to 0.

(h) The size of the value of y gets larger and larger without limit (though the numbers being negative actually get lower).

(i) A calculator will show an error message of some kind. This is because you cannot divide by 0.

(j) A sketch such as:

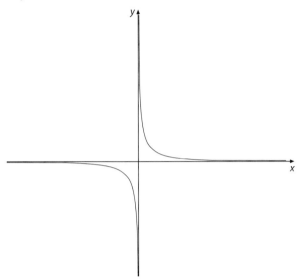

(k) Yes; the mirror lines are $y = x$ and $y = {}^-x$.

(l) Yes; the centre is the origin $(0, 0)$ and the order of rotation symmetry is 2.

B2 (a) (i) 1   **(ii)** $^-1$

    (b) A and R, B and P, C and S, D and Q

B3 (a) Comments on the graphs of $y = x^2$ and $y = \dfrac{1}{x^2}$

    (b) Comments on the graphs of $y = x^3 - x$ and $y = \dfrac{1}{x^3 - x}$

    (c) Comments on the graph of any function and its reciprocal

Test yourself (p 29)

T1 (a) $\frac{1}{4}$ or 0.25   **(b)** 10   **(c)** 2

    (d) $\frac{7}{3}$ **(e)** $\frac{3}{4}$

T2 $x = 4.8$

4 Arc, sector and segment

A Arc and sector of a circle (p 30)

A1 (a) (i) 2.0 cm   **(ii)** 3.9 cm^2
    (b) (i) 12.0 cm   **(ii)** 36.1 cm^2
    (c) (i) 30.8 cm   **(ii)** 107.8 cm^2
    (d) (i) 36.9 cm   **(ii)** 119.8 cm^2
    (e) (i) 9.6 cm   **(ii)** 31.3 cm^2
    (f) (i) 18.2 cm   **(ii)** 47.2 cm^2

A2 (a) 7.0 m^2 **(b)** 3.4 m

A3 (a) 12.0 m^2 **(b)** 9.6 m

A4 (a) 18.4 cm^2 **(b)** 18.7 cm

A5 492 cm^2

A6 (a) 4π cm   **(b)** 3π cm^2

A7 (a) 5π cm   **(b)** 2.5 cm

A8 5.6 cm

A9 6.8 cm

A10 160°

A11 60 cm

B Segment of a circle (p 32)

B1 (a) 111.7 cm^2
    (b) PX = XR = 8.99 cm, OX = 4.38 cm
    (c) 39.4 cm^2
    (d) 72 cm^2 (to the nearest cm^2)

B2

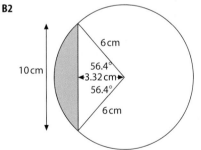

      Area of segment = 18.8 cm^2 or 18.9 cm^2

B3 (a) 135 cm^2 **(b)** 144 cm^2 **(c)** 125 cm^2

B4 (a) 1.9 m^2 **(b)** 2.1 m

C Part of a cylinder (p 33)

C1 354 cm^3

C2 (a) 51.3 cm^2 **(b)** 58.6 cm^2 **(c)** 217.3 cm^2

C3 **(a)** $1429\,\text{m}^2$

(b) Rectangular face $1219\,\text{m}^2$
Each segment shaped face $73\,\text{m}^2$
Total of the three faces $1365\,\text{m}^2$

(c) 824 tonnes

Test yourself (p 33)

T1 $78.0°$ (to 1 d.p.)

T2 $6.9\,\text{cm}^2$ (to 1 d.p.)

5 Investigating and identifying graphs

A Investigating graphs (p 34)

A1 Negative values of a give upside-down parabolas.
The size of a tells you how steep the graph will be.
Large (positive or negative) values of a such as 4 or $^-5$
give steep parabolas and fractional values of a such as $\frac{1}{2}$
and $^-\frac{1}{4}$ give much shallower parabolas. All graphs with
equations of the form $y = ax^2$ have the y-axis as a line
of symmetry and go through $(0, 0)$.

A2 The value of a gives the information outlined in A1.
The value of c gives the y-intercept of the graph. All
graphs with equations of the form $y = ax^2 + c$ have the
y-axis as a line of symmetry.

A3 A and R, B and S, C and P, D and Q

A4 **(a)** $y = x^2 - 3$

(b) $x = 1$

(c) For both equations, when $x = 0$, $y = ^-3$; so both
have a y-intercept of $^-3$.

(d) **(i)**

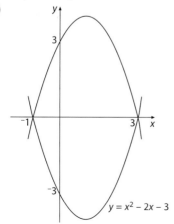

$y = x^2 - 2x - 3$

(ii) All the y-values have changed sign in the
reflected graph so the equation is
$y = ^-(x^2 - 2x - 3)$ which is equivalent to
$y = ^-x^2 + 2x + 3$.

A5 C

A6 All the graphs are the same basic shape of a curve with
a kink in the middle. The curves all have rotation
symmetry of order 2. Positive values of p give curves in
this orientation:

Negative values of p give curves in this orientation:

As with quadratics, the size of p tells you how steep the
graph will be. Large (positive or negative) values of p
such as 4 or $^-5$ give steep curves and fractional values
of p such as $\frac{1}{2}$ and $^-\frac{1}{4}$ give much shallower curves. The
value of q gives the y-intercept of the graph.

A7 **(a)** A and W, B and Z, C and X, D and Y

(b) W $(0, 0)$, X $(0, 1)$, Y $(0, 1)$, Z $(0, 0)$

A8 Negative values of b give graphs with a wiggle in the
middle like this

The larger the negative value of b in size, the more
pronounced the wiggle is.
Positive values of b give graphs with a small kink in the
middle. The larger the positive value of b, the more
stretched out in the y-direction the graph is.
All graphs with equations of the form $y = x^3 + bx$ have
rotation symmetry of order 2 about $(0, 0)$.

A9 A and R, B and P, C and Q

A10 $p = 4$, $q = 4\frac{1}{2}$, $r = ^-2$

A11 Negative values of k give upside-down graphs. The size of k tells you how stretched out in the y-direction the graph is. The value of c affects the vertical position of the graph. The x-intercept of the graph of $y = \frac{k}{x} + c$ is $\left(-\frac{k}{c}, 0\right)$. The graph has rotation symmetry of order 2 about $(0, c)$.

A12 A and M, B and L, C and N

B Identifying graphs (p 36)

B1 A and U, B and T, C and Q, D and P, E and R, F and S

B2
$y = x^2 + 3x$ D
$y = x - x^3$ C
$y = x^3 - 2x$ E
$y = x^2 + 2x - 4$ F
$y = \frac{4}{x}$ A
$y = x^2 + 3$ B

Test yourself (p 38)

T1 (a) $y = 2 - x^3$ (b) $y = \frac{2}{x}$

T2 (a) C   (b) D   (c) B

T3 Graph A: $y = x^3 + 4$
Graph B: $y = 4 - 3x$
Graph C: $y = x^2 - x - 6$

6 Combining probabilities

A Review: finding probabilities (p 39)

A1 (a) $\frac{1}{2}$ (b) $\frac{1}{4}$ (c) $\frac{1}{5}$ (d) $\frac{1}{8}$

A2 (a) $\frac{75}{140} = \frac{15}{28}$ (b) $\frac{80}{140} = \frac{4}{7}$
(c) $\frac{40}{140} = \frac{2}{7}$ (d) $\frac{55}{140} = \frac{11}{28}$

A3 (a) $\frac{1}{3}$ (b) 1, 2, 2, 3, 3, 4

A4 (a) 0.096 or $\frac{12}{125}$ (b) 0.924 or $\frac{231}{250}$ (c) 0.656 or $\frac{82}{125}$

B Mutually exclusive events (p 40)

B1 (a) No
(b) No
(c) (i) No   (ii) Yes   (iii) Yes   (iv) No

B2 (a) $\frac{1}{4}$ (b) $\frac{1}{4}$ (c) $\frac{7}{16}$

B3 (a) (i) No   (ii) No   (iii) No   (iv) Yes   (v) Yes
(b) $\frac{1}{2}$
(c) Jake is not right. You cannot add the probabilities because the events are not mutually exclusive.

B4 (a) 0.06   (b) 0.54   (c) 0.6   (d) 0.32

B5 (a) (i) $\frac{120}{600} = \frac{1}{5}$ (ii) $\frac{340}{600} = \frac{17}{30}$
(iii) $\frac{330}{600} = \frac{11}{20}$ (iv) $\frac{410}{600} = \frac{41}{60}$
(b) (i) 270   (ii) $\frac{120}{270} = \frac{4}{9}$

C Independent events (p 42)

C1 (a) $\frac{1}{2}$ (b) $\frac{1}{2}$ (c) $\frac{1}{4}$

C2 (a) $\frac{1}{3}$ (b) $\frac{1}{4}$ (c) $\frac{1}{12}$

C3 (a) $\frac{1}{4}$ (b) $\frac{1}{5}$ (c) $\frac{1}{20}$

C4 (a) $\frac{2}{5}$ (b) $\frac{2}{15}$ (c) $\frac{4}{15}$ (d) $\frac{1}{5}$

C5 (a) $\frac{1}{8}$ (b) $\frac{1}{8}$ (c) $\frac{1}{16}$

C6 (a) $\frac{6}{35}$ (b) $\frac{12}{35}$

C7 (a) $\frac{6}{25}$ (b) $\frac{6}{25}$

C8 (a) 0.7   (b) 0.14   (c) 0.06   (d) 0.56

D Tree diagrams (p 44)

D1 (a)

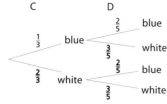

(b) (i) $\frac{8}{15}$ **(ii)** $\frac{7}{15}$

D2 (a)

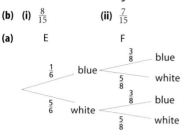

(b) $\frac{21}{40}$

D3 (a)

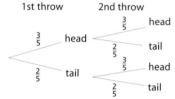

(b) $\frac{12}{25}$

D4 (a) $\frac{7}{10}$ **(b)** $\frac{3}{50}$ **(c)** $\frac{19}{50}$

D5 (a) Completed tree diagram with probabilities $\frac{1}{3}, \frac{1}{3}, \frac{1}{3}$ for A and $\frac{1}{6}, \frac{1}{2}, \frac{1}{3}$ for B

    (b) $\frac{1}{3}$

    (c) $\frac{5}{18}$

D6 (a) 0.02   **(b)** 0.98   **(c)** More likely

E Dependent events (p 46)

E1 (a) $\frac{7}{15}$ **(b)** $\frac{8}{15}$

E2 (a) Tree diagram   **(b)** $\frac{8}{20}$ or $\frac{2}{5}$ **(c)** $\frac{12}{20}$ or $\frac{3}{5}$

E3 $\frac{42}{90}$ or $\frac{7}{15}$

E4 (a)

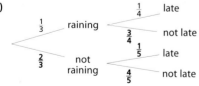

    (b) $\frac{13}{60}$

E5 (a) 0.48   **(b)** 0.52

E6 (a) $\frac{3}{10}$ **(b)** $\frac{27}{50}$

E7 $\frac{1}{2}$

F Mixed questions (p 48)

F1 The events 'even' and 'less than 6' are not mutually exclusive.

F2 The events 'male' and 'wearing a skirt' are not independent.

F3 (a) $\frac{20}{33}$ **(b)** $\frac{4}{13}$ **(c)** $\frac{1}{13}$ **(d)** $\frac{3}{8}$

F4 0.79

F5 $\frac{3}{5}$

Test yourself (p 49)

T1 (a) 0.85

    (b) 110

    (c) (i) 0.09   **(ii)** 0.33

T2 (a) $\frac{4}{7}$ **(b)** $\frac{3}{7}$ **(c)** $\frac{1}{7}$ **(d)** $\frac{6}{7}$

T3 (a)

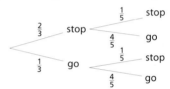

    (b) $\frac{4}{15}$

T4 $\frac{33}{95}$ or 0.347 (to 3 d.p.)

T5 0.432

Review 1 (p 50)

1 $a = 5.7\,\text{cm}$, $b = 7.2\,\text{cm}$

2 (a) £94.24   **(b)** 14

3 (a) $^-3, ^-2, ^-1, 0, 1, 2, 3, 4$ **(b)** 0, 1, 2

4 (a) A sketch such as:

The volume is $12\,\text{cm}^3$.

(b) A full-size drawing of

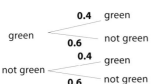

5 $^-7$

6 (a) $\frac{1}{5}$ **(b)** $\frac{5}{2}$ **(c)** $\frac{1}{100}$ **(d)** $\frac{5}{6}$

7 $y = ^-\frac{1}{2}x + 4$ or $2y + x = 8$

8 (a) $(3, 7)$ **(b)** $(1, 6)$ **(c)** 4.47 units **(d)** $(2, 4)$

9 (a)

First set   Second set

- 0.7 green
  - 0.4 green
  - 0.6 not green
- 0.3 not green
  - 0.4 green
  - 0.6 not green

(b) (i) 0.18   **(ii)** 0.54

10 (a) 54

(b) Lower quartile 44, upper quartile 63

(c) About 89%

11 $x \leq 7$

12 £8.06

13 $x^2 + 6x$

14 (a) $\angle PTS = \angle PRQ$ (corresponding angles)
$\angle PST = \angle PQR$ (corresponding angles)
So triangles PTS and PRQ are similar (equal angles).

(b) 14 cm

(c) 16 cm

15 (a) $\frac{5}{8}$ **(b)** 3   **(c)** $1\frac{1}{5}$ or $\frac{6}{5}$ **(d)** $\frac{9}{10}$

16 (a) $9x + 5$ cm

(b) $9x + 5 = 32$, leading to $x = 3$

(c) 12 cm

17 3.7% increase

18 $3a + c = 12$
$2a + 4c = 13$
or equivalent (letters other than a and c may be used)
$a = 3.5$ and $c = 1.5$ so the cost of an adult ticket is £3.50 and the cost of a child ticket is £1.50

19 (a), (c)

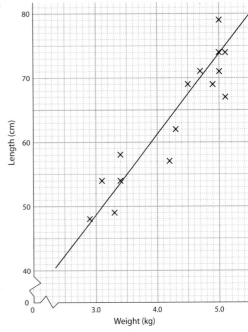

(b) Positive correlation

(d) About 5.1 kg

20 (a) $\frac{8}{3}$ **(b)** 2.667

21 40°

22 (a) 0.19   **(b)** 135

23 $x = 5, y = ^-2$

24 606.3 g (to the nearest 0.1 g)

25 (a) £$(x + 10)$

(b) Kelly has £$3x$ so the total number of pounds is
$x + (x + 10) + 3x = 5x + 10$
which factorises to give $5(x + 2)$ as required

26 $\frac{2}{5}$

27 (a) $y = x + 1$

(b) $y \leq x + 1, x \leq 3, y \geq 0$

(c)

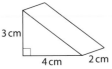

28 (a) 78.5 cm (to the nearest 0.1 cm)

(b) 3839.7 cm^2 (to the nearest 0.1 cm^2)

(c) 2.4 kg (to the nearest 0.1 kg)

29 $3xy(2x + 5y)$

30 $\frac{3}{10}$

31 (a) $2x$ **(b)** x^2 **(c)** 2

(d) $4x + 2$ (or $2(2x + 1)$) **(e)** $x - 7$

32 (a) 76 kg

(b) 76.7 kg (to the nearest (0.1 kg)

33 (a), (b) (i)

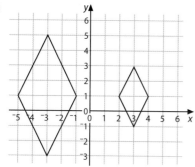

(ii) $(^-3, 5)$

(iii) 16 square units

34 (a) $x^2 + 5x - 15$ **(b)** $3n - n^2 - 6$ **(c)** $9p$

35 25 000 cm^2

36 A: S B: Q C: R D: T E: P

37 (a) $\frac{2}{9}$ **(b)** 18 (12 boys and 6 girls)

7 Direct and inverse proportion

A Review: ratio (p 55)

A1 (a) 2:1 **(b)** 3:5 **(c)** 3:5 **(d)** 8:1 **(e)** 2:5

A2 (a) 1.2 **(b)** 2.5 **(c)** 0.625

A3 40

A4 (a) £24, £36 **(b)** £48, £12 **(c)** £10, £15, £

A5 (a) 4:1 **(b)** 3.5:1 **(c)** 0.8:1

A6 15:8

B Quantities related by a rate (p 56)

B1 (a) £7.50

(b) £300

(c) $\frac{2}{15}$ hour

(d)

T	6	1	40	$\frac{2}{15}$	12	30
W	45	**7.50**	**300**	1	90	**225**

(e)

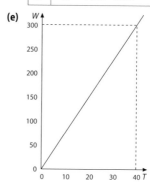

(f) $W = 7.5T$

(g) (i) £112.50 **(ii)** 8 hours

B2 (a)

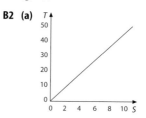

(b) $T = 4.5S$

(c) (i) 135 **(ii)** 12

C Direct proportion (p 57)

C1 Graph C (straight line through $(0, 0)$)

C2 (a) True **(b)** False **(c)** False

(d) True **(e)** False

C3 (a) Yes, $Q = 4P$ **(b)** No **(c)** No

(d) Yes, $Q = 2P$ **(e)** No **(f)** Yes, $Q = 3.5$

D Calculating with direct proportion (p 58)

D1 (a) $V = 50T$ **(b)** 225 **(c)** 525 **(d)** 9.5

D2 (a) $P = \frac{3}{40}A$ or $P = 0.075A$ **(b)** 10.5

D3 (a) $L = 1.75H$ **(b)** 6.65 m **(c)** 4.2 m

D4 (a) $I = 0.6V$ **(b)** 2.7 **(c)** 11.5

D5 (a) 8 **(b)** 224 **(c)** 0.5625

D6 (a) 3.6

(b)

X	5	1	3.33	11
Y	18	3.6	12	39.6

D7 (a) £12.60 **(b)** 100 km

E $Q \propto P^2, Q \propto P^3, \ldots$ (p 59)

E1 (a), (c)

S	0	20	40	60	80
S^2	0	400	1600	3600	6400
L	0	200	800	1800	3200

(b) $k = \frac{1}{2}$, so $L = \frac{1}{2}S^2$

(d) 30 km/h

E2 (a) $s = 5t^2$

(b)

t	0	4	7	14
t^2	0	16	49	196
s	0	80	245	980

E3 (a) $R = 1.5S^2$

(b)

S	10	30	40	44
S^2	100	900	1600	1936
R	150	1350	2400	2904

E4 (a)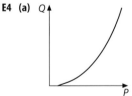

(b) $Q = 5.5P^2$

(c) (i) 352 **(ii)** 18

E5 (a) $Y = 0.6X^2$ **(b)** 101.4 **(c)** 290.4 **(d)** 17

E6 (a) $T = 2\sqrt{L}$

(b)

L	4	6.25	9	625
$\sqrt{L}$	2	2.5	3	25
T	4	5	6	50

E7 (a) $d = \dfrac{20L^3}{3\,375\,000}$ or $d = \dfrac{L^3}{168\,750}$
or $d = 0.000\,005\,93\,L^3$ (to 3 s.f.)

(b) 136 (to 3 s.f.)

F Inverse proportion (p 61)

F1 (a) $PQ = 60$ for all pairs in the table

(b) For example, when P is multiplied by 5 (from 4 to 20), then Q is divided by 5 (from 15 to 3).

(c) (i) 30 **(ii)** 20 **(iii)** 60 **(iv)** 120

F2 (a) 40

(b) 5, 2 and 1

(c) (i) 1.6 **(ii)** 32

F3 (a) Direct proportion, $Q = 1.5P$

(b) Neither

(c) Inverse proportion, $PQ = 100$

(d) Inverse proportion, $PQ = 0.36$

F4 (a) $FL = 8000$ **(b)** 500 **(c)** 64 **(d)** 8

F5 (a) 7.5 **(b)** 120

F6 (a) 4 **(b)** 4.8

F7 (a) A^2B is 360.

(b) $A^2B = 360$

(c)

...	5	6
...	25	36
...	14.4	10

F8 (a) $D\sqrt{M} = 20$

(b)

M	4	25	16	0.25
$\sqrt{M}$	2	5	4	0.5
D	10	4	5	40

F9 (a) 0.75

F10 (a) $V\sqrt{U} = 80$ or $V = \dfrac{80}{\sqrt{U}}$

(b) (i) 20 **(ii)** 256

F11 (a) $VU^2 = 72$ or $V = \dfrac{72}{U^2}$

(b) (i) 0.18 **(ii)** 6

F12 (a) 5.76 **(b)** $\frac{12}{7} = 1.71$ (to 2 d.p.)

F13 P is multiplied by $1\frac{1}{2}$.
So Q is divided by $1\frac{1}{2}$ (or multiplied by $\frac{2}{3}$).
So Q is reduced by $33\frac{1}{3}\%$.

G Identifying a proportional relationship (p 64)

G1 (a) 8 **(b)** 27
(c) U^3 **(d)** $V = \frac{1}{2}U^3$

G2 (a) For example, when S goes from 2 to 4 ($\times 2$) T goes from 180 to 45 ($\div 4$).

(b) For example, when S goes from 2 to 6 ($\times 3$) T goes from 180 to 20 ($\div 9$).

(c) $TS^2 = 720$ or $T = \dfrac{720}{S^2}$

G3 (a) $Q \propto P^2$, $Q = 5P^2$

(b) $Q \propto \frac{1}{P}$, $QP = 36$ or $Q = \frac{36}{P}$

(c) $Q \propto \frac{1}{P^2}$, $QP^2 = 72$ or $Q = \frac{72}{P^2}$

(d) $Q \propto P^3$, $Q = 5P^3$

(e) $Q \propto P$, $Q = 3.5P$

(f) $Q \propto P^2$, $Q = 6P^2$

Test yourself (p 65)

T1 (a) £3.84   **(b)** Graph C

T2 (a) $t = 0.8\sqrt{d}$ **(b)** 6.4 s   **(c)** 100 m

T3 When t is multiplied by 3, h is multiplied by 9, which is 3^2, so rule B $h \propto t^2$ fits. The equation is $h = 2.5t^2$.

T4 (a) (i) $DP = 2700$ or $D = \frac{2700}{P}$ **(ii)** 270

(b)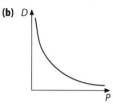

T5 (a) $yx^2 = 48$ or $y = \frac{48}{x^2}$ **(b)** 1.92

T6 (a) $yx^3 = 320$ or $y = \frac{320}{x^3}$

(b) (i) 40   **(ii)** 10

8 Quadratic expressions and equations 1

A Review: simple quadratic expressions and equation
(p 66)

A1 (a) $x^2 + 7x + 12$ **(b)** $x^2 - 25$ **(c)** $x^2 - 8x +$

A2 (a) $(x + 3)(x + 2)$ **(b)** $(x - 6)(x + 5)$

(c) $(x + 4)(x - 4)$

A3 (a) $(x + 6)(x - 3) = 0$ so $x = {}^-6, 3$

(b) $(x + 4)(x + 3) = 0$ so $x = {}^-4, {}^-3$

(c) $x(x + 11) = 0$ so $x = 0, {}^-11$

(d) $(x + 1)(x - 10) = 0$ so $x = {}^-1, 10$

(e) $(x + 3)^2 = 0$ so $x = {}^-3$

(f) $(x - 5)(x - 8) = 0$ so $x = 5, 8$

A4 (a) $(x + 4)(x - 1) = 0$ so $x = {}^-4, 1$

(b) $(x - 4)^2 = 0$ so $x = 4$

(c) $x(x - 1) = 0$ so $x = 0, 1$

(d) $(x - 2)(x - 3) = 0$ so $x = 2, 3$

(e) $(x + 1)(x - 11) = 0$ so $x = {}^-1, 11$

(f) $x(x - 3) = 0$ so $x = 0, 3$

A5 (a) Length $\times$ width $=$ area
so $(x + 7)(x - 4) = 42$
so $x^2 + 3x - 28 = 42$
so $x^2 + 3x - 70 = 0$ as required

(b) $x = 7, {}^-10$; since length cannot be negative, $x = 7$ gives dimensions 3 cm by 14 cm.

A6 (a) $x + 7$

(b) (i) $x(x + 7) = 44$ which rearranges to give $x^2 + 7x - 44 = 0$ with solution $x = 4, {}^-11$

(ii) 30 cm

A7 Sketch of a parabola through $({}^-4, 0)$ and $(5, 0)$; $b = {}^-1$ and $c = {}^-20$

B Multiplying out expressions such as $(2n - 3)(4n + 5)$
(p 67)

B1 (a) $2x^2 + 7x + 3$ **(b)** $4x^2 + 11x + 6$

(c) $3x^2 + 13x - 10$ **(d)** $2x^2 - x - 3$

(e) $2x^2 - 13x + 20$ **(f)** $5x^2 - 12x + 4$

B2 (a) $6n^2 + 11n + 4$ **(b)** $25n^2 + 25n + 6$

(c) $8n^2 + 6n - 5$ **(d)** $6n^2 - 5n - 4$

(e) $6n^2 - 19n + 15$ **(f)** $10n^2 - 17n + 3$

B3 (a) $5m^2 - 49m - 10$ **(b)** ${}^-6c^2 + 7c + 20$

(c) $6a^2 - 5a + 1$

B4 $(2x + 3)^2 = (2x + 3)(2x + 3)$
$$= 4x^2 + 6x + 6x + 9$$
$$= 4x^2 + 12x + 9$$

B5 (a) $4x^2 + 20x + 25$ **(b)** $9x^2 - 6x + 1$
    (c) $16x^2 - 8x + 1$

B6 The area of the lawn is the area of the garden minus the area of the pond:
$$(5x + 3)(x + 7) - 21$$
$$= 5x^2 + 35x + 3x + 21 - 21$$
$$= 5x^2 + 38x \text{ as required}$$

B7 The area of the patio is the total area minus the area of the pond:
$$(3x + 2)(x + 2) - x^2$$
$$= 3x^2 + 6x + 2x + 4 - x^2$$
$$= 2x^2 + 8x + 4 \text{ as required}$$

B8 (a) $(2x + 1)(x + 3) = 2x^2 + 7x + 3$
    (b) $(3x + 2)(2x + 5) = 6x^2 + 19x + 10$
    (c) $(2x + 1)(3x - 1) = 6x^2 + x - 1$
    (d) $(3x - 2)(5x - 4) = 15x^2 - 22x + 8$

B9 (a) $3x + 1$ and $x + 5$ **(b)** $3x + 5$ and $x + 1$
    (c) $2x + 5$ and $x + 5$ **(d)** $3x + 1$ and $2x + 1$

B10 (a) $2x + 3$ and $x - 1$ **(b)** $2x + 1$ and $x - 1$
    (c) $2x - 1$ and $x - 1$ **(d)** $2x - 1$ and $2x - 3$

C Factorising quadratic expressions (p 69)

C1 (a) $(2x + 1)(x + 7)$ **(b)** $(3x + 1)(x + 3)$
    (c) $(2x + 1)(x + 4)$ **(d)** $(3x + 2)(x + 2)$
    (e) $(3x + 4)(x + 1)$ **(f)** $(5x + 2)(x + 3)$

C2 (a) $(2k + 3)(2k + 1)$ **(b)** $(4m + 1)(m + 3)$
    (c) $(10n + 7)(n + 1)$ **(d)** $(4p + 1)(4p + 1)$
    (e) $(2x + 3)(2x + 3)$ **(f)** $(3y + 10)(2y + 1)$

C3 (a) $(2x + 5)(x - 1)$ **(b)** $(3x - 1)(x + 3)$
    (c) $(3x - 5)(x + 1)$ **(d)** $(5x + 1)(x - 2)$
    (e) $(2x - 1)(x - 3)$ **(f)** $(3x - 1)(x - 7)$

C4 (a) $(3k + 5)(2k - 1)$ **(b)** $(2m - 1)(2m - 1)$
    (c) $(3n - 8)(n + 1)$ **(d)** $(2p - 1)(p - 6)$
    (e) $(2x - 5)(2x - 3)$ **(f)** $(2y - 3)(3y + 2)$

C5 (a) $2(2x + 1)(x + 3)$ **(b)** $5(x + 1)(x + 1)$
    (c) $3(3x - 1)(x - 4)$

C6 (a) (i) $4x^2 - 1$ **(ii)** $9x^2 - 4$ **(iii)** $9 - 16x^2$
    (b) A comment such as 'There is no term involving x, just the first term squared minus the second term squared.'
    (c) (i) $(2x + 3)(2x - 3)$ **(ii)** $(3x + 1)(3x - 1)$
    (iii) $(4 + 5x)(4 - 5x)$

C7 (a) $16, 49, 100$
    (b) $9n^2 + 6n + 1 = (3n + 1)^2$ which is a square number when n is an integer so all the terms in the sequence are square.

C8 (a) (i) 272 **(ii)** 16×17
    (b) (i) $(3n + 1)(3n + 2)$
    (ii) $9n^2 + 9n + 2$ can be written as the product $(3n + 1)(3n + 2)$. $3n + 1 + 1 = 3n + 2$ so $3n + 1$ and $3n + 2$ are consecutive numbers.

D Solving equations by factorising (p 71)

D1 (a) $(2x - 1)(x + 5) = 0$ so $x = \frac{1}{2}, \text{-}5$
    (b) $(2x + 1)(x + 5) = 0$ so $x = \frac{\text{-}1}{2}, \text{-}5$
    (c) $(3x - 1)(x + 7) = 0$ so $x = \frac{1}{3}, \text{-}7$
    (d) $2x(x - 3) = 0$ so $x = 0, 3$
    (e) $(2x - 1)(x - 11) = 0$ so $x = \frac{1}{2}, 11$
    (f) $(5x - 7)(x + 1) = 0$ so $x = \frac{7}{5}, \text{-}1$

D2 (a) $(4x + 1)(x + 1) = 0$ so $x = \frac{\text{-}1}{4}, \text{-}1$
    (b) $(2x - 1)(2x - 3) = 0$ so $x = \frac{1}{2}, \frac{3}{2}$
    (c) $(2x - 3)(x - 5) = 0$ so $x = \frac{3}{2}, 5$
    (d) $(3x + 2)(x - 1) = 0$ so $x = \frac{\text{-}2}{3}, 1$
    (e) $(4x - 1)^2 = 0$ so $x = \frac{1}{4}$
    (f) $2x(2x + 7) = 0$ so $x = 0, \frac{\text{-}7}{2}$
    (g) $(2x - 1)(2x + 9) = 0$ so $x = \frac{1}{2}, \frac{\text{-}9}{2}$
    (h) $(2x - 3)(2x - 5) = 0$ so $x = \frac{3}{2}, \frac{5}{2}$
    (i) $(3x - 4)(x - 5) = 0$ so $x = \frac{4}{3}, 5$

D3 (a) $2(x + 5)(x + 4) = 0$ so $x = \text{-}5, \text{-}4$
    (b) $2(2x - 1)(x - 3) = 0$ so $x = \frac{1}{2}, 3$
    (c) $3(3x + 1)(x - 5) = 0$ so $x = \frac{\text{-}1}{3}, 5$

D4 (a) $(2x - 1)(x + 6) = 0$ so $x = \frac{1}{2}, \text{-}6$
    (b) $(3y + 1)(y + 4) = 0$ so $y = \frac{\text{-}1}{3}, \text{-}4$
    (c) $(5m - 3)(m + 7) = 0$ so $m = \frac{3}{5}, \text{-}7$
    (d) $5k(k + 6) = 0$ so $k = 0, \text{-}6$
    (e) $2(5p + 1)(p - 3) = 0$ so $p = \frac{\text{-}1}{5}, 3$
    (f) $(3a + 5)(3a - 7) = 0$ so $y = \frac{\text{-}5}{3}, \frac{7}{3}$

D5 A: $(\text{-}4, 0)$ and B: $\left(\frac{1}{3}, 0\right)$

D6 $(1, 0)$ and $\left(\frac{3}{2}, 0\right)$

D7 (a) Area $=$ length $\times$ width
$$= (2x + 1)(x + 2)$$
$$= 2x^2 + 4x + x + 2$$
$$= 2x^2 + 5x + 2 \text{ as required}$$

(b) (i) $2x^2 + 5x + 2 = 14$ rearranges to
$2x^2 + 5x - 12 = 0$.
The solution is $x = \frac{3}{2}, ^-4$.

(ii) The length is $4\,\mathrm{cm}$ and the width is $3\frac{1}{2}\,\mathrm{cm}$.

D8 (a) The area of the six faces is
$2[x(x + 3) + x(x - 1) + (x + 3)(x - 1)]$
$= 2(x^2 + 3x + x^2 - x + x^2 - x + 3x - 3)$
$= 2(3x^2 + 4x - 3)$
$= 6x^2 + 8x - 6$ as required

(b) (i) The surface area is $184\,\mathrm{cm}^2$
so $6x^2 + 8x - 6 = 184$
so $6x^2 + 8x - 190 = 0$
so $2(3x^2 + 4x - 95) = 0$
so x satisfies the equation $3x^2 + 4x - 95 = 0$
as required.

(ii) $160\,\mathrm{cm}^3$

D9 (a) (i) $(4x - 1)(x - 9)$ **(ii)** $x = \frac{1}{4}, 9$

(b) The equation $4y^4 - 37y^2 + 9 = 0$ is obtained by
replacing x by y^2 in the equation in part (a) and so
the solutions are obtained by solving $y^2 = \frac{1}{4}$ and
$y^2 = 9$. This gives $y = \frac{1}{2}, \frac{^-1}{2}, 3$ and $^-3$.

E Quadratic expressions that use two letters (p 72)

E1 (a) $2x^2 + 5xy + 3y^2$ **(b)** $2x^2 + 5xy + 2y^2$
(c) $3x^2 - 5xy - 2y^2$ **(d)** $2p^2 + pq - q^2$
(e) $2p^2 + 7pq - 15q^2$ **(f)** $5p^2 - 6pq + q^2$
(g) $4a^2 - 8ab + 3b^2$ **(h)** $a^2 + 2ab + b^2$
(i) $4a^2 - 4ab + b^2$ **(j)** $4y^2 - 12xy + 9x^2$
(k) $4x^2 - y^2$ **(l)** $25x^2 - 4y^2$

E2 (a) $a^2 - b^2$
(b) (i) $99^2 - 1^2 = (99 + 1)(99 - 1)$
$= 100 \times 98$
$= 9800$
(ii) $99^2 = 9800 + 1 = 9801$

E3 (a) $998\,000$ **(b)** $998\,001$ **(c)** 9600
(d) 9604 **(e)** $996\,004$

E4 (a) $(a + b)(a - b)$ **(b)** $(2x + y)(2x - y)$
(c) $(3p + 4q)(3p - 4q)$ **(d)** $(h + 5k)(h - 5k)$
(e) $5(g + h)(g - h)$ **(f)** $2(3a + b)(3a - b)$
(g) $3(x + 2y)(x - 2y)$ **(h)** $2(p + 10q)(p - 10q)$

E5 (a) $(3x + y)(x + 2y)$ **(b)** $(2a + b)(a - b)$
(c) $(3p + 2q)(2p - q)$

E6 (a) $xy + 2x + 3y + 6$ **(b)** $5a + ab + 5b + b^2$
(c) $p^2 - pq + 6p - 6q$ **(d)** $2h^2 + 2hk - h - k$
(e) $16g - 4gh + 20 - 5h$ **(f)** $2x^2 - 10xy + x - 5y$

E7 (a) $(p + 3)(p + q)$ **(b)** $(p + q)(p + 1)$
(c) $(2p - 3)(p - q)$

Test yourself (p 73)

T1 $2p^2 + p - 10$

T2 (a) $6x^2 - 7x - 20$ **(b)** $9n^2 - 30n + 25$
(c) $3x^2 - 13xy - 30y^2$

T3 (a) $(2n - 3)(n - 4)$ **(b)** $(5x - 3)(x + 4)$
(c) $(3x - 1)(3x - 1) = (3x - 1)^2$

T4 (a) $y = \frac{1}{3}, ^-2$ **(b)** $x = 0, \frac{5}{2}$ **(c)** $x = \frac{7}{2}, 14$

T5 (a) $(x + 3y)(x - 3y)$ **(b)** $(1 + 5a)(1 - 5a)$

T6 (a) The area of the shape is
$(3x - 2)(2x + 5) + 2(3x - 2)$
$= 6x^2 + 15x - 4x - 10 + 6x - 4$
$= 6x^2 + 17x - 14$
Since the area is $25\,\mathrm{cm}^2$ then $6x^2 + 17x - 14 = 25$
which is equivalent to $6x^2 + 17x - 39 = 0$ as
required.

(b) (i) $x = \frac{3}{2}, \frac{^-13}{3}$ **(ii)** $8\,\mathrm{cm}$

T7 $3(5p + q)(5p - q)$

T8 (a) $x^2 - y^2$ **(b)** $560\,000$

9 Dimension of an expression

A Length, area and volume (p 74)

A1 (a) ab (b) $2(a + b)$ (c) $2a + 4b$
(d) $ab + b^2$ (e) $ab - b^2$

A2 (a) $[length]^3$ (b) $[length]^1$ (c) $[length]^3$
(d) $[length]^1$ (e) $[length]^1$

A3 Length: $a + 3b$; area: $2ab$; volume: a^2b;
pure number: $\dfrac{ab}{c^2}$

A4 (a) $[length]^2$ (b) $[length]^1$
(c) $[length]^2$ (d) $[length]^3$

A5 (a) Area   (b) Length
(c) Pure number   (d) Volume
(e) Inconsistent

A6 (a) Area   (b) Area   (c) Area
(d) Volume   (e) Area   (f) Length
(g) Volume

A7 (a) $[length]^1$ (b) $[length]^2$ (c) $[length]^1$
(d) $[length]^2$ (e) No dimension

A8 (a) Volume   (b) Length   (c) Area
(d) Length   (e) Pure number

Test yourself (p 77)

T1 (a) Area   (b) None of these   (c) Volume

T2 $2\pi b^2$, πab, $2(a^2 + b^2)$

T3 $\dfrac{\pi ab^2}{6}$; its dimension is $[length]^3$.

T4 (a) Volume   (b) Area   (c) Length

T5 (a) (i) D   (ii) C
(b) 2

10 Sequences

A Linear sequences (p 78)

A1 (a) 2, 9, **16**, 23, **30**, …   (b) 20, 18, **16**, 14, 12, …
(c) 1, **7**, **13**, 19, **25**, …   (d) 30, **27**, **24**, **21**, 18, …

A2 (a) (i) $2n + 3$ (ii) $3n - 2$ (iii) $n - 4$
(iv) $7n + 1$ (v) $20 - n$ (vi) $25 - 2n$
(b) (i) 23   (ii) 28   (iii) 6
(iv) 71   (v) 10   (vi) 5

A3 (a) $5n - 1$
(b) 99
(c) An explanation such as:
$5n - 1 = 1000$ leads to $n = 200.2$ which is not a
whole number.
or:
The 200th term is 999 and the 201st term is 1004
so 1000 cannot be a term in the sequence.
(d) 100 terms

B Quadratic sequences (p 79)

B1 A, D

B2 (a) 18, 24   (b) 38, 51

B3 (a) (i) $n^2 + 4$ (ii) $n^2 - 1$ (iii) $2n^2$
(iv) $3n^2 - 2$ (v) $n^2 + 3n$ (vi) $2n^2 + n - 1$
(b) (i) 104   (ii) 99   (iii) 200
(iv) 298   (v) 130   (vi) 209

C Mixed sequences (p 80)

C1 (a) $^-4, ^-1, 2, 5, 8$ (b) 2, 9, 28, 65, 126
(c) $^-3, ^-2, 3, 12, 25$ (d) 0, 8, 28, 66, 128
(e) 0, 12, 72, 240, 600   (f) 12, 6, 4, 3, 2.4 $\left(\text{or } 2\tfrac{2}{5}\right)$
(g) $\tfrac{1}{2}, \tfrac{2}{3}, \tfrac{3}{4}, \tfrac{4}{5}, \tfrac{5}{6}$ (h) 4, 10, 28, 82, 244

C2 (a) 1, 3, 5
(b) 1, 3, 5
(c) The first three terms are the same.
(d) 7 and 13

C3 (a) 1, 8, 27   (b) $6n^2 - 11n + 6$

C4 $4n + 1$

C5 (a) n^2 (b) $n^2 + 1$ (c) $n^2 + n + 1$

C6 $n^2 - 3$

C7 (a) $\tfrac{3}{8}, \tfrac{6}{10} \left(\text{or } \tfrac{3}{5}\right)$ (b) The 6th term

C8 (a) $\dfrac{n}{n + 2}$ (b) $\dfrac{1}{3n^2}$

D Analysing spatial patterns (p 81)

D1 An explanation such as:
The diagram shows that pattern 4 can be split into 4 lots of 3 matches + 1. The sequence increases by adding on 3 matches each time. So pattern n can be split up into n lots of 3 matches + 1 giving $3n + 1$ matches.

D2 An explanation such as:
Pattern 3 can be split up into two 'staircase' shapes that can be fitted together to make a 3 by 3 square. Hence the number of squares in pattern 3 is $3^2 = 9$.

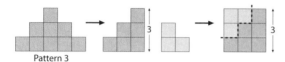

Pattern 3

Pattern n can be split up and the pieces fitted together in the same way to make a n by n square. Hence the number of squares in pattern n is n^2.

D3 (a) The number of cubes in the nth model is $4n + 4$.
An explanation such as:
The nth model can be divided into four identical 'rods', each with n cubes and 4 extra cubes at the corners.

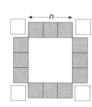

Hence the total number of cubes in the nth model is $4n + 4$.

Alternatively:
The nth model is a square of cubes that is $(n + 2)$ by $(n + 2)$ with the central n by n square removed. Hence the total number of cubes in model n is $(n + 2)^2 - n^2$ which is equivalent to $n^2 + 4n + 4 - n^2$ and simplifies to $4n + 4$.

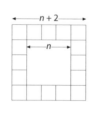

Also the sequence of cubes must be linear as the number of cubes goes up by 4 each time (an extra cube is added to each side). The nth term of the linear sequence 8, 12, 16, 20, ... is $4n + 4$.

(b) The number of hidden faces in the nth model is $8n + 8$. One explanation is that each cube in a model has 2 hidden faces. Hence the number of hidden faces in model n is twice the number of cubes, i.e. $2(4n + 4)$ or $8n + 8$.

(c) No, because $4n + 4 = 150$ does not have a whole-number solution.

D4 (a) The number of cubes in the nth model is $2n(n + 1)$ or $2n^2 + 2n$. The models can be turned into rectangles $2n$ by $(n + 1)$ so the nth term is $2n(n+ 1)$.

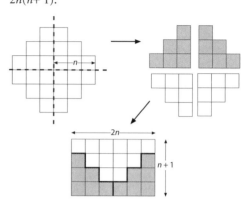

(b) 220 cubes

D5 (a) 1, 3, 6, 10, 15, 21

(b) The nth triangle number is $\frac{1}{2}n(n + 1)$ or $\frac{1}{2}n^2 + \frac{1}{2}n$. If you double each triangle number, you can arrange the cubes in a rectangle n by $(n + 1)$ so the formula is $\frac{1}{2}n(n + 1)$.

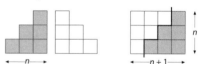

Alternatively, the sequence of first differences for the triangle numbers is 2, 3, 4, 5, ... and it is clear that this will continue. So the sequence is quadratic and analysis of the differences produces an nth term of $\frac{1}{2}n^2 + \frac{1}{2}n$.

(c) 5050

(d) 39

D6 (a) The number of matches in the nth pattern is $n(n + 1)$ or $n^2 + n$. We can argue from differences as the sequence of first differences is the linear sequence 4, 6, 8, ... or note that it's essentially the triangle numbers × 2 (two matches for each cube in D5).

(b) The number of matches in the nth pattern is $\frac{1}{2}n^2 + \frac{5}{2}n$ or $\frac{1}{2}n(n + 5)$. The sequence of matches that are added on is:

which gives a simple linear sequence with first differences of 1. So the second differences of the sequence are a constant 1 and hence the sequence is quadratic. The methods of section B give the nth term of $\frac{1}{2}n^2 + \frac{5}{2}n$.

D7 (a) Yes

(b) You can make 1, 2 and 4 regions with 1, 2 and 3 points respectively.

(c) 16

(d) The sequence of regions is 1, 2, 4, 8, 16, … Lee probably thinks that the number of regions will continue to double and so the maximum number of regions with 6 points will be $2 \times 16 = 32$. In fact a diagram with 6 points and 32 regions cannot be drawn: the maximum number of regions is 31.

(e) 57

Test yourself (p 83)

T1 $5n + 1$

T2 (a) $3, ^-3$ **(b)** 0 **(c)** $4n + 1$

T3 (a) Pattern 1 is a 1 by 3 rectangle. The sequence of patterns is obtained by adding 1 dot to each edge of the rectangle each time. So the width of pattern n is n dots and the height of pattern n is $n + 2$ dots. Hence the number of dots in the nth pattern is $n(n + 2)$ dots.

(b) $n(n + 3)$

T4 (a) $n^2 + 1$ **(b)** $4n^2$

T5 $n^2 + 2n - 1$

T6 $n^2 + 2n$

11 Enlargement, area and volume

A Enlargement and area (p 84)

A1 (a) $18\,cm^2$

(b)

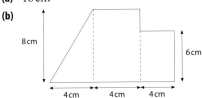

(c) $72\,cm^2$; the area has been multiplied by 4.

(d) $162\,cm^2$; the area has been multiplied by 9.

(e) $40.5\,cm^2$; the area has been multiplied by 2.25.

(f) Each area factor is the square of the scale factor.

A2 (a)

Original shape	Scaled shape	Scale factor	Original area	Scaled area	Area factor
P	Q	$\frac{2}{3}$	$18\,cm^2$	$8\,cm^2$	$\frac{4}{9}$
P	R	$\frac{1}{3}$	$18\,cm^2$	$2\,cm^2$	$\frac{1}{9}$
Q	R	$\frac{1}{2}$	$8\,cm^2$	$2\,cm^2$	$\frac{1}{4}$

(b) The area factor is the square of the scale factor.

A3 (a) 28 square units

(b)

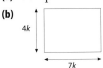

(c) $28k^2$ square units

(d) k^2

A4 (a) $3k$ **(b)** $\pi \times (3k)^2 = 9\pi k^2$ **(c)** k^2

A5 (a) 8.5 square units

(b)

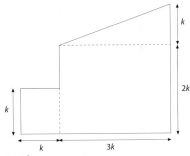

(c) $8.5k^2$ square units

(d) k^2

(e) k can be more than 1 or less than 1.

A6 (a)

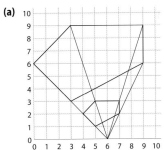

(b) 4 square units

(c) 36 square units

(d) The area factor is 9. As expected, this is the square of the scale factor.

A7 (a) 4.17 (to 2 d.p.) **(b)** 17.4 (to 1 d.p.)

A8 (a) 25 **(b)** 81 **(c)** 10 000

(d) 20.25 **(e)** 3

A9 $1100\,cm^2$

A10 $3500\,cm^2$

A11 (a) 2　　　　　　**(b)** $\sqrt{2}$, which is approximately 1.41

A12 (a) 4　　　　　　**(b)** 10　　　　**(c)** 6.5

　　　(d) 200　　　　**(e)** $\sqrt{5}$, which is approximately 2.24

A13 1:20 or $\frac{1}{20}$ (or an equivalent scale such as 1 cm
　　　represents 20 cm)

A14 (a) 5　　　　　　　　**(b)** $\frac{1}{5}$ or 0.2

A15 (a) $\frac{1}{16}$　**(b)** 0.36　**(c)** $\frac{9}{16}$　**(d)** 0.04　**(e)** 0.01

A16 (a) $9.2\,m^2$　　　　　**(b)** 0.75

A17 (a) $\frac{1}{5}$　　　　　　　**(b)** 0.32 (to 2 d.p.)

A18 (a) 3:2　　　　　　　**(b)** 2.5:1

A19 (a) Appropriate estimates

　　　(b) Shield A: scale factor ≈ 0.7; area factor ≈ 0.5
　　　　　Shield B: scale factor ≈ 0.65; area factor ≈ 0.42
　　　　　Shield C: scale factor ≈ 0.6; area factor ≈ 0.36
　　　　　Shield A has half its area shaded.

B Enlargement and volume (p 88)

B1 (a) $24\,cm^3$

　　　(b)

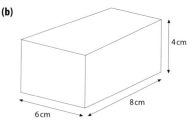

　　　(c) Volume = $192\,cm^3$, volume factor = 8
　　　(d) Volume = $648\,cm^3$, volume factor = 27
　　　(e) Volume = $81\,cm^3$, volume factor = 3.375
　　　(f) Volume = $3\,cm^3$, volume factor = 0.125
　　　(g) Volume = $24k^3\,cm^3$, volume factor = k^3

B2 (a) 2.5　　　　**(b)** 15.625　　**(c)** $3750\,cm^3$

B3 (a) 64　　　　　**(b)** 125　　　**(c)** 19683
　　　(d) 1000　　　**(e)** 125000

B4 $270\,cm^3$

B5 (a) 5.832　　　　　**(b)** $350\,cm^3$

B6 (a) 1.331　　　　　**(b)** 333 g (to the nearest g)

B7 (a) 75000 litres　　**(b)** $110\,m^2$

B8 6

B9 (a) 10　**(b)** 7　**(c)** 20　**(d)** 100　**(e)** 50

B10 1.260 (to 3 d.p.)

B11 (a) 1.2　　　　　　**(b)** 1.063 (to 3 d.p.)

B12 (a) $\frac{1}{8}$　**(b)** $\frac{1}{27}$　**(c)** $\frac{27}{64}$　**(d)** 0.512　**(e)** 0.001

B13 (a) 0.064
　　　(b) About 50 g (calculated as 51.2 g)

B14 $96\,cm^3$

B15 The volume factors are A 0.50, B 0.28, C 0.15.
　　　So, surprisingly, A shows the glass half full.

B16 (a) Golden plover $21.5\,cm^3$, Yellow wagtail $1.05\,cm^3$,
　　　　Canada goose $97.1\,cm^3$
　　　(b) Golden plover $50.1\,cm^2$, Yellow wagtail $6.7\,cm^2$,
　　　　Canada goose $136.9\,cm^2$

B17

	Dolls' house	Real house
Height of front door	6 cm	3 m
Number of windows	4	**4**
Total area of windows	$96\,cm^2$	**$24\,m^2$**
Height of chimney	**2 cm**	1 m
Capacity of water tank	12 ml	**1500 litres**
Number of roof tiles	**1600**	1600
Area of one roof tile	$0.45\,cm^2$	**$1125\,cm^2$**
Volume of roof space	$3024\,cm^3$	**$378\,m^3$**
Percentage of floor carpeted	**80%**	80%
Total area of carpet	**$740\,cm^2$**	$185\,m^2$

B18 3:7

B19 (a) 125:27　　　　**(b)** $108\,cm^3$

B20 Various criticisms can be made. For example the barrel
　　　on the far right is about 6.4 times the height of the
　　　barrel on the far left. If these were similar-shaped
　　　barrels the volume factor would be about 260. But the
　　　far right price is about 5.53 times the far left price,
　　　so the impression given by the volumes is a gross
　　　exaggeration.

C Mixed units (p 93)

C1 (a) $1.5\,m^2$　　　　**(b)** $272\,cm^2$

C2 (a) $600\,000\,m^2$　　**(b)** $0.6\,km^2$

C3 (a) $36\,cm^2$　　　　**(b)** $144\,cm^2$

C4 $10\,200\,m^2$

C5 $781.25\,cm^3$

C6 $9.3\,m^3$

C7 $610\,cm^3$ or 0.61 litres or $0.000\,61\,m^3$

C8 1:10 000 000 (or $\frac{1}{10\,000\,000}$ or an equivalent scale such
　　　as 1 cm represents 100 km)

Test yourself (p 94)

T1 (a) 44%　　　　　**(b)** 72.8%

T2 $1600\,cm^3$

T3 6.25

T4 7.5 cm

12 Algebraic fractions and equations 1

A Simplifying by cancelling (p 95)

A1 (a) $5x^4$ (b) $\dfrac{b}{2}$ (c) $\dfrac{3n}{2}$ (d) $\dfrac{x}{y^3}$ (e) $\dfrac{2b^4}{5a^3}$

A2 (a) 6 (b) $x + 5$ (c) $5(x - 7)$ (d) $\frac{1}{4}$

     (e) $(a + b)^2$ (f) $\dfrac{1}{a - b}$ (g) $\dfrac{x - 1}{2}$ (h) $\dfrac{2}{3(x + 7)}$

A3 (a) $x + 1$ (b) $5(x + 5)$ (c) $\dfrac{x + 1}{x + 8}$

     (d) $\dfrac{x}{x - 1}$ (e) $\dfrac{2x + 1}{x}$ (f) $3x - 1$

B Factorising then simplifying (p 96)

B1 (a) $\frac{2}{3}$ (b) $\frac{1}{2}$ (c) 7

B2 (a) (i) A:5, B:5, C:5, D:5

     (ii) A:7, B:$7\frac{1}{2}$, C:5, D:13

     (iii) A:2, B:$1\frac{1}{4}$, C:5, D:$-\frac{1}{3}$

     (b) $\dfrac{5x + 10}{x + 2} = \dfrac{5(x + 2)}{x + 2} = 5$ so the value of $\dfrac{5x + 10}{x + 2}$ is 5 for all values of x (except for $x = {}^-2$).

B3 $2x + 1 \neq 2 \times (x + 1)$ so $x + 1$ cannot be 'cancelled'.

B4 (a) $\dfrac{5(x + 2)}{(x + 1)(x + 2)} = \dfrac{5}{x + 1}$ (b) $\dfrac{x + 3}{(x + 3)(x + 5)} = \dfrac{1}{x + 5}$

     (c) $\dfrac{(x + 1)(2x + 5)}{4(x + 1)} = \dfrac{2x + 5}{4}$ (d) $\dfrac{x(x + 5)}{(x + 2)(x + 5)} = \dfrac{x}{x + 2}$

     (e) $\dfrac{x(x + 3)}{(x + 3)(x + 3)} = \dfrac{x}{x + 3}$ (f) $\dfrac{(x + 5)(3x + 4)}{2x(x + 5)} = \dfrac{3x + 4}{2x}$

B5 (a) $\frac{1}{4}$

     (b) $\dfrac{x + 4}{x^2 + 6x + 8} = \dfrac{x + 4}{(x + 4)(x + 2)} = \dfrac{1}{x + 2}$

     which is a unit fraction when x is an integer.

B6 (a) $\dfrac{(x + 1)(x + 2)}{(x + 1)(x + 3)} = \dfrac{x + 2}{x + 3}$ (b) $\dfrac{(x + 3)(x + 2)}{(x + 3)(x + 4)} = \dfrac{x + 2}{x + 4}$

     (c) $\dfrac{(x + 1)(2x + 9)}{(x + 1)(x + 1)} = \dfrac{2x + 9}{x + 1}$

B7 (a) $\dfrac{x(x - 2)}{(x + 7)(x - 2)} = \dfrac{x}{x + 7}$ (b) $\dfrac{(x + 6)(x - 5)}{x(x + 6)} = \dfrac{x - 5}{x}$

     (c) $\dfrac{x(x - 5)}{(x - 2)(x - 5)} = \dfrac{x}{x - 2}$ (d) $\dfrac{(x - 2)(x + 1)}{(x + 1)(x + 5)} = \dfrac{x - 2}{x + 5}$

     (e) $\dfrac{(x + 4)(x - 3)}{(x + 2)(x - 3)} = \dfrac{x + 4}{x + 2}$ (f) $\dfrac{(x - 5)(x - 1)}{(x - 5)(x - 3)} = \dfrac{x - 1}{x - 3}$

     (g) $\dfrac{(2x + 1)(x + 3)}{(x - 1)(x + 3)} = \dfrac{2x + 1}{x - 1}$ (h) $\dfrac{(x - 5)(x + 3)}{(2x - 1)(x - 5)} = \dfrac{x + 3}{2x - 1}$

     (i) $\dfrac{(3x + 1)(x - 1)}{(3x + 1)(x - 6)} = \dfrac{x - 1}{x - 6}$

B8 (a) $(x + 2)(x - 2)$

     (b) $\dfrac{x(x + 2)}{(x + 2)(x - 2)} = \dfrac{x}{x - 2}$

B9 (a) $\dfrac{(x + 5)(x - 5)}{x(x - 5)} = \dfrac{x + 5}{x}$

     (b) $\dfrac{(x + 3)(x - 3)}{(x + 5)(x - 3)} = \dfrac{x + 3}{x + 5}$

     (c) $\dfrac{(x - 7)(x + 1)}{(x - 1)(x + 1)} = \dfrac{x - 7}{x - 1}$

     (d) $\dfrac{(2x + 3)(2x - 3)}{(2x + 3)(2x + 1)} = \dfrac{2x - 3}{2x + 1}$

     (e) $\dfrac{3x(2x - 5)}{(2x + 5)(2x - 5)} = \dfrac{3x}{2x + 5}$

     (f) $\dfrac{(3x + 2)(3x - 2)}{5(3x + 2)} = \dfrac{3x - 2}{5}$

B10 (a) $\dfrac{(2x - 1)(x + 4)}{(x - 2)(x + 4)} = \dfrac{2x - 1}{x - 2}$

     (b) $\dfrac{(x + 5)(x - 5)}{(3x - 1)(x + 5)} = \dfrac{x - 5}{3x - 1}$

     (c) $\dfrac{x(x + 1)}{7(x + 1)(x - 1)} = \dfrac{x}{7(x - 1)}$

     (d) $\dfrac{x(x - 7)}{(x - 7)(x + 5)} = \dfrac{x}{x + 5}$

     (e) $\dfrac{(2x + 1)(x - 1)}{(x + 10)(x - 1)} = \dfrac{2x + 1}{x + 10}$

     (f) $\dfrac{x(5 - x)}{2(5 + x)(5 - x)} = \dfrac{x}{2(5 + x)}$

B11 (a) $(2a + b)(2a - b)$

     (b) $\dfrac{(2a + b)(2a - b)}{5(2a - b)} = \dfrac{2a + b}{5}$

B12 (a) $\dfrac{(x + y)(x - y)}{2(x + y)} = \dfrac{x - y}{2}$

     (b) $\dfrac{(3p + q)(3p - q)}{2p(3p - q)} = \dfrac{3p + q}{2p}$

     (c) $\dfrac{(5a + 2b)(5a - 2b)}{3(5a + 2b)} = \dfrac{5a - 2b}{3}$

C Multiplying and dividing (p 98)

C1 (a) 2 (b) $\dfrac{a^2}{2}$ (c) $\dfrac{5a^2}{8}$ (d) $\dfrac{3ab}{4}$

     (e) $\frac{3}{2}$ (f) $\dfrac{a^2}{2}$ (g) $\dfrac{5b}{8}$ (h) $\dfrac{5b}{8}$

C2 (a) b (b) $\dfrac{1}{b}$ (c) $\dfrac{x}{2\pi z}$

     (d) $7c$ (e) 3 (f) $2y$

C3 $\dfrac{3a}{10} \div \dfrac{6a^2}{5} = \dfrac{3a}{10} \times \dfrac{5}{6a^2} = \dfrac{1}{4a}$

C4 (a) $\dfrac{a^2}{8}$ (b) $\dfrac{3}{2}$ (c) $\dfrac{3a^3}{50}$ (d) $\dfrac{4a^2}{15}$

(e) $\dfrac{a^3}{2}$ (f) $\dfrac{1}{2b}$ (g) $\dfrac{2b}{a}$ (h) $\dfrac{4}{a^2}$

C5 (a) $\dfrac{1}{y}$ (b) $\dfrac{y}{x^3}$ (c) $\dfrac{a}{3b}$ (d) $\dfrac{1}{ab}$

C6 (a) $(x+4)(x-4)$

(b) (i) $\dfrac{x}{x-4}$ (ii) 2

D Solving equations that contain fractions (p 99)

D1 (a) $x=\frac{1}{2}$ (b) $x=^-8$ (c) $x=1$

(d) $x=3$ (e) $x=5$ (f) $x=7$

(g) $x=7$ (h) $x=\frac{1}{3}$ (i) $x=0$

D2 (a) $x=6$ (b) $x=^-2$ (c) $x=^-3$

D3 (a) $x=^-4,3$ (b) $x=^-2,4$ (c) $x=^-\frac{3}{2},2$

(d) $x=^-5,2$ (e) $x=1,9$ (f) $x=^-4,^-3$

(g) $x=0,11$ (h) $x=^-5,5$ (i) $x=^-\frac{4}{3},0$

Test yourself (p 100)

T1 $\dfrac{2x-1}{x-1}$

T2 (a) $\dfrac{x-4}{x}$ (b) $\dfrac{5x}{x+4}$

T3 $\dfrac{5x-1}{x-3}$

T4 (a) $(3x-1)^2$ (b) $\dfrac{2x+3}{3x-1}$

T5 (a) $(x+2y)(x-2y)$ (b) $\dfrac{x-2y}{5}$

T6 (a) $\dfrac{2ab}{3}$ (b) $\dfrac{3yz}{\pi}$ (c) $3p$ (d) $\dfrac{5}{b}$

(e) $\dfrac{2}{a-1}$ (f) $\dfrac{x^4}{5}$ (g) $\dfrac{x^2}{10}$ (h) $\dfrac{1}{a^2}$

T7 $\dfrac{x(x-2)}{2}$

T8 (a) $x=7$ (b) $\dfrac{2x}{2x+3}$

T9 (a) $x=\frac{1}{2}$ (b) $x=^-3$ (c) $x=^-1,\frac{5}{2}$ (d) $x=0,7$

13 Time series

A Trend and moving average (p 101)

A1 (a) The remaining values are 8, 8.5, 9.5, 10, 11, 11.5.

(b) The trend is upwards.

A2 (a)

Year	2005			2006				2007	
Quarter	2	3	4	1	2	3	4	1	2
Visitors (000)	16	23	10	7	15	21	11	3	1
Moving average (000)		14	13.75	13.25	13.5	12.5	12		

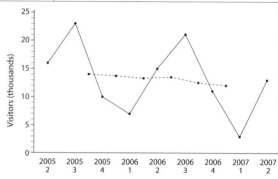

(b) The trend is downwards.

A3 (a)

Year	2005			2006				2007	
Quarter	2	3	4	1	2	3	4	1	2
Visitors (000)	7	9	14	22	10	10	17	25	1
Moving average (000)		13	13.75	14	14.75	15.5	15.75		

Data and moving average shown on a graph

(b) The trend is upwards.

A4 (a) 12-point moving average:
17, 17.17, 17.42, 17.08, 16.67, 16.33, 16.08, 16.25, 16.33

(b) The trend increased, then fell and fluctuated around 16.2.

Test yourself (p 104)

T1 28, 25.6, 26.6

T2 (a),(b) Here are the values of the moving average. The first is plotted between 2005 2nd quarter and 3rd quarter.
51.5, 51, 52.25, 52.75, 52.5, 54, 54.5

(c) There is an upward trend.

Review 2 (p 105)

1 $C = 3(n + 2)$ or $C = 3n + 6$

2 28

3 The data collected in question 1 is very likely to be grouped into intervals such as '$0 < a \leq 15$' and '$15 < a \leq 30$' so it would be more useful to collect the information in that form.
In the same way, the data collected in question 2 is very likely to be grouped into intervals such as '$0 < n \leq 5$' and '$5 < n \leq 10$' so it would be more useful to collect the information in that form. Also, it might be difficult for some people to decide what their 'average' meat consumption is. It might be better to ask people to estimate how many times they ate meat in the previous week.

4 (a) $6x^2 + x - 2$ (b) $4x^2 + 20x + 25$ (c) $9x^2 - 1$

5 076°

6 (a) $7n - 2$
(b) $7n - 2 = 60$ does not have a positive integer solution so 60 is not a term in the sequence.

7 (a) 18.25, 18.5, 19.5, 19.5, 20.5
(b) Increasing

8 (a) The line through A and B has the equation $y = -\frac{1}{2}x + 4$ or $2y + x = 8$.
The line through C and D has the equation $y = \frac{1}{3}x - 1$ or $3y = x - 3$.
(b) $(6, 1)$

9 $V = 3\sqrt{U}$

10 (a) 36°
(b) 7.3 cm (to the nearest 0.1 cm)
(c) 36.3 cm (to the nearest 0.1 cm)

11 (a) $\frac{b}{2}$ (b) $\frac{b}{12}$ (c) $\frac{a^2 b}{2}$ (d) $\frac{3}{a}$ (e) $\frac{2}{b}$

12 (a) 1.26
(b) Height: 2.5 cm, length: 5.0 cm, width: 3.8 cm (all to the nearest 0.1 cm)

13 (a) $(3x + 2)(x + 5)$ (b) $(3y - 4)(2y + 3)$
(c) $(3m + n)(3m - n)$

14 $2bh$, $3b^2$, $h\sqrt{a^2 + b^2}$, $h(a + b)$

15 $x = \frac{3}{2}, -6$

16 15.625

17 (a) $2[x(x - 2) + 2(x - 2) + 2x]$ which simplifies to $2x^2 + 4x - 8$
(b) $2x^2 + 4x - 8 = 62$ is equivalent to $x^2 + 2x - 35 = 0$ which has solutions $x = 5$ and $x = -7$. Since length is positive the value of x is 5.
(c) 30 cm³

18 $y = -\frac{1}{2}x$ or $2y + x = 0$

19 (a) $[(22.5 \times 5) + (27.5 \times 9) + (32.5 \times 17) + (37.5 \times 7) + (42.5 \times 2)] \div (5 + 9 + 17 + 7 + 2) = 1260 \div 40 = 31.5$ so an estimate of the mean weight is 31.5 kg.
(b) $30 < w \leq 35$
(c)

Weight, w kg	Cumulative frequency
$20 < w \leq 25$	5
$20 < w \leq 30$	14
$20 < w \leq 35$	31
$20 < w \leq 40$	38
$20 < w \leq 45$	40

(d)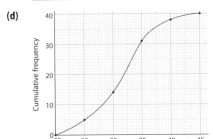

(e) About 16 boys

20 14.4

21 (a) 3 (b) $\frac{1}{c + 2}$ (c) $\frac{5x - 3}{x - 1}$ (d) $\frac{3x - 4}{2x + 1}$

22 500 000 m² or 0.5 km²
(or 5 000 000 000 cm² which would be very unusual units for the area of a reservoir)

23 (a) 110
(b) $n(n + 1)$ or $n^2 + n$
(c) $n^2 + n = 100$ is equivalent to $n^2 + n - 100 = 0$. The expression $n^2 + n - 100$ does not factorise so the equation has no integer solutions. So a step pattern cannot be made with 100 tiles. An alternative approach is to note that pattern 9 uses 90 tiles and pattern 10 uses 110 tiles so a pattern with 100 tiles is not possible.

24 $r(s + 2t)$: area, $\pi(r + s)$: length, $r^2 + s^2$: area, $\pi s(s + t)$: area, $\pi s^2 t$: volume

25 (a) $x = \frac{9}{5}$ or 1.8 (b) $x = -1, \frac{5}{3}$ (c) $x = -1$

14 Trigonometric graphs

A The sine graph (p 108)

A1 Values close to the following from the sine graph on sheet H2–2

   (a) 0.91 **(b)** 0.97 **(c)** 0.45 **(d)** ⁻0.53 **(e)** ⁻0.97

A2 Calculator checks

A3 **(a)** There are two angles, approximately 53° and 127°.

   (b) The calculator only gives the answer 53.13…°. The graph is needed to get the second value.

A4 **(a)** 124° **(b)** 68° **(c)** 241° **(d)** 341° **(e)** 169°

   (f) 289° **(g)** 254° **(h)** 98° **(i)** 79° **(j)** 219°

A5 **(a)** 44.4°, 135.6°   **(b)** 11.5°, 168.5°

   (c) 0.0°, 180.0°, 360.0°   **(d)** 90.0°

   (e) 36.9°, 143.1°

A6 252°, 288°

A7 43°, 137°

A8 Values close to the following

   (a) 0.87 **(b)** ⁻0.94 **(c)** ⁻0.26 **(d)** 0.50 **(e)** ⁻0.26

   (f) ⁻0.94 **(g)** 0.34 **(h)** ⁻0.34 **(i)** 0.87 **(j)** 0.98

A9 Calculator checks

A10 The completed graph

A11 **(a)** 200°, 340°   **(b)** 50°, 130°   **(c)** 70°, 110°

   (d) 265°, 275°   **(e)** 208°, 332°

A12 **(a)** ⁻323.1°, ⁻216.9°   **(b)** ⁻156.4°, ⁻23.6°

   (c) ⁻354.3°, ⁻185.7°   **(d)** ⁻14.5°, ⁻165.5°

   (e) ⁻270°   **(f)** ⁻150°, ⁻30°

   (g) ⁻159.5°, ⁻20.5   **(h)** ⁻288.2°, ⁻251.8°

   (i) ⁻174.3°, ⁻5.7   **(j)** ⁻90°

A13

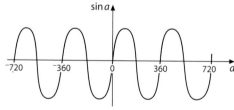

   (a) ⁻720°, ⁻540°, ⁻360°, ⁻180°, 0°, 180°, 360°, 540°, 720°

   (b) ⁻630°, ⁻270°, 90°, 450°

   (c) ⁻450°, ⁻90°, 270°, 630°

A14 17.5°, 162.5°, 377.5°, 522.5°, ⁻197.5°, ⁻342.5°, ⁻557.5°, ⁻702.5°

A15 You get an error message. A sine cannot be greater than 1 (or less than ⁻1) because it is defined by the *y*-coordinates of points on a circle with radius 1.

A16 **(a)** 44.4°, 135.6°   **(b)** 30.0°, 150.0°

   (c) 197.5°, 342.5°   **(d)** 194.5°, 345.5°

   (e) 48.6°, 131.4°   **(f)** 203.6°, 336.4°

A17 It could be between 36.9° and 143.1° or between 396.9 and 503.1°.

B The cosine graph (p 111)

B1 Values close to the following from the cosine graph on sheet H2–2

   (a) 0.57 **(b)** ⁻0.09 **(c)** ⁻0.84 **(d)** ⁻0.88 **(e)** 0.57

B2 Calculator checks

B3 **(a)** There are two angles, approximately 46° and 314°.

   (b) The calculator only gives the answer 45.57…°. The graph is needed to get the second value.

B4 **(a)** 298° **(b)** 252° **(c)** 59° **(d)** 165° **(e)** 358°

B5 **(a)** ⁻272°, ⁻88°, 88°   **(b)** ⁻355°, ⁻5°, 5

   (c) ⁻289°, ⁻71°, 289°   **(d)** ⁻261°, ⁻99°, 261°

   (e) ⁻317°, ⁻43°, 43°   **(f)** ⁻350°, 10°, 350°

   (g) ⁻110°, 110°, 250°   **(h)** ⁻50°, 50°, 310°

   (i) ⁻275°, 85°, 275°   **(j)** ⁻328°, 32°, 328°

B6 **(a)** ⁻306.9°, ⁻53.1°, 53.1°, 306.9°

   (b) ⁻240°, ⁻120°, 120°, 240°

   (c) ⁻275.7°, ⁻84.3°, 84.3°, 275.7°

   (d) ⁻243.3°, ⁻116.7°, 116.7°, 243.3°

   (e) ⁻360°, 0°, 360°

   (f) ⁻318.6°, ⁻41.4°, 41.4°, 318.6°

   (g) ⁻258.5°, ⁻101.5°, 101.5°, 258.5°

   (h) ⁻180°, 180°

   (i) ⁻287.5°, ⁻72.5°, 72.5°, 287.5°

   (j) ⁻270°, ⁻90°, 90°, 270°

B7 ⁻256°, ⁻104°, 104°, 256°

B8 ⁻280°, ⁻80°, 80°, 280°

B9

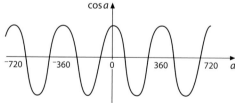

   (a) ⁻630°, ⁻450°, ⁻270°, ⁻90°, 90°, 270°, 450°, 630°

   (b) ⁻720°, ⁻360°, 0, 360°, 720°

   (c) ⁻540°, ⁻180°, 180°, 540°

B10 ⁻653.6°, ⁻426.4°, ⁻293.6°, ⁻66.4°, 66.4°, 293.6°, 426.4°, 653.6°

B11 (a) 84.3°, 275.7° **(b)** 81.8°, 278.2°
(c) 104.5°, 255.5° **(d)** 101.5°, 258.5°
(e) 48.2°, 311.8° **(f)** 143.1°, 216.9°

B12 It could be between 126.9° and 233.1° or between 486.9° and 593.1°.

B13 a and b differ by 180° (or, more generally, differ by $(360n + 180)°$).

B14 $q = {}^-p$ (or, more generally, $q = 360n° - p$ where n is an integer)

C The tangent graph (p 113)

C1 (a) 3.73 **(b)** 255°, 435°

C2 (a) 210°, 390° **(b)** 80°, 260° **(c)** 20°, 380°
(d) 100°, 280° **(e)** ⁻30°, 330° **(f)** ⁻60°, 120°
(g) 228°, 408° **(h)** 39°, 219° **(i)** ⁻37°, 323°
(j) 153°, 333°

C3 (a) 42.0° (to 1 d.p.) **(b)** 222.0°, 402.0°

C4 (a) 31.0°, 211.0°, 391.0° **(b)** 59.5°, 239.5°, 419.5°
(c) 88.7°, 268.7°, 448.7° **(d)** 0.6°, 180.6°, 360.6°
(e) ⁻21.8°, 158.2°, 338.2° **(f)** ⁻68.2°, 111.8°, 291.8°
(g) ⁻78.7°, 101.3°, 281.3° **(h)** ⁻5.7°, 174.3°, 354.3°
(i) ⁻2.9°, 177.1°, 357.1° **(j)** ⁻75.2°, 104.8°, 284.8°

C5 117°, 297°

C6 66°, 246°

C7 (a) 89.4°, 269.4° **(b)** 153.4°, 333.4°
(c) 58.0°, 238.0° **(d)** 104.0°, 284.0°
(e) 168.7°, 348.7° **(f)** 146.3°, 326.3°

C8 180°

D Graphs based on trigonometric functions (p 116)

D1 (a)

x	0°	45°	90°	135°	180°	225°
$\sin x$	0	0.71	1	0.71	0	⁻0.71
$3 \sin x$	0	2.13	3	2.13	0	⁻2.13

	270°	315°	360°
	⁻1	⁻0.71	0
	⁻3	⁻2.13	0

(b)

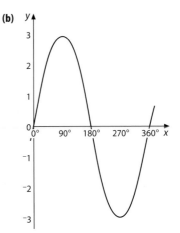

(c) It is stretched vertically by a factor of 3.

D2 (a)

x	0°	90°	180°	270°	360°
$\cos x$	1	0	⁻1	0	1
$\cos x + 1$	2	1	0	1	2

(b)

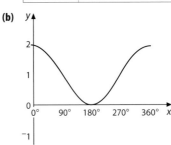

(c) It is lifted up by one unit.

D3 (a)

x	0°	90°	180°	270°	360°
$\sin x$	0	1	0	⁻1	0
$^-\sin x$	0	−1	0	1	0

(b)

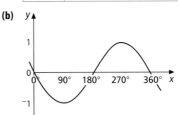

(c) It consists of the graph of $y = \sin x$ reflected in the x-axis.

D4 (a)

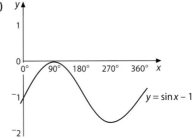

$y = \sin x - 1$

(b)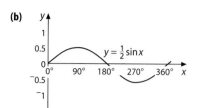

$y = \frac{1}{2}\sin x$

(c)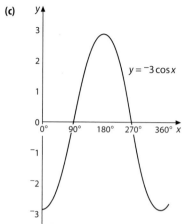

$y = ^-3\cos x$

(d)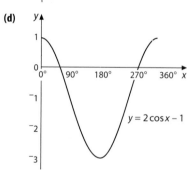

$y = 2\cos x - 1$

D5 P: $y = 2\sin x + 1$ Q: $y = ^-2\cos x$
    R: $y = ^-\sin x - 1$ S: $y = \cos x - 2$
    T: $y = ^-\cos x + 1$ U: $y = 2\sin x + 2$

D6 **(a)** $h = ^-63\cos x + 71$ (or $h = 71 - 63\cos x$)
    (b) **(i)** $81.9\,\text{m}$ **(ii)** $102.5\,\text{m}$

D7 **(a)** $p = 3,\ q = 2$ **(b)** $120°,\ 240°$

D8 **(a)**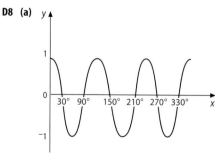

(b)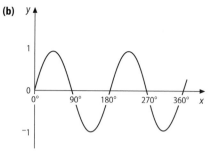

(c)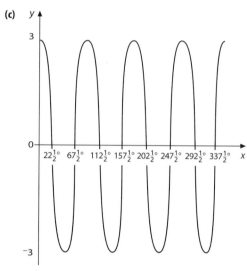

(d)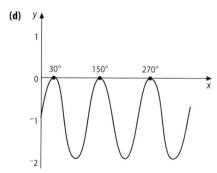

D9 P: $y = 2\sin(2x)$ Q: $y = \cos(2x)$
    R: $y = \sin(2x) - 1$ S: $y = ^-2\cos(2x)$

D10 **(a)**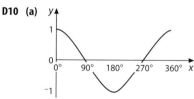

(b)

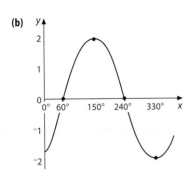

D11 $a = 3, b = 30°$

Test yourself (p 120)

T1 (a)

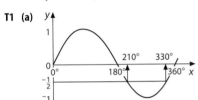

(b) 36.9°, 143.1° (to 1 d.p.)

T2 $^-\tan 145° = \tan 35° = \tan 215°$
$^-\tan 35° = \tan 145° = \tan 325°$

T3 (a) $y = 2\cos x$ **(b)** $y = \cos(2x)$ **(c)** $y = \cos x + 1$

15 Pyramid, cone and sphere

A Pyramid and cone (p 121)

A1 (a) $\frac{1}{6}a^3$ **(b)** a^2 **(c)** $\frac{1}{2}a$

A2 (a) $700\,\text{cm}^3$ **(b)** $78\,\text{cm}^3$
 (c) $118\,\text{cm}^3$ (to the nearest cm^3)

A3 $25\,\text{m}^2$

A4 5.6 million tonnes (to the nearest 0.1 million tonnes)

A5 (a) $45\,\text{m}^3$ **(b)** $90\,\text{m}^3$

A6 (a) $8.24\,\text{cm}$ **(b)** $223\,\text{cm}^2$
 (c) $818\,\text{cm}^3$

A7 (a) $50.27\,\text{cm}^2$ **(b)** $168\,\text{cm}^3$

A8 $128\,\text{cm}^3$

A9 (a) πr^2 **(b)** $\frac{1}{3}\pi r^2 h$

A10 $60\,\text{cm}^2$

A11 (a) $8\,\text{cm}^2$ **(b)** $80\,\text{cm}^2$

A12 (a) $\frac{1}{2}bl$ **(b)** $\frac{1}{2}nbl$

A13 (a) $70\,\text{cm}^2$ **(b)** $210\,\text{cm}^2$
 (c) $79\,\text{cm}^2$

A14 $80\,\text{cm}$

A15 (a) $157.1\,\text{cm}$ **(b)** $3142\,\text{cm}^2$

A16 (a) $2\pi r$ **(b)** πrl

A17 (a) $110\,\text{cm}^2$ **(b)** $238\,\text{cm}^2$
 (c) $989\,\text{cm}^2$

A18 $7.0\,\text{cm}$

A19 $7.9\,\text{cm}$

A20 (a) $13\,\text{cm}$ **(b)** $204\,\text{cm}^2$

A21 (a) $\pi rl + \pi r^2$ **(b)** $\pi r(l + r)$

A22 (a) $188\,\text{cm}^2$ **(b)** $243\,\text{cm}^2$
 (c) $118\,\text{m}^2$

A23 $16.4\,\text{m}^3$

A24 (a) $190\,\text{cm}^3$ **(b)** $198\,\text{cm}^2$

B Sphere (p 126)

B1 (a) $1257\,\text{cm}^2$ **(b)** $765\,\text{cm}^2$
 (c) $3058\,\text{cm}^2$

B2 (a) 499 million km^2 **(b)** 349 million km^2

B3 $5.7\,\text{cm}$

B4 (a) $524\,\text{cm}^3$ **(b)** $2855\,\text{cm}^3$
 (c) $13\,306\,\text{cm}^3$

B5 2145 litres

B6 48%

B7 33%

B8 $620\,\text{cm}$ or $6.20\,\text{m}$

B9 (a) $6.9\,\text{cm}^3$ **(b)** $39\,\text{cm}^2$

Test yourself (p 128)

T1 $8.9\,\text{cm}$

T2 (a) $288\pi\,\text{cm}^3$ **(b)** $2.88\,\text{cm}$

T3 $640\,\text{cm}^2$

16 Rearranging a formula

A Review: rearranging a simple formula (p 129)

A1 (a) $b = \dfrac{a+3}{6}$ (b) $d = \dfrac{w-10}{5}$

(c) $j = \dfrac{2h+3}{5}$ (d) $f = \dfrac{3e-21}{4}$

A2 (a) $x = 5 - y$ (b) $x = 3 - 2y$

(c) $x = \dfrac{12-3y}{2}$ (d) $x = \dfrac{1-6y}{5}$

A3 $n = \dfrac{5-d}{3}$

A4 (a) $p = 8 - q$ (b) $p = \dfrac{10-q}{2}$

(c) $p = \dfrac{4q-24}{3}$ (d) $p = \dfrac{8-3q}{7}$

A5 (a) (i) $x = \dfrac{y-5}{2}$ (ii) $\left(\dfrac{-5}{2}, 0\right)$

(b) (i) $x = 10 - y$ (ii) $(10, 0)$

(c) (i) $x = \dfrac{11-3y}{5}$ (ii) $\left(\dfrac{11}{5}, 0\right)$

(d) (i) $x = \dfrac{10-5y}{4}$ (ii) $\left(\dfrac{5}{2}, 0\right)$

A6 (a) $s = 3(t - 12)$ (b) $j = 5h + 2$

(c) $y = \dfrac{2(x+1)}{3}$ (d) $b = \dfrac{3(a+5)}{2}$

A7 (a) $z = \dfrac{y-2x}{5}$ (b) $\dfrac{8}{5}$

A8 (a) $q = p + r$ (b) $r = q - p$ (c) $p = m - 2n$

(d) $n = \dfrac{m-p}{2}$ (e) $v = 2u - w$ (f) $v = w(u + 3)$

(g) $v = \dfrac{u-x}{w}$ (h) $w = \dfrac{10-u}{v}$

B Choosing the first step in a rearrangement (p 130)

B1 (a) $x = \dfrac{y+10}{5}$ or $x = \dfrac{y}{5} + 2$

(b) $x = \dfrac{p+6r}{6}$ or $x = \dfrac{p}{6} + r$

(c) $x = \dfrac{4z-y}{4}$ or $x = z - \dfrac{y}{4}$

(d) $x = \dfrac{A+5}{10}$ or $x = \dfrac{A}{10} + \dfrac{1}{2}$ $\left(\text{or } x = \dfrac{\frac{A}{5}+1}{2}\right)$

B2 (a) (i) $x = 4(y + 3)$ (ii) $x = 4y + 12$

(b) $4(y + 3) = 4 \times y + 4 \times 3$
$= 4y + 12$

B3 (a) $q = \dfrac{p}{r-2}$ (b) $r = \dfrac{p}{q} + 2$

(c) $x = \dfrac{2y}{1-z}$ (d) $z = 1 - \dfrac{2y}{x}$

B4 $c = \dfrac{3a}{b} - 5$

B5 (a) $h = \dfrac{V}{lw}$ (b) $w = \dfrac{V}{lh}$ (c) $a = \dfrac{P+3}{2b}$

(d) $q = \dfrac{V}{\pi^2 p}$ (e) $y = \dfrac{3P}{\pi x}$ (f) $x = \dfrac{6V}{\pi y}$

(g) $b = \dfrac{2R-y}{\pi c^2}$ (h) $y = \dfrac{3(R+x^2)}{r^2}$

B6 C: $k = \dfrac{a}{h-j}$

B7 (a) $b = \dfrac{2a}{l}$ (b) $c = \dfrac{ab}{3m}$

(c) $y = \dfrac{\pi}{rxz}$ (d) $e = \dfrac{d^2}{h-1}$

B8 D: $r = \dfrac{g}{w-s}$

B9 (a) $t = \dfrac{l}{1-s}$ (b) $c = \dfrac{d}{2b-a}$

(c) $h = \dfrac{f}{e-\frac{1}{4}d}$ or $h = \dfrac{4f}{4e-d}$ (d) $r = \dfrac{2\pi}{\theta(ab-z)}$

B10 $y = \dfrac{a}{x-c}$

$y(x - c) = a$

$x - c = \dfrac{a}{y}$

$x = \dfrac{a}{y} + c$

B11 (a) $d = \dfrac{b}{a} - c$ (b) $y = 6 - \dfrac{2z}{5x}$

(c) $y = \dfrac{2z}{x+3} - 5$ (d) $u = \dfrac{t+2}{w} + 3$

C Simplifying squares and square roots (p 132)

C1 (a) $25a^2$ (b) $4a^6b^2$ (c) $\frac{1}{4}a^2b^2$

(d) $\dfrac{9a^2}{b^2}$ (e) $\dfrac{4a^2}{25b^2}$

C2 (a) $9p$ (b) $3p$ (c) $\frac{1}{4}ab$ (d) $\dfrac{2}{a^2}$ (e) $\dfrac{z}{3}$

C3 (a) $4x$ (b) $5p^2$ (c) ab^2 (d) $\dfrac{a}{2}$ (e) $\dfrac{\sqrt{p}}{10}$

D Formulas involving squares and square roots (p 133)

D1 9.77 cm

D2 (a) $r = \sqrt{\dfrac{A}{4\pi}}$ (b) 28 cm

D3 (a) $h = \sqrt{4(S-3)}$ or $2\sqrt{S-3}$ (b) $h = \sqrt{\dfrac{xr}{9}}$ or $h = \dfrac{\sqrt{xr}}{3}$

(c) $h = \sqrt{\dfrac{V+10}{7\pi x}}$ (d) $h = \sqrt{l^2 - 2rx}$

D4 (a) $x = y^2 - 1$ (b) $x = (y-1)^2$

(c) $x = \dfrac{y^2}{3}$ (d) $x = \left(\dfrac{y}{3}\right)^2$ or $x = \dfrac{y^2}{9}$

(e) $x = 2y^2$ (f) $x = (2y)^2$ or $x = 4y^2$

(g) $x = \left(\dfrac{y}{3\pi}\right)^2$ or $x = \dfrac{y^2}{9\pi^2}$ (h) $x = y^2 - 3\pi$

D5 (a) $p = q\left(\dfrac{T}{\pi}\right)^2$ or $p = \dfrac{qT^2}{\pi^2}$

(b) $c = \dfrac{b}{a^2}$

(c) $z = \dfrac{y^2 r}{2}$

(d) $r = \dfrac{2z}{y^2}$

(e) $m = \left(\dfrac{V}{3\pi}\right)^2$ or $m = \dfrac{V^2}{9\pi^2}$

(f) $g = \left(\dfrac{5hV}{\pi}\right)^2$ or $g = \dfrac{25h^2V^2}{\pi^2}$

(g) $x = \dfrac{z - y^2}{2}$

(h) $x = \left(\dfrac{S}{2\pi r}\right)^2 - y^2$

D6 (a) $x = \pm\sqrt{\dfrac{y+50}{2}}$ or $x = \pm\sqrt{\dfrac{y}{2}+25}$

(b) $(^-5, 0)$ and $(5, 0)$

D7 (a) $x = \pm\sqrt{9 - y^2}$

(b) $x = \pm\sqrt{3zy}$

(c) $x = \pm\sqrt{y - 5z}$

(d) $x = \pm\sqrt{\dfrac{1-9y^2}{4}}$ or $x = \dfrac{\pm\sqrt{1-9y^2}}{2}$

E Formulas where the new subject appears more than once (p 134)

E1 (a) $n = \dfrac{f}{3+d}$ (b) $n = \dfrac{3T}{\pi + k}$ (c) $n = \dfrac{s+6}{p-3}$

(d) $n = \dfrac{3e}{3-r}$ (e) $n = \dfrac{Ft}{v-u}$ (f) $n = \dfrac{a}{ap-2}$

(g) $n = \dfrac{m}{mk-1}$ (h) $n = \dfrac{S}{pk + \frac{1}{3}y^2}$ or $n = \dfrac{3S}{3pk + y^2}$

E2 $v = \dfrac{b-5}{3-a}$

E3 $y = \dfrac{b-d}{a-c}$

E4 (a) $x^2(3+y)$ (b) $x = \pm\sqrt{\dfrac{7z}{3+y}}$

E5 (a) $r = \dfrac{P-7}{3+a}$ (b) $r = \dfrac{H-ax}{1-k}$

(c) $r = \pm\sqrt{\dfrac{A+y^2}{x+\pi}}$

E6 (a) $f = \dfrac{2a}{3-a}$

(b) $f = \dfrac{3u + uq}{q-3}$ or $f = \dfrac{u(3+q)}{q-3}$

(c) $f = \dfrac{2-k}{1+2k}$

(d) $f = \dfrac{g+6}{2-g}$

E7 $y = \dfrac{10x - 3z}{3+x}$

E8 $r = \dfrac{7s + 12}{2s + 3}$

E9 (a) $k = \dfrac{s}{s-3}$

(b) $k = \dfrac{4}{t-1}$

(c) $k = \dfrac{P+3}{P+1}$

(d) $k = \dfrac{5y+4}{y-2}$

(e) $k = \dfrac{hn-g}{2-h}$ or $k = \dfrac{g-hn}{h-2}$

(f) $k = \dfrac{2n - Rn}{R+3}$ or $k = \dfrac{n(2-R)}{R+3}$

(g) $k = \dfrac{n(n-Y)}{mY-1}$ or $k = \dfrac{n(Y-n)}{1-Ym}$ or either of the unfactorised versions

(h) $k = \dfrac{abe}{ab - d}$

E10 (a) 0.94 or 0.9 (b) $q = \dfrac{8p}{pt - 8}$

E11 $z = \dfrac{Ry}{xy + R}$

E12 (a) $x = \pm\sqrt{\dfrac{y^2}{1-y^2}}$ or $x = \dfrac{y}{\pm\sqrt{1-y^2}}$

(b) $x = \dfrac{100S}{100 + rt}$

(c) $x = \pm\sqrt{\dfrac{k(t+1)}{t^2}}$ or $x = \dfrac{\pm\sqrt{k(t+1)}}{t}$

(d) $x = \pm\sqrt{\dfrac{n^2}{1+m^2}}$ or $x = \dfrac{n}{\pm\sqrt{1+m^2}}$

F Forming and manipulating formulas (p 136)

F1 **(a)** Area of the trapezium
= area of square + area of triangle
$= x^2 + \frac{1}{2}x^2$
$= \frac{3}{2}x^2$

(b) $x = \sqrt{\dfrac{2A}{3}}$

(c) $x = 3.65\,\text{cm}$ (to 2 d.p.)

F2 **(a)** Area of top is $2a \times b = 2ab$
Area of side is $2a \times a = 2a^2$
Area of front is $a \times b = ab$
So total surface area is
$2(2ab + 2a^2 + ab)$
$= 2(3ab + 2a^2)$
$= 6ab + 4a^2$ as required

(b) $b = \dfrac{A - 4a^2}{6a}$

(c) 4 cm by 7 cm by 2 cm

F3 **(a)** **(i)** The square has an edge length of $2r$ so the total length of the straight edge is $2r \times 3 = 6r$.
The length of the curved edge is $\dfrac{2\pi r}{2} = \pi r$.
So $P = \pi r + 6r$

(ii) $r = \dfrac{P}{\pi + 6}$

(iii) $r = 1.09\,\text{m}$ (to 2 d.p.)

(b) **(i)** $A = 4r^2 + \frac{1}{2}\pi r^2$ **(ii)** $r = \sqrt{\dfrac{2A}{8 + \pi}}$

F4 **(a)** $A = \frac{3}{4}\pi r^2$ **(b)** $r = \sqrt{\dfrac{4A}{3\pi}}$

F5 $V = \frac{4}{3}\pi x^3$
so $3V = 4\pi x^3$
so $\dfrac{3V}{4\pi} = x^3$
so $x = \sqrt[3]{\dfrac{3V}{4\pi}}$

F6 **(a)** $V = \pi r^3$ **(b)** $r = \sqrt[3]{\dfrac{V}{\pi}}$

F7 **(a)** $\pi r^2 h$
(b) $36\pi r^3$
(c) $\pi r^2 h = 36\pi r^3$
so $h = \dfrac{36\pi r^3}{\pi r^2}$
$= 36r$ as required

F8 $\frac{2}{3}x$

F9 The total surface area of the cylinder is
$\pi x^2 \times 2 + 2\pi x \times 8x$
$= 2\pi x^2 + 16\pi x^2$
$= 18\pi x^2$
The surface area of the sphere is $4\pi r^2$.
So $18\pi x^2 = 4\pi r^2$
So $x^2 = \dfrac{4\pi r^2}{18\pi}$
$= \frac{2}{9}r^2$
so $x = \sqrt{\frac{2}{9}r^2}$
$= \dfrac{\sqrt{2}}{3}r$ as required

Test yourself (p 138)

T1 $u = \dfrac{D - kt^2}{t}$ or $u = \dfrac{D}{t} - kt$

T2 $d = \dfrac{t - c^2}{2}$

T3 $L = G\left(\dfrac{T}{2\pi}\right)^2$ or $L = \dfrac{GT^2}{4\pi^2}$

T4 $a = \dfrac{7 - 12b}{2}$

T5 **(a)** $r = \sqrt{\dfrac{3V}{\pi h}}$ **(b)** $v = \dfrac{u}{uf - 1}$

T6 **(a)** 24.8   **(b)** $r = \dfrac{P - 2a}{\pi + 2}$

T7 **(a)** $c = \pm\sqrt{\dfrac{E}{m}}$

(b) $m = \dfrac{E}{gh + \frac{1}{2}v^2}$ or $m = \dfrac{2E}{2gh + v^2}$

T8 $r = \dfrac{\pi t + 3}{1 + 2\pi}$

T9 $x = \dfrac{3y + 4}{y - 3}$

T10 $a = \dfrac{n(n - P)}{P - 1}$ or $a = \dfrac{n(P - n)}{1 - P}$ or either of the unfactorised versions

T11 $t = \dfrac{1}{g - 3}$

T12 $h = 32x$

17 Sampling

B Random sampling (p 140)

There are no answers for B1–B6 as these are class activities.

B7 Jason could go through the registers for his year group numbering the students. He could generate random numbers until he has selected 50 students for the sample.

D Stratified sampling (p 143)

D1 23 males and 27 females

D2 Year 7: 38, year 8: 34, year 9: 28

D3 (a) 103   (b) 43

Test yourself (p 144)

T1 North: 145, South: 125, East: 97, West: 133

T2 (a) Managers: 4, craftsmen: 21, labourers: 9, administrators: 6 (or 4, 21, 8, 7 or 4, 20, 9, 7)

     (b) Number the workers within each group and use random numbers to select each sub-sample (or put names of each group in a box and pick out required number at random).

18 Using graphs to solve equations

A Review: graphs and simple equations (p 145)

A1 (a)

x	-1	0	1	2	3	4
y	8	0	-4	-4	0	8

     (b) The graph of $y = 2x^2 - 6x$ drawn for the values in the table above

     (c) An estimate close to 3.7

A2 (a)

x	-1	0	1	2	3	4	5	6
y	9	3	-1	-3	-3	-1	3	9

     (b) The graph of $y = x^2 - 5x + 3$ drawn for the values in the table above

     (c) Estimates close to -0.2 and 5.2

A3 (a)

     (b) 3

     (c) An explanation such as:
The minimum value of $x^2 - 2x + 4$ is 3 so there is no value of x such that $x^2 - 2x + 4 = 2$.

B Intersection of a linear and a curved graph (p 146)

B1 (a)

x	-3	-2	-1	0	1	2	3
y	8	3	0	-1	0	3	8

     (b) The graph of $y = x^2 - 1$ drawn for the values in the table above

     (c) The graph of $y = 2x$ drawn on the same set of axes as in (b)

     (d) Estimates close to -0.4 and 2.4

     (e) (i) $x^2 - 2x - 1 = 0$ (ii) $x = 2.41$ (to 2 d.p.)

B2 (a) Estimates close to -0.9, 0.8 and 4.1

     (b) (i) $x^3 - 4x^2 + 4 = x + 1$ rearranges to
$x^3 - 4x^2 + 4 - x - 1 = 0$ which simplifies to
$x^3 - 4x^2 - x + 3 = 0$

        (ii) $x = 4.06$ (to 2 d.p.)

B3 (a)

x	$^-4$	$^-3$	$^-2$	$^-1$	$^-0.5$	$^-0.25$
$\frac{3}{x} + 1$	0.25	**0**	**$^-$0.5**	$^-2$	**$^-$5**	**$^-$11**

0.25	0.5	1	2	3	4
13	7	**4**	**2.5**	**2**	**1.75**

(b), (c) and (d)

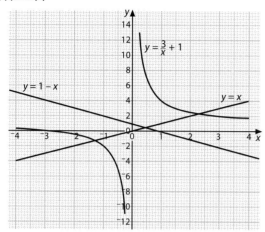

(c) Estimates close to $^-$1.3 and 2.3

(d) The graphs of $y = \frac{3}{x} + 1$ and $y = 1 - x$ do not intersect so there is no solution to the equation $\frac{3}{x} + 1 = 1 - x$.

B4 (a) (i) The line $y = 2x - 1$ drawn on sheet H2–4 leading to estimates close to $^-$0.6 and 4.6

(ii) $x^2 - 2x - 4 = 2x - 1$ rearranges to
$x^2 - 2x - 4 - 2x + 1 = 0$ which simplifies to
$x^2 - 4x - 3 = 0$.

(b) (i) The line $y = 4 - \frac{1}{2}x$ drawn on sheet H2–4 leading to estimates close to $^-$2.2 and 3.7

(ii) $x^2 - 2x - 4 = 4 - \frac{1}{2}x$ rearranges to
$x^2 - 2x - 4 + \frac{1}{2}x - 4 = 0$ which simplifies to
$x^2 - 1\frac{1}{2}x - 8 = 0$. Multiplying both sides by 2
gives $2x^2 - 3x - 16 = 0$ so the solutions to
$x^2 - 2x - 4 = 4 - \frac{1}{2}x$ also satisfy $2x^2 - 3x - 16 = 0$.

C Deciding which linear graph to draw (p 148)

C1 (a) A, C and D **(b)** $y = 6 - x$

C2 $y = 4x$

C3 $y = 2 - 4x$

C4 (a)

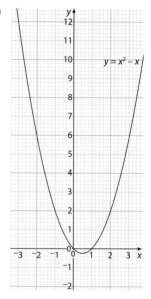

(b) (i) Estimates close to $^-$1.8 and 2.8

(ii) The line $y = 1 - 2x$ drawn on the graph from (a) leading to estimates close to $^-$1.6 and 0.6

(iii) The line $y = 3x - 1$ drawn on the graph from (a) leading to estimates close to 0.3 and 3.7

C5 (a) (i) The line $y = x$ drawn on sheet H2–6 leading to an estimate close to 1.5

(ii) The graphs of $y = x^3 - 2$ and $y = x$ intersect at only one point so there is just one solution to the equation $x^3 - x - 2 = 0$.

(iii) $x = 1.52$ (to 2 d.p.)

(b) (i) The line $y = 3x - 3$ drawn on sheet H2–6 leading to estimates close to 0.3 and 1.5

(ii) The graphs of $y = x^3 - 2$ and $y = 3x - 3$ will intersect at three points so there are three solutions to the equation $x^3 - 3x + 1 = 0$.

(c) The line $y = 1 - x$ drawn on sheet H2–6 leading to an estimate close to 1.2

C6 (a) The line $y = 4x$ drawn on sheet H2–6 leading to an estimate close to 0.7

(b) The equation $\frac{2}{x} - 4x$ rearranges to give $4x = \frac{2}{x}$.
Multiplying both sides by x gives $4x^2 = 2$ and
dividing both sides by 4 gives $x^2 = \frac{1}{2}$.
Hence the positive solution is $x = \sqrt{\frac{1}{2}}$.

C7 (a) and (c) (ii)

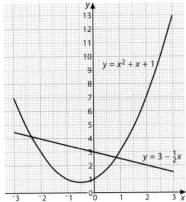

(b) A and D

(c) (i) $y = 3 - \frac{1}{2}x$

   (ii) The line $3 - \frac{1}{2}x$ drawn on the graph from (a)
        leading to estimates close to $^-2.4$ and 0.9

C8 $y = \frac{1}{3}x + 1$

C9 $y = 10x - 11$

C10 The graphs of $y = \frac{1}{x} + 1$ and $y = 7 - x^2$ intersect where
$\frac{1}{x} + 1 = 7 - x^2$.

Multiplying both sides by x gives $1 + x = 7x - x^3$ which
rearranges to $x^3 + 1 + x - 7x = 0$.
This simplifies to $x^3 - 6x + 1 = 0$ as required.

D Forming equations and using graphs to solve problems (p 150)

D1 (a) The area is $64\,m^2$ so the length of the pen is $\frac{64}{x}$.
    Hence the total length of fencing is
    $x + x + \frac{64}{x} = 2x + \frac{64}{x}$ as required.

(b)

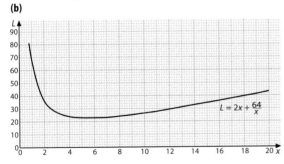

(c) Estimates close to 2.6 m and 12.4 m

(d) An estimate of the total length close to 22.6 m with
    an estimate of the width close to 5.7 m

D2 (a) $2x^2 + lx$

(b) (i) The total area is $9\,m^2$ so $2x^2 + lx = 9$.
        This rearranges to $lx = 9 - 2x^2$.
        Dividing both sides by x gives $l = \frac{9}{x} - 2x$ as
        required.

   (ii) The total volume is $x^2l = x^2\left(\frac{9}{x} - 2x\right) = 9x - 2x^3$
        as required.

(c)

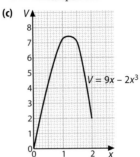

(d) Estimates close to 0.5 and 1.8

(e) (i) Estimate close to 1.2

   (ii) Estimate close to $7.3\,m^3$

(f) (i) 1.22

   (ii) $7.348\,304\,m^3$ with a comment on the accuracy
        of the estimate in part (e) (ii)

D3 (a) The length of the base will be $30 - 2x\,cm$.
    The width of the base will be $21 - 2x\,cm$.
    The height will be $x\,cm$. Hence the volume is given
    by the product $x(21 - 2x)(30 - 2x)$.

(b)

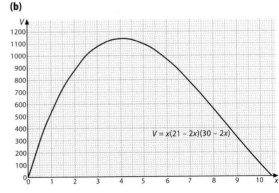

(c) An estimate of the value of x close to 4.1 and an
    estimate of the volume close to $1140\,cm^3$

(d) (i) 4.06

   (ii) $1144.17\,cm^3$ with a comment on the accuracy
        of the estimate for the maximum volume in
        part (c)

D4 (a) (i) x^2l

   (ii) The total volume is $100\,m^3$ so $x^2l = 100$.
        This rearranges to $l = \frac{100}{x^2}$ as required.

(b) $2x^2 + 4xl$

(c) The total surface area is 200 m² so $2x^2 + 4xl = 200$
Substituting $\frac{100}{x^2}$ for l gives $2x^2 + 4x\left(\frac{100}{x^2}\right) = 200$
This simplifies to $2x^2 + \frac{400}{x} = 200$.
Multiplying both sides by x gives $2x^3 + 400 = 200x$.
Dividing both sides by 2 and rearranging gives
$x^3 - 100x + 200 = 0$ so x satisfies the equation
$x^3 - 100x + 200 = 0$.

(d) (i)

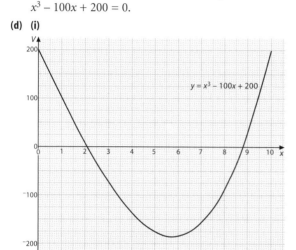

(ii) The two different blocks have approximate
dimensions 2.1 m by 2.1 m by 22.7 m and
8.8 m by 8.8 m by 1.3 m.

Test yourself (p 152)

T1 (a)

x	-2	-1	0	1	2	3	4
y	11	**5**	1	-1	**-1**	1	5

(b) The graph of $y = x^2 - 3x + 1$ drawn for the values
in the table above

(c) An estimate close to $^-1.25$

(d) The line $y = 2x - 4$ added to the diagram to obtain
estimates close to 1.4 and 3.6

T2 (a) An estimate close to 1.4

(b) The line $y = 1 - 2x$ added to the diagram on sheet
H2–7 to obtain an estimate close to 0.6

T3 (a) The perimeter is 14 cm so the sum of the length
and the width is 7 cm. Since the length is x cm, the
width must be $7 - x$ cm. The area is 9 cm².
Hence $x(7 - x) = 9$ which expands to $7x - x^2 = 9$
and rearranges to $x^2 - 7x + 9 = 0$.

(b)

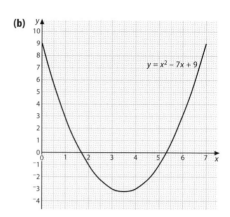

(c) An estimate of the dimensions close to 1.7 cm by
5.3 cm

19 Histograms

A Reading a histogram using an 'area scale' (p 153)

A1

Height, h cm	Frequency
$95 < h \le 100$	4
$100 < h \le 110$	12
$110 < h \le 115$	12
$115 < h \le 120$	10
$120 < h \le 130$	6

A2

Weight, w kg	Frequency
$1.0 < w \le 2.0$	40
$2.0 < w \le 2.5$	60
$2.5 < w \le 3.0$	120
$3.0 < w \le 4.0$	60
$4.0 < w \le 4.5$	10

A3 (a) 50   **(b)** 195

A4

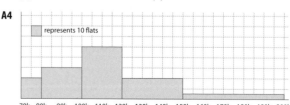

A5 (a)
$$\frac{0.5\times 34 + 1.5\times 13 + 3.5\times 12 + 7.5\times 10 + 15\times 4}{73} = \frac{213.5}{73}$$
= 2.9 minutes (to 1 d.p.)

(b)

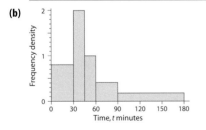

B Frequency density (p 155)

B1 (a) 4, 8, 12, 16, 20, 24   **(b)** 6

B2

Weight, w g	Frequency
$100 < w \le 150$	**25**
$150 < w \le 250$	**100**
$250 < w \le 300$	**175**
$300 < w \le 450$	**225**

B3

Height, h cm	Frequency
$120 < h \le 130$	**1**
$130 < h \le 155$	**5**
$155 < h \le 175$	**12**
$175 < h \le 190$	**6**

B4 2

B5 (a) 0.2   **(b)** 0.5   **(c)** 0.6   **(d)** 0.2

C Drawing a histogram (p 157)

C1 (a)

Time, t minutes	Frequency density
$0 < t \le 30$	**24 ÷ 30 = 0.8**
$30 < t \le 45$	**30 ÷ 15 = 2**
$45 < t \le 60$	**15 ÷ 15 = 1**
$60 < t \le 90$	**12 ÷ 30 = 0.4**
$90 < t \le 180$	**18 ÷ 90 = 0.2**

(b)

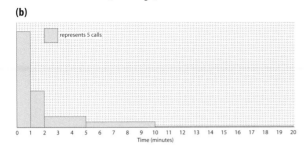

C2 (a) Frequency densities 1.6, 4.8, 7.2, 1.4, 0.6

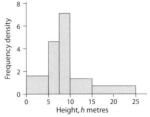

(b) About 10

C3 (a), (c)

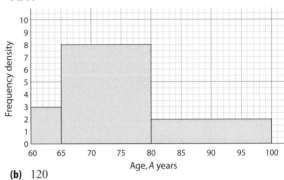

(b) 120

Test yourself (p 158)

T1 (a)

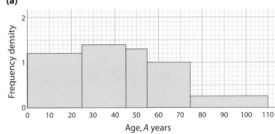

(b) $30 + 1.2\times 15 = 48$ per cent, approximately

T2 (a)

Age (x) in years	Frequency
$0 < x \le 10$	160
$10 < x \le 25$	**60**
$25 < x \le 30$	**40**
$30 < x \le 40$	100
$40 < x \le 70$	120

(b)

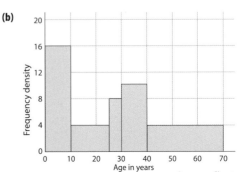

20 Quadratic expressions and equations 2

A Perfect squares (p 159)

A1 (a) $x^2 + 10x + 25$ (b) $x^2 - 8x + 16$
(c) $x^2 - 6x + 9$ (d) $x^2 + 24x + 144$

A2 (a) $(x - 5)^2 = x^2 + 10x + 25$
(b) $(x + 6)^2 = x^2 + 12x + 36$
(c) $(x + 4)^2 = x^2 + 8x + 16$
(d) $(x - 2)^2 = x^2 - 4x + 4$
(e) $(x + 8)^2 = x^2 + 16x + 64$
(f) $(x - 7)^2 = x^2 - 14x + 49$

A3 (a) A: $x^2 + 2x + 1$
C: $x^2 - 12x + 36$
D: $x^2 - 18x + 81$
E: $x^2 + 6x + 9$
(b) A: $x^2 + 2x + 1 = (x + 1)^2$
C: $x^2 - 12x + 36 = (x - 6)^2$
D: $x^2 - 18x + 81 = (x - 9)^2$
E: $x^2 + 6x + 9 = (x + 3)^2$

A4 (a) $x^2 + 2ax + a^2$ (b) $x^2 - 2bx + b^2$

A5 (a) 4   (b) 9   (c) 16   (d) 1
(e) 4   (f) 9   (g) 1   (h) 25

A6 (a) 5   (b) 3   (c) 6   (d) 6
(e) 20   (f) 7

A7 (a) 1   (b) 4   (c) 16

B Using a perfect square to solve a quadratic equation (p 160)

B1 (a) $x = 2, 8$ (b) $x = 2, ^-6$
(c) $x = 5.646, 0.354$ (d) $x = 2.162, ^-4.162$

B2 (a) 7   (b) $x = ^-0.354, ^-5.646$

B3 (a) 5   (b) $x = 1.236, ^-3.236$

B4 (a) $x = ^-0.708, ^-11.292$ (b) $x = 0.477, ^-10.477$
(c) $x = 0.796, ^-8.796$

B5 Using perfect squares gives $(x + 1)^2 = ^-2$. This cannot be solved as the square root of $^-2$ cannot be found.

B6 (a) $x = 4.449, ^-0.449$ (b) $x = 12.403, ^-0.403$
(c) $x = 4.414, 1.586$

B7 (a) $x^2 - x + \frac{1}{4}$ (b) $x = 2.303, ^-1.303$

B8 $x = 0.562, ^-3.562$

B9 $2x^2 + 8x + 2 = 0$
$x^2 + 4x + 1 = 0$
$x^2 + 4x + 4 = 3$
$(x + 2)^2 = 3$
$x + 2 = \pm\sqrt{3}$
$x = \pm\sqrt{3} - 2$
$x = ^-0.268, ^-3.732$

B10 (a) $x = ^-0.354, ^-5.646$ (b) $x = 8.123, ^-0.123$
(c) $x = 2.618, 0.382$

C Using a formula to solve a quadratic equation (p 161)

C1 (a) $x = ^-0.697, ^-4.302$ (b) $x = ^-0.303, 3.303$
(c) $x = 10.110, 0.890$ (d) $x = 0.291, ^-2.291$
(e) $x = 0.458, ^-5.458$ (f) $x = 1.290, 0.310$

C2 (a) $x = 1.230, ^-1.897$ (b) $x = 1.707, 0.293$
(c) $x = 3.236, ^-1.236$

C3 (a) (i) Factorising to obtain $x = ^-5, ^-6$
(ii) Factorising to obtain $x = 1, \frac{1}{3}$
(b) Using the formula to obtain the solutions above

C4 (a) $x = 1, ^-7$ (b) $x = ^-0.153, ^-2.180$
(c) $x = ^-0.214, ^-3.120$ (d) $x = \frac{10}{3}, \frac{^-3}{2}$
(e) $x = 3, ^-1.4$ (f) $x = 2.851, ^-0.351$

C5 (a) When the graph of $y = x^2 - 5x - 5$ cuts the x-axis, the value of y is 0 so the corresponding values of x are the solutions to $x^2 - 5x - 5 = 0$.
(b) $(^-0.9, 0), (5.9, 0)$

C6 $(^-1, 0), (0.8, 0)$

C7 (a) $x = 1.5$ (b) B

C8 (a) $b^2 - 4ac = (^-2)^2 - 4 \times 1 \times 5 = ^-16$ and the square root of $^-16$ cannot be found.
(b) The graph does not meet the x-axis.

D Solving problems (p 163)

D1 (a) Area $=$ length $\times$ width so
$A = (x + 4)(x - 1)$
$= x^2 - x + 4x - 4$
$= x^2 + 3x - 4$ as required
(b) 6.53 cm

D2 (a) (i) $(x + 1)^2 + x^2 = (x + 3)^2$
(ii) $(x + 1)^2 + x^2 = (x + 3)^2$
$x^2 + 2x + 1 + x^2 = x^2 + 6x + 9$
$x^2 + 2x + 1 = 6x + 9$
$x^2 - 4x - 8 = 0$
(b) (i) $x = 5.464, ^-1.464$ (to 3 d.p.)
(ii) 8.5 (to 1 d.p.)

D3 (a) $13 - y$

(b) Area = length × width
$$= y(13 - y)$$
$$= 13y - y^2$$
The area is $35\,\text{cm}^2$ so $13y - y^2 = 35$.
Adding y^2 and subtracting $13y$ from each side gives
$0 = y^2 - 13y + 35$ or $y^2 - 13y + 35 = 0$ as required.

(c) Length $9.19\,\text{cm}$, width $3.81\,\text{cm}$

D4 (a) The length of the pen is $50 - 2x$ metres.
Area = length × width
$$= x(50 - 2x)$$
$$= 50x - 2x^2$$
The area is $250\,\text{m}^2$ so $50x - 2x^2 = 250$.
Dividing both sides by 2 gives $25x - x^2 = 125$.
Adding x^2 and subtracting $25x$ from each side gives
$x^2 - 25x + 125 = 0$ as required.

(b) $x = 6.9, 18.1$ (to 1 d.p.) are the possible values.

D5 $10.6\,\text{cm}$

E Simultaneous equations (p 164)

E1 (a) $x = 2, y = 4$ and $x = 3, y = 9$

(b) $x = 5, y = 32$ and $x = {}^-2, y = 11$

(c) $x = 4, y = 11$ and $x = {}^-2, y = {}^-1$

(d) $x = 0.35, y = 8.75$ and $x = {}^-2.85, y = {}^-7.25$ (to 2 d.p.)

E2 (a) $(3, 5), ({}^-4, 12)$

(b) $(2.79, {}^-2.21), ({}^-1.79, {}^-6.79)$

(c) $(0.8, 3.4), ({}^-2, 9)$

(d) $(2.35, {}^-1.53), ({}^-0.85, 3.28)$

E3 (a) $x = 2$

(b) There is only one solution so the line meets the curve at just one point.

E4 (a) The line $y = x - 1$ meets the curve $y = 4x^2 + 5x$ when $4x^2 + 5x = x - 1$. This rearranges to $4x^2 + 4x + 1 = 0$ which factorises to $(2x + 1)^2 = 0$. This equation has only one solution so the line meets the curve at only one point.

(b) $({}^-0.5, {}^-1.5)$

E5 The line $y = x - 3$ meets the curve $y = x^2 + 2x + 1$ when $x^2 + 2x + 1 = x - 3$. This rearranges to $x^2 + x + 4 = 0$. $b^2 - 4ac = 1^2 - 4 \times 4 = {}^-15$ and the square root of ${}^-15$ cannot be found so trying to use the formula shows that the equation has no solutions. Hence the line does not meet the curve.

Test yourself (p 165)

T1 (a) 36

(b) $x = 12.24, {}^-0.24$

T2 $x = 10.48, {}^-0.48$

T3 $x = 6.27, {}^-1.27$

T4 (a) Area $= \dfrac{2x \times (x + 20)}{2}$
$$= x(x + 20)$$
$$= x^2 + 20x$$
The area is $400\,\text{cm}^2$ so $x^2 + 20x = 400$ as required.

(b) $x = 12.361$

T5 (a) The surface area of the cuboid is
$$2 \times [x(x - 1) + 3x + 3(x - 1)]$$
$$= 2 \times [x^2 - x + 3x + 3x - 3]$$
$$= 2 \times [x^2 + 5x - 3]$$
$$= 2x^2 + 10x - 6$$
The surface area is $63\,\text{cm}^2$ so $2x^2 + 10x - 6 = 63$ which rearranges to $2x^2 + 10x - 69 = 0$ as required.

(b) (i) $x = 3.88, {}^-8.88$ (to 2 d.p.)

(ii) $3.88\,\text{cm}$ by $2.88\,\text{cm}$ by $3\,\text{cm}$

T6 $x = 1, y = 3$ and $x = {}^-\frac{2}{3}, y = \frac{4}{3}$

T7 $x = 2.0, y = 5.0$ and $x = {}^-8.5, y = 15.5$

Review 3 (p 166)

1 (a) 60   **(b)** $\frac{39}{60} = \frac{13}{20}$

2 £1.01

3 (a) $q = \frac{ts - p}{r}$

  (b) $q = \pm\sqrt{6p}$

  (c) $q = \frac{s^2}{4} - b$ or $\left(\frac{s}{2}\right)^2 - b$ or $\frac{s^2 - 4b}{4}$

  (d) $q = \pm\frac{\sqrt{s}}{3}$ $\left(\text{or} \pm\sqrt{\frac{s}{9}}\right)$

4 No. During the week, schoolchildren are at school at this time so they are likely to be under-represented in the sample. Also many adults have a break for lunch at this time and may visit the library so they are likely to be over-represented in the sample.

5 $y = \frac{2}{3}x - 1$ or $3y = 2x - 3$

6 (a) 0.5 km   **(b)** 3 km/h   **(c)** 5 minutes
  (d) 2 km   **(e)** 20 km/h   **(f)** 10 km/h

7 (a) $x = ^-1.61, 5.61$ **(b)** $x = ^-3.64, 0.14$
  (c) $x = ^-0.90, 1.40$
       all values given to 2 d.p.

8 (a) 45° (alternate angles)
  (b) 70° (corresponding angles)
  (c) 65°

9 (a) Rounding to one significant figure gives
     $\frac{30 + 6}{3^2} = \frac{36}{9} = 4$
  (b) 4.16

10 (a) ab^2 **(b)** $16a^8b^4$ **(c)** $8a^3b^4$ **(d)** $\frac{3x}{2}$

11 (a) 3
  (b) $2^2 \times 3 \times 7$
  (c) (i) 4   **(ii)** 840

12 44 minutes

13 1.64×10^{11} km³

14 Year 9: 37 students; year 10: 44 students; year 11: 39 students

15 (a) 4   **(b)** $^-1$ **(c)** 4   **(d)** 4

16 (a) A full-size drawing of this isosceles triangle

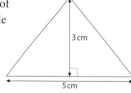

  (b) 25 cm³

17 (a) $r = \frac{V}{3 + q}$ **(b)** $r = \frac{P + 2}{5 + \pi}$ **(c)** $r = \pm\sqrt{\frac{A}{9 -}}$

18 (a) 30°, 150°   **(b)** 78.5°, 281.5°   **(c)** 19.5°, 160.
  (d) 63.4°, 243.4°   **(e)** 138.6°, 221.4°   **(f)** 168.7°, 348

19 $s = 4l^2f^2d$ or $s = (2lf)^2d$

20 358

21 (a) 138 cm (to the nearest cm)

  (b)

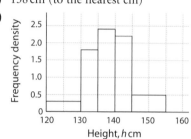

22 $(^-2.35, 0), (0.85, 0)$

23 26%

24 (a) $t = \frac{a - ba}{b}$ or $\frac{a(1 - b)}{b}$ or $\frac{a}{b} - a$

  (b) $t = \frac{a}{b - 1}$

  (c) $t = \frac{ab}{a - b}$

  (d) $t = \frac{ab - a}{b + 1}$ or $\frac{a(b - 1)}{b + 1}$

25 (a) $x^2 + 4xh$
  (b) $x^2 + 4xh = 50$
      so $4xh = 50 - x^2$
      so $h = \frac{50 - x^2}{4x}$

  (c) $V = x^2h = x^2 \times \left(\frac{50 - x^2}{4x}\right) = \frac{x(50 - x^2)}{4}$

  (d) The graph of $V = \frac{x(50 - x^2)}{4}$ from (0, 0) to (7, 1.75

  (e) $x \approx 4.1$ giving an approximate maximum volume o 34 cm³

26 5.6 cm (to the nearest 0.1 cm)

27 (a)

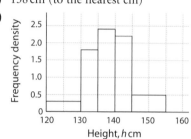

  (b) 720°
  (c) 120°

28 25 m/s

29 **(a)** The area is $\frac{1}{2}x(x-2)$ so x satisfies the equation $\frac{1}{2}x(x-2) = 30$. Multiplying both sides by 2 gives $x(x-2) = 60$ and expanding and rearranging gives $x^2 - 2x - 60 = 0$.

 (b) 8.81

30 **(a)** $y = x - 1$

 (b) An accurate graph of $y = x^3 - 2x^2$ and $y = x - 1$ on the same axes giving approximate solutions of $^-0.8$, 0.6 and 2.2

 (c) 2.25

31 **(a)** Radius of curved surface $= \sqrt{r^2 + h^2}$

 Length of arc $= 2\pi r$

 $$A = \frac{2\pi r \times \pi \left(\sqrt{r^2 + h^2}\right)^2}{2\pi \sqrt{r^2 + h^2}}$$

 which simplifies to $A = \pi r \sqrt{r^2 + h^2}$

 (b) $h = \sqrt{\left(\dfrac{A}{\pi r}\right)^2 - r^2}$

 (c) $h = 22.4$ cm, volume $= 586$ cm^3 (to the nearest cm^3)

32 **(a)** $x = \frac{-1}{3}$, $y = \frac{1}{3}$; $x = 1$, $y = 3$

 (b) $x = ^-4$, $y = 28$; $x = 3$, $y = 14$

 (c) $x = \frac{1}{3}$, $y = \frac{19}{9}$; $x = ^-1$, $y = 3$

33 20°

34 **(a)** 3.57×10^{-5} **(b)** 1.5×10^9 **(c)** 8×10^{-3}

21 Working with rounded quantities

A Lower and upper bounds (p 170)

A1 **(a)** 6.05, 6.15   **(b)** 6.95, 7.05

A2 5.65 cm, 5.75 cm

A3 3350 kg, 3450 kg

A4 3.275, 3.285

A5 **(a)** 3.455 m, 3.465 m   **(b)** 3.75 kg, 3.85 kg
 (c) 1525 litres, 1535 litres   **(d)** 3.95 km, 4.05 km
 (e) 4.575 m, 4.585 m

A6 **(a)** 74 249   **(b)** 74 150

A7 3.505 ohm, 3.495 ohm

B Calculating with rounded quantities (p 171)

B1 1302 g, 1298 g

B2 19.75 m, 19.25 m

B3 250 g, 246 g

B4 39.5 cm, 36.5 cm

B5 880.342 875 cm^3, 852.602 625 cm^3

B6 12.81 cm, 11.45 cm

C Subtracting (p 173)

C1 252 g, 254 g

C2 570 g, 590 g

C3 35.55 m

C4 **(a)** 11.25 cm, 11.35 cm
 (b) Eight bricks could measure as much as $8 \times 11.35 = 90.8$ cm. The shelf could be as little as 90.5 cm long.

C5 189.5 cm, 210.5 cm

D Dividing (p 174)

D1 197.9 litres per minute, 186.0 litres per minute

D2 8.086 g/cm^3, 7.595 g/cm^3

D3 $\frac{13.95}{8.55} = 1.6315\ldots$

D4 **(a)** **(i)** 6.375   **(ii)** 6.365
 (b) 3.927 729 772…
 (c) 0.617 082 446…

Test yourself (p 175)

T1 242.5 miles

T2 50

T3 **(a)** 341.5 g, 342.5 g   **(b)** 4098 g, 4110 g

T4 **(a)** $\dfrac{12.25}{15.65 - 7.195} = 1.448\,846\ldots$
 (b) Maximum total weight of boxes
 $= 3 \times 141.5 + 7 \times 150.5 = 1478$ kg.
 Lower bound of safe load $= 1475$ kg, so it cannot safely carry these boxes.

T5 0.020 547…

T6 $\dfrac{3 \times 414.5}{\pi \times 5.85^2} = 11.566\,02\ldots$ cm

22 Using exact values

A Showing π in a result (p 176)

A1 **(a)** π cm **(b)** 4π cm

A2 All lengths are in cm.
B: 4π C: $3\pi + 4$ D: $2\pi + 4$
E: $4\pi + 2$ F: $2\pi + 4$ G: $\pi + 8$

A3 **(a)** $\frac{1}{2}\pi$ cm^2 **(b)** 2π cm^2 **(c)** 3π cm^2

A4 All areas are in cm^2.
B: $2\pi + 4$ C: $3\pi + 4$ D: $\pi + 4$
E: $2\pi + 4$ F: $\pi + 5$ G: $\pi + 5$

A5 **(a)** 4 cm^2 **(b)** π cm^2
(c) $(4 - \pi)$ cm^2 **(d)** $(\pi + 4)$ cm

A6 **(a)** **(i)** $(9 - \pi)$ cm^2 **(ii)** $(2\pi + 4)$ cm
(b) **(i)** $(9 - \pi)$ cm^2 **(ii)** $(\pi + 8)$ cm
(c) **(i)** 8 cm^2 **(ii)** 4π cm
(d) **(i)** 3π cm^2 **(ii)** 6π cm
(e) **(i)** 4 cm^2 **(ii)** $(2\pi + 4)$ cm

A7 $(5\pi + 20)$ cm

A8

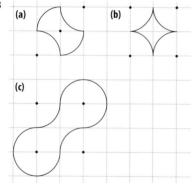

B Showing a surd in a result (p 178)

B1 **(a)** $\sqrt{40}$ cm   **(b)** $\sqrt{5}$ cm

B2 **(a)** $\sqrt{17}$ cm   **(b)** $\sqrt{17}$ cm
(c) $(2\sqrt{17} + 2)$ cm

B3 P and R $(2\sqrt{65} + 2)$ cm; Q and S $(2\sqrt{85} + 4)$ cm;
T and U $(2\sqrt{50} + 4)$ cm

B4 **(a)** $\sqrt{21}$ cm   **(b)** $\sqrt{33}$ cm   **(c)** $\sqrt{7}$ cm

B5 **(a)** $(\sqrt{21} + 7)$ cm   **(b)** $(\sqrt{33} + 11)$ cm
(c) $(\sqrt{7} + 7)$ cm

B6 **(a)** $\sqrt{21}$ cm^2 **(b)** $2\sqrt{33}$ cm^2
(c) $\frac{3\sqrt{7}}{2}$ cm^2 or $\frac{3}{2}\sqrt{7}$ cm^2

B7 **(a)** $\frac{1}{\sqrt{2}}$
(b) **(i)** $\frac{1}{\sqrt{2}}$ **(ii)** $\frac{-1}{\sqrt{2}}$

B8 **(a)**

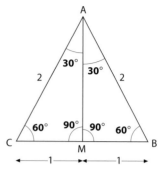

(b) $\sqrt{3}$
(c) **(i)** $\frac{\sqrt{3}}{2}$ **(ii)** $\frac{1}{2}$ **(iii)** $\sqrt{3}$ **(iv)** $\frac{1}{2}$ **(v)** $\frac{\sqrt{3}}{2}$ **(vi)** $\frac{1}{\sqrt{3}}$
(d) **(i)** $\frac{\sqrt{3}}{2}$ **(ii)** $\frac{-1}{2}$ **(iii)** $-\sqrt{3}$ **(iv)** $\frac{1}{2}$ **(v)** $\frac{-\sqrt{3}}{2}$ **(vi)** $\frac{-1}{\sqrt{3}}$
(e) $\sqrt{3}$

B9 The hypotenuse of the given triangle is $\sqrt{5}$ long.
This is a $\times 2$ enlargement of it.

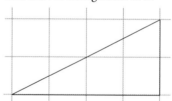

Its hypotenuse is $\sqrt{4 + 16} = \sqrt{20}$. So $\sqrt{20} = 2\sqrt{5}$.

B10

The larger triangle is a $\times 4$ enlargement of the smaller.
Hypotenuse of smaller $= \sqrt{3^2 + 1^2} = \sqrt{10}$
Hypotenuse of larger $= \sqrt{12^2 + 4^2} = \sqrt{160}$
So $\sqrt{160} = 4\sqrt{10}$

C Mixed questions (p 181)

C1 **(a)** Area $= (\pi + 1)$ cm^2, perimeter $= (\pi + \sqrt{5} + 3)$ cm
(b) Area $= \left(\frac{3}{4}\pi + \frac{1}{2}\right)$ cm^2, perimeter $= \left(\frac{3\pi}{2} + \sqrt{2}\right)$ cm
(c) Area $= 7\frac{1}{2}$ cm^2, perimeter $= (10 + \sqrt{10})$ cm
(d) Area $= (\pi + 6)$ cm^2, perimeter $= (\pi + 3\sqrt{8})$ cm
or $(\pi + 6\sqrt{2})$ cm

C2 $3\pi a^2$

C3 Curved surface area $= \pi rl = 136\pi$
Base surface area $= \pi r^2 = 64\pi$
So total surface area $= 200\pi$

C4 Radius $= \sqrt{2}$ cm. So area $= \frac{1}{2}\pi r^2 = \pi$ cm^2

C5 $\sqrt{\dfrac{10}{\pi}}$

C6 (a) These are possible lengths.

(b) (i) $\dfrac{\sqrt{7}}{4}$ **(ii)** $\dfrac{\sqrt{7}}{3}$

D Exact relationships between variables (p 182)

D1 (a) $\dfrac{\pi}{4}$ **(b)** $\dfrac{2}{\pi}$

D2 $a = 3b$

D3 (a) $\dfrac{5}{2}$ **(b)** $\dfrac{125}{6}\pi$

D4 $\dfrac{2}{3}$

D5 (a) Surface area of cylinder $= 2\pi rh + 2\pi r^2$
$= 10\pi y^2 + 2\pi y^2$
$= 12\pi y^2$
Surface area of sphere $= 4\pi r^2$
Since the areas are equal, $4\pi r^2 = 12\pi y^2$
Dividing both sides by 4π, $r^2 = 3y^2$
(b) $2\sqrt{3}$

Test yourself (p 183)

T1 (a) $\sqrt{61}$ cm   **(b)** $\sqrt{23}$ cm

T2   Area (cm^2)   Perimeter (cm)

(a) $2 + \dfrac{\pi}{2}$ $2 + 2\sqrt{2} + \pi$

(b) $5\frac{1}{2}$ $5 + \sqrt{2} + \sqrt{13}$

(c) $7 - \dfrac{\pi}{2}$ $2 + 2\sqrt{5} + \pi$

(d) $1 + \frac{3}{2}\pi$ $2 + 2\sqrt{2} + 3\pi$

T3 $\sin x = \dfrac{3}{\sqrt{10}}, \cos x = \dfrac{1}{\sqrt{10}}$

T4 $\dfrac{3}{\sqrt{2}} \left(\text{or } \dfrac{3\sqrt{2}}{2}\right)$

T5 $\dfrac{14}{\sqrt{\pi}}$

23 Fractional indices

A Review: positive and negative indices (p 184)

A1 (a) 5^7 **(b)** 5^6 **(c)** 5^4 **(d)** 5^{12} **(e)** 5^{-8}

A2 (a) $\frac{1}{8}$ **(b)** 27 **(c)** $\frac{1}{27}$ **(d)** $\frac{8}{27}$ **(e)** 8

A3 (a) 2^3 **(b)** 2^{-3} **(c)** 2^{-5} **(d)** 2^{-4} **(e)** 2^{-6}

A4 (a) $n = 2$ **(b)** $n = 6$ **(c)** $n = 0$ **(d)** $n = -1$
    (e) $n = -2$ **(f)** $n = 3$ **(g)** $n = 3$ **(h)** $n = 2$

B Roots (p 184)

B1 (a) 4 **(b)** $\frac{1}{2}$ **(c)** 1 **(d)** $\frac{1}{2}$ **(e)** $\frac{2}{3}$

B2 (a) 2 **(b)** 1 **(c)** $\frac{1}{3}$ **(d)** 3 **(e)** $\frac{1}{2}$

B3 $\frac{1}{3}$

B4 2

C Fractional indices of the form 1/n or $^{-}$1/n (p 185)

C1 (a) 3 **(b)** 5 **(c)** $\frac{1}{4}$ **(d)** $\frac{1}{10}$ **(e)** 3

C2 (a) 5^1 or 5 **(b)** $\sqrt[3]{5}$

C3 (a) 81^1 or 81 **(b)** $\sqrt[4]{81}$ (or 3)

C4 (a) $3^{\frac{1}{2}}$ **(b)** $5^{\frac{1}{4}}$

C5 (a) (i) 3 **(ii)** 5 **(iii)** 10
    (b) (i) $\frac{1}{3}$ **(ii)** $\frac{1}{5}$ **(iii)** $\frac{1}{2}$

C6 (a) 2 **(b)** $\frac{1}{2}$ **(c)** 2 **(d)** $\frac{1}{2}$ **(e)** 5
    (f) $\frac{1}{10}$ **(g)** $\frac{1}{2}$ **(h)** $\frac{1}{3}$ **(i)** 5 **(j)** 2

C7 (a) 1 **(b)** $\frac{4}{3}$ **(c)** $\frac{8}{3}$ **(d)** 18

C8 (a) $n = \frac{1}{2}$ **(b)** $n = \frac{1}{3}$ **(c)** $n = \frac{-1}{3}$
    (d) $n = \frac{1}{2}$ **(e)** $n = \frac{-1}{2}$

C9 (a) $64^{\frac{1}{2}}$ **(b)** $64^{\frac{1}{6}}$ **(c)** 64^0 **(d)** $64^{-\frac{1}{2}}$ **(e)** $64^{-\frac{1}{3}}$

C10 $81^{-\frac{1}{4}}$

C11 $81^{\frac{3}{4}}$

D Fractional indices of the form p/q or $^{-}$p/q (p 187)

D1 (a) $27^{\frac{2}{3}} = \left(27^{\frac{1}{3}}\right)^2 = 3^2$ **(b)** 9

D2 (a) 4 **(b)** 27 **(c)** 8 **(d)** 100 **(e)** 125
    (f) $\frac{1}{9}$ **(g)** $\frac{1}{64}$ **(h)** $\frac{1}{27}$ **(i)** $\frac{1}{16}$ **(j)** $\frac{1}{8}$
    (k) $\frac{1}{4}$ **(l)** $\frac{1}{64}$ **(m)** $\frac{8}{27}$ **(n)** 27 **(o)** $\frac{25}{4}$

D3 $8\sqrt{2} = 2^3 \times 2^{\frac{1}{2}} = 2^{\frac{7}{2}} \left(\text{or } 2^{3\frac{1}{2}}\right)$

D4 (a) $2^{\frac{5}{2}}$ **(b)** $2^{\frac{7}{3}}$ **(c)** $2^{\frac{3}{2}}$ **(d)** $2^{\frac{7}{2}}$ **(e)** $2^{-\frac{3}{2}}$
    (f) $2^{-\frac{2}{3}}$ **(g)** $2^{-\frac{5}{3}}$ **(h)** $2^{\frac{2}{3}}$ **(i)** $2^{-\frac{1}{3}}$ **(j)** $2^{\frac{1}{6}}$

D5 (a) $2^{\frac{3}{2}}$ **(b)** $2^{\frac{5}{2}}$ **(c)** $2^{\frac{4}{3}}$ **(d)** $2^{\frac{3}{4}}$ **(e)** $2^{-\frac{2}{5}}$

D6 (a) $n = \frac{7}{2}$ **(b)** $n = 5$

    (c) $n = 32$ **(d)** $n = \frac{1}{32}$ or 2^{-5}

D7 (a) $x = \frac{5}{2}$ **(b)** $x = \frac{4}{3}$ **(c)** $n = \frac{1}{4}$

    (d) $k = \frac{-2}{3}$ **(e)** $y = \frac{2}{3}$

E Powers and roots on a calculator (p 188)

E1 (a) 3.873   **(b)** 1.149   **(c)** 1.778

    (d) 33.37   **(e)** 0.8459

E2 Ramanujan's approximation gives 3.141 592 653 (to 9 d.p.) which agrees with the value of π to eight decimal places.

E3 (a) $x = 2.115$ **(b)** $x = 1.585$ **(c)** $x = 2.201$

    (d) $x = 1.631$ **(e)** $x = 1845$

Test yourself (p 188)

T1 (a) 4   **(b)** 8

T2 (a) 8   **(b)** $\frac{1}{3}$

T3 64

T4 (a) 1   **(b)** 4   **(c)** $\frac{1}{3}$

T5 $\frac{5}{3}$

T6 (a) (i) 1   **(ii)** 8   **(iii)** $\frac{1}{16}$

    (b) $n = \frac{5}{2}$

T7 (a) (i) 13   **(ii)** 1

    (b) $x = {}^{-}3$

    (c) $y = \frac{3}{2}$

24 Exponential growth and decay

A Exponential growth (p 189)

A1 (a) 1059 (to 4 s.f.)   **(b)** 291.3 (to 4 s.f.)

A2 (a) $6.5\,\text{m}^2$

    (b) 5%

    (c) $8.1\,\text{m}^2$

    (d) $5.9\,\text{m}^2$ is the area of the patch 2 weeks before the first measurement.

A3 (a) $P = 247\,000 \times 1.09^t$

    (b)

t	0	1	2	3	4	5
P	247 000	269 230	293 461	319 872	348 661	380 040

(c) The graph of P against t

(d) About 2.3

(e) $247\,000 \times 1.09^{2.3} = 301\,000$ (to 3 s.f.)

A4 (a) 2600×1.15^t **(b)** 4240

A5 £8500

A6 $1.02^{35} = 2.000$ (to 4 s.f.)

A7 (a) The graphs have the same basic shape, either   or

    (b) Values of k greater than 1 give the curve on the left and the higher the value of k the steeper the curve. Values of k less than 1 give the curve on the right and the lower the value of k the steeper the curve. When $k = 1$, the graph is the straight line $y = 1$.

    (c) The y-intercept is always 1. When $x = 0$, $y = k^0$ and $k^0 = 1$ for all values of k.

    (d) The problem is that $y = k^x$ is not defined for all values of x when k is negative. For example, if $k = {}^{-}2$, then the equation is $y = ({}^{-}2)^x$ which is not defined when $x = 0.5$, as the square root of a negative number cannot be found.

    (e) The graph of $y = k^{-x}$ is a reflection of the graph of $y = k^x$ in the y-axis.

B Exponential decay (p 190)

B1 (a) 20 600   **(b)** $P = 24\,300 \times 0.96^t$

    (c) 26 400 (to 3 s.f.)

B2 Graph C; it is the only one that has a smaller rate of decrease as time goes on, and does not meet the time axis.

B3 (a)

t	0	1	2	3	4	5	6
P	10 000	9200	8464	7787	7164	6591	6064

    (b) The graph of P against t

    (c) About 4.3 years

    (d) 11 815

    (e) $P = 10\,000 \times 0.92^t$

B4 (a) It decreases by 5%.   **(b)** 2018

Test yourself (p 191)

T1 (a) Graph of $y = 2^x$ **(b)** $x = 2.4$ (to 1 d.p.)

T2 (a) $R = 4.51$ **(b)** £1205.86

25 Angle properties of a circle

A Angles of a triangle (p 192)

A1 $a = 135°, b = 35°, c = 76°$

A2 The quadrilateral shown is
split into 2 triangles.
Angles of the quad are
$p, q + s, t$ and $u + r$.
Angle sum is $p + q + s + t + u + r$
$= (p + q + r) + (s + t + u) = 180° + 180° = 360°$

B Angles in a circle (p 193)

B1 (a) Isosceles (b) 20°
 (c) 40° (d) 30°
 (e) 60° (f) 100°; $\angle$AOB is twice $\angle$APB.

B2 (a) Isosceles (b) 40°
 (c) 80° (d) 45°
 (e) 90° (f) 170°; again, $\angle$AOB is twice $\angle$APB.

B3 (a) a
 (b) $2a$
 (c) It equals $2b$.
 (d) $\angle$AOC $= 2a$ and $\angle$BOC $= 2b$ so $\angle$AOB $= 2a + 2b$,
   which is $2(a + b)$, which is $2 \times \angle$APB.

B4 $a = 112°, b = 62°, c = 192°, d = 105°, e = 240°, f = 100°$

B5 (a) $\angle$AOB $= 180°$.
 (b) $\angle$APB is half of 180°, or 90°.

B6 $\angle$AP$_1$B and $\angle$AP$_2$B are both half of $\angle$AOB.

B7 $p = 33°, q = 60°, r = 80°, s = 62°, t = 44°, u = 106°,$
 $v = 90°, w = 53°, x = 42°, y = 48°, z = 48°$

C Angles of a cyclic quadrilateral (p 196)

C1 (a) $x = 80°$ (twice angle at circumference)
   $y = 280°$ (angles at a point add up to 360°)
   $z = 140°$ (half angle at centre)
 (b) $x = 100°, y = 260°, z = 130°$
 (c) $x = 120°, y = 240°, z = 120°$
 (d) $\angle$BAD and $\angle$BCD add up 180°.

C2 (a) $x = 2a$
 (b) $y = 2b$
 (c) $x + y = 360°$
 (d) $2a + 2b = 360°$, so $2(a + b) = 360°$, so $a + b = 180°$

C3 $e = a$

C4 $a = 88°, b = 124°, c = 95°, d = 107°, e = 97°, f = 94°,$
 $g = 83°, h = 87°, i = 70°, j = 119°, k = 92°, l = 107°,$
 $m = 73°, n = 53°, p = 140°$

C5 (a) 80°
 (b) 80°
 (c) 100°
 (d) Reflection symmetry
 (e) If the angle at B is x, the angle at C is $180° − x$
   (supplementary angles formed with parallel lines),
   the angle at D is also $180° − x$ (opposite angles of
   cyclic quad) and the angle at A is x (opposite angles
   of a cyclic quad), hence the symmetry.

C6 They are both 90°.

C7 (a) $\angle$ABC $= 90°$ (angle in a semicircle)
   So $\angle$ACB $= 180° − 90° − 42° = 48°$ (angles of a
   triangle)
   So $\angle$ADB $= 48°$ (angles in same segment)
 (b) $\angle$ACD $= 62°$ (half angle at centre)
   $\angle$BAC $= 62° − 32° = 30°$
   (exterior angle property of triangle ABC)
 (c) Draw line ON to make two isosceles triangles.
   $\angle$LNM $= 38° + 25° = 63°$ (angles of isosceles
   triangles)
   $\angle$LOM $= 2 \times 63° = 126°$ (angle at centre is twice
   angle at circumference)
 (d) $a = 180° − 97° = 83°$ (lines RQ and OP are parallel)
   Reflex $\angle$ROP $= 194°$ (twice angle at circumference)
   so $b = 360° − 194° = 166°$ (angles at a point add up
   to 360°)
   $c = 180° − 166° = 14°$ (lines RQ and OP are parallel)
   or $c = 360° − 97° − 83° − 166° = 14°$ (angles of a
   quad add up to 360°)
 (e) $\angle$FEH $= 180° − 72° = 108°$ (angles on straight line)
   $\angle$FGH $= 180° − 108° = 72°$ (opposite angles of
   cyclic quadrilateral)
   $\angle$GFH $+ \angle$GHF $= 180° − 72° = 108°$ (angles of a
   triangle)
   But $\angle$GFH $= \angle$GHF (isosceles triangle)
   So $\angle$GHF $= 54°$, so $l = 54°$
 (f) $\angle$CDF $= 180° − 42° = 138°$ (angles on a straight
   line)
   $\angle$EBA $= 42°$ (angle in the same segment as $\angle$EDA)
   $\angle$CBF $= 180° − 42° = 138°$ (angles on a straight
   line)
   $\angle$DFB $= 360° − 27° − 138° − 138° = 57°$ (angle sum
   of quad)
   So $h = 57°$ (vertically opposite to $\angle$DFB)

C8 (a) $\angle$DAB $= \angle$BCG $= 76°$ (exterior angle of cyclic quad
   is equal to opposite interior angle)
   $\angle$BEF $= \angle$DAB $= 76°$ (exterior angle of cyclic quad)
 (b) $\angle$BCG $= \angle$DAB $= \angle$BEF, so CD is parallel to EF
   (alternate angles)

D Tangent to a circle (p 199)

D1 (a) $\angle$LKN = 65° (alternate segment)

(b) $\angle$QPR = 58° (alternate segment)

(c) $\angle$ABD = 76° (angles of a triangle)
$\angle$ADE = 76° (alternate segment)

(d) $\angle$QSR = 78° (alternate segment)
$\angle$QRS = 51° (angles of isosceles triangle)

(e) $\angle$ABD = 39° (tangent perpendicular to radius)
$\angle$DEB = 39° (alternate segment)

(f) $\angle$STQ = 47° (alternate segment)
$\angle$TQU = 47° (alternate angles with parallel lines)

(g) $\angle$BDF = 66° (alternate segment)
$\angle$DBF = 180° − 66° − 46° = 68° (angles of a triangle)
$\angle$DFE = 68° (alternate segment)

(h) $\angle$SQP = 83° (alternate segment)
$\angle$QSR = 83° − 44° = 39° (exterior angle of triangle
= sum of opposite interior angles)

(i) $\angle$RQU = 54° (alternate segment)
$\angle$SQU = 180° − 68° − 54° = 58° (angles on a straight line)
$\angle$STU = 180° − 58° = 122° (opposite angles of cyclic quad)

D2 (a) AOB is an isosceles triangle.

(b) The tangent AT is perpendicular to the radius OA.

(c) $\angle$AOB = 180° − 2y (angle sum of triangle AOB)

(d) $\angle$ACB = 90° − y (half angle at centre)

(e) From $x + y = 90°$, we get $x = 90° − y$, so $\angle$ACB = x.

E Mixed questions (p 201)

E1 $a = 140°$, $b = 47°$, $c = 68°$, $d = 22°$

E2 $p = 78°$, $q = 140°$, $r = 51°$

E3

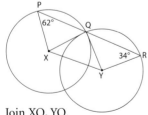

Join XQ, YQ.
$\angle$XQP = 62° (isosceles triangle)
So $\angle$PXQ = 180° − 2×62° = 56°
$\angle$YQR = 34° (isosceles triangle)
So $\angle$QYR = 180° − 2×34° = 112°
$\angle$XQY = 180° − 62° − 34° = 84°
So $\angle$QXY and $\angle$QYX are each $\frac{1}{2}$(180° − 84°) = 48°
(isosceles triangle)
$\angle$PXY = 56° + 48° = 104°
$\angle$RYX = 112° + 48° = 160°

E4 $\angle$SAB + $\angle$TAD = 180° − $\angle$BAD = $\angle$BCD (opposite angles of cyclic quad)

Test yourself (p 202)

T1 (a) $\angle$AOC = 116°

(b) The angle at the centre is twice the angle at the circumference.

T2 $p = 92°$, $q = 83°$, $r = 26°$, $s = 51°$

T3 $\angle$QPR = 90° (angle in a semicircle)
$\angle$PQR = 180° − 90° − 19° = 71° (angles of a triangle)
$e = \angle$PQR = 71° (angle in alternate segment)
$f = 36°$ (angle in alternate segment)
So $\angle$BAC = 36° (angles of isosceles triangle)
So $g = 180° − 36° − 36° = 108°$ (angles of a triangle)

T4 (a) (i) $\angle$ABC = 180° − 132° = 48°

(ii) Opposite angles of cyclic quad add up to 180°.

(b) (i) $\angle$CBD = 18°

(ii) $\angle$ABD = 30° (alternate segment),
so $\angle$CBD = 48° − 30° = 18°

(c) AC is not a diameter because $\angle$ABC is not equal to 90°.

T5 (a) $\angle$ABD = 31° (angle at centre = twice angle at circumference)

(b) $\angle$ADC = 90° (angle in a semicircle)

(c) $\angle$ACD = $\angle$ABD = 31° (angles in same segment are equal)
$\angle$CAD = 180° − 90° − 31° = 59° (angles in triangle ACD)
or $\angle$CAD = $\angle$ODA (base angles of isosceles triangle)
$\angle$CAD = $\frac{1}{2}$(180° − 62°) = 59°

(d) $\angle$CDP = 59° (alternate segment)
or $\angle$ODC = $\angle$OCD = 31° (isosceles triangle)
$\angle$ODP = 90° (tangent perpendicular to radius)
$\angle$CDP = $\angle$ODP − $\angle$ODC = 90° − 31° = 59°

26 Algebraic fractions and equations 2

Algebraic fractions are given in their simplest form, where appropriate.

A Adding and subtracting algebraic fractions (p 204)

A1 (a) (i) $\dfrac{b}{6} = \dfrac{4b}{24}$ (ii) $\dfrac{5b}{8} = \dfrac{15b}{24}$

(b) $\dfrac{19b}{24}$

A2 (a) $\dfrac{3a}{4}$ (b) $\dfrac{a}{12}$ (c) $\dfrac{5a}{3}$ (d) $\dfrac{29a}{14}$

A3 (a) $\dfrac{2a+b}{4}$ (b) $\dfrac{5x-3y}{15}$

(c) $\dfrac{12a+5b}{16}$ (d) $\dfrac{4p-15q}{10}$

A4 (a) $\dfrac{3a+4}{4}$ (b) $\dfrac{5a-4}{12}$ (c) $\dfrac{3a+2}{4}$ (d) $\dfrac{a+2}{2}$

A5 (a) $2 = \dfrac{10}{5}$ (b) $\dfrac{10+3a}{5}$

A6 (a) $\dfrac{12+a}{4}$ (b) $\dfrac{2a+3}{4}$ (c) $\dfrac{5a}{3}$ (d) $\dfrac{16-a}{2}$

A7 (a) $\dfrac{4a+3}{4}$ (b) $\dfrac{3a-5}{6}$

(c) $\dfrac{1}{6}$ (d) $\dfrac{5(a+1)}{18}$ or $\dfrac{5a+5}{18}$

A8 $\dfrac{a+13}{2}$

A9 (a) $\dfrac{3}{2a}$ (b) $\dfrac{1}{12a}$ (c) $\dfrac{1-3a}{a^2}$ (d) $\dfrac{-1}{2a}$

(e) $\dfrac{3b+2a}{6ab}$ (f) $\dfrac{b-a}{ab}$ (g) $\dfrac{10a^2+1}{8a}$ (h) $\dfrac{2-a^2}{2a}$

A10 A and E; B and F; C and D; G and H

B More complex denominators (p 206)

B1 (a) $\dfrac{2x+3}{x(x+3)}$ (b) $\dfrac{2-13x}{3x(x+1)}$

(c) $\dfrac{4x+3}{(x+5)(3x-2)}$ (d) $\dfrac{2x}{(x+6)(x+2)}$

B2 (a) $\dfrac{x^2+6x-2}{(x-2)(x+5)}$ (b) $\dfrac{4x^2-x+9}{(x-3)(2x+1)}$

(c) $\dfrac{2x+11}{x+5}$ (d) $\dfrac{x^2-5}{(x+1)(x+5)}$

B3 $\dfrac{x}{x+1} + \dfrac{1}{x-1}$

$= \dfrac{x(x-1)+x+1}{(x+1)(x-1)}$

$= \dfrac{x^2-x+x+1}{x^2-1}$

$= \dfrac{x^2+1}{x^2-1}$ as required

B4 (a) $\dfrac{x^2+2x+2}{x(x+2)}$

(b) $\dfrac{x^2+3x-2}{x(2x-1)}$

(c) $\dfrac{x^2+4x+8}{x^2-4}$ or $\dfrac{x^2+4x+8}{(x+2)(x-2)}$

(d) $\dfrac{5-9x}{(x+3)(x-1)}$

B5 $\dfrac{x}{x-1} - \dfrac{4}{x}$

$= \dfrac{x^2-4(x-1)}{x(x-1)}$

$= \dfrac{x^2-4x+4}{x(x-1)}$

$= \dfrac{(x-2)^2}{x(x-1)}$

B6 (a) $\dfrac{8-3x}{(1-x)^2}$

(b) $\dfrac{3(2x-3)}{x^2-4}$ or $\dfrac{3(2x-3)}{(x+2)(x-2)}$

(c) $\dfrac{x^2}{3(x+3)(x-3)}$ or $\dfrac{x^2}{3(x^2-9)}$

B7 The length of the rectangle is $\dfrac{20}{x}$ so the perimeter is

$2\left(x + \dfrac{20}{x}\right)$

$= 2\left(\dfrac{x^2+20}{x}\right)$

$= \dfrac{2(x^2+20)}{x}$

B8 The total time is $\dfrac{20}{x} + \dfrac{30}{x+5}$

$= \dfrac{20(x+5)+30x}{x(x+5)}$

$= \dfrac{50x+100}{x(x+5)}$

$= \dfrac{50(x+2)}{x(x+5)}$

C Solving equations containing fractions (p 207)

C1 (a) $x = 11$ (b) $x = 7$ (c) $x = 14$

C2 (a) $x = \frac{1}{4}$ (b) $x = 9$ (c) $x = \frac{5}{2}$

   (d) $x = \frac{-1}{4}$ (e) $x = {}^-1$ (f) $x = \frac{2}{5}$

C3 (a) $x = 9, 6$ (b) $x = 5, {}^-2$ (c) $x = 2, \frac{{}^-8}{5}$

   (d) $x = 2, \frac{1}{2}$ (e) $x = 2, {}^-3$ (f) $x = {}^-2, {}^-3$

C4 (a) $x = 10.77, 2.23$ (b) $x = 2.24, {}^-2.24$

   (c) $x = 4.47, {}^-3.47$

C5 (a) $\dfrac{100}{x} + \dfrac{60}{x+10}$

   (b) $\dfrac{100}{x} + \dfrac{60}{x+10} = 3$

      So $100(x + 10) + 60x = 3x(x + 10)$

          $100x + 1000 + 60x = 3x^2 + 30x$

              $160x + 1000 = 3x^2 + 30x$

      $3x^2 + 30x - 160x - 1000 = 0$

         $3x^2 - 130x - 1000 = 0$

   (c) $x = 50, \frac{{}^-20}{3}$

      Speeds cannot be negative so the two speeds are 50 m.p.h. and 60 m.p.h.

C6 9 km/h

C7 It could be 8 or 40 apples (40 apples is less likely though as it would make the mean weight 16 g which is a small apple).

D Rearranging formulas containing fractions (p 208)

D1 $p = \dfrac{q}{qr + 1}$

D2 (a) $x = \dfrac{a(b + y)}{b}$

   (b) $x = \dfrac{y}{5y - 3}$

   (c) $x = \dfrac{y}{zy + 1}$

   (d) $x = \dfrac{3yz}{4(1 - 6y)}$

   (e) $x = \pm\sqrt{\dfrac{z}{4 + yz}}$

   (f) $x = \pm\sqrt{\dfrac{y^2}{3y^2 - 1}}$ or $x = \dfrac{y}{\pm\sqrt{3y^2 - 1}}$

D3 Multiplying both sides of $\dfrac{1}{f} = \dfrac{1}{u} + \dfrac{1}{v}$ by fuv gives

    $uv = fv + fu$

    So $uv = f(v + u)$

    So $f = \dfrac{uv}{v + u}$ as required

D4 $x = \dfrac{hy}{2y - h}$

Test yourself (p 209)

T1 (a) $\dfrac{11}{15x}$ (b) $\dfrac{5x + 7}{(x - 1)(2x + 1)}$

   (c) $\dfrac{5x}{(x - 3)(x + 2)}$ (d) $\dfrac{x^2}{x - 1}$

T2 (a) $1\frac{1}{4}$ hours

   (b) (i) $\dfrac{12}{x} + \dfrac{25}{x + 4}$

       (ii) $\dfrac{12}{x} + \dfrac{25}{x + 4} = 2$

       Multiplying both sides by $x(x + 4)$ gives

          $12(x + 4) + 25x = 2x(x + 4)$

          $12x + 48 + 25x = 2x^2 + 8x$

            $37x + 48 = 2x^2 + 8x$

        $2x^2 + 8x - 37x - 48 = 0$

        $2x^2 - 29x - 48 = 0$ as required

       (iii) $x = 16, \frac{{}^-3}{2}$ but speed cannot be negative so the speed is 16 m.p.h.

T3 $x = 5$

T4 $x = \frac{4}{5}$

T5 $x = 12, 4$

T6 $x = \frac{{}^-1}{2}, {}^-4$

T7 (a) $x = \frac{9}{4}$ (b) $y = \frac{5}{2}, \frac{{}^-1}{2}$

T8 $P = \dfrac{2R}{3(RQ - 1)}$

27 Vectors

A Vector notation (p 210)

A1 $\overrightarrow{EF}$

A2 $\overrightarrow{GH}$

A3 (a) $\overrightarrow{CD}$ (b) $\overrightarrow{IJ}$ (c) $\overrightarrow{MN}$

A4 $\overrightarrow{OP}$

A5 (a) $\overrightarrow{WX}$ (b) $\overrightarrow{QR}$

A6 (a) $4\mathbf{a}$ (b) $3\mathbf{b}$ (c) $^-\mathbf{b}$ (d) $^-2\mathbf{b}$

A7 (a) They are all parallel to **a**.

   (b) They are all parallel to **b**.

A8 Diagrams showing

(a) $2\mathbf{c} = \begin{bmatrix} -4 \\ 8 \end{bmatrix}$ (b) $3\mathbf{d} = \begin{bmatrix} -9 \\ -6 \end{bmatrix}$ (c) $^-\mathbf{c} = \begin{bmatrix} 2 \\ -4 \end{bmatrix}$

(d) $^-\mathbf{d} = \begin{bmatrix} 3 \\ 2 \end{bmatrix}$ (e) $^-2\mathbf{c} = \begin{bmatrix} 4 \\ -8 \end{bmatrix}$ (f) $^-4\mathbf{d} = \begin{bmatrix} 12 \\ 8 \end{bmatrix}$

A9 (a) (i) $\begin{bmatrix} 8 \\ 2 \end{bmatrix}$ (ii) $\begin{bmatrix} -9 \\ 6 \end{bmatrix}$ (iii) $\begin{bmatrix} -4 \\ -1 \end{bmatrix}$ (iv) $\begin{bmatrix} 6 \\ -4 \end{bmatrix}$

(b) (i) $3\mathbf{e}$ (ii) $2\mathbf{f}$ (iii) $^-\mathbf{f}$ (iv) $^-4\mathbf{e}$

A10 (a) A vector equivalent to $\mathbf{s}$

(b) (i) $\mathbf{s}$ (ii) $3\mathbf{s}$ (iii) $4\mathbf{t}$ (iv) $^-\mathbf{s}$

(v) $^-\mathbf{t}$ (vi) $2\mathbf{t}$ (vii) $^-2\mathbf{t}$ (viii) $^-3\mathbf{s}$

B Adding vectors (p 212)

B1 (a) $\begin{bmatrix} -1 \\ 9 \end{bmatrix}$ (b) $\begin{bmatrix} 0 \\ 2 \end{bmatrix}$ (c) $\begin{bmatrix} -3 \\ -1 \end{bmatrix}$ (d) $\begin{bmatrix} -2 \\ 5 \end{bmatrix}$

A diagram should be drawn for each one.

B2 (a) (i) 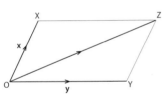 (ii)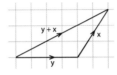

(b) Yes

(c) Yes. For any two vectors $\mathbf{x}$ and $\mathbf{y}$, we can construct a parallelogram OXZY where $\overrightarrow{OX} = \mathbf{x}$ and $\overrightarrow{OY} = \mathbf{y}$.

Now $\overrightarrow{OZ} = \overrightarrow{OX} + \overrightarrow{XZ} = \mathbf{x} + \mathbf{y}$.
Also $\overrightarrow{OZ} = \overrightarrow{OY} + \overrightarrow{YZ} = \mathbf{y} + \mathbf{x}$.
So for any two vectors $\mathbf{x} + \mathbf{y} = \mathbf{y} + \mathbf{x}$.

B3 (a) Diagrams showing

(i) $\mathbf{f} + \mathbf{g} = \begin{bmatrix} -3 \\ 6 \end{bmatrix}$ (ii) $3\mathbf{f} + \mathbf{g} = \begin{bmatrix} -1 \\ 14 \end{bmatrix}$

(iii) $\mathbf{f} + 2\mathbf{g} = \begin{bmatrix} -7 \\ 8 \end{bmatrix}$ (iv) $2\mathbf{f} + 2\mathbf{g} = \begin{bmatrix} -6 \\ 12 \end{bmatrix}$

(b) (i) $\begin{bmatrix} -2 \\ 10 \end{bmatrix}$ (ii) $\begin{bmatrix} 0 \\ 18 \end{bmatrix}$ (iii) $\begin{bmatrix} -10 \\ 14 \end{bmatrix}$ (iv) $\begin{bmatrix} -3 \\ 24 \end{bmatrix}$

B4 (a) $\overrightarrow{AR} = \overrightarrow{AQ} + \overrightarrow{QR}$ (b) $\overrightarrow{AR} = 2\mathbf{p} + \mathbf{q}$

B5 $\overrightarrow{AL}, \overrightarrow{IT}, \overrightarrow{EP}$

B6 (a) $\mathbf{p} + \mathbf{q}$ (b) $\mathbf{p} + 2\mathbf{q}$ (c) $2\mathbf{p} + 3\mathbf{q}$ (d) $2\mathbf{p} + 2\mathbf{q}$

C Subtracting vectors (p 213)

C1 (a) 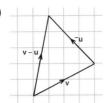 (b)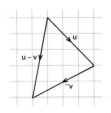

C2 (a) $\overrightarrow{CB}, \overrightarrow{ED}$

(b) (i) $\overrightarrow{HD} = \overrightarrow{HE} + \overrightarrow{ED}$ (ii) $\mathbf{j} - \mathbf{k}$

(c) (i) $\mathbf{j} - \mathbf{k}$ (ii) $\mathbf{k} - \mathbf{j}$

(d) $\overrightarrow{CH}, \overrightarrow{BG}$

(e) (i) $\overrightarrow{HA} = \overrightarrow{HC} + \overrightarrow{CA}$ (ii) $2\mathbf{j} - 2\mathbf{k}$

(f) $\overrightarrow{HB} = \overrightarrow{HC} + \overrightarrow{CB} = 2\mathbf{j} - \mathbf{k}$

(g) $^-\mathbf{j} - \mathbf{k}$ or $^-\mathbf{k} - \mathbf{j}$

C3 (a) $\mathbf{n} - \mathbf{m}$ (b) $\mathbf{m} - \mathbf{n}$ (c) $\mathbf{m} + \mathbf{n}$ (d) $^-\mathbf{m} - \mathbf{n}$

C4 (a) $\overrightarrow{AE}$

(b) (i) $2\mathbf{u}$ (ii) $\mathbf{v} - \mathbf{u}$ (iii) $\mathbf{u} - \mathbf{v}$

(iv) $2\mathbf{v} - \mathbf{u}$ (v) $2\mathbf{u} - \mathbf{v}$ (vi) $2\mathbf{u} - 2\mathbf{v}$

C5 (a) (i) $2\mathbf{m}$ (ii) $^-\mathbf{n}$ (iii) $^-2\mathbf{n}$

(iv) $\mathbf{n} - \mathbf{m}$ (v) $\mathbf{m} - \mathbf{n}$ (vi) $^-\mathbf{n} - \mathbf{m}$

(b) (i) $\overrightarrow{CE} = \overrightarrow{CF} + \overrightarrow{FE}$ (ii) $2\mathbf{n} - \mathbf{m}$

(c) (i) $2\mathbf{m} - \mathbf{n}$ (ii) $\mathbf{m} - 2\mathbf{n}$ (iii) $\mathbf{n} - 2\mathbf{m}$

C6 (a) $\mathbf{x} - \mathbf{y}$ (b) $2\mathbf{y}$ (c) $2\mathbf{y} - \mathbf{x}$

C7 (a) AC is a line with B as the mid-point.

(b) AC is a line and B is a point $\frac{2}{3}$ of the way along it from A.

(c) AC is a line with B as the mid-point.

(d) A and C are the same point.

D Fractions of a vector (p 215)

D1 (a)

(b)

(c)

(d)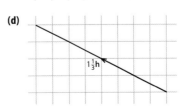

(e)

$-\frac{2}{3}\mathbf{h}$

(f)

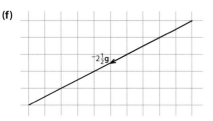

$-2\frac{1}{2}\mathbf{g}$

D2 (a) (i) $\frac{2}{3}\mathbf{p}$ (ii) $\frac{1}{2}\mathbf{q}$ (iii) $\frac{-1}{3}\mathbf{p}$

     (b) (i) $\mathbf{p} + \frac{1}{2}\mathbf{q}$ (ii) $\frac{1}{3}\mathbf{p} + \mathbf{q}$ (iii) $\frac{2}{3}\mathbf{p} + \mathbf{q}$

     (iv) $\frac{1}{3}\mathbf{p} + \frac{1}{2}\mathbf{q}$ (v) $\mathbf{p} - \frac{1}{2}\mathbf{q}$ (vi) $\frac{-1}{2}\mathbf{q} - \frac{1}{3}\mathbf{p}$

D3 (a)–(d)

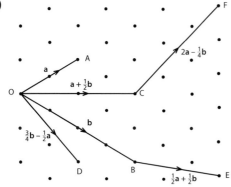

$2\mathbf{a} - \frac{1}{4}\mathbf{b}$

$\mathbf{a} + \frac{1}{2}\mathbf{b}$

$\frac{3}{4}\mathbf{b} - \frac{1}{2}\mathbf{a}$

$\frac{1}{2}\mathbf{a} + \frac{1}{2}\mathbf{b}$

D4 (a) $\frac{1}{2}\mathbf{a}$ (b) $\mathbf{b} + \frac{1}{2}\mathbf{a}$ (c) $\frac{1}{3}\mathbf{b}$

     (d) $\mathbf{a} + \frac{1}{3}\mathbf{b}$ (e) $\frac{2}{3}\mathbf{b}$ (f) $^{-}\mathbf{a} + \frac{2}{3}\mathbf{b}$

E Vector algebra (p 216)

E1 (a) $3\mathbf{a} + 5\mathbf{b}$ (b) $2\mathbf{a} + \mathbf{b}$

     (c) $4\mathbf{a} + 4\mathbf{b}$ or $4(\mathbf{a} + \mathbf{b})$ (d) $\mathbf{a} - 3\mathbf{b}$

     (e) $\mathbf{a} + \frac{2}{3}\mathbf{b}$ (f) $\frac{5}{6}\mathbf{a} + \frac{1}{6}\mathbf{b}$

E2 (a) $6\mathbf{a} - 3\mathbf{b}$ (b) $\frac{1}{2}\mathbf{a} + \mathbf{b}$ (c) $2\mathbf{a} + 2\mathbf{b}$

E3 (a) $\mathbf{b} - \mathbf{a}$ (b) $\frac{1}{3}\mathbf{b} - \frac{1}{3}\mathbf{a}$ or $\frac{1}{3}(\mathbf{b} - \mathbf{a})$

     (c) $\frac{2}{3}\mathbf{a} + \frac{1}{3}\mathbf{b}$

E4 (a) (i) $2\mathbf{u}$ (ii) $\mathbf{v} - \mathbf{u}$ (iii) $2\mathbf{u} + \mathbf{v}$ (iv) $\mathbf{u} + \mathbf{v}$

     (b) (i) $\frac{1}{2}\mathbf{u} + \frac{1}{2}\mathbf{v}$ or $\frac{1}{2}(\mathbf{u} + \mathbf{v})$ (ii) $\frac{3}{2}\mathbf{u} + \frac{1}{2}\mathbf{v}$

     (iii) $\frac{3}{2}\mathbf{u} - \frac{1}{2}\mathbf{v}$

E5 (a) $\mathbf{b} - \mathbf{a}$ (b) $\frac{1}{3}\mathbf{a} + \frac{2}{3}\mathbf{b}$

E6 $\frac{3}{2}\mathbf{a} - \frac{1}{2}\mathbf{b}$

E7 (a) (i) $\mathbf{b} - \mathbf{a}$ (ii) $\mathbf{a} - \mathbf{b}$ (iii) $\frac{1}{3}\mathbf{a} + \frac{1}{3}\mathbf{b}$

         (iv) $\frac{1}{3}\mathbf{a} - \frac{2}{3}\mathbf{b}$ (v) $\frac{-2}{3}\mathbf{a} + \frac{1}{3}\mathbf{b}$

     (b) (i) $\frac{1}{2}\mathbf{b} - \frac{1}{2}\mathbf{a}$ (ii) $\frac{-1}{6}\mathbf{a} - \frac{1}{6}\mathbf{b}$

E8 (a) $2\mathbf{p} - \mathbf{q} + \mathbf{p} + \mathbf{q} = 3\mathbf{p}$ (b) $\begin{bmatrix} 9 \\ 6 \end{bmatrix}$

     (c) $\begin{bmatrix} 3 \\ 2 \end{bmatrix}$ (d) $\begin{bmatrix} 1 \\ -2 \end{bmatrix}$

F Proof by vectors (p 218)

F1 (a) $\overrightarrow{AB} = \mathbf{b} - \mathbf{a}$

         $\overrightarrow{CD} = \frac{2}{3}\mathbf{b} - \frac{2}{3}\mathbf{a} = \frac{2}{3}(\mathbf{b} - \mathbf{a})$

     (b) AB and CD are parallel but CD is $\frac{2}{3}$ of the length of AB.

F2 (a)

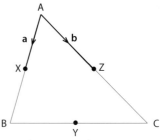

     (b) (i) $\overrightarrow{ZX} = \mathbf{a} - \mathbf{b}$, $\overrightarrow{CB} = 2\mathbf{a} - 2\mathbf{b}$

         (ii) ZX and CB are parallel but CB is twice the length of ZX.

     (c) $\overrightarrow{AY} = \mathbf{a} + \mathbf{b}$

F3 (a) $\mathbf{y} - \mathbf{x}$

     (b) $\frac{1}{2}\mathbf{x}$

     (c) $\frac{1}{2}(\mathbf{y} - \mathbf{x})$

     (d) They are parallel and AB is half the length of ST.

F4 (a) $\mathbf{b} - \mathbf{a}$

     (b) $n = 3$

     (c) AB and CD are parallel so
       $\angle$OBA = $\angle$ODC and $\angle$OAB = $\angle$OCD
       (pairs of corresponding angles). Angles BOA and DOC are identical. As the triangles have the same angles, they are similar.

F5 (a) (i) $2\mathbf{a} + \mathbf{b}$ (ii) $2\mathbf{a} - 2\mathbf{b}$

     (b) $\overrightarrow{SQ} = 3\mathbf{a} - 3\mathbf{b} = 3(\mathbf{a} - \mathbf{b})$ and
       $\overrightarrow{SX} = 2\mathbf{a} - 2\mathbf{b} = 2(\mathbf{a} - \mathbf{b})$. So SX and SQ are parallel. Since they both go through S, the points must be on the same line.

F6 (a) $\overrightarrow{AM} = \frac{1}{2}\mathbf{u} + \frac{3}{2}\mathbf{v}$, $\overrightarrow{NM} = \frac{1}{2}(\mathbf{u} - \mathbf{v})$

     (b) $\overrightarrow{NO} = 2(\mathbf{u} - \mathbf{v})$

     (c) $\overrightarrow{NM}$ and $\overrightarrow{NO}$ are parallel and, since both go through N, must be on the same line.

     (d) Since $\overrightarrow{NM} = \frac{1}{2}(\mathbf{u} - \mathbf{v})$ and $\overrightarrow{NO} = 2(\mathbf{u} - \mathbf{v})$,
       NM = $\frac{1}{4}$NO.

F7 (a) (i) $\mathbf{a} + \mathbf{b}$ (ii) $2\mathbf{a} + \mathbf{b}$ (iii) $\mathbf{b} - \mathbf{a}$

     (b) $2\mathbf{b} + \mathbf{a}$

(c) $\overrightarrow{OF} = \overrightarrow{OC} + \overrightarrow{CF} = 2\mathbf{a} + \mathbf{b} + 2\mathbf{b} + \mathbf{a}$
$= 3\mathbf{a} + 3\mathbf{b} = 3(\mathbf{a} + \mathbf{b}) = 3\overrightarrow{OD}$. So OD and OF are
parallel and both go through O. So the points O, D
and F lie on the same line.

F8

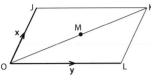

$\overrightarrow{OK} = \overrightarrow{OL} + \overrightarrow{LK} = \mathbf{x} + \mathbf{y}$ so $\overrightarrow{OM} = \frac{1}{2}(\mathbf{x} + \mathbf{y})$
$\overrightarrow{JM} = \overrightarrow{JO} + \overrightarrow{OM} = {}^-\mathbf{x} + \frac{1}{2}(\mathbf{x} + \mathbf{y}) = \frac{1}{2}\mathbf{y} - \frac{1}{2}\mathbf{x} = \frac{1}{2}(\mathbf{y} - \mathbf{x})$
$\overrightarrow{JL} = \overrightarrow{JO} + \overrightarrow{OL} = \mathbf{y} - \mathbf{x}$
So $\overrightarrow{JM} = \frac{1}{2}\overrightarrow{JL}$ showing that M is the mid-point of JL

F9 (a) $\overrightarrow{OQ} = \frac{1}{2}(\mathbf{a} + \mathbf{b})$, $\overrightarrow{OP} = \frac{1}{3}(\mathbf{a} + \mathbf{b})$

(b) $\overrightarrow{AR} = \frac{1}{2}\mathbf{b} - \mathbf{a}$

(c) $\overrightarrow{AT} = \frac{1}{3}\mathbf{b} - \frac{2}{3}\mathbf{a}$

(d) $\overrightarrow{OT} = \frac{1}{3}(\mathbf{a} + \mathbf{b})$

(e) T and P are the same point.

(f) $\overrightarrow{OX} = \frac{1}{3}(\mathbf{a} + \mathbf{b})$
Proof:
$\overrightarrow{BS} = \frac{1}{2}\mathbf{a} - \mathbf{b}$
$\overrightarrow{BX} = \frac{1}{3}\mathbf{a} - \frac{2}{3}\mathbf{b}$
$\overrightarrow{OX} = \mathbf{b} + \frac{1}{3}\mathbf{a} - \frac{2}{3}\mathbf{b} = \frac{1}{3}(\mathbf{a} + \mathbf{b})$

Test yourself (p 221)

T1 (a) (i) $\mathbf{r} - \mathbf{s}$ **(ii)** $\frac{3}{4}(\mathbf{r} - \mathbf{s})$

(b) $\frac{3}{4}\mathbf{r} + \frac{1}{4}\mathbf{s}$

T2 (a) (i) $\mathbf{a} + \mathbf{b}$ **(ii)** $\mathbf{b} - \mathbf{a}$ **(iii)** $\mathbf{a} + 2\mathbf{b}$

(b) (i)

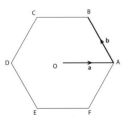

(ii) $3\mathbf{b}$

T3 (a) (i) $\mathbf{a} - 2\mathbf{b}$ **(ii)** $\frac{1}{3}\mathbf{a} + \frac{1}{3}\mathbf{b}$ **(iii)** $\frac{2}{3}\mathbf{a} + \frac{2}{3}\mathbf{b}$

(b) $\overrightarrow{MQ}$ and $\overrightarrow{OP}$ are both multiples of $\mathbf{a} + \mathbf{b}$ and so are
parallel. Hence OMQP is a trapezium.

T4 (a) $2\mathbf{a} + 4\mathbf{c}$

(b) $\overrightarrow{OM} = \overrightarrow{OC} + \overrightarrow{CM} = 6\mathbf{c} + 3\mathbf{a} = 3\mathbf{a} + 6\mathbf{c}$
$\overrightarrow{OP} = \frac{2}{3}\overrightarrow{OM}$ so OM and OP are parallel and both go
through O. So OPM is a straight line.

Review 4 (p 222)

1 Greatest possible height: 142.5 cm
Least possible height: 137.5 cm

2 (a) $AB^2 + BC^2 = 4.5^2 + 6^2 = 20.25 + 36 = 56.25$
$AC^2 = 7.5^2 = 56.25$
So $AB^2 + BC^2 = AC^2$ showing that $\angle ABC = 90°$ and
so is the angle in a semicircle with diameter AC.
This puts B on the circumference.

(b) An accurate full-size drawing of the required triangle

(c) (i) The mid-point of AC found and marked by use
of straight-edge and compasses

(ii) The circle drawn as shown

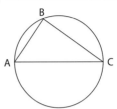

3 A (0, 3, 0)   B (2, 3, 0)   C (2, 0, 0)   D (2, 0, 1)
E (0, 0, 1)   F (0, 3, 1)   O (0, 0, 0)

4 (a) 19.5%   **(b)** 917

5 3.86

6

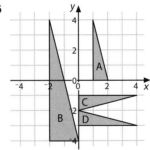

(a) Scale factor 2, centre of enlargement (4, 4)

(b) (i) Triangle C marked on the diagram as above

(ii) Rotation of 90° clockwise about (0, 0)

(c) Triangle D marked on the diagram as above

7 (a) 52° (Angle at the centre is double the angle at the
circumference so $\angle ABC = 104° \div 2$)

(b) 128° (Opposite angles of a cyclic quadrilateral add
up to 180° so $\angle ADC = 180° - 52°$)

(c) 38° (Triangle OAC is isosceles so
$\angle OCA = (180° - 104°) \div 2$)

(d) 12° (Triangle OBC is isosceles so
$\angle OBC = \angle OCB = 40°$.
$\angle ABC = 52°$ so $\angle OBA = 52° - 40° = 12°$.
Triangle OAB is isosceles so $\angle OAB = \angle OBA$.)

8 (a) $\dfrac{8+a^2}{4a}$ (b) $\dfrac{5x+4}{6}$

   (c) $-\dfrac{1}{(p+1)(2p+1)}$ (d) $\dfrac{3y^2+2y+1}{(y+1)(y-1)}$

9 (a) 75° ($\angle$DBC = $\angle$CDE = 35° (alternate segment) so
     $\angle$BCD = 180° − (70° + 35°) (angles in a triangle))

   (b) 105° ($\angle$BAD = 180° − 75° as BAD and BCD are
     opposite angles in a cyclic quadrilateral.)

10 (a) 240 watts   (b) 19.3%

11 (a) $^-2m + 2p$ or $2p - 2m$ (b) $^-p + m$ or $m - p$
   (c) $m + p$

12 (a) (i) 5   (ii) 2   (iii) $\frac{4}{5}$

   (b) (i) $^-4$ (ii) $\frac{1}{2}$ (iii) $\frac{-1}{2}$ (iv) $\frac{2}{3}$

13 (a) $x = 7$ (b) $x = 12$ (c) $x = {}^-1.5, 3$
   (d) $x = 0, 2$ (e) $x = 5$ (f) $x = {}^-0.48, 4.15$

14 Radius: $\sqrt{13}$ units
   Area: 13π square units
   Circumference: $2\sqrt{13}\,\pi$ units

15 (a) 9.7 cm   (b) 36°   (c) 54°

16 (a) (i) $\frac{2}{9}$ (ii) 4   (iii) 2

   (b) $5\frac{5}{2}$

   (c) 9

17 (a) (i) $\frac{1}{2}b$ (ii) $\frac{-1}{6}a$ (iii) $\frac{1}{2}b - \frac{1}{6}a$ (iv) $b - \frac{1}{3}a$

   (b) The line segments are parallel and DF is twice as
     long as EG.

18 48.84 m.p.h.

19 $\dfrac{120}{\pi}$ cm

20 (a) $t = \dfrac{d}{a_1} + \dfrac{d}{a_2}$ (b) $d = \dfrac{a_1 a_2 t}{a_1 + a_2}$

28 Circles and equations

A Equation of a circle (p 225)

A1 When $x = 3$ and $y = 4$, $x^2 + y^2 = 3^2 + 4^2 = 9 + 16 = 25$
   so $(3, 4)$ is a point on the circle $x^2 + y^2 = 25$.

A2 (a) A
   (b) B: $x^2 + y^2 = 9$, C: $x^2 + y^2 = 16$

A3 (a) A sketch of circle with centre $(0, 0)$ and radius 7
   (b) The point $(3, 2)$ is inside the circle so any straight
     line through this point must cut the circle in two
     places.

A4 (a) $(^-10, 0)$ and $(10, 0)$
   (b) $(0, {}^-10), ({}^-6, {}^-8), \left(1, {}^-\sqrt{99}\right), \left({}^-5, \sqrt{75}\right)$

A5 (a) 8   (b) 20   (c) $\sqrt{11}$

A6 (a) $x^2 + y^2 = 36$ (b) $x^2 + y^2 = 1$ (c) $x^2 + y^2 =$
   (d) $x^2 + y^2 = 7$ (e) $x^2 + y^2 = 18$

B Intersection of a line and a circle (p 226)

B1 (a) At the points of intersection,
$$x^2 + (x + 5)^2 = 17$$
$$x^2 + x^2 + 10x + 25 = 17$$
$$2x^2 + 10x + 8 = 0$$
     and dividing both sides by 2 gives
$$x^2 + 5x + 4 = 0$$

   (b) G $(^-4, 1)$, H $(^-1, 4)$

B2 (a) A sketch of circle with centre $(0, 0)$ and radius 3
   (b) $y = 2x - 3$ added to the sketch
   (c) $(0, {}^-3), (2\frac{2}{5}, 1\frac{4}{5})$

B3 P $(1, 7)$, Q $(^-7, {}^-1)$ (or vice versa)

B4 (a) A $(^-1.8, {}^-0.8)$, B $(0.8, 1.8)$
   (b) A $(^-1.82, {}^-0.82)$, B $(0.82, 1.82)$

B5 P $(0.77, 2.54)$, Q $(^-1.57, {}^-2.14)$ (or vice versa)

B6 (a) The quadratic has no real solutions.
   (b) The line and the
     circle do not meet.

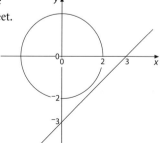

B7 (a) $x = 2, y = 1$
   (b) The line and the circle touch at just one point.

B8 (a) $x = 4, y = 3$ and $x = {}^-3, y = {}^-4$

    (b) $x = 2, y = 1$ and $x = 2.2, y = 0.4$

    (c) $x = 1.8, y = {}^-1.6$ and $x = {}^-1.4, y = {}^-3.2$

B9 (a) $x^2 + y^2 = 81$

    (b) $y = 5 - x$

    (c) A $({}^-3.35, 8.35)$, B $(8.35, {}^-3.35)$

B10 (a) $x = 3, y = 1$ and $x = 1, y = 3$

    (b) $x = 2, y = 1$ and $x = {}^-1, y = {}^-2$

    (c) $x = 1.4, y = {}^-0.2$ and $x = {}^-1, y = {}^-1$

Test yourself (p 228)

T1 (a) A sketch of circle with centre $(0, 0)$ and radius 11

    (b) $(0, 11), (0, {}^-11)$

T2 $x^2 + y^2 = 9$

T3 (a) At the points of intersection,
$$x^2 + (2x - 1)^2 = 2$$
$$x^2 + 4x^2 - 4x + 1 = 2$$
which rearranges to $5x^2 - 4x - 1 = 0$

    (b) A $({}^-\frac{1}{5}, {}^-1\frac{2}{5})$, B $(1, 1)$

T4 (a) The radius is $\sqrt{50}$.

Now $\sqrt{50}$ is between $\sqrt{49}$ and $\sqrt{64}$ so the radius is between 7 and 8.

    (b) (i) 50

        (ii)

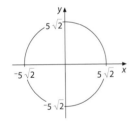

or

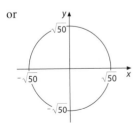

    (c) $x = 7, y = 1$ and $x = {}^-1, y = {}^-7$

T5 A $(2.30, 5.89)$, B $({}^-1.70, {}^-6.09)$ (or vice versa) correct to 2 d.p.

T6 (a) At the points of intersection x would satisfy the equation $x^2 + 6^2 = 25$. The equation rearranges to $x^2 = {}^-11$ which has no real solutions. Hence Bill is incorrect.

    (b) $x = {}^-1\frac{2}{5}, y = {}^-4\frac{4}{5}$ and $x = 3, y = 4$

T7 $x = 2, y = 5$ and $x = {}^-5, y = {}^-2$

T8 (a) (i) $\sqrt{3^2 + 4^2} = 5$ so, by Pythagoras, the point $(3, 4)$ is 5 units from $(0, 0)$. The centre of the circle is $(0, 0)$ and its radius is $\sqrt{27}$ which is greater than 5. Hence $(3, 4)$ is inside the circle.

        (ii) $3 + 4 = 7$ so the point $(3, 4)$ is on the line $x + y = 7$. As this point is inside the circle then the line goes through the circle and hence cuts it at two points.

    (b) $(2.38, 4.62)$ and $(4.62, 2.38)$

29 Congruent triangles

A 'Fixing' a triangle (p 230)

A1 A and H (SSS), B and G (ASA), C and E (RHS), D and F (SAS)

B Proving that two triangles are congruent (p 232)

B1 (a) AM = MB (given)
OM = OM (common side)
OA = OB (equal radii)
So triangle OAM is congruent to triangle OBM (SSS).

    (b) AMB is a straight line,
so $\angle$OMA + $\angle$OMB = 180°.
$\angle$OMA and $\angle$OMB are equal, so they are both right angles.

B2 PQ = SR (given)
$\angle$PQT = $\angle$SRT (alternate)
$\angle$QPT = $\angle$RST (alternate)
So triangle PTQ is congruent to triangle STR (ASA).

B3 JK = JL (sides of equilateral triangle)
KM = LN (given)
$\angle$JKM = $\angle$JLN (both 120°)
So triangle JKM is congruent to triangle JLN (SAS).

C Proving by congruent triangles (p 233)

C1 AB = AC (given)
AM = AM (common side)
BM = CM (given)
So triangle ABM is congruent to triangle ACM (SSS).

C2 (a) PQ = PS (given)
QR = SR (given)
PR = PR (common side)
So triangle PQR is congruent to triangle PSR (SSS).

(b) ∠PSR

C3 (a) ∠AXP = ∠AXQ = 90° (given)
AX = AX (common side)
AP = AQ (hypotenuse, given)
So triangle XAP is congruent to triangle XAQ (RHS).

(b) XP = XQ

C4 (a) VA = VB (given)
∠VAK = ∠VBL (alternate)
∠VKA = ∠VLB (alternate)
So triangle VAK is congruent to triangle VBL (ASA).

(b) AK = BL, VK = VL

C5 (a) PQ = PR (given)
∠QPS = ∠RPS (given)
PS = PS (common side)
So triangle PQS is congruent to triangle PRS (SAS).

(b) QS = RS, ∠QSP = ∠RSP, ∠PQS = ∠PRS

C6 (a) ∠AXO = ∠AYO = 90° (tangent perpendicular to radius)
AO = AO (common side, hypotenuse)
OX = OY (equal radii)
So triangle AOX and AOY are congruent (RHS).

(b) AX = AY

C7 AP = AQ (equal radii)
BP = BQ (equal radii)
AB = AB (common side)
So triangle APB is congruent to triangle AQB (SSS).
So ∠APB = ∠AQB.

C8 ∠OPA = ∠OPB = 90° (given)
OA = OB (equal radii)
OP = OP (common side)
So triangle OPA is congruent to triangle OPB (RHS).
So PA = PB, so P is the mid-point of AB.

D Justifying ruler-and-compasses constructions (p 235)

D1 Join **BD** and **CD**.
In the triangles ABD and **ACD**,
AD = **AD** (common side)
AB = AC (equal radii)
BD = **CD** (**equal radii**)
So triangles ABD and **ACD** are congruent (reason: **SSS**)
So angle DAB = angle **DAC**

D2 (a) PC = PC (common side)
PA = PB (equal radii)
AC = BC (equal radii)
So triangle APC is congruent to triangle BPC (SSS)
So ∠APC = ∠BPC

(b) APB is a line segment, so ∠APC + ∠BPC = 180°, and since they are equal each angle is a right angle.

D3 (a) (i) PA = PB (equal radii)
AD = BD (equal radii)
PD = PD (common side)
So triangle APD is congruent to triangle BPD (SSS).

(ii) So ∠APD = ∠BPD

(b) (i) PA = PB (equal radii)
PE = PE (common side)
∠APE = ∠BPE (proved)
So triangle PEA is congruent to triangle PEB (SAS).

(ii) So ∠PEA = ∠PEB
AEB is a line segment so ∠PEA + ∠PEB = 180° so each angle is a right angle.

D4

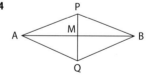

In triangles APQ and BPQ,
AP = BP (equal radii)
AQ = BQ (equal radii)
PQ = PQ (common side)
So triangle APQ is congruent to triangle BPQ (SSS).
So ∠APQ = ∠BPQ
In triangles APM and BPM,
AP = BP (equal radii)
PM = PM (common side)
∠APM = ∠BPM (proved above)
So triangle APM is congruent to triangle BPM (SAS).
So AM = BM and ∠PMA = ∠PMB
AMB is a line segment, so ∠PMA and ∠PMB are right angles.
So PQ is the perpendicular bisector of AB.

T1 (a) The required diagram

(b) AB = CD (given)
OA = OC (equal radii)
OB = OD (equal radii)
So triangle AOB is congruent to triangle COD (SSS).
So ∠AOB = ∠COD

T2 (a) OA = OC (equal radii)
OB = OB (common side)
∠OAB = ∠OCB = 90°
(tangent perpendicular to radius)
So triangle OAB is congruent to triangle OCB (RHS).
So AB = CB

(b) (i) ∠AOB = (360° − 250°) ÷ 2 = 55°
(angles round point = 360°)
so x = 180°− 90° − 55° = 35°
(angles in a triangle)

(ii) y = 55° (angle at centre = twice angle at circumference)

T3 In triangles BQC and CPB,
∠QCB = ∠PBC (given)
CB = BC (common)
∠QBC = ∠PCB (each half of the angles given as equal)
So triangles BQC and CPB are congruent (ASA).
So PB = QC

T4 (a) ∠ABC and ∠EBG are right angles.
So ∠ABG = 90° + ∠CBG
and ∠CBE = ∠CBG + 90°
So ∠ABG = ∠CBE

(b) ∠ABG = ∠CBE (proved in (a))
AB = CB (sides of square ABCD)
BG = BE (sides of square BEFG)
So triangle ABG is congruent to triangle CBE (SAS).
So AG = CE

30 Proof

A Proving a statement is false with a counterexample
(p 238)

A1 Statement C is false: for example, $3 \times 5 = 15$ where 3 and 5 are odd but 15 is not even.

A2 There are many counterexamples: for example, for $n = 6$, $6n − 1 = 35$, which is 5×7 (not prime).

A3 No: for example, $\sqrt{0.25} = 0.5$ but 0.5 is greater than 0.25.

A4 For each of these there are many counterexamples. Only one is given in each case.
(a) For $n = 3$, $3n + 1 = 10$ (even)
(b) For $n = 1.5$, $2n = 3$ (odd)
(c) For $n = {}^-1$, $2^n = \frac{1}{2}$ (less than 1)
(d) For $n = 11$, $2n^2 + 11 = 253$ which is 11×23 (not prime)

A5 A counterexample is: for $x = 2$ and $y = 4$,
$(x + y)^2 = 6^2 = 36$ but $x^2 + y^2 = 2^2 + 4^2 = 20$.
Alternatively, $(x + y)^2 = x^2 + y^2 + 2xy \neq x^2 + y^2$ in general.

A6 For each of these there are many counterexamples. Only one is given in each case.
(a) $k = {}^-3$ is a number that makes $k^2 > 0$ true as $({}^-3)^2 = 9 > 0$. However $k > 0$ is false as ${}^-3$ is not greater than 0.
(b) $k = 6$ is an even number but $\frac{k}{2} = 3$, which is not even.
(c) $p = 13$ is a prime number but $p + 2 = 15$, which is not prime.
(d) $a = {}^-2$ is less than 1 and $b = {}^-3$ is less than 1 but $ab = {}^-2 \times {}^-3 = 6$, which is not less than 1.

B Algebraic proof (p 239)

Only one proof is given in each case. There may be alternative valid proofs.

B1 An odd and an even number can be written $2a + 1$ and $2b$ where a and b are integers. The product is $2b(2a + 1) = 2(2ab + b)$, which is even.

B2 B, C, D, E and F

B3 (a) The sum of an odd and an even number is odd. Hence $P + Q$ is odd and so $P + Q − 1$ is even.

(b) $P = 1$ is an odd number and $Q = 2$ is an even number, giving $P + Q − 1 = 2$, which is prime.

B4 The sum of seven consecutive numbers can be written $k + (k + 1) + (k + 2) + (k + 3) + (k + 4) + (k + 5) + (k + 6)$ for some integer k. The sum simplifies to $7k + 21 = 7(k + 3)$, which is divisible by 7.

B5 **(a)** The sum of two consecutive even numbers can be written $2k + (2k + 2)$ for some integer k. The sum simplifies to $4k + 2$. Hence the remainder on dividing by 4 is 2 so the sum is not divisible by 4.

 (b) The sum of two consecutive odd numbers can be written $(2k + 1) + (2k + 3)$ for some integer k. The sum simplifies to $4k + 4 = 4(k + 1)$, which is divisible by 4.

B6 Three consecutive numbers can be written $k, k + 1$ and $k + 2$. Multiplying the first and last and adding 1 gives $k(k + 2) + 1$ which expands to $k^2 + 2k + 1$ and factorises to $(k + 1)^2$, which is the middle number squared.

B7 Four consecutive numbers can be written $k, k + 1, k + 2$ and $k + 3$. The product of the first and last is $k(k + 3)$, which expands to $k^2 + 3k$. The product of the middle two numbers is $(k + 1)(k + 2)$, which expands to $k^2 + 3k + 2$. This is 2 more than the product of the first and last.

B8 **(a)** $(k + 1)^2$

 (b) $(k + 1)^2 - k^2 = k^2 + 2k + 1 - k^2 = 2k + 1$ which is odd.

B9 The sum of three consecutive squares can be written $k^2 + (k + 1)^2 + (k + 2)^2$, which expands to $k^2 + k^2 + 2k + 1 + k^2 + 4k + 4$ and simplifies to $3k^2 + 6k + 5$. The expression $3k^2 + 6k + 5$ can be written as $3(k^2 + 2k + 2) - 1$, which is one less than a multiple of 3.

B10 **(a)** Out of three consecutive numbers either one is odd and two are even or one is even and two are odd. In both cases at least one of the numbers is even.

 (b) Every third integer is a multiple of 3 so it is impossible to have three consecutive numbers where none of them is a multiple of 3.

 (c) Since at least one of the numbers is even, the product must be a multiple of 2. Since one of the numbers is a multiple of 3, the product must be a multiple of 3. A number which is a multiple of 2 and 3 is also multiple of 6.

B11 **(a)** $(p + q)(p - q)$

 (b) $n^2 - 1$

 (c) The product of two consecutive terms of this sequence can be written $(k^2 - 1)((k + 1)^2 - 1)$. As each expression is a difference of two squares it can be factorised to $(k + 1)(k - 1)((k + 1) + 1)((k + 1) - 1)$ or $(k + 1)(k - 1)(k + 2)(k)$, which rearranges to $(k - 1)k(k + 1)(k + 2)$, namely the product of four consecutive numbers.

B12 $k^2 - 1$ can be written as $(k + 1)(k - 1)$. When $k = 1$, $(k + 1)(k - 1) = 2 \times 0 = 0$ which is not prime. When $k = 2$, $(k + 1)(k - 1) = 3 \times 1 = 3$ which is prime. When $k > 2$, both $(k + 1)$ and $(k - 1)$ are greater than 1 so the product cannot be prime (having at least two factors greater than 1). Hence there is only one prime number of the form $k^2 - 1$.

B13 A triangle number can be written $\frac{1}{2}k(k + 1)$ for some integer k. $8 \times \frac{1}{2}k(k + 1) + 1 = 4k(k + 1) + 1 = 4k^2 + 4k + 1 = (2k + 1)^2$ which is the square of an odd number. An odd number squared is itself an odd number so the result is an odd square number.

Test yourself (p 241)

T1 **(a)** Any multiple of 4 will show that Jo is wrong. For example, when $k = 4$, $\frac{1}{2}k + 1 = 3$, which is odd.

 (b) Any counterexample where a or b is 2. For example, $a = 2$ and $b = 3$ are both prime numbers and $a + b = 5$, which is odd.

T2 p is an odd number so p^2 is the product of two odd numbers and hence odd. So $p^2 + 1$ is even.

T3 In any pair of consecutive multiples of 3, one number is even and one is odd. The product of an even and an odd number is even, so the product of any pair of consecutive multiples of 3 is even.

T4 Three consecutive numbers can be written $k, k + 1$ and $k + 2$ where k is an integer. The sum is $k + (k + 1) + (k + 2) = 3k + 3 = 3(k + 1)$, which is divisible by 3.

T5 $(n + 1)^2 - (n - 1)^2 = (n^2 + 2n + 1) - (n^2 - 2n + 1) = 4n$ which is a multiple of 4 when n is a positive integer.

T6 Three consecutive numbers can be written $k, k + 1$ and $k + 2$. The difference between the squares of the first and last is $(k + 2)^2 - k^2$ which expands and simplifies to $4k + 4$ and factorises to $4(k + 1)$, which is 4 times the middle number.

T7 (a) (i) n and $n + 1$ are consecutive integers. In any pair of consecutive integers, one is even and one is odd. The product of an even and an odd number is even, so $n(n + 1)$, which is the product of any pair of consecutive integers, is even.

(ii) $2n$ is an even number for any positive integer n. Hence $2n + 1$ is odd (being one more than an even number).

(b) $(2n + 1)^2 = 4n^2 + 4n + 1$

(c) Where n is an integer, $2n + 1$ is an odd number whose square is $4n^2 + 4n + 1$.
Now $4n^2 + 4n + 1 = 4n(n + 1) + 1$. If n is even then $4n$ is a multiple of 8 and so $4n(n + 1)$ is a multiple of 8. If n is odd then $(n + 1)$ is even and so $4n(n + 1)$ is a multiple of 8. In either case, $4n(n + 1) + 1$ is 1 more than a multiple of 8 and so the square of any odd number is always 1 more than a multiple of 8.

T8 (a) $(2a - 1)^2 - (2b - 1)^2$
$= (4a^2 - 4a + 1) - (4b^2 - 4b + 1)$
$= 4a^2 - 4a - 4b^2 + 4b$
$= 4(a^2 - a - b^2 + b)$
$4(a - b)(a + b - 1)$
$= 4(a^2 + ab - a - ba - b^2 + b)$
$= 4(a^2 - a - b^2 + b)$
Hence $(2a - 1)^2 - (2b - 1)^2 = 4(a - b)(a + b - 1)$

(b) Where a and b are integers, $2a - 1$ and $2b - 1$ are odd numbers. The difference between the squares of these odd numbers is $(2a - 1)^2 - (2b - 1)^2$ which is equivalent to $4(a - b)(a + b - 1)$.
If a and b are both odd or both even, then $a - b$ is even and hence $4(a - b)$ is a multiple of 8. If one of a and b is odd and one is even, then $a + b - 1$ is even and hence $4(a + b - 1)$ is a multiple of 8.
In either case $4(a - b)(a + b - 1)$ is a multiple of 8 and so the difference between the squares of any two odd numbers is a multiple of 8.

31 Extending trigonometry to any triangle

A Revision: trigonometry and Pythagoras (p 242)

A1 (a) 7.3 cm   **(b)** 6.2 cm   **(c)** 23.6 cm
(d) 12.1 cm   **(e)** 14.3 cm   **(f)** 11.8 cm
(g) 17.0 cm   **(h)** 11.7 cm

A2 (a) 47°   **(b)** 42°   **(c)** 31°

A3 (a) $w \tan A$ **(b)** $k \cos P$ **(c)** $\dfrac{m}{\sin L}$
(d) $\dfrac{g}{\cos B}$ **(e)** $d \tan M$ **(f)** $\dfrac{v}{\tan D}$

B The sine rule: finding a side (p 243)

B1 (a) 5.142 cm   **(b)** 5.7 cm
(c) A drawing and check

B2 (a) $b \sin A$ **(b)** $a \sin B$

B3 (a) 3.8 cm   **(b)** 7.1 cm   **(c)** 3.8 cm

B4 (a) 80°   **(b)** 5.7 cm   **(c)** 6.7 cm

B5 $x = 10.6$ cm, $p = 9.2$ cm, $q = 7.6$ cm, $m = 6.0$ cm, $n = 8.3$ cm

B6 (a) 5.8 cm   **(b)** 12.5 cm   **(c)** 14.4 cm

B7 (a) 192.6 m   **(b)** 110 m to the nearest metre

C The sine rule: finding an angle (p 246)

C1 (a) 0.8586...; 59° and 121°; it has to be 59° because 121° + 75° is greater than 180°.
(b) 0.6439...; 40° and 140°; it has to be 40° because 140° + 105° is greater than 180°.

C2 (a) 0.8668...; 60° and 120°; either seems possible: 60° + 52° =112° so angle P = 68°, and 120° + 52° = 172° so angle P = 8°.
(b) If RP is drawn first and the line from R on which Q will lie is drawn second, and then an arc is drawn from P with radius 10 cm, the arc crosses the second line in two places. These are the two possible positions for Q, so there are two possible triangles.

C3 **(a)** 1.1367...; as this is greater than 1 no angle has this value as its sine.

(b) Using the drawing approach as in C2, the 5.5 cm radius arc does not reach the required line. It is not possible to have a triangle with the given measurements, hence the impossible sine.

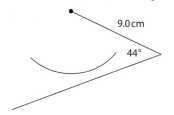

9.0 cm

44°

D The cosine rule (p 247)

D1 **(a)** 2.113 cm **(b)** 4.532 cm **(c)** 6.887 cm **(d)** 8.2 cm

D2 **(a)** $b - x$ **(b)** $a^2 - (b - x)^2$ **(c)** $c^2 - x^2$

D3 $a^2 = (b - x)^2 + c^2 - x^2$
$= b^2 - 2bx + x^2 + c^2 - x^2$
$= b^2 + c^2 - 2bx$

D4 $c \cos A$

D5 $a^2 = 67.96...$, so $a = 8.2$ cm (to 1 d.p.), the same answer as for D1(d)

D6 **(a)** 4.1 cm **(b)** 12.4 cm **(c)** 7.6 cm

D7 10.3 cm (to 1 d.p.)

D8 28.7 km (to 1 d.p.)

D9 **(a)** 47° **(b)** 102° **(c)** 73°

D10 $a = 5$ cm using the cosine rule. But this is also the result you would expect from Pythagoras. This happens because $\cos A = 0$ when $A = 90°$, so the term $2bc \cos A$ disappears.

E The sine formula for the area of a triangle (p 250)

E1 16 cm²

E2 **(a)** 7.518 cm **(b)** 38 cm²

E3 **(a)** $c \sin A$ **(b)** $\frac{1}{2} bc \sin A$

E4 **(a)** 36 cm² **(b)** 59 cm² **(c)** 116 cm²

E5 42.4 cm² (to 1 d.p.)

F Mixed questions (p 251)

F1 **(a)** Cosine rule
(b) Sine rule
(c) Cosine rule
(d) Sine rule
(e) Sine rule (two different triangles may be drawn)

F2 **(a)** 27.9 cm² (to 1 d.p.) **(b)** 11.0 cm (to 1 d.p.)
(c) 175° to the nearest degree

F3 7.9 cm (to 1 d.p.)

F4 19 km (to 2 s.f.)

F5 **(a)** 56.4 cm² **(b)** 7.84 cm

F6 **(a)** 127° to the nearest degree
(b) 16.1 cm

F7 **(a)** 6.54 m **(b)** 41.4 m

Test yourself (p 252)

T1 **(a)** 7.5 m (to 1 d.p.) **(b)** 15.6 m (to 1 d.p.)
(c) 76.9 m² (to 1 d.p.)

T2 Bearing = 322° to the nearest degree, distance = 21 km to the nearest km

32 Transforming graphs

A Working with quadratic expressions in the form $(x + a)^2 + b$ (p 253)

A1 **(a)** **(i)** 4 **(ii)** 16 **(iii)** 9 **(iv)** 49 **(v)** 0
(b) 0
(c) **(i)** 7 **(ii)** 1 **(iii)** ⁻5

A2 **(a)** Minimum value 3 at $x = 4$
(b) Minimum value 5 at $x = ⁻2$
(c) Minimum value ⁻6 at $x = 3$
(d) Minimum value 0 at $x = ⁻1$

A3 **(a)** **(i)** $(x + 3)^2 = x^2 + 6x + 9$
(ii) $(x + 3)^2 - 5 = x^2 + 6x + 9 - 5$
$= x^2 + 6x + 4$
(b) ⁻5

A4 **(a)** $(x - 5)^2 + 1$ **(b)** 1

A5 A and Y, B and Z, C and X

A6 **(a)** $y = (x - 4)^2 + 2$ **(b)** $(0, 18)$

A7 A sketch of a parabola which has a minimum shown a ($⁻4, 1$) and cuts the y-axis at $(0, 17)$

A8 $(x-3)^2 - 16 = 0$

$(x-3)^2 = 16$

$x - 3 = \pm 4$

$x = \pm 4 + 3$

So the solutions are $x = 7$ and $x = {}^-1$

A9 (a) $x = 1, 7$ (b) $x = 6, {}^-2$ (c) $x = 2, {}^-8$

A10 (a) The minimum point of the graph of
$y = (x-5)^2 + 1$ is $(5, 1)$ which is above the x-axis
so the graph does not cut the x-axis.

(b) At points $(4, 0)$ and $(6, 0)$

B Completing the square (p 255)

B1 A and D

B2 (a) $x^2 + 4x + 5 = (x+2)^2 + 1$

(b) $x^2 - 8x + 19 = (x-4)^2 + 3$

(c) $x^2 + 10x + 11 = (x+5)^2 - 14$

(d) $x^2 - 6x + 2 = (x-3)^2 - 7$

B3 (a) $(x+3)^2 + 6$ has a minimum of 6.

(b) $(x+1)^2 + 4$ has a minimum of 4.

(c) $(x+4)^2 + 4$ has a minimum of 4.

(d) $(x+2)^2 - 3$ has a minimum of $^-3$.

(e) $(x+5)^2 - 17$ has a minimum of $^-17$.

(f) $(x+6)^2 - 32$ has a minimum of $^-32$.

B4 (a) $(x-2)^2 + 3$ has a minimum of 3.

(b) $(x-1)^2 + 4$ has a minimum of 4.

(c) $(x-3)^2 + 5$ has a minimum of 5.

(d) $(x-2)^2 - 1$ has a minimum of $^-1$.

(e) $(x-5)^2 - 17$ has a minimum of $^-17$.

(f) $(x-7)^2 - 9$ has a minimum of $^-9$.

B5 $(x-4)^2 + 5; a = 4, b = 5$

B6 $(x+3)^2 - 7; p = 3, q = 7$

B7 (a) $x^2 + 6x - 1 = (x+3)^2 - 10$

(b) $x^2 - 8x - 3 = (x-4)^2 - 19$

(c) $x^2 + 8x = (x+4)^2 - 16$

(d) $x^2 - 14x = (x-7)^2 - 49$

B8 $(x+4)^2 = x^2 + 8x + 16$ so $x^2 + 8x + 11 = (x+4)^2 - 5$
If $(x+4)^2 - 5 = (x+p)^2 + q$ then $p = 4$ and $q = {}^-5$.

B9 (a) $(x+2)^2 - 2; a = 2, b = {}^-2$

(b) $(x+1)^2 - 4; a = 1, b = {}^-4$

(c) $(x+4)^2 - 19; a = 4, b = {}^-19$

(d) $(x-3)^2 + 4; a = {}^-3, b = 4$

(e) $(x-1)^2 - 6; a = {}^-1, b = {}^-6$

(f) $(x-5)^2 - 30; a = {}^-5, b = {}^-30$

B10 (a) $a = 6, b = {}^-16$

(b) $(6, {}^-16)$

(c) A sketch of a parabola which has a minimum
$(6, {}^-16)$ and cuts the y-axis at $(0, 20)$

B11 (a) $y = (x-2)^2 - 7$

(b) A sketch of a parabola which has a minimum
$(2, {}^-7)$ and cuts the y-axis at $(0, {}^-3)$

B12 (a) $(x+2)^2 - 9$

(b) (i) From part (a), $x^2 + 4x - 5 = 0$ is equivalent to
$(x+2)^2 - 9 = 0$. Adding 9 to each side gives
$(x+2)^2 = 9$.

(ii) $x = 1, {}^-5$

B13 (a) $(x-3)^2 - 2$ (b) $x = 1.59, 4.41$

B14 (a) $9x^2 + 12x + 4$ (b) $(3x+2)^2 + 1$

B15 (a) $x^2 + 3x + 2 = \left(x+\frac{3}{2}\right)^2 - \frac{1}{4}$ or $(x+1.5)^2 - 0.25$

(b) $x^2 - 5x + 7 = \left(x-\frac{5}{2}\right)^2 + \frac{3}{4}$ or $(x-2.5)^2 + 0.75$

C Transforming quadratic graphs (p 256)

C1 (a) $y = x^2 + 2$ (b) $y = (x-2)^2$

(c) $y = (x-2)^2 - 1$ (d) $y = (x+3)^2 + 1$

C2 $y = (x+4)^2$

C3 $\begin{bmatrix} {}^-5 \\ 1 \end{bmatrix}$

C4 $y = (x-3)^2 - 4$

C5 (a) $y = {}^-x^2$ (b) $y = x^2$

C6 (a) Coordinates of five points on $y = x^2$

(b) Points from (a) with y-values multiplied by 2

(c) Graphs of $y = x^2$ and $y = 2x^2$

(d) $y = 2x^2$

C7 A stretch by a factor of 3 in the y-direction

C8 (a) Coordinates of three points on $y = x^2$

(b) Points from (a) with y-values multiplied by $\frac{1}{2}$

(c) Graphs of $y = x^2$ and $y = \frac{1}{2}x^2$

(d) $y = \frac{1}{2}x^2$

C9 (a) Coordinates of five points on $y = x^2$

(b) Points from (a) with x-values multiplied by 2

(c) Graphs of $y = x^2$ and $y = \frac{1}{4}x^2$

(d) D: $y = \frac{1}{4}x^2$

C10 (a) Graphs of $y = x^2$ and $y = 4x^2$

(b) C: $y = 4x^2$

C11 $y = 9x^2$

C12 A sketch of $y = 5 - x^2$ labelled with its equation

C13 $y = 4x^2 + 3$

D Transforming graphs in general (p 259)

D1 (a) $y = ^-\sin x$ (b) $y = \frac{1}{2}\sin x$

D2 $y = x^3 - 4$

D3 (a) $y = \cos x + 1$ (b) $y = 2\cos x$

D4 $y = \cos(x - 90°)$

D5 (a) $y = (x + 3)^2$ (b) $y = \sin(x + 3)$ (c) $y = \dfrac{1}{x + 3}$

D6 A sketch of $y = \sin x$ translated 30 units to the right

D7 $y = \cos\left(\frac{1}{2}x\right)$

D8 (a) $y = \left(\frac{1}{3}x\right)^3$ or $y = \frac{1}{27}x^3$

     (b) $y = \left(\frac{1}{3}x\right)^2 + 1$ or $y = \frac{1}{9}x^2 + 1$

     (c) $y = 3\left(\frac{1}{3}x\right)$ or $y = x$

D9 $y = \sin(4x)$

D10 (a) $y = (2x)^2$ or $y = 4x^2$

     (b) $y = (2x)^3 - 1$ or $y = 8x^3 - 1$

     (c) $y = \dfrac{1}{2x}$

D11 $y = \sin(3x)$

D12 (a) $y = (^-x)^2$ or $y = x^2$ (b) $y = \cos(^-x)$ or $y = \cos x$

     (c) $y = 2(^-x)^3$ or $y = ^-2x^3$

D13 $y = \sin(^-x)$ is a reflection of $y = \sin x$ in the y-axis.

$y = ^-\sin x$ is a reflection of $y = \sin x$ in the x-axis.

Both reflections produce the same image here so $\sin(^-x) = ^-\sin x$.

E Function notation (p 262)

E1 (a) 1   (b) 7   (c) $^-3$

E2 (a) 7   (b) 7   (c) $^-9$

E3 (a) 1   (b) $^-1$ (c) 0

E4 (a) (i) 16   (ii) 0

     (b) (i) 0   (ii) 49

     (c) B: $y = (x + 5)^2$

E5 (a) (i) 32   (ii) 2   (iii) 50

     (b) $y = 2x^2$

E6 (a) 1

     (b) (i) 1   (ii) 0.5

     (c) $y = \sin(2x)$

E7 (a) $y = x^2 + 3$ (b) $y = x^2 - 6x + 10$

     (c) $y = 4x^2 + 1$

E8 (a) (i) 25   (ii) 0

     (b) $y = (x + 2)^2$ or $y = x^2 + 4x + 4$

     (c) Sketches of $y = x^2$ and $y = (x + 2)^2$

F Transforming functions (p 263)

F1 (a) A translation by $\begin{bmatrix} 0 \\ 1 \end{bmatrix}$

     (b) (i) A translation by $\begin{bmatrix} -1 \\ 0 \end{bmatrix}$

        (ii)

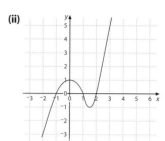

     (c) (i)

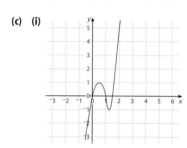

        (ii)

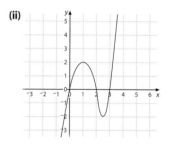

        (iii)

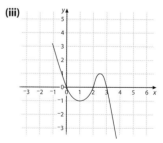

        (iv)

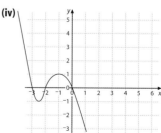

F2 (a) $(3, 10)$ (b) $(6, 8)$ (c) $(^-3, 8)$ (d) $(1, 8)$

F3 (a) P has coordinates $(^-4, 5)$.

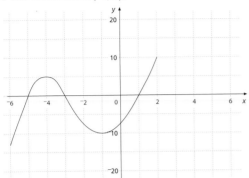

(b) P has coordinates $(^-1, 10)$.

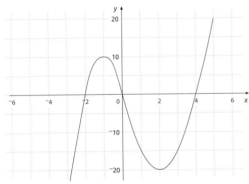

(c) P has coordinates $(^-1, ^-5)$.

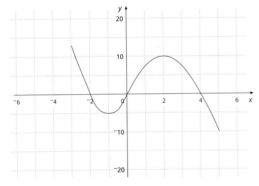

F4 (Sheet H2–8)

(a)

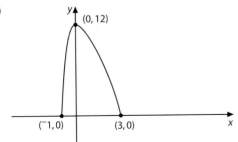

(b)

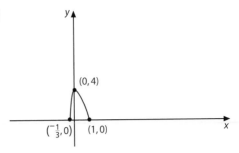

(c)

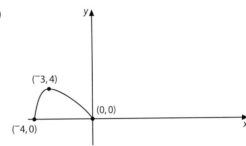

F5 (a) (i) $(5, ^-4)$ **(ii)** $(2, ^-9)$ **(iii)** $(2, 4)$ **(iv)** $(1, ^-4)$

(b) $f(x) = (x - 2)^2 - 4$ or $f(x) = x^2 - 4x$

F6 (a) $(4, 1)$

(b) (i) $(4, 3)$ **(ii)** $(3, 1)$ **(iii)** $(1, 1)$ **(iv)** $(16, 1)$

(c) $(0, 37)$

Test yourself (p 265)

T1 (a) $a = 2, b = 25$

(b) Minimum value $^-25$ at $x = 2$

T2 (a) $p = 3, q = ^-16$ **(b)** $x = ^-7, 1$

T3 Sketch of $y = (x - 2)^3$ with intercepts $(0, ^-8)$ and $(2, 0)$ clearly labelled with their coordinates

T4 $y = (x + 2)^2 + 3$ or $y = x^2 + 4x + 7$

T5 A: $y = (x - 3)^2$ or $y = x^2 - 6x + 9$
B: $y = (x + 3)^2$ or $y = x^2 + 6x + 9$
C: $y = ^-x^2$
D: $y = 3 - x^2$

T6 (a) $y = f(2x)$ **(b)** $y = f(x + 2)$

T7 (a)

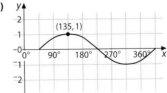

(b)

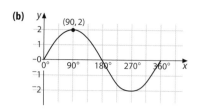

T8 (a) (i) 3 **(ii)** 5

  (b) $(3, 5)$

  (c) 5

  (d) (i) $(4, 5)$ **(ii)** $(0, 21)$

T9 A stretch by a factor of $\frac{1}{2}$ in the x-direction

33 Rational and irrational numbers

A Review: fractions to decimals (p 268)

A1 (a) 0.6 **(b)** 0.28 **(c)** 0.78 **(d)** 0.625 **(e)** 0.225

A2 (a) $0.\dot{3}$ **(b)** $0.\dot{2}\dot{3}$ **(c)** $0.2\dot{3}$ **(d)** $0.\dot{3}2\dot{1}$ **(e)** $0.3\dot{2}\dot{1}$

A3 (a) 0.833 333... or $0.8\dot{3}$

  (b) 0.181 818... or $0.\dot{1}\dot{8}$

  (c) 0.142 857 142 857... or $0.\dot{1}42 85\dot{7}$

  (d) 0.545 454... or $0.\dot{5}\dot{4}$

  (e) 0.233 333... or $0.2\dot{3}$

A4 (a) $\frac{1}{9} = 0.111111...$

  $\frac{3}{9} = 0.333333...$

  $\frac{5}{9} = 0.555555...$

  $\frac{7}{9} = 0.777777...$

  (b) $\frac{9}{9}$ or 1

A5 (a) $\frac{1}{2} = 0.5$ (terminating)

  $\frac{1}{3} = 0.333333...$

  $\frac{1}{4} = 0.25$ (terminating)

  $\frac{1}{5} = 0.2$ (terminating)

  $\frac{1}{6} = 0.1666666...$

  $\frac{1}{7} = 0.142857142857...$

  $\frac{1}{8} = 0.125$ (terminating)

  $\frac{1}{9} = 0.111111...$

  $\frac{1}{10} = 0.1$ (terminating)

  $\frac{1}{11} = 0.090909...$

  $\frac{1}{12} = 0.08333333...$

  $\frac{1}{13} = 0.076923076923...$

  $\frac{1}{14} = 0.0714285714285...$

  $\frac{1}{15} = 0.0666666...$

  $\frac{1}{16} = 0.0625$ (terminating)

  $\frac{1}{17} = 0.\dot{0}58823529411764\dot{7}$

  $\frac{1}{18} = 0.0555555...$

  $\frac{1}{19} = 0.\dot{0}52631578947368421\dot{1}$

  $\frac{1}{20} = 0.05$ (terminating)

  (b) If the denominator of a fraction is a product of only 2s and/or 5s, the decimal equivalent will terminate.

  (c) $\frac{9}{20}, \frac{7}{8}, \frac{1}{25}, \frac{1}{80}, \frac{3}{64}$

A6 No. It does not have a group of recurring digits.

B Recurring decimals to fractions (p 269)

B1 (a) $\frac{7}{10}$ **(b)** $\frac{17}{20}$ **(c)** $\frac{3}{100}$ **(d)** $\frac{231}{250}$ **(e)** $\frac{1}{40}$

B2 (a) $\frac{8}{9}$ **(b)** $\frac{5}{33}$ **(c)** $\frac{3}{11}$ **(d)** $\frac{49}{333}$ **(e)** $\frac{2}{9}$

  (f) $\frac{4}{11}$ **(g)** $\frac{1}{333}$ **(h)** $\frac{326}{999}$

B3 (a) $f = 0.1555555...$

    $10f = 1.5555555...$

    $100f = 15.5555555...$

    $90f = 14$

  (b) $\frac{7}{45}$

B4 (a) $\frac{8}{45}$ **(b)** $\frac{2}{45}$ **(c)** $\frac{229}{900}$ **(d)** $\frac{103}{330}$ **(e)** $\frac{1}{30}$

  (f) $\frac{47}{110}$ **(g)** $\frac{8}{495}$ **(h)** $\frac{1648}{1665}$

B5 (a) $\frac{5}{9}$ **(b)** $\frac{5}{90}$

B6 (a) $\frac{1}{3}$ **(b)** $\frac{1}{10}$ **(c)** $\frac{1}{3} + \frac{1}{10} = \frac{13}{30}$

B7 (a) $\frac{2}{3}$ **(b)** $\frac{2}{5}$ **(c)** $\frac{2}{3} - \frac{2}{5} = \frac{4}{15}$

B8 5 and 6

C Irrational numbers (p 270)

C1 $\sqrt{8}, 4\sqrt{7}, \frac{\pi}{2}, \sqrt{125}, \sqrt[3]{25}, \sqrt{3}+4, \pi^2+1$

C2 $\sqrt{5}+\sqrt{5}=2\sqrt{5}$
$6\sqrt{5}-2\sqrt{5}=4\sqrt{5}$
$2(\sqrt{5}+2)=2\sqrt{5}+4$
$(2\sqrt{5})^2=20$

C3 (a) $2\sqrt{7}$ (b) 7 (c) $3\sqrt{7}$
(d) $3\sqrt{7}+6$ (e) 7 (f) $2\sqrt{7}+8$

C4 $\pi-1, \sqrt{5}, \sqrt{8}, \sqrt{12}-1$

C5 Irrational numbers between:
(a) 4 and 5, such as $\sqrt{17}, \pi+1$
(b) 5 and 6, such as $\sqrt{26}, \pi+2$
(c) 0 and 1, such as $\frac{\sqrt{2}}{2}, \frac{\pi}{4}$
(d) 10 and 11, such as $\sqrt{120}$

C6 It is irrational. Although the digits after the decimal point follow a pattern, there will never be a group of recurring digits.

C7 (i) Rational: it is equivalent to the fraction $\frac{1}{10}$.
(ii) Irrational: although the digits after the decimal point follow a pattern, there will never be a group of recurring digits.
(iii) Rational: it is equivalent to the fraction $\frac{41}{333}$.

C8 (a) $\sqrt{10}$ cm   (b) $\sqrt{3}$ cm   (c) 4 m
(d) $\sqrt{101}$ mm   (e) 9 cm

C9 $\sqrt{18}$ cm or $3\sqrt{2}$ cm

C10 A proof such as:
Suppose it did go through the point (a, b) where a and b are integers. Then the gradient would be $\frac{b}{a}$ and so $\frac{b}{a}$ would be equivalent to $\sqrt{3}$. But this is impossible as $\sqrt{3}$ is irrational. So the line never goes through the intersection of two grid lines.

C11 A proof such as:
Suppose the square has edge length of 1 unit; the diagonal is $\sqrt{2}$ units long. Imagine the journey of each insect stretched out in one dimension as below.

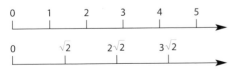

Each mark represents an insect at a vertex. So the insects can only meet if two marks coincide. This can only happen if there exist two integers so that $a = b\sqrt{2}$, that is if $\sqrt{2} = \frac{a}{b}$. But we know that is impossible because $\sqrt{2}$ is irrational. So the insects never meet again.

C12 A proof such as:
Suppose there are two integers a and b, such that $a^2 = 2b^2$. Then $\frac{a^2}{b^2} = 2$ and $\frac{a}{b} = \sqrt{2}$. But this is impossible as $\sqrt{2}$ is irrational. So there is no square number that is double another square number.

D Simplifying expressions containing square roots
(p 271)

D1 (a) $\sqrt{15}$ (b) $\sqrt{14}$ (c) $\sqrt{24}$ (d) $\sqrt{50}$

D2 (a) 5   (b) 3   (c) 4   (d) 10

D3 (a) 6   (b) 42   (c) $3\sqrt{10}$ (d) $8\sqrt{10}$

D4 (a) 11   (b) 3   (c) 10

D5 (a) $3\sqrt{3}$ (b) $5\sqrt{2}$ (c) $4\sqrt{5}$ (d) $7\sqrt{2}$ (e) $10\sqrt{3}$

D6 (a) $6\sqrt{2}$ (b) $8\sqrt{2}$ (c) $6\sqrt{5}$ (d) $18\sqrt{2}$ (e) $20\sqrt{5}$

D7 Comments such as: $\sqrt{9}+\sqrt{9}=3+3=6$ and $\sqrt{18}\neq 6$.

D8 (a) $2\sqrt{5}$ (b) $3\sqrt{6}$ (c) $5\sqrt{3}$ (d) 6

D9 (a) $2\sqrt{3}$ (b) $7\sqrt{3}$

D10 $7\sqrt{3}$

D11 (a) $3\sqrt{2}$ (b) $\sqrt{3}$ (c) $6\sqrt{5}$ (d) $6\sqrt{2}$

D12 (a) $5\sqrt{3}$ (b) $\sqrt{3}$

D13 (a) $6\sqrt{3}$ (b) $3\sqrt{3}$

D14 (a) $\sqrt{3}$ (b) 3   (c) $\sqrt{5}$ (d) $2\sqrt{2}$ (e) $2\sqrt{2}$

E Multiplying out brackets containing square roots
(p 273)

E1 (a) $4\sqrt{3}+\sqrt{6}$ (b) $\sqrt{10}+2$
(c) $10+\sqrt{5}$ (d) 12

E2 (a) $8+5\sqrt{2}$ (b) $1-3\sqrt{5}$ (c) 22
(d) $12-6\sqrt{7}$ (e) $9+4\sqrt{5}$ (f) $4-2\sqrt{3}$

E3 $2\sqrt{3}$ cm

E4 (a) $2+\sqrt{3}+2\sqrt{2}+\sqrt{6}$ (b) $6+6\sqrt{5}-\sqrt{3}-\sqrt{15}$
(c) 2   (d) 32
(e) $8-2\sqrt{15}$ (f) 32

E5 6

E6 (a) $6+2\sqrt{5}$
(b) An explanation, for example:
$(1+\sqrt{5})^2-2(1+\sqrt{5})-4$
$=(6+2\sqrt{5})-2(1+\sqrt{5})-4$
$=6+2\sqrt{5}-2-2\sqrt{5}-4=0$
so $x=1+\sqrt{5}$ is a solution to $x^2-2x-4=0$

E7 (a) $4\sqrt{3}$ (b) $26-8\sqrt{3}$

E8 $15+10\sqrt{2}$

E9 $18+6\sqrt{5}$

F Further simplifying with square roots (p 274)

F1 (a) $\sqrt{6}$ (b) 2 (c) $\sqrt{5}$

F2 (a) $\frac{3}{5}$ (b) $\frac{9}{12}$ or $\frac{3}{4}$ (c) $\frac{4}{11}$

F3 $\frac{\sqrt{3}}{4}$

F4 $\frac{5}{\sqrt{2}}$

F5 (a) $\frac{7\sqrt{5}}{5}$ (b) $\frac{\sqrt{3}}{3}$ (c) $3\sqrt{2}$

(d) $\sqrt{7}$ (e) $\frac{\sqrt{10}}{2}$ (f) $\frac{\sqrt{30}}{3}$

F6 $3\sqrt{3}$

F7 (a) $\frac{3\sqrt{5}+5}{5}$ (b) $1+3\sqrt{2}$ (c) $\frac{3-4\sqrt{3}}{3}$

F8 $\frac{1}{\sqrt{2}}+\frac{\sqrt{2}}{6}=\frac{\sqrt{2}}{2}+\frac{\sqrt{2}}{6}$

$=\frac{3\sqrt{2}}{6}+\frac{\sqrt{2}}{6}$

$=\frac{4\sqrt{2}}{6}=\frac{2\sqrt{2}}{3}$ as required

F9 $3\sqrt{3}$

G Surd solutions to quadratic equations (p 275)

G1 $4\pm\sqrt{13}$

G2 (a) $2\pm\sqrt{2}$ (b) $3\pm\sqrt{6}$

(c) $1\pm\sqrt{3}$ (d) $^-4\pm\sqrt{13}$

G3 (a) $(x-3)^2-7$ (b) $x=3\pm\sqrt{7}$

G4 (a) $(x+6)^2-32$ (b) $x=^-6\pm4\sqrt{2}$

G5 (a) $^-2\pm\sqrt{3}$ (b) $^-3\pm\sqrt{5}$

(c) $5\pm\sqrt{23}$ (d) $\frac{3}{2}\pm\frac{\sqrt{13}}{2}$

G6 $2\pm\frac{1}{2}\sqrt{10}$

G7 (a) $1\pm\frac{1}{2}\sqrt{2}$ (b) $\frac{3}{4}\pm\frac{1}{4}\sqrt{33}$ (c) $\frac{2}{3}\pm\frac{1}{3}\sqrt{7}$

G8 (a) $2(x+2)^2-3$

(b) $2(x+2)^2-3=0$

$2(x+2)^2=3$

$(x+2)^2=\frac{3}{2}$

$x+2=\pm\sqrt{\frac{3}{2}}=\pm\sqrt{\frac{3\times2}{2\times2}}=\pm\frac{1}{2}\sqrt{6}$

$x=^-2\pm\frac{1}{2}\sqrt{6}$

H Mixed questions (p 276)

H1 $2\sqrt{6}$ cm

H2 (a) Area $\sqrt{21}$ cm^2, perimeter $2(\sqrt{3}+\sqrt{7})$ cm

(b) Area 4 cm^2, perimeter $6\sqrt{2}$ cm

H3 (a) $\frac{14}{33}$ (b) $\frac{49}{66}$

H4 $x=2\pm\sqrt{3}$

H5 (a) $2\sqrt{2}$

(b) $\frac{\sqrt{72}-\sqrt{32}}{\sqrt{18}+\sqrt{8}}=\frac{2\sqrt{2}}{3\sqrt{2}+2\sqrt{2}}=\frac{2\sqrt{2}}{5\sqrt{2}}=\frac{2}{5}$

H6 (a) Yes, $\sqrt{2}\times\sqrt{6}=\sqrt{12}=\sqrt{4}\times\sqrt{3}=2\sqrt{3}$

(b) No. The expression in column A is equivalent to $\sqrt{5}$ which is irrational. The number in column B is a terminating decimal and so cannot be equivalent to $\sqrt{5}$.

(c) Yes, $\sqrt{\frac{144}{121}}=\frac{12}{11}$ and division shows that

$\frac{12}{11}=1.090\,909\,09\ldots$

H7 (a) (i) $2\sqrt{3}$ (ii) Irrational

(b) (i) 1 (ii) Rational

Test yourself (p 277)

T1 (a) $\frac{1}{6}$, $\frac{2}{3}$

(b) $0.\dot{2}$

(c) $f=0.154\,545\,4\ldots$

$10f=1.545\,454\ldots$

$1000f=154.5454\ldots$

$990f=153$

$f=\frac{153}{990}=\frac{17}{110}$

T2 (a) $\frac{5}{11}$

(b) (i) $12+2\sqrt{35}$ (ii) Irrational

T3 (a) 5 (b) 18

T4 $f=1.207\,207\,207\ldots$

$1000f=1\,207.207\,207\ldots$

$999f=1206$

$f=\frac{1206}{999}=1\frac{207}{999}=1\frac{23}{111}$

T5 (a) $2\sqrt{2}$ (b) $1+2\sqrt{2}$

T6 $\frac{3}{\sqrt{6}}+\frac{\sqrt{6}}{3}=\frac{3\sqrt{6}}{6}+\frac{2\sqrt{6}}{6}=\frac{5\sqrt{6}}{6}=\frac{5}{\sqrt{6}}$

T7 $\frac{2\sqrt{3}+3}{3}=\frac{2}{3}\sqrt{3}+1$

T8 $\sqrt{22}$

T9 $x=3\pm2\sqrt{3}$

34 Pythagoras and trigonometry in three dimensions

A Solving problems using a grid (p 278)

A1 **(a)** 15 cm, giving a rectangle 15 cm by 5 cm

(b) The calculated length is 15.8 cm.

(c) $\angle$BEC is 18.4° (to 1 d.p.) ($\sin^{-1}$ or $\cos^{-1}$ can be used to find this angle but $\tan^{-1}$ is 'safer' here because it does not rely on earlier, approximated results.)

A2 **(a)** 8.6 cm by 9 cm

(b) 12.4 cm

(c) 46.3°

(Although the results given in answers should be sensibly rounded as here, it is wise to keep a record of them with some extra significant figures for use in later calculations, as in part (c) of this question.)

A3 **(a)** Rectangle GACF

(b)

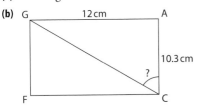

$\angle$GCA is 49.4°.

(c) Angle GCA is the angle between line CG and the plane **ABCD**.

A4 Plane GACF

A5 Plane JBCI

A6 **(a)** 11.4 cm **(b)** 25.9°

A7 64.1°

A8 34.7°

A9 **(a)** 10.3 cm **(b)** 60.1° **(c)** 61.8 cm²

A10 **(a)** **(i)** 10.296 cm **(ii)** 11.402 cm **(iii)** 8.602 cm

(b) The constructed triangle

(c) **(i)** 74° **(ii)** 46° **(iii)** 60°

A11 **(a)** GI = 7.071 cm, IF = 10.296 cm, FG = 10.296 cm

(b) $\angle$IFG = 40°, $\angle$FGI = 70°, $\angle$GIF = 70°

B Solving problems without a grid (p 280)

B1 $DE^2 = 29$

Using Pythagoras in the plane DEFC,

$$CE^2 = DE^2 + CD^2$$
$$= 29 + 9 = 38$$

So CE $= \sqrt{38}$, as expected

B2 $\sqrt{165}$

B3 $\sqrt{l^2 + b^2 + h^2}$ (This can now be used as a standard formula for the length of the diagonal between opposite vertices of a cuboid.)

B4 $\sqrt{304}$ cm

B5 $\sqrt{12}$

B6 **(a)** 51° **(b)** 4.695 cm

(c) 8.829 cm **(d)** 165.8 cm³

B7 **(a)** 22.4 m (to 1 d.p.) **(b)** 26° to the nearest degree

B8 The key step in finding the angle between a given line and a given plane is to identify the plane in which the trigonometry is to be done and draw a sketch of it with vertices and known dimensions labelled. Some people find it helpful to rotate the three-dimensional problem mentally so the given plane becomes the horizontal ground; the given line is thought of as a rod held loosely at the point where it meets the ground; the angle the rod would fall through if it was 'dropped' is the one required. Alternatively the task can now be seen as finding an angle of elevation. Either way, the plane in which the trigonometry must be done usually becomes obvious. Another approach is to remember that the triangle to be worked on must have these as its sides: the given line; a line in the given plane; a line at right angles to the given plane.

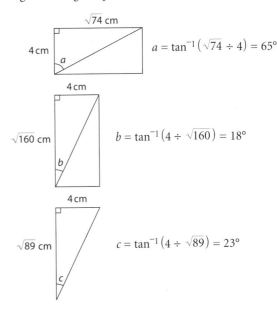

B9 **(a)** PT = 70 ÷ tan 32° = 112 m

QT = 70 ÷ tan 35° = 100 m

Using the cosine rule,

$PQ^2 = 112^2 + 100^2 - 2 \times 112 \times 100 \times \cos 134° = 38\,104$

so PQ = 195 m, to the nearest metre

(b) 22° to the nearest degree

B10 (a)

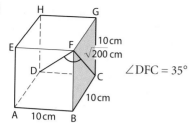

$\angle DFC = 35°$

(b)

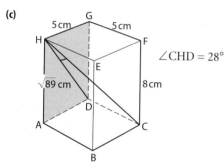

$\angle TVU = 58°$

(c)

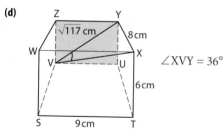

$\angle CHD = 28°$

(d)

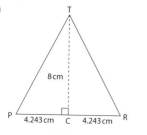

$\angle XVY = 36°$

B11 (a) Length $= \sqrt{50^2 + 120^2 + 120^2} = 177$ cm to the nearest cm

(b) Angle $= \tan^{-1}(120 \div \sqrt{16\,900}) = 43°$ to the nearest degree

B12 (a) PR $= 8.485$ cm, PC $= 4.243$ cm

(b)

T

8 cm

P 4.243 cm C 4.243 cm R

(i) 9.1 cm

(ii) 62°

(c) TM $= \sqrt{8^2 + 3^2} = 8.544$ cm, area $= 25.6$ cm^2 (to 1 d.p.)

B13 (a) 1.732 unit
(b) 1.732 unit
(c) 70.53°
(d) 1.414 square unit
(e) 1.633 unit
(f) 0.94 cubic unit

B14 (a) VA $= 6.887$ cm (using the sine rule on triangle AVB
VO $= 6.887 \sin 20° = 2.355$ cm (to 3 d.p.)

(b) VB $= 5.870$ cm (using the sine rule on triangle AVB
$\angle$VBO $= \sin^{-1}(2.355 \div 5.870) = 24°$ to the nearest degree

B15 191 cm^3 to the nearest cm^3

C Using coordinates in three dimensions (p 284)

C1 5.39 units

C2 K 6.16 units, L 11.18 units, M 9.43 units, N 11.00 units

C3 (a) $\sqrt{99}$ units in every case

(b) All four points are the same distance ($\sqrt{99}$ units) from the origin. This is true of all points on a sphere of radius $\sqrt{99}$ units, centre the origin.

C4 7.07 units

C5 (a) A $(1, 0, 1)$, M $(3, 1, 2)$, B $(5, 2, 3)$

(b) In going from A to M, the x-coordinate increases by 2, the y-coordinate by 1 and the z-coordinate by 1; in going from M to B the coordinates increase by these same amounts: so A to M and M to B are the same three-dimensional translation (or vector), so have the same length and direction.

(c) It is halfway between them, or the mean of them. The same is true for the y-coordinate and the z-coordinate.

C6 (a) $(2, 5, 4)$
(b) $\left(6, 5\frac{1}{2}, 1\right)$

C7 (a) $\left(0, 3\frac{1}{2}, 3\frac{1}{2}\right)$

(b) AB $= 5$, BC $= \sqrt{10}$, CA $= \sqrt{41}$

(c) 29° (to the nearest degree)

(d) 7.8 square units

Test yourself (p285)

T1 (a) 20.6° (to 1 d.p.)
(b) 13.9 cm (to 1 d.p.)
(c) 12.4° (to 1 d.p.)

T2 13 cm

Review 5 (p 286)

1 (a) $8.856 \, \text{m}^3$ **(b)** 8856 litres

2 (a) True   **(b)** True   **(c)** False

3 $-4\frac{1}{2} < x \le 4$

4 20

5 (a) $x^2 + y^2 = 100$ **(b)** $(6, 8), (-8, -6)$

6 (a)

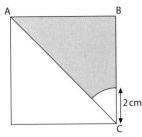

(b) (i) $\left(18 - \frac{1}{2}\pi\right) \text{cm}^2$

(ii) The fraction is $\dfrac{18 - \frac{1}{2}\pi}{36}$. Multiplying the top and bottom by 2 gives $\dfrac{36 - \pi}{72}$ as required.

7 (a) $\frac{3}{8}$ **(b)** $\frac{19}{40}$

8 £36

9 $2\sqrt{7}$

10 (a)

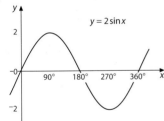

(b)

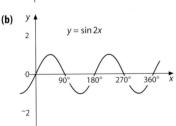

(c)

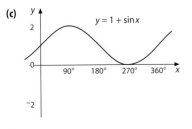

11 (a) OB = OA as both are radii of the circle. Also AP = BP as both are tangents to the circle from the same external point. So the shape has two pairs of adjacent sides that are equal in length and hence shape OBPA is a kite.

(b) $\angle OBP = 90°$ as BP is a tangent and OB is a radius. Hence $\angle BPO = 180° - (57° + 90°) = 33°$.

(c) $\angle ACB = 57°$ ($\angle AOP = 57°$ as triangles OBP and OAP are congruent so $\angle AOB = 57° + 57° = 114°$. Hence $\angle ACB = 114° \div 2$ as $\angle ACB$ is half the size of $\angle AOB$.)

12 $\left(n + \frac{1}{2}\right)^2 = n^2 + n + \frac{1}{4} = n(n + 1) + \frac{1}{4}$ proving the rule works

13 $20\sqrt{2}$

14 (a) Max. $(-2, 3)$, min. $(4, 1)$

(b) Max. $(-3, 1)$, min. $(3, -1)$

(c) Max. $(-2, 2)$, min. $(4, -2)$

(d) Max. $(-1, 1)$, min. $(2, -1)$

15 (a) $\frac{6}{7}$ **(b)** $\dfrac{\sqrt{13}}{6}$

16 3.2

17 (a) Since ABCD is a kite, AB = AD, BC = DC and $\angle ABC = \angle ADC$. Hence triangles ABC and ADC are congruent (SAS).

(b) $90°$

(c) (i) $\angle ADC = \angle ABC = 90°$. Hence a circle with diameter AC goes through B and D (angles in a semicircle are $90°$). This gives a circle with A, B, C and D on its circumference.

(ii) The mid-point of AC

18 (a) $a = 5, b = -28$

(b) The minimum value is -28 and it occurs when $x = -5$.

19 (a)

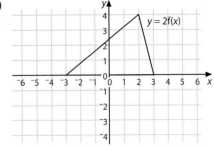

(b)

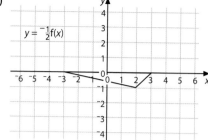

$y = -\frac{1}{2}f(x)$

(c)

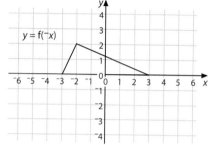

$y = f(-x)$

(d)

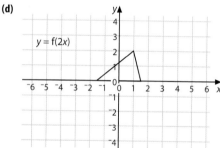

$y = f(2x)$

(e)

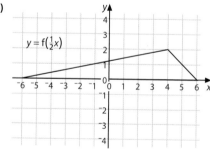

$y = f(\frac{1}{2}x)$

20 (a) 60   **(b)** $9 + 6\sqrt{2}$

21 (a) 43°   **(b)** 7.1 km

22 $x = -\frac{1}{5}, y = \frac{7}{5}; x = -1, y = -1$

23 The sum of three consecutive numbers can be written as $n + (n + 1) + (n + 2)$ where n is an integer. The sum simplifies to $3n + 3$. Three times the middle number is $3(n + 1) = 3n + 3$, proving that the sum of three consecutive numbers is always three times the middle number.

24 (a) $0.8\overset{..}{1}$

    (b) Let $n = 0.\overset{..}{1}\overset{..}{2}$
Then $100n = 12.\overset{..}{1}\overset{..}{2}$
Subtracting gives $99n = 12$ so $n = \frac{12}{99}$ which simplifies to $\frac{4}{33}$ as required.

    (c) (i) $\frac{4}{9}$ **(ii)** $\frac{3}{11}$ **(iii)** $\frac{3}{110}$

25 (a) $\angle BAX = \angle CDX$ (alternate angles)
$\angle ABX = \angle DCX$ (alternate angles)
$\angle CXD = \angle BXA$ (vertically opposite angles)
Since triangles ABX and DCX have the same angles, they are similar.

    (b) 7 cm

    (c) 8.4 cm² (to the nearest 0.1 cm²)

26 $x = 1 \pm \sqrt{2}$

27 (a) An accurate construction of this parallelogram

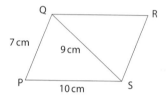

    (b) 76° (to the nearest degree)

    (c) (i) The perpendicular from R to QS constructed on the parallelogram

    (ii) 6.8 cm (to the nearest 0.1 cm)

28 (a) $\frac{125}{64}$ **(b)** $4\sqrt{10}$

29 (a) 20.6° (to the nearest 0.1°)

    (b) 11.7 cm (to the nearest 0.1 cm)

    (c) 14.9° (to the nearest 0.1°)

30 22 m.p.h., 30 m.p.h.

Index